THE FUNCTIONS OF INTERNATIONAL ADJUDICATION AND INTERNATIONAL ENVIRONMENTAL LITIGATION

This book uses environmental disputes as a focus to develop a novel comparative analysis of the functions of international adjudication. Paine focuses on three challenges confronting international tribunals: managing change in applicable legal norms or relevant facts, determining the appropriate standard and method of review when scrutinising State conduct for compliance with international obligations, and contributing to wider processes of dispute settlement. The book compares how tribunals manage these challenges across four key sites of international adjudication: adjudication in the World Trade Organization and under the United Nations Convention on the Law of the Sea, International Court of Justice litigation, and investment treaty arbitration. It shows that while international tribunals perform several key functions in the contemporary international legal order, they are subject to significant constraints. Paine makes a genuine addition to literature on the role of international adjudication in international law, which will benefit academics, practitioners, and policymakers.

JOSHUA PAINE is Senior Lecturer in Law at the University of Bristol. His research focuses on international dispute settlement and international economic law. He has published widely in leading peer-reviewed journals and in edited volumes.

CAMBRIDGE STUDIES IN INTERNATIONAL AND COMPARATIVE LAW: 189

Established in 1946, this series produces high quality, reflective and innovative scholarship in the field of public international law. It publishes works on international law that are of a theoretical, historical, cross-disciplinary or doctrinal nature. The series also welcomes books providing insights from private international law, comparative law and transnational studies which inform international legal thought and practice more generally.

The series seeks to publish views from diverse legal traditions and perspectives, and of any geographical origin. In this respect it invites studies offering regional perspectives on core *problématiques* of international law, and in the same vein, it appreciates contrasts and debates between diverging approaches. Accordingly, books offering new or less orthodox perspectives are very much welcome. Works of a generalist character are greatly valued and the series is also open to studies on specific areas, institutions or problems. Translations of the most outstanding works published in other languages are also considered.

After seventy years, Cambridge Studies in International and Comparative Law sets the standard for international legal scholarship and will continue to define the discipline as it evolves in the years to come.

A list of books in the series can be found at the end of this volume.

THE FUNCTIONS OF INTERNATIONAL ADJUDICATION AND INTERNATIONAL ENVIRONMENTAL LITIGATION

JOSHUA PAINE
University of Bristol

CAMBRIDGE
UNIVERSITY PRESS

CAMBRIDGE
UNIVERSITY PRESS

Shaftesbury Road, Cambridge CB2 8EA, United Kingdom

One Liberty Plaza, 20th Floor, New York, NY 10006, USA

477 Williamstown Road, Port Melbourne, VIC 3207, Australia

314–321, 3rd Floor, Plot 3, Splendor Forum, Jasola District Centre, New Delhi – 110025, India

103 Penang Road, #05-06/07, Visioncrest Commercial, Singapore 238467

Cambridge University Press is part of Cambridge University Press & Assessment, a department of the University of Cambridge.

We share the University's mission to contribute to society through the pursuit of education, learning and research at the highest international levels of excellence.

http://www.cambridge.org
Information on this title: http://www.cambridge.org/9781108493499

DOI: 10.1017/9781108655651

First published 2024

A catalogue record for this publication is available from the British Library

Library of Congress Cataloging-in-Publication Data
Names: Paine, Joshua, author.
Title: The functions of international adjudication and international environmental litigation / Joshua Paine, University of Bristol.
Description: New York : Cambridge University Press, 2024. | Series: Cambridge studies in international and comparative law | Includes bibliographical references and index.
Identifiers: LCCN 2023048351 (print) | LCCN 2023048352 (ebook) | ISBN 9781108493499 (hardback) | ISBN 9781108737272 (paperback) | ISBN 9781108655651 (epub)
Subjects: LCSH: Arbitration (International law) | Jurisdiction (International law) | International commerical arbitration. | International courts. | Environmental law, International. | World Trade Organization. | Investments, Foreign–Law and legislation. | United Nations Convention on the Law of the Sea (1982 December 10)
Classification: LCC KZ6115 .P35 2024 (print) | LCC KZ6115 (ebook) | DDC 344.04/6–dc23/eng/20231013
LC record available at https://lccn.loc.gov/2023048351
LC ebook record available at https://lccn.loc.gov/2023048352

ISBN 978-1-108-49349-9 Hardback

For Fiona, and for my parents, Bruce and Nicole

This book is a must-read for anybody seeking a better understanding of the problems faced by modern-day international law adjudication, and exploring solutions to them. Joshua Paine develops a powerful argument that comparative approaches that scrutinize the law and practice of various international courts and tribunals hold the key to such endeavors and can make a real difference, for states, but also the courts and tribunals themselves.

Stephan Schill, University of Amsterdam

International environmental litigation has emerged as an emotive topic of contestation. Deftly addressing the intricate legal details of these judicial and arbitral processes with rigour and clarity, Dr Paine's monograph serves to temper the debate. An excellent book.

Gleider Hernández, Catholic University of Leuven (KU Leuven)

Paine has presented a richly researched and insightful examination of the functions of international courts and tribunals. His book is a significant contribution to the literature and essential reading for those studying and working in international dispute settlement, international trade law, investment treaty law, the law of the sea and international environmental law.

Natalie Klein, UNSW Sydney

Joshua Paine's book is timely and most welcome when environmental disputes are at the forefront of the adjudicatory agenda. The book helps us understand and navigate through the various functions that ICJ, ITLOS and arbitral tribunals, WTO Dispute Settlement Mechanism and investment arbitral tribunals can play, as well as the legal techniques they can resort to, while underlining the particularities of each one's contribution. Last but not least, Paine stresses how some of these judicial institutions aim at furthering cooperation between the parties in a post-adjudicatory phase. Paine's book is a must read on a topic which will undoubtedly grow in importance.

Laurence Boisson de Chazournes, University of Geneva

This fine book rewards with important insights into international law's capacity to adapt to complexity and change. With deftness in traversing international trade and investment regimes, the law of the sea, and general international law, Dr Joshua Paine helpfully compares and evaluates contemporary judicial functions and practices.

Margaret Young, University of Melbourne

This timely study exploring the adjudication of environmental disputes across a range of influential international courts and tribunals offers an invaluable guide for both scholars and litigators. Joshua Paine's detailed comparative analysis provides a much-needed mapping of the ways in which institutional contexts shape the conduct and outcomes of international environmental litigation.

Anne Orford, University of Melbourne

In this broad-ranging work, Joshua Paine unpacks the case law and practice of four adjudicatory settings to identify the key factors influencing dispute settlement concerning environmental matters. The insightful analysis addresses the core challenges facing international courts and tribunals as they seek to meet the needs of the international community in an era of mounting environmental problems, whilst simultaneously striving to maintain their legitimacy as judicial actors.

James Harrison, University of Edinburgh

This important work offers a deeply insightful contribution to understanding how international adjudicative bodies have balanced the competing imperatives of stability and change in addressing both perennial and novel challenges facing the international legal order.

Tim Stephens, University of Sydney

CONTENTS

ACKNOWLEDGEMENTS

This book has been over a decade in the making and there are numerous people to thank. The book began its life as a PhD thesis completed at the University of Melbourne between 2013 and 2017. Professors Anne Orford and Margaret Young were diligent supervisors and consistently read my work and provided detailed comments, pushing me to develop my thinking further. My PhD examiners, Professor Tim Stephens (University of Sydney) and Professor Ellen Hey (Erasmus University Rotterdam), both provided detailed written reports with numerous constructive suggestions for reworking the PhD thesis for publication. In 2014 I also benefited from a fellowship at the Max Planck Institute for Comparative Public Law and International Law in Heidelberg, Germany, which provided sustained time to refine the scope of the project and access to additional literature.

Two anonymous peer reviewers who were engaged by Cambridge University Press during 2018 provided detailed written reports with numerous constructive suggestions for reworking the thesis manuscript into a book. While I do not know their identity, I thank those two reviewers, whose reports I have returned to repeatedly in the last five years. The editors of the Cambridge Studies in International and Comparative Law series also provided a helpful suggestion on revising the book's title. At Cambridge University Press I thank Tom Randall, Marianne Nield, Biju Singh and Franklin Mathews Jebaraj. Immediately after completing my PhD, I spent almost three years (2017–19) as a Senior Research Fellow at the Max Planck Institute Luxembourg. I am grateful to Professor Hélène Ruiz Fabri who offered me a post-doctoral position in Luxembourg. I learnt a great deal from Hélène and from other researchers at the Institute about international adjudication during my time there. I also thank the library staff at the Max Planck Institute Luxembourg, who provided excellent support. While I did not manage to complete the book during my time in Luxembourg, the foundations of the book project were laid there.

I took up a lectureship at the University of Bristol Law School in January 2020. Initially, the shift to a full-time teaching and research position meant that most of my time was devoted to teaching, including developing a new LLM unit in International Investment Law and redesigning several units in the teaching changes that occurred in successive academic years due to the Covid pandemic. Nevertheless, being able to teach intensively in my areas of research between 2020 and 2023 has indirectly benefited my research. I am grateful to my prior students and to Professor Ken Oliphant, who has been an understanding and fair-minded Head of School. Numerous colleagues at Bristol have provided friendly advice on aspects of academic life, including Pat Capps, Lawrence Hill-Cawthorne, Clair Gammage, Lee McConnell, Greg Messenger, Jule Mulder, Tonia Novitz, and Albert Sanchez Graells.

During the ten years I have been working on this project, I have benefited from informal exchanges with numerous colleagues interested in similar issues, either at conferences and workshops or via email, which have informed my thinking. Above all I must thank Esmé Shirlow who was kind enough to provide detailed comments on several draft chapters of the book during 2023. I also wish to thank Jonathan Bonnitcha, Caroline Foster, Caroline Henckels, Moshe Hirsch, Jürgen Kurtz, Lan Nguyen, Stephan Schill, and Elizabeth Sheargold. Inevitably I will have left some names off this list.

This book draws on aspects of several prior publications; however, in all instances the material has been reworked and significantly developed for this book, involving additional research, thinking, and (re-)writing. Limited aspects of my ideas regarding the functions of international adjudication, covered in Chapter 1(B), were published in 'International Adjudication as a Global Public Good?' (2018) 29(4) European Journal of International Law 1223–49. Some of the material on necessity testing and proportionality analysis in WTO law and in investment treaty arbitration, covered, respectively, in Chapter 2(C)(2) and Chapter 5(C)(2), was published in 'Autonomy to Set the Level of Regulatory Protection in International Investment Law' (2021) 70(3) International and Comparative Law Quarterly 696–736. Earlier versions of part of the material covered in Chapter 3(B) and (C), and limited aspects of Chapter 4(B)(1) and (C)(2)(a), were published in 'The Judicial Dimension of Regime Interaction beyond Systemic Integration', in Seline Trevisanut, Nikolaos Giannopoulos, and Rozemarijn Roland Holst (eds), *Regime Interaction in Ocean Governance: Problems, Theories and Methods* (Brill Nijhoff 2020) 184–221. Chapter 5(B) draws partly on ideas and material first published in 'On Investment Law and Questions of Change' (2018) 19(2) Journal of World Investment & Trade 173–207. Some of the material on standards of review in this book, particularly in relation to investment treaty arbitration (Chapter 5(C)(1)), draws on my 'Standard of Review: Investment Arbitration', in Hélène Ruiz Fabri (ed), *Max Planck Encyclopedia of International Procedural Law* (Oxford University Press 2019), and 'Standard of Review', in Hélène Ruiz Fabri and Edoardo Stoppioni (eds), *International Investment Law: An Analysis of Major Decisions* (Hart 2022) 327–41. Much earlier, very limited aspects of my thinking on standards of review and proportionality analysis in investment treaty arbitration were also published in 'The Project of System-Internal Reform in International Investment Law: An Appraisal' (2015) 6(2) Journal of International Dispute Settlement 332–54, 342–47.

Substantive aspects of the book were finalised in July 2023, and the book takes account of developments in case law and literature available to me up to 1 July 2023.

On a personal note, I must, above all, thank my partner Fiona, who has provided unfailing love and support, including through several international moves and the daily ups and downs of an academic career. I also wish to thank my parents, Bruce and Nicole, without whose support my academic pursuits would not have been possible; my sister Laura; and my aunts Carrie and Cathy.

TABLE OF CASES

International Court of Justice and Permanent Court of International Justice

Aerial Herbicide Spraying (Ecuador v Colombia), Order of 13 September 2013, ICJ Rep [2013] 278 154
Alleged Violations of Sovereign Rights and Maritime Spaces in the Caribbean Sea (Nicaragua v Colombia), Judgment, ICJ Rep [2022] 266 172
Case Concerning the Factory at Chorzów (Germany v Poland), Claim for Indemnity – Jurisdiction, PCIJ Rep Series A No 9 [1927] 15
Certain Activities Carried Out by Nicaragua in the Border Area (Costa Rica v Nicaragua) and Construction of a Road in Costa Rica along the San Juan River (Nicaragua v Costa Rica), Judgment, ICJ Rep [2015] 665 2, 180–1, 191, 283
Certain Activities Carried Out by Nicaragua in the Border Area (Costa Rica v Nicaragua), Compensation, Judgment, ICJ Rep [2018] 15 192
Certain Iranian Assets (Islamic Republic of Iran v United States of America), Judgment, 30 March 2023 184, 186, 279
Certain Phosphate Lands in Nauru (Nauru v Australia), Preliminary Objections, Judgment, ICJ Rep [1992] 240 154
Delimitation of the Maritime Boundary in the Gulf of Maine Area (Canada/United States of America), Judgment, ICJ Rep [1984] 286 193, 195
Dispute over the Status and Use of the Waters of the Silala (Chile v Bolivia), Judgment, ICJ Rep [2022] 614 2, 193–4
Dispute regarding Navigational and Related Rights (Costa Rica v Nicaragua), Judgment, ICJ Rep [2009] 213 113, 171–2, 183–4, 186, 196–7, 199, 264, 275, 279
Fisheries Jurisdiction (*Federal Republic of Germany v Iceland*), Merits, Judgment, ICJ Rep [1974] 175 187–8, 200, 283
Fisheries Jurisdiction (Spain v Canada), Jurisdiction of the Court, Judgment, ICJ Rep [1998] 432 154
Fisheries Jurisdiction (*United Kingdom v Iceland*), Merits, Judgment ICJ Rep [1974] 3 187–8, 200, 283
Gabčikovo-Nagymaros (Hungary/Slovakia), Judgment, ICJ Rep [1997] 7 2, 169–70, 185–7, 189–90, 196–7, 263–4, 280, 283, 289
Kasikili/Sedudu Island (Botswana/Namibia), Judgment, ICJ Rep [1999] 1045 172

Investor-State Arbitration

United Nations Convention on the Law of the Sea

World Trade Organization and General Agreement on Tariffs and Trade

Other International Cases

Commission v Ireland, Case C-459/03, Judgment of 30 May 2006, [2006] ECR I-04635 139

Dispute Concerning Access to Information under Article 9 of the OSPAR Convention (Ireland v United Kingdom), Final Award (2003) 126 ILR 334 139

In the Arbitration Regarding the Iron Rhine ("Ijzeren Rijn") Railway (Belgium v Netherlands), Award (24 May 2005), 140 ILR 130 26, 197

Indus Waters Kishenganga Arbitration (Pakistan v India), Partial Award (18 February 2013) 154 ILR 1 197

L.F.H. Neer and Pauline E. Neer v Mexico, US–Mexico Claims Commission, Opinion (15 October 1926) IV RIAA 60 218

MOX Plant Case (Ireland v United Kingdom), Order No 3 (2003) 126 ILR 310 139

Domestic Cases

United Mexican States v Metalclad [2001] BCSC 664 225

ABBREVIATIONS

AB	Appellate Body
AJIL	American Journal of International Law
ALOP	appropriate level of protection
ASF	African swine fever
ASIL Proceedings	Proceedings of the Annual Meeting – American Society of International Law
BIT	bilateral investment treaty
CBD	Convention on Biological Diversity
CCAMLR	Convention on the Conservation of Antarctic Marine Living Resources
CCSBT	Convention for the Conservation of Southern Bluefin Tuna
CETA	Comprehensive Economic and Trade Agreement between Canada and the European Union
CPTPP	Comprehensive and Progressive Agreement for Trans-Pacific Partnership
CUP	Cambridge University Press
DSB	Dispute Settlement Body
DSS	dispute settlement system
DSU	Dispute Settlement Understanding
EC	European Communities
ECT	Energy Charter Treaty
EEZ	Exclusive Economic Zone
EIA	environmental impact assessment
EJIL	European Journal of International Law
EU	European Union
FET	fair and equitable treatment
FTA	free trade agreement
GATS	General Agreement on Trade in Services
GATT	General Agreement on Tariffs and Trade
GWILR	George Washington International Law Review
ICJ	International Court of Justice
ICSID	International Centre for Settlement of Investment Disputes

ICSID Convention	Convention on the Settlement of Investment Disputes between States and Nationals of Other States
IIA	international investment agreement
IJMCL	International Journal of Marine and Coastal Law
ILC	International Law Commission
ILR	International Law Reports
ISDS	investor–State dispute settlement
ITLOS	International Tribunal for the Law of the Sea
IUU fishing	illegal, unreported, and unregulated fishing
IWC	International Whaling Commission
JIDS	Journal of International Dispute Settlement
JIEL	Journal of International Economic Law
JWIT	Journal of World Investment and Trade
JWT	Journal of World Trade
LJIL	Leiden Journal of International Law
LPICT	The Law and Practice of International Courts and Tribunals
MFN	most-favoured-nation
MJIL	Melbourne Journal of International Law
MPA	marine protected area
MPIA	Multi-Party Interim Appeal Arrangement
MST	minimum standard of treatment
NAFTA	North American Free Trade Agreement
NYUJILP	New York University Journal of International Law and Politics
ODIL	Ocean Development and International Law
OUP	Oxford University Press
PTA	preferential trade agreement
RdC	*Recueil des cours* (Collected Courses of the Hague Academy of International Law)
RECIEL	Review of European Community and International Environmental Law
SBT	southern bluefin tuna
SPS	sanitary and phytosanitary
SPS Agreement	Agreement on the Application of Sanitary and Phytosanitary Measures
SRFC	Sub-Regional Fisheries Commission
TAC	total allowable catch
TBT Agreement	Agreement on Technical Barriers to Trade
TPP	tobacco plain packaging
UK	United Kingdom
UN	United Nations
UNCITRAL	United Nations Commission on International Trade Law

UNCLOS	United Nations Convention on the Law of the Sea
UNCTAD	United Nations Conference on Trade and Development
US	United States
VCLT	Vienna Convention on the Law of Treaties
Whaling Convention	International Convention for the Regulation of Whaling
WTO	World Trade Organization
WTO Agreement	Marrakesh Agreement Establishing the World Trade Organization
WTR	World Trade Review

1

Introduction

A. Focus and Contributions of the Book

At the broadest level, this book considers how international tribunals might perform their functions given the limitations of their roles and the demands they are being confronted with across several areas of international law. More specifically, the book uses the focus of environmental disputes to reflect upon three cross-cutting challenges confronting international tribunals across four key sites of contemporary international adjudication. The book analyses how tribunals across the World Trade Organization (WTO), United Nations Convention on the Law of the Sea (UNCLOS), International Court of Justice (ICJ), and investment treaty contexts manage the problems of change in relevant legal norms or facts, review of State conduct for compliance with international obligations, and dispute resolution, and why their practices differ.[1]

A WTO panel or the Appellate Body decides a dispute concerning an environmental measure that restricts international trade.[2] A dispute concerning marine environmental harm is brought before the International Tribunal for the Law of the Sea (ITLOS) or an arbitral tribunal under

[1] For a conceptualisation of the notion of 'international judicial practices', drawing on earlier applications of practice theory to international relations, see Jeffrey L Dunoff and Mark A Pollack, 'International Judicial Practices: Opening the "Black Box" of International Courts' (2018) 40 Mich. J. Int'l L. 47, esp. 55–56, 62. See also Tommaso Soave, 'The Social Field of International Adjudication: Structures and Practices of a Conflictive Professional Universe' (2023) 36 LJIL 565, 586–90.

[2] Eg Appellate Body Report, *United States – Measures Concerning the Importation, Marketing and Sale of Tuna and Tuna Products*, WT/DS381/AB/R, adopted 13 June 2012; Appellate Body Report, *United States – Import Prohibition of Certain Shrimp and Shrimp Products*, WT/DS58/AB/R, adopted 6 November 1998; Appellate Body Report, *United States – Standards for Reformulated and Conventional Gasoline*, WT/DS2/AB/R, adopted 20 May 1996; *European Union – Certain Measures Concerning Palm Oil and Oil Palm Crop-Based Biofuels*, WT/DS593/9, Request for the Establishment of a Panel by Indonesia, 24 March 2020.

UNCLOS.[3] A dispute concerning environmental harm is brought before the ICJ.[4] A State's refusal on environmental grounds of a permit required for an investment to operate is challenged by a foreign investor before an arbitral tribunal under an investment treaty.[5] In each case, the international tribunal is faced with adjudicating the international obligations of a State (or States) in a dispute involving an environmental component. While all the tribunals operate within distinct institutional contexts, they are likely to face, to a greater or lesser degree, several common challenges confronting international tribunals today. How do changes in international law, or changes in relevant facts, affect the tribunal's task of interpreting and applying obligations under an applicable treaty? How much deference, if any, should the international tribunal afford to determinations made by domestic authorities who may have greater familiarity with local conditions, have applied specialist forms of non-legal expertise, or enjoy greater legitimacy? How should adjudicators scrutinise measures that further one legally protected interest under the relevant regime but undermine another? Should adjudicators apply a test for reasonableness, necessity or least restrictive means, or engage in proportionality balancing stricto sensu? Finally, should adjudicators aim to dispose completely of the parties' dispute, or should they clarify con-

[3] Eg *South China Sea Arbitration (Philippines v China)*, Award (2016) 170 ILR 180; *Case Concerning Land Reclamation by Singapore in and around the Straits of Johor (Malaysia v Singapore)* (Provisional Measures, Order of 8 October 2003) ITLOS Reports 2003, p. 10; *MOX Plant (Ireland v United Kingdom)* (Provisional Measures, Order of 3 December 2001) ITLOS Reports 2001, p. 95; *Request for an Advisory Opinion submitted by the Commission of Small Island States on Climate Change and International Law*, Request for Advisory Opinion, 12 December 2022.

[4] Eg *Dispute over the Status and Use of the Waters of the Silala (Chile v Bolivia)*, Judgment, ICJ Rep [2022] 614; *Certain Activities Carried Out by Nicaragua in the Border Area (Costa Rica v Nicaragua) and Construction of a Road in Costa Rica along the San Juan River (Nicaragua v Costa Rica)*, Judgment, ICJ Rep [2015] 665; *Pulp Mills on the River Uruguay (Argentina v Uruguay)*, Judgment, ICJ Rep [2010] 14; *Gabčikovo-Nagymaros (Hungary/Slovakia)*, Judgment, ICJ Rep [1997] 7; *Obligations of States in respect of Climate Change*, Request for Advisory Opinion, 12 April 2023.

[5] Eg *William Ralph Clayton, William Richard Clayton, Douglas Clayton, Daniel Clayton and Bilcon of Delaware, Inc v Canada*, PCA Case No 2009–04, Award on Jurisdiction and Liability (17 March 2015); *Crystallex International Corporation v Venezuela*, ICSID Case No ARB[AF]/11/2, Award (4 April 2016); *Lone Pine Resources Inc. v Canada*, ICSID Case No UNCT/15/2, Award (21 November 2022); *Ruby River Capital LLC v Canada*, ICSID Case No ARB/23/5, Request for Arbitration (17 February 2023).

tested issues of law and fact and hand parts of the dispute back to the parties for further negotiation or cooperation?[6]

The overall argument this book develops is that international tribunals perform several crucial roles or functions in the contemporary international legal order by incrementally adapting international norms, scrutinising State conduct for compliance with international obligations, and contributing to broader processes of dispute resolution. However, international tribunals are subject to significant constraints. These include constraints imposed by States as system designers and controllers, constraints imposed by adjudicators themselves, and other practical limitations.[7] For example, international tribunals may lack the legitimacy or specialist knowledge needed to engage in significant law-making, weigh competing values, or resolve a dispute in its entirety.

Addressing how international tribunals might discharge their functions is important because international adjudication is at a crossroads. International adjudication has become increasingly central to some areas of international law and international relations over the past

[6] A note on terminology: this book uses the terms 'adjudicators' and 'tribunals' interchangeably, unless otherwise specified. Partly this is to avoid the repetition of referring only to 'tribunals'. It also reflects that adjudicators are in the driving seat in the key activity of composing the decisions of a tribunal, with the bench typically deciding collectively on the tribunal's decisions (by majority vote if needed). Using the term 'adjudicators' tends to emphasise the agency of the individuals who serve as judges and arbitrators. However, I acknowledge that for some purposes a meaningful distinction may be drawn between 'adjudicators' and the 'tribunals' to which they belong. For example, in some tribunals the registry or secretariat also plays a major role in the practices of the tribunal (including the drafting of judgments). Additionally, individual adjudicators are shaped and constrained by the institutional practices of a tribunal to which they belong. On these wider theoretical issues see generally Salvatore Caserta and Mikael Rask Madsen, 'The Situated and Bounded Rationality of International Courts: A Structuralist Approach to International Adjudicative Practices' (2022) 35 LJIL 931, esp. 932, 939–40; Dunoff and Pollack (n 1) esp. 62–64, 83–85. See also Cesare PR Romano, Karen J Alter and Yuval Shany, 'Mapping International Adjudicative Bodies, the Issues, and Players' in Cesare PR Romano, Karen J Alter and Yuval Shany (eds), *The Oxford Handbook of International Adjudication* (OUP 2013) 4–5, 24–25.

[7] On the constraints or control mechanisms that international tribunals are subject to see e.g. Laurence R Helfer and Anne-Marie Slaughter, 'Why States Create International Tribunals: A Response to Professors Posner and Yoo' (2005) 93 Calif LR 899, 942–55; Jacob Katz Cogan, 'Competition and Control in International Adjudication' (2008) 48 Virginia JIL 411, 420–37; Tom Ginsburg, 'Bounded Discretion in International Judicial Lawmaking' (2005) 45 Va. J. Int'l L. 631, 657–71. See also from a different theoretical perspective Caserta and Madsen (n 6) 932–33, 939–40; Soave (n 1) 589–90.

25–30 years.[8] International tribunals are frequently asked to determine how States' treaty obligations are affected by changes in international law or relevant facts, or to determine the legality of domestic regulatory measures that are based on specialised forms of expertise and/or strike a contestable balance between competing values. However, substantial concerns have arisen about the desirability of 'court-based governance of international relations'[9] in light of its operation in recent decades. Many have raised concerns over the legitimacy of the significant power exercised by international tribunals through their development of legal principles that affect the rights and obligations of actors far beyond the disputing parties.[10] For example, a tribunal's decision may restrict the policy space of States who were not parties to a case.[11] Another common concern is that tribunals embedded within particular regimes – as most contemporary international tribunals are – may promote values specific to their own regime, at the cost of other concerns.[12] Others have posed the question of whether more flexible modes of dispute resolution, such as negotiation, mediation or conciliation, would be better suited

[8] Yuval Shany, 'No Longer a Weak Department of Power? Reflections on the Emergence of a New International Judiciary' (2009) 20 EJIL 73, 73, 75–76, 83–84; Benedict Kingsbury, 'International Courts: Uneven Judicialisation in Global Order' in James Crawford and Martti Koskenniemi (eds), *The Cambridge Companion to International Law* (CUP 2012) 210–12; Karen J Alter, *The New Terrain of International Law: Courts, Politics, Rights* (Princeton UP 2014) 3–4.

[9] Yuval Shany, *Assessing the Effectiveness of International Courts* (OUP 2014) 3.

[10] See e.g. Nienke Grossman, 'The Normative Legitimacy of International Courts' (2013) 86 Temple Law Review 61, 68–73; Armin von Bogdandy and Ingo Venzke, *In Whose Name? A Public Law Theory of International Adjudication* (OUP 2014) 106–08, 112–19; Caroline E Foster, *Global Regulatory Standards in Environmental and Health Disputes: Regulatory Coherence, Due Regard, and Due Diligence* (OUP 2021) 287.

[11] Benedict Kingsbury and Stephan Schill, 'Investor-State Arbitration as Governance: Fair and Equitable Treatment, Proportionality and the Emerging Global Administrative Law' in Albert Jan van den Berg (ed), *50 Years of the New York Convention* (Kluwer Law International 2009) 5–6, 23–26; Foster (n 10) ibid.

[12] See e.g. von Bogdandy and Venzke (n 10) 134–35; Andreas Paulus, 'International Adjudication' in Samantha Besson and John Tasioulas (eds), *The Philosophy of International Law* (OUP 2010) 214–15; Tim Stephens, *International Courts and Environmental Protection* (CUP 2009) 309–10, 355–56. Where this study uses the term 'regime' I understand this to mean 'sets of norms, decision-making procedures and organisations coalescing around functional issue-areas and dominated by particular modes of behaviour, assumptions and biases': see Margaret A Young, 'Introduction: The Productive Friction between Regimes' in Margaret A Young (ed), *Regime Interaction in International Law: Facing Fragmentation* (CUP 2012) 4–11.

to resolving some of the disputes coming before international tribunals.[13] Far from being issues only of academic interest, these issues are central to ongoing policy debates over reform of existing adjudicatory mechanisms, particularly in relation to investor–State dispute settlement (ISDS) and WTO dispute settlement.[14]

International tribunals continue to be presented with a large number of disputes across a variety of institutional contexts. Contemporary adjudicators are, on the whole, acutely sensitive to the broader concerns surrounding their work and often seek to address such concerns in their decisions.[15] Thus, a crucial challenge facing international adjudication is to develop legal doctrines and techniques that respond to the demands facing the contemporary legal order, including by addressing concerns and potential shortcomings that have arisen from the increased adjudicatory activity of recent decades.[16]

In addressing these wider issues, this book makes three more specific contributions to our understanding of the functions of contemporary international adjudication. First, this book contributes to debates concerning the role played by international tribunals in incrementally adapting treaty obligations over time, given changes in international law or relevant facts, and, in so doing, balancing the competing interests of stability and change. I explain why this is a key challenge for tribunals in the context of international law's limited processes for law adjustment

[13] Vaughan Lowe, 'The Function of Litigation in International Society' (2012) 61 ICLQ 209, 220–22; Anna Spain, 'Integration Matters: Rethinking the Architecture of International Dispute Resolution' (2010) 32 Univ. of Pennsylvania JIL 1; Daniel Bethlehem, 'The Greening of International Dispute Settlement? Stepping Back a Little' (2020) 114 ASIL Proceedings 225, 231–32; Shany (n 8) 88–89.

[14] As outlined in Chapter 5, since 2017 Working Group III of the United Nations Commission on International Trade Law has been working on a mandate for reform of ISDS, which operates alongside other efforts to reform ISDS: see Chapter 5, text at nn 12–14. As outlined in Chapter 2, due to the United States blocking all appointments to the WTO Appellate Body from 2017 onwards – leading to the AB's demise in 2019 – numerous proposals for reform of WTO dispute settlement have been developed and some WTO members have developed an alternative system for appellate arbitration: see Chapter 2(A)(2)(b).

[15] Similarly: Andrew Lang, 'Twenty Years of the WTO Appellate Body's "Fragmentation Jurisprudence"' (2015) 14 Journal of International Trade Law and Policy 116, 120–21; Sivan Shlomo-Agon, 'Clearing the Smoke: The Legitimation of Judicial Power at the WTO' (2015) 49 JWT 539, 582–87; Christina Voigt, 'International Courts and the Environment: The Quest for Legitimacy' in Christina Voigt (ed), *International Judicial Practice on the Environment* (Cambridge University Press 2019) 20.

[16] Shany (n 8) 91.

and why it plays out differently across the four contexts studied. Second, in relation to the interrelated problems of the appropriate standard and method of review, which arise when adjudicators scrutinise State conduct for compliance with applicable international obligations,[17] this book adds to existing debates that largely focus on WTO dispute settlement and investment treaty arbitration by connecting them to more recent debates over these issues in the ICJ and UNCLOS contexts. This part of the analysis reveals significant opportunities for comparatively informed learning. For example, I will demonstrate that a small number of functionally similar balancing techniques are used across the four contexts studied in scrutinising State measures for compliance with international obligations and suggest that certain lessons emerge regarding how such techniques might be employed. Third, the book adds to understandings of how adjudicators might, through their decisions, contribute to broader processes of dispute resolution. It builds on literature that suggests that international tribunals may in some circumstances play a partly facilitative role by clarifying key questions of law and fact and providing the parties a framework for resolving their dispute and rebuilding their relationship.[18] These three challenges have been selected because they are issues of significance in their own right but also provide a useful proxy for developing a broader comparative assessment of the functions of international adjudication.

A broader, overall contribution made by this book is to analyse how international tribunals might discharge their functions given the varied contexts and constraints within which they operate. Contemporary international tribunals have markedly different design features, reflecting strategic choices made by the States who created them.[19] For example, the control mechanisms that States can exercise, such as deciding upon (re)appointments to a tribunal or agreeing upon authoritative

[17] The concepts of the standard and method of review are explained below: text at nn 74–76 and 86–89.

[18] See literature cited below nn 101–106.

[19] See e.g. Andrew T Guzman, 'International Tribunals: A Rational Choice Analysis' (2008) 157 Univ. of Pennsylvania LR 171, 203; Jeffrey L Dunoff and Mark A Pollack, 'The Judicial Trilemma' (2017) 111 AJIL 225, 229–31 (overview of rational design literature relevant to international tribunals); Barbara Koremenos, Charles Lipson and Duncan Snidal, 'The Rational Design of International Institutions' (2001) 55 International Organization 761, 761–62, 766–67.

interpretations of a treaty, differ significantly across contexts.[20] Our understanding of the functions of international tribunals must be sensitive to the marked variations that characterise contemporary international adjudication. In the chapters that follow, I will develop conclusions regarding how the particular context in which each of the tribunals operates shapes how the three selected challenges manifest themselves and are responded to by adjudicators. The analysis also identifies elements that are common across the contexts studied and provide broader insights into the functions performed by international adjudication.[21]

For several reasons, the category of environmental cases provides an ideal lens for the comparative study just described. Environmental disputes lack a dedicated international tribunal and are adjudicated across a variety of 'borrowed' fora with diverse design features and functional orientations.[22] A substantial number of environmental cases have been litigated in each of the adjudication settings considered and no one institution or professional community has dominated such cases.[23] Accordingly, this category of cases is representative of the sectorial and decentralised nature of contemporary international adjudication,[24] and the familiarity with multiple subsystems of international law that this demands of international lawyers.[25] Environmental cases highlight the problem of how to respond to change because they often require adjudicators to interpret legal rules agreed at an earlier point – when

20 See e.g. Helfer and Slaughter (n 7) 946–53; Katz Cogan (n 7) 420–25; Ginsburg (n 7) 657–68.

21 Cf Ruti Teitel and Robert Howse, 'Cross-Judging: Tribunalization in a Fragmented but Interconnected Global Order' (2009) 41 NYUJILP 959, 966 (on the possibility of identifying elements that are 'common and distinctive in the legalist's way of seeing international problems').

22 Pierre-Marie Dupuy and Jorge E Viñuales, *International Environmental Law* (2nd ed., CUP 2018) 300, 303.

23 Alan Boyle, 'The Environmental Jurisprudence of the International Tribunal for the Law of the Sea' (2007) 22 IJMCL 369, 372; James Harrison, 'Reflections on the Role of International Courts and Tribunals in the Settlement of Environmental Disputes and the Development of International Environmental Law' (2013) 25 Journal of Environmental Law 501, 502–03.

24 Ellen Hey, *Reflections on an International Environmental Court* (Kluwer Law International 2000) 24.

25 Suzannah Linton and Firew Kebede Tiba, 'The International Judge in an Age of Multiple International Courts and Tribunals' (2008) 9 Chicago JIL 407, 464 (international lawyers need 'to be as versatile as Swiss Army knives in terms of their knowledge of the various subsystems of international law'); Martti Koskenniemi, 'The Case for Comparative International Law' (2011) 20 Finnish YBIL 1, 6–7 (suggesting contemporary international lawyers need expertise in multiple regimes).

environmental norms were less well developed – in new ways,[26] and because the application of such norms often depends on facts that are prone to change, such as scientific knowledge or technical capacity.[27] Additionally, because environmental norms are often vague or 'standard-like', environmental cases force adjudicators, in concretising the content of such principles, to walk 'a tight-rope between application and development of the law'.[28] Environmental disputes also pose acutely the question of how intensely international adjudicators should scrutinise domestic-level determinations based on the application of specialised forms of non-legal expertise, an assessment of local circumstances, or the exercise of discretion. Thus, this category of cases foregrounds the problem of the appropriate standard or intensity of review. As environmental disputes typically involve competing economic and ecological interests,[29] they also raise the question of which legal techniques international tribunals might use to balance partially competing interests and whether adjudicators should ever themselves weigh the relative importance of competing regulatory aims. Finally, environmental cases have repeatedly raised the question of whether it is appropriate for international tribunals to decide disputes with a partly prospective focus, and, for example, order the parties to cooperate in conducting further environmental monitoring or negotiations.[30]

Existing international law literature concerning international environmental adjudication largely focuses on the conditions under which international adjudication might act as an effective mechanism for protecting

[26] Anna Spain, 'Beyond Adjudication: Resolving International Resource Disputes in an Era of Climate Change' (2011) 30 Stanford Environmental LJ 343, 362.

[27] See e.g. Bradly J Condon, *Environmental Sovereignty and the WTO: Trade Sanctions and International Law* (Transnational Publishers 2006) 38–40; Markus Vordermayer, '"Gardening the Great Transformation": The Anthropocene Concept's Impact on International Environmental Law Doctrine' (2014) 25 Ybk IEL 79 (on the challenge of adapting existing treaties given evolving scientific understandings of the environment).

[28] Voigt (n 15) 8. Similarly: Natalie Klein and Danielle Kroon, 'Settlement of International Environmental Law Disputes' in Malgosia Fitzmaurice, Marcel Brus and Panos Merkouris (eds), *Research Handbook on International Environmental Law* (2nd ed., Edward Elgar 2021) 244–45; Philippe Sands, 'Litigating Environmental Disputes: Courts, Tribunals and the Progressive Development of International Environmental Law' in Tafsir Malick Ndiaye, Rüdiger Wolfrum and Chie Kojima (eds), *Law of the Sea, Environmental Law, and Settlement of Disputes: Liber Amicorum Judge Thomas A. Mensah* (Martinus Nijhoff 2007) 314–15.

[29] Klein and Kroon (n 28) 232; Richard Bilder, 'The Settlement of Disputes in the Field of the International Law of the Environment' (1975) 144 RdC 140, 154–55.

[30] Klein and Kroon (n 28) 248–49.

environmental interests.[31] This book has a different focus as it uses environmental cases as a lens for reflecting back on the functions performed by international adjudication, and how those functions might be discharged, given the varied contexts in which the selected tribunals operate. In short, environmental disputes are used here as a useful terrain for studying the role of adjudication in international law; strictly this is not a book about environmental law.

The remainder of this chapter explains how the book achieves these aims. Section B situates this book in relation to existing debates concerning the functions of international adjudication and expands further on the three challenges facing tribunals that are traced throughout the book. Section C explains how this study has defined what counts as an environmental case and why the four adjudication settings focused upon have been selected. Section D explains certain basic insights the book has incorporated from methodological debates in comparative law. Section E provides an overview of the chapters to come.

B. The Varied Functions of Contemporary International Adjudication

By analysing how adjudicators address the three selected challenges across the four contexts studied, this book investigates the functions that these international tribunals perform. By 'functions' I mean the roles played by international tribunals in deciding cases, or what they are doing,[32] and how their decisions serve particular ends or purposes,[33] as one part of the broader international legal order.[34] Thinking in terms of

[31] Cesare PR Romano, *The Peaceful Settlement of International Environmental Disputes: A Pragmatic Approach* (Kluwer Law International 2000) xlv, 30; Stephens (n 12) 2, 365; Yasuhiro Shigeta, *International Judicial Control of Environmental Protection: Standard Setting, Compliance Control, and the Development of International Environmental Law by the International Judiciary* (Kluwer Law International 2010) 4, 8, 351; Justine Bendel, *Litigating the Environment: Process and Procedure before International Courts and Tribunals* (Edward Elgar 2023) 1, 7–8, 12–13, 249.

[32] Lowe (n 13) 211.

[33] Stephan Wittich, 'The Judicial Functions of the International Court of Justice' in Isabelle Buffard and others (eds), *International Law between Universalism and Fragmentation: Festschrift in Honour of Gerhard Hafner* (Martinus Nijhoff 2008) 985–86.

[34] von Bogdandy and Venzke (n 10) 5, 7; Theresa Squatrito and others, 'A Framework for Evaluating the Performance of International Courts and Tribunals' in Theresa Squatrito and others (eds), *The Performance of International Courts and Tribunals* (CUP 2018) 10. Typically the ends served by adjudicatory decisions will be more specific than, and make an incremental contribution to, the ultimately aims of a legal order: Lowe (n 13) 211.

the functions of international adjudication is useful because international tribunals are designed with different purposes that must be analysed in an institution-specific manner,[35] and a tribunal's specific functions, established by relevant constitutive instruments, are an important influence on how adjudicators perform their roles.[36] Furthermore, the decisions of international tribunals are typically multifunctional in that a single decision often has 'a series of legal and social consequences that one can regard as functions',[37] which are distinct yet overlapping and frequently in tension with each other.[38]

A primary function of international tribunals is to settle the disputes presented to them in accordance with the applicable law.[39] For example, the function of dispute settlement has an explicit basis in both the Statute of the ICJ and the WTO Dispute Settlement Understanding, and both the ICJ and WTO panels and the AB have affirmed this task in their case law.[40] A traditional view sees the dispute settlement function as limited

On the functions of international law generally, see e.g. Dana Burchardt, 'The Functions of Law and Their Challenges: The Differentiated Functionality of International Law' (2019) 20 German LJ 409. In limited respects Section B of this chapter draws on ideas and material from Joshua Paine, 'International Adjudication as a Global Public Good?' (2018) 29 EJIL 1223.

35 Shany (n 9) 48; Wittich (n 33) 988; Dinah Shelton, 'Form, Function, and the Powers of International Courts' (2008) 9 Chicago JIL 537, 571.

36 Wittich (n 33) 987; José E Alvarez, *The Impact of International Organizations on International Law* (Brill Nijhoff 2017) 341–42. However, note that it is well recognised that an international tribunal may perform functions that are not expressly assigned to it: see e.g. Hersch Lauterpacht, *The Development of International Law by the International Court* (rev ed., Stevens & Sons 1958) 5; von Bogdandy and Venzke (n 10) 7–8. Note also that the literature recognises that there are certain core or generic functions that most international tribunals perform: Shany (n 9) 37–38; Yaël Ronen, 'Functions and Access' in William A Schabas and Shannonbrooke Murphy (eds), *Research Handbook on International Courts and Tribunals* (Edward Elgar 2017) 463.

37 von Bogdandy and Venzke (n 10) 5, 7.

38 Wittich (n 33) 989, 1000. But see Shelton (n 35) 539–40 (arguing there is always a dominant function at a given time).

39 Manley O Hudson, *International Tribunals: Past and Future* (Carnegie Endowment for International Peace 1944) 236.

40 Statute of the International Court of Justice (1945) 33 UNTS 993, art 38(1) ('ICJ Statute'); Understanding on Rules and Procedures Governing the Settlement of Disputes, Marrakesh Agreement Establishing the World Trade Organisation, Annex 2 (1994) 1869 UNTS 401, arts 3.3, 3.4, 3.7 ('DSU' and 'WTO Agreement'). See e.g. *LaGrand (Germany v United States of America)*, Judgment, ICJ Rep [2001] 466, [52]; *Nuclear Tests (New Zealand v France)*, Judgment, ICJ Rep [1974] 457, [58], [60]; *Northern Cameroons (Cameroon v United Kingdom)*, Preliminary Objections, Judgment, ICJ Rep [1963] 15, 33–34; Panel Report, *European Communities – Regime for the Importation, Sale and Distribution of Bananas, Complaint by Ecuador*, WT/DS27/R/ECU, adopted

and private, whereby the task of tribunals 'is "to do justice" between the litigant States, and to render a judgment or award which takes account of all relevant facts, which is limited to the *petitum* of the dispute, and which is made with final and binding force'.[41] However, in the course of deciding disputes, tribunals typically perform, even if only indirectly, a variety of other more public functions.[42] To begin with, even the dispute settlement function is not solely of a private and bilateral nature. The peaceful settlement of disputes arguably serves a broader community interest beyond the disputing parties by preventing disputes festering and escalating into broader international tensions or even violent conflict.[43] In some circumstances, tribunals' decisions might also enable future dispute settlement or 'bargaining in the shadow' of such decisions, including by parties who were not involved in the original case.[44]

A second key function served by international tribunals is that they act as 'agents' in the development of international law.[45] There are important differences between other types of law-making, such as concluding treaties or agreeing on treaty amendments or authoritative interpretations, and the far more constrained law-making in which international tribunals have an opportunity to engage.[46] In particular, international tribunals are constrained by the cases that are brought before them and how those cases are argued by the disputing parties, and there is a strong expectation that tribunals' decisions will be related to existing legal

25 September 1997, [7.32]; Appellate Body Report, *United States – Measure Affecting Imports of Woven Wool Shirts and Blouses from India*, WT/DS33/AB/R, adopted 23 May 1997, 18–19.

41 Chester Brown, *A Common Law of International Adjudication* (OUP 2007) 72.

42 Ibid 72–78; A Neil Craik, 'Recalcitrant Reality and Chosen Ideals: The Public Function of Dispute Settlement in International Environmental Law' (1997) 10 Georgetown Int'l Envtl. L. Rev. 551, 562ff. Caron suggested distinguishing between the singular judicial task of adjudicators, namely 'resolving disputes according to preexisting legal norms', and the various social functions that are furthered indirectly as a result of adjudicators' activity: David D Caron, 'The Multiple Functions of International Courts and the Singular Task of the Adjudicator' (2017) 111 ASIL Proceedings 231, 233–34.

43 Wittich (n 33) 990; Shany (n 9) 41–42; Hudson (n 39) 237–39.

44 See e.g. Andrea K Schneider, 'Bargaining in the Shadow of (International) Law: What the Normalization of Adjudication in International Governance Regimes Means for Dispute Resolution' (2008) 41 NYUJILP 789, 817–19; Sara McLaughlin Mitchell and Andrew P Owsiak, 'Judicialization of the Sea: Bargaining in the Shadow of UNCLOS' (2021) 115 AJIL 579, 598–99.

45 See e.g. Philippa Webb, *International Judicial Integration and Fragmentation* (OUP 2013) 206; Christian J Tams and Antonios Tzanakopoulos, '*Barcelona Traction* at 40: The ICJ as an Agent of Legal Development' (2010) 23 LJIL 781, 785.

46 von Bogdandy and Venzke (n 10) 109.

materials and make use of recognised methods of legal reasoning.[47] The influence of their decisions also depends, to a greater degree than other forms of law-making, on how they are received in subsequent legal practice.[48] International courts and tribunals also 'lack the legitimacy, deliberative character' and representative nature of some other law-making processes (e.g. multilateral diplomatic fora).[49] Yet, despite these qualifications, international tribunals are bodies with immense 'semantic authority', or ability to shape legal meanings and establish their communications as 'authoritative reference points in legal discourse'.[50] By deciding cases, international tribunals contribute, at least incrementally, to the clarification and development of principles that prospectively shape the rights and obligations of actors well beyond the disputing parties.[51] This aspect of contemporary international adjudication has given rise to major legitimacy concerns. Unlike domestic courts, whose decisions can typically be overridden by legislation, international tribunals are largely not under equivalent forms of direct political control because treaties cannot be authoritatively interpreted in the absence of consensus amongst the treaty parties, and treaty amendment procedures typically either require consensus or a specified majority.[52]

[47] Ibid 109–11; Foster (n 10) 288–93; Christian J Tams, 'The ICJ as a "Law-Formative Agency": Summary and Synthesis' in Christian J Tams and James Sloan (eds), *The Development of International Law by the International Court of Justice* (OUP 2013) 392; James Harrison, 'Judicial Law-Making and the Developing Order of the Oceans' (2007) 22 IJMCL 283, 284–85; Alan Boyle, 'Progressive Development of International Environmental Law: Legislate or Litigate?' (2019) 62 German Ybk. Int'l L. 305, 322–24; Oliver J Lissitzyn, *The International Court of Justice: Its Role in the Maintenance of International Peace and Security* (Carnegie Endowment for International Peace 1951) 16–17.

[48] Webb (n 45) 206; Tams (n 47) 380; José E Alvarez, *International Organizations as Law-Makers* (OUP 2006) 550–51.

[49] Boyle (n 47) 322; Foster (n 10) 287–90.

[50] Ingo Venzke, *How Interpretation Makes International Law: On Semantic Change and Normative Twists* (OUP 2012) 63.

[51] See e.g. Grossman (n 10) 68; Lowe (n 13) 212–14; von Bogdandy and Venzke (n 10) 106, 207; Boyle (n 47) 322; Geert De Baere, Anna-Luise Chane and Jan Wouters, 'International Courts as Keepers of the Rule of Law: Achievements, Challenges, and Opportunities' (2016) 48 NYUJILP 715, 780–86; Alvarez (n 36) 286. Note in this regard that the reasoning employed by an international tribunal arguably 'has a broad conditioning effect on the way states themselves engage in legal reasoning': Sean D Murphy, 'International Judicial Bodies for Resolving Disputes between States' in *The Oxford Handbook of International Adjudication* (n 6) 198–99.

[52] von Bogdandy and Venzke (n 10) 124–25. On the point that subsequent agreement and subsequent practice under Articles 31(3)(a) and (b) of the Vienna Convention on the Law of Treaties require the agreement of all treaty parties see International Law Commission

This aspect of the adjudicatory function is broadly where the first cross-cutting challenge traced by this book arises. I argue that adjudicators, in interpreting and applying applicable legal norms, face a challenge of ensuring 'legal certainty through predictable interpretation of the law and at the same time to make allowance for legal change, without which law cannot live'.[53] The challenge of responding to demands for change while providing a sufficient degree of legal certainty and stability has been recognised as one of the key problems facing international adjudication by various commentators who have reflected on the functions of international adjudication over the last century.[54] Similarly to

(ILC), Draft Conclusions on Subsequent Agreements and Subsequent Practice in relation to the Interpretation of Treaties with Commentaries, [2018] II(2) ILC Ybk 25, 63–67, Conclusion 10 and commentary; Article IX:2 of the WTO Agreement empowers the Ministerial Conference and General Council to adopt interpretations of WTO covered agreements by a three-fourths majority of members. However, this power has never been used, including as in practice these bodies operate via consensus: see e.g. Claus-Dieter Ehlermann and Lothar Ehring, 'The Authoritative Interpretation under Article IX:2 of the Agreement Establishing the World Trade Organization: Current Law, Practice and Possible Improvements' (2005) 8 JIEL 803, 813–18. Multilateral treaty amendment procedures that permit some form of majority voting may also provide that amendments only enter into force for parties that ratify the amendment: e.g. UNCLOS arts 312(2), 316 (1); WTO Agreement art X(1), (3).

53 Ilmar Tammelo, *Treaty Interpretation and Practical Reason: Towards a General Theory of Legal Interpretation* (Law Book Company 1967) 53–54. See also Gleider I Hernández, *The International Court of Justice and the Judicial Function* (OUP 2014) 157–59, 187–91 (discussing how the practice of relying on precedent ensures stability and legal certainty but also has a forward-looking aspect, whereby judges consider how their reasoning will affect similar cases that may arise in future); Letizia Lo Giacco, *Judicial Decisions in International Law Argumentation: Between Entrapment and Creativity* (Hart 2022) 6, 33, 61–62 (discussing international criminal tribunals' recurrent emphasis on ensuring legal certainty and predictability as a reason for preferring certain interpretations); Klara Polackova Van der Ploeg, 'International Law through Time: On Change and Facticity of International Law' in Luca Pasquet, León Castellanos-Jankiewicz and Klara Polackova Van der Ploeg (eds), *International Law and Time: Narratives and Techniques* (Springer 2022) 325–26 (noting that equating stability with legal certainty may not always be correct as '[s]o long as law provides clear mechanisms for its modification, change can remain predictable' and change in international law may be needed 'to facilitate stability in the international domain').

54 Important discussions include Hersch Lauterpacht, *The Function of Law in the International Community* (OUP 1933) 254–57 and generally Pt IV ('Stability and Change in International Law'); C Wilfred Jenks, 'Orthodoxy and Innovation in the Law of Nations' (1971) 57 Proceedings of the British Academy 215, 222–33; RP Anand, *Studies in International Adjudication* (Vikas Publications 1969) 168–71, 178–90. More recently, see e.g. Peter Van den Bossche, 'Is There Evolution in the Evolutionary Interpretation of WTO Law?' in Georges Abi-Saab and others (eds), *Evolutionary Interpretation and International Law* (Hart 2019) 221–22. See also Gregory Messenger,

these earlier perspectives, this book argues that balancing the competing interests of stability and legal certainty on the one hand, and change and responsiveness to new demands on the other, is a pressing problem for international adjudication. In addition to contemporary international law being expected to be responsive to an increasing range of social demands,[55] in many areas of international law there is little new treaty law being agreed,[56] compared to the large number of disputes being adjudicated,[57] meaning the burden of responding to demands for change is frequently placed on adjudicators.[58] Through their decisions, international tribunals clarify the content of abstract norms and adapt them to changed circumstances.[59] As Lowe has suggested, international litigation often operates 'as an alternative to, or substitute for, law reform and treaty-making'.[60] For example, we will see in Chapter 2 that despite the

'The Development of International Law, Perception, and the Problem of Time' in *International Law and Time* (n 53) 340–41, 349, 352 (highlighting the fundamental nature of the 'functional tension' between stability and change for international law and that it places certain 'demands on interpreters', particularly judicial bodies); Van der Ploeg (n 53) 316, 325–27 (unpacking the distinct aspects of change and stability in international law).

55 Campbell McLachlan, 'The Evolution of Treaty Obligations in International Law' in Georg Nolte (ed), *Treaties and Subsequent Practice* (OUP 2013) 72; Christian Djeffal, *Static and Evolutive Treaty Interpretation: A Functional Reconstruction* (CUP 2015) 210–11; Irina Buga, *Modification of Treaties by Subsequent Practice* (OUP 2018) 2–3.

56 See Joost Pauwelyn, Ramses A Wessel and Jan Wouters, 'When Structures Become Shackles: Stagnation and Dynamics in International Lawmaking' (2014) 25 EJIL 733, esp. 734–37; McLachlan, ibid 70–72; Andreas Motzfeldt Kravik, 'An Analysis of Stagnation in Multilateral Law-Making – and Why the Law of the Sea Has Transcended the Stagnation Trend' (2021) 34 LJIL 935.

57 See Alter (n 8) 105 (charting binding rulings issued by permanent international courts by year up until 2011, excluding the exceptionally active European Court of Human Rights and European Court of Justice. This shows that more rulings were issued in each year from 2003 than had been issued between 1945 and 1989. Notably, Alter's data excludes investor–State arbitration, which has been an exceptionally active site of international adjudication in the last twenty-five years).

58 Caron (n 42) 236.

59 Shany (n 9) 38–39; Shelton (n 35) 553; Robert Kolb, *The International Court of Justice* (Alan Perry tr, Hart 2013) 1141–43; Christopher G Weeramantry, 'The Function of the International Court of Justice in the Development of International Law' (1997) 10 LJIL 309, 313–19 (judge as 'the instrument of change through which the process of adaptation takes place to the needs of the time').

60 Lowe (n 13) 214. See also Paul F Diehl and Charlotte Ku, *The Dynamics of International Law* (CUP 2010) 64–70, 147–50 (noting this role of international tribunals within a theory of international legal change whereby major changes occur infrequently, for example through the adoption of multilateral treaties, and stability in the international legal system is the norm); Alvarez (n 48) 533–34; Nico Krisch, 'The Dynamics of

negotiating processes within the WTO having been largely stalled since the conclusion of the Uruguay Round agreements, WTO law has continued to develop, including through adjudicators interpreting WTO agreements.[61] While judges in any legal system try to avoid being seen to make law, this pressure is 'particularly heavy' for international adjudicators,[62] including because their institutional position ultimately relies upon State consent.[63]

In analysing the challenge that adjudicators face in balancing the competing interests of stability and change it is useful to distinguish between the questions of changes in legal norms themselves and changes in facts that affect the application of such norms. Where the meaning of a legal norm changes – for example if the meaning of a treaty term is tied to another legal concept that may change – we are dealing with change or evolution in the law.[64] In contrast, the broad meaning of a legal norm may remain constant but the norm may be applied to changing factual circumstances that will affect what the norm requires at any particular time.[65] As we will see, environmental cases have frequently raised both

International Law Redux' (2021) 74 Current Legal Problems 269 (general account of change in international law that views 'the judicial path' as being one of several different pathways through which international law changes).

61 See e.g. Gregory Messenger, *The Development of World Trade Organization Law: Examining Change in International Law* (OUP 2016) 61–67, 193.

62 Tammelo (n 53) 53.

63 Lauterpacht (n 36) 75–76; Boyle (n 47) 324; Alvarez (n 48) 564–65.

64 Panos Merkouris, '(Inter)Temporal Considerations in the Interpretative Process of the VCLT: Do Treaties Endure, Perdure or Exdure?' (2014) 45 Netherlands YBIL 121, 132–33.

65 Sondre Torp Helmersen, 'Evolutive Treaty Interpretation: Legality, Semantics and Distinctions' (2013) 6 EJLS 161, 162; Graham Cook, 'The Illusion of "Evolutionary Interpretation" in WTO Dispute Settlement' in *Evolutionary Interpretation and International Law* (n 54) 182–84. The distinction between changes in law and changes in relevant facts is not always clear-cut; see Robert Kolb, 'Evolutionary Interpretation in International Law: Some Short and Less than Trail-Blazing Reflections' in *Evolutionary Interpretation and International Law* (n 54) 16–18. Further distinctions are possible. For a useful taxonomy of the variety of types of change that fall within the broad category of evolutionary interpretation, see Gabrielle Marceau, 'Evolutive Interpretation by the WTO Adjudicator' (2018) 21 JIEL 791, 803–13. Within debates on treaty interpretation a distinction is recognised between the interrelated processes of interpretation, which involves 'determining the meaning of a rule', and application, which involves 'determining the consequences which the rule attaches to the occurrence of a given fact': *Case Concerning the Factory at Chorzów (Germany v Poland)*, Claim for Indemnity – Jurisdiction, PCIJ Rep Series A No 9 [1927], Diss. Op. Ehrlich 39. For discussion, see e.g. Anastasios Gourgourinis, 'The Distinction between Interpretation and Application of Norms in International Adjudication' (2011) 2 JIDS 31, 43–48.

the question of potential changes in legal norms and that of changes in facts that affect the application of legal norms.

Another key function of international tribunals is scrutinising the conduct of State authorities for compliance with international law.[66] The particular manifestation of this function that has attracted substantial attention in recent years is the scenario where a State enjoys a degree of discretion under applicable international legal norms (often a treaty) and an international tribunal must determine whether the State has acted within the limits imposed on its discretion.[67] Some authors suggest that this 'compliance monitoring' role is more present in some contexts, such as WTO adjudication or regional human rights courts, than others, such as the ICJ and ITLOS, which are characterised as primarily concerned with dispute settlement.[68] This book demonstrates, however, that in the UNCLOS and ICJ contexts adjudicators also frequently grapple with issues that are central to the compliance-monitoring function, such as how to calibrate the appropriate standard or intensity of review and which methods of review to employ.

It is important to emphasise that while throughout this book I refer to a 'review' function or similar, whereby international tribunals scrutinise State conduct for compliance with international norms, I do not assume that this can be equated with judicial review as occurs in certain domestic

[66] von Bogdandy and Venzke (n 10) 14–15; Armin von Bogdandy and Ingo Venzke, 'On the Functions of International Courts: An Appraisal in Light of Their Burgeoning Public Authority' (2013) 26 LJIL 49, 57–58; Ronen (n 36) 469–70; Shany (n 9) 469–70; De Baere, Chane and Wouters (n 51) 775.

[67] Robert Kolb, 'Short Reflections on the ICJ's Whaling Case and the Review by International Courts and Tribunals of "Discretionary Powers"' (2014) 32 AYBIL 135, 135–36; Erietta Scalieri, 'Discretionary Power of Coastal States and the Control of Its Compliance with International Law by International Tribunals' in Angela Del Vecchio and Roberto Virzo (eds), *Interpretations of the United Nations Convention on the Law of the Sea by International Courts and Tribunals* (Springer 2019) 349–62; Vladyslav Lanovoy, 'Standards of Review in the Practice of International Courts and Tribunals' in Gábor Kajtár, Basak Çali and Marko Milanovic (eds), *Secondary Rules of Primary Importance in International Law* (OUP 2022) 42; Deborah Russo, 'The Use of Proportionality in the Recent Case-Law of the ICJ' (2015), University of Oslo Faculty of Law Legal Studies Research Paper Series No 2015-15 http://ssrn.com/abstract=2614316. Neil Craik, 'The Duty to Cooperate in International Environmental Law: Constraining State Discretion through Due Respect' (2019) 30 Ybk IEL 22, esp. 29–30, 34–35, 44.

[68] Yuval Shany, 'One Law to Rule Them All: Should International Courts Be Viewed as Guardians of Procedural Order and Legal Uniformity?' in Ole Kristian Fauchald and André Nollkaemper (eds), *The Practice of International and National Courts and the (De-)Fragmentation of International Law* (Hart 2012) 19–20; Shelton (n 35) 564–66.

systems of public law. Rather, while an analogy with domestic judicial review has animated much of the international law literature concerning the standard or intensity of review, this analogy does not necessarily hold in all respects.[69] As Shirlow and Foster have both observed, the analogy with domestic judicial review relies upon a conferred or delegated powers model of sovereignty, whereby a State's powers are limited rather than plenary, and a tribunal's task is to determine whether the terms of the delegation have been respected.[70] Whether this view of sovereignty can be transposed to the international plane is debatable. Relatedly, Fahner has developed an important claim that due to the limited purposes of international courts and tribunals, and their limited powers to directly affect domestic legal systems (e.g. by annulling domestic legal acts), international adjudication, with the exception of regional human rights courts, is not comparable to judicial review in the domestic context.[71] In Fahner's account, whereas judicial review in domestic systems serves the purpose of 'legitimising the exercise of public power in a constitutional sense by providing checks on political institutions', most international courts and tribunals serve the limited purpose of settling disputes in accordance with the norms established by particular sectorial regimes.[72]

The function of international tribunals of scrutinising State conduct for compliance with applicable international norms is where the second problem traced by this book arises, which is twofold. Specifically, across the four contexts considered I analyse tribunals' approaches to the interrelated issues of the standard or intensity of review and the methods of review employed.[73] The standard of review refers to the intensity of

[69] Esmé Shirlow, *Judging at the Interface: Deference to State Decision-Making Authority in International Adjudication* (CUP 2021) 222–24. See also Shai Dothan, *International Judicial Review: When Should International Courts Intervene?* (CUP 2020) 8, 138.

[70] Shirlow (n 69) 225–27. Foster links this view of sovereignty as conferred power to the implicit use by international tribunals, in adjudicating States' regulatory powers, of one aspect the abuse of rights doctrine, focusing on misuse of powers (ie use of a right for a purpose other than the purpose for which it was created): Foster (n 10) 8–9, 30–32, 294–96, 307–09.

[71] Johannes Hendrik Fahner, *Judicial Deference in International Adjudication: A Comparative Analysis* (Hart 2020) 190–212.

[72] Ibid 205–09; Johannes Hendrik Fahner, 'The Limited Utility of Deference in International Dispute Settlement' (2022) 21 LPICT 467, 475–77. For a similar argument see Başak Çalı, 'International Judicial Review' in Anthony Lang and Antje Wiener (eds), *Handbook on Global Constitutionalism* (Edward Elgar 2017) esp. 291–97.

[73] The point that these issues are interrelated, meaning one cannot be analysed without considering the other, is well recognised: e.g. Valentina Vadi, *Proportionality, Reasonableness and Standards of Review in International Investment Law and*

the scrutiny applied by international adjudicators to prior determinations made by another decision-maker, typically an organ of the State whose conduct is being scrutinised for compliance with international obligations.[74] The standard or intensity of review applied can fall on a variety of points 'on a continuum bounded by total deference to justifications provided or analysis performed by a primary decision-maker at one end, and substitutionary (*de novo*) review of the relevant measure and its justification at the other'.[75] In this book I use the term standard of review, however there are other concepts that are largely synonymous, which also arise in some of the case law analysed, most obviously the 'margin of appreciation' doctrine as developed in the jurisprudence of the European Court of Human Rights. These terms are manifestations of the broader concept of 'deference', which, as Shirlow puts it, encompasses a wide range of 'techniques used by international adjudicators to recognise a domestic actor's superior "authority" to decide issues relevant to the settlement of the dispute brought before the international adjudicator'.[76]

The question of the standard or intensity of review is of central importance for the role played by international adjudication because it directly affects the division of decision-making power between the international and national levels.[77] Furthermore, the applicable standard or intensity of review

Arbitration (Edward Elgar 2018) 253; Caroline Henckels, *Proportionality and Deference in Investor-State Arbitration: Balancing Investment Protection and Regulatory Autonomy* (CUP 2015) 31; Julian Rivers, 'Proportionality and Discretion in International and European Law' in Nicholas Tsagourias (ed), *Transnational Constitutionalism: International and European Perspectives* (CUP 2007) 108–09.

74 Wouter Werner and Lukasz Gruszczynski, 'Introduction' in Lukasz Gruszczynski and Wouter Werner (eds), *Deference in International Courts and Tribunals: Standard of Review and Margin of Appreciation* (OUP 2014) 1–2; Henckels (n 73) 29–30.

75 Caroline Henckels, 'Balancing Investment Protection and the Public Interest: The Role of the Standard of Review and the Importance of Deference in Investor-State Arbitration' (2013) 4 JIDS 197, 201; Werner and Gruszczynski (n 74) 1–2. Note that even those who argue that the development of refined standards of review adds little to the normal exercise of interpreting and applying applicable international legal norms nevertheless recognise that deference may be appropriate in some cases, for example based on the greater expertise or accountability of other decision-makers, and will involve something short of de novo review: Fahner (n 72) 479.

76 Shirlow (n 69) 16. See also Stephan W Schill, 'Deference in Investment Treaty Arbitration: Re-conceptualizing the Standard of Review' (2012) 3 JIDS 577, 582; Fahner (n 71) 5–7, 148.

77 See e.g. Michael Ioannidis, 'Beyond the Standard of Review: Deference Criteria in WTO Law and the Case for a Procedural Approach' in Gruszczynski and Werner (eds), *Deference in International Courts and Tribunals* (n 74) 92–93; Henckels (n 73) 30; Shirlow (n 69) 270–71, 273; Werner and Gruszczynski (n 74) 2.

is at most partly resolved by applicable treaties and is to a significant degree determined by international adjudicators themselves.[78] As we will see, the prospect of international tribunals scrutinising, and potentially second-guessing, sensitive domestic determinations, such as determinations concerning environmental risks and how to respond to such risks, raises acute concerns regarding the relative expertise and legitimacy of adjudicators.

The problem of the applicable standard or intensity of review is persistent in the context of the adjudication of a complex and 'inward-looking' international law of cooperation, where international law increasingly regulates issues that are the subject of domestic decision-making processes.[79] Determining whether States have complied with their international obligations frequently requires tribunals to consider contested questions based on specialised forms of expertise, often of a scientific or technical character, which adjudicators are not well placed to answer themselves.[80] Other actors, including national-level decision-makers who are not courts, and thus not constrained by the inherent limitations of an adjudicatory process, may possess greater subject-specific expertise for answering such questions.[81] Compared to international tribunals, domestic decision-makers also enjoy proximity to local conditions, which can be relevant to applying international norms, particularly in the context of open-ended or standard-type norms the application of which is inherently context specific.[82] Finally, it is widely recognised that compared to international adjudicators, domestic decision-makers may enjoy greater legitimacy to make certain kinds of determinations, for example discretionary, value-laden determinations such as determining what is in the domestic public interest.[83]

78 Werner and Gruszczynski (n 74) 1; Yuval Shany, 'Toward a General Margin of Appreciation Doctrine in International Law?' (2005) 16 EJIL 907, 911.

79 See e.g. Shirlow (n 69) 253–54 (on how the subject matter regulated by international law affects deference); Fahner (n 71) 1; Shany (n 78) 920–21 (on the connection between 'inward-looking' international norms and deference); Lanovoy (n 67) 42, 63.

80 Makane Moïse Mbengue and Rukmini Das, 'The ICJ's Engagement with Science: To Interpret or Not to Interpret?' (2015) 6 JIDS 568, 568–69, 576; Joel P Trachtman, 'International Legal Control of Domestic Administrative Action' (2014) 17 JIEL 753, 754–55, 784.

81 See e.g. Shirlow (n 69) 20–24; Shany (n 78) 918; Henckels (n 73) 39–41.

82 Shirlow (n 69) 24; Shany (n 78) 913–15. Note, however, that the independence of international adjudicators from national processes can also be an important argument against deference to national processes: e.g. Henckels (n 73) 38.

83 Schill (n 76) 599–601; Henckels (n 73) 37–38; Andreas von Staden, 'The Democratic Legitimacy of Judicial Review beyond the State: Normative Subsidiarity and Judicial Standards of Review' (2012) 10 ICON 1023, 1026–27, 1037–38.

The issue of the standard of review is already the subject of a substantial literature, particularly in the trade and investment contexts.[84] The essential move made by this book is to demonstrate that the same basic dilemmas concerning the division of decision-making power between international tribunals and States, and the relative knowledge and legitimacy of international adjudicators, also arise in 'fact-intensive' environmental disputes in the UNCLOS and ICJ contexts.[85] This aspect of the book explains how contextual differences across the four settings studied shape how the problem of the standard of review arises in each context and reveals significant opportunities for comparatively informed learning.

In analysing how adjudicators scrutinise State conduct for compliance with international norms across the four contexts studied, I also trace the related issue of the methods of review, or legal tests, employed by tribunals when faced with balancing two competing legally protected interests.[86] To varying degrees, across all the adjudication settings studied, there are debates, fuelled by developments in case law, concerning the appropriateness of a limited number of methods of review or legal tests that can be used by adjudicators to strike a balance between two (or more) competing interests both protected by a legal regime. Typically, such tests only have a limited basis in any applicable treaty and are 'read into the law' by tribunals.[87] For example, Foster speaks of 'regulatory standards' that are elaborated by international tribunals in successive disputes to give greater determinacy to open-ended international obligations and to provide a formula 'establishing how competing legal rights and interests are to be balanced under the applicable international legal provisions and rules'.[88] Examples of such methods of review developed by international tribunals include reasonableness-based tests, requirements for a rational relationship between a measure and a permissible

[84] See e.g. the literature cited above nn 73–83.

[85] Similarly: Jacqueline Peel, 'Of Apples and Oranges (and Hormones in Beef): Science and the Standard of Review in WTO Disputes under the SPS Agreement' (2012) 61 ICLQ 427, 457–58.

[86] My terminology draws particularly on Henckels (n 73) 6, 31 (method of review as 'a technique used by adjudicators (such as proportionality analysis) to determine the permissibility of interference with a right or interest'). For similar use of this term, including the distinction with the standard or intensity of review, see Vadi (n 73) xvi–xvii, 253; Aileen Kavanagh, *Constitutional Review under the UK Human Rights Act* (CUP 2009) 237–38; Mads Andenas and Stefan Zleptnig, 'Proportionality: WTO Law in Comparative Perspective' (2007) 42 Texas ILJ 371, 392–93.

[87] Foster (n 10) 33–34.

[88] See ibid 20–21, 34–36, 347, 349.

aim, necessity or least restrictive means testing, and proportionality balancing stricto sensu.[89] What is common to these methods of review is that they require a State's measures to bear a particular relationship to a permissible policy objective.[90] Additionally, as Foster suggests, such methods of review (or in her terminology 'regulatory standards') may be understood as requiring States to engage in 'internal balancing processes' and to give some degree of consideration to 'the legal rights and interests of other States and their populations'.[91] While the latter point is particularly clear in relation to requirements of 'due regard', a concept that has been developed by some of the UNCLOS jurisprudence considered in Chapter 3, other methods of review, such as proportionality analysis or reasonableness tests, also implicitly require a State to balance its own interests with other legally protected rights and interests.[92]

The basic reason why the problem of the appropriate method of review arises across the legal regimes studied is that all the regimes protect a variety of competing interests, often expressed through treaty provisions drafted at a high level of generality and which use inherently context-specific terms such as 'reasonable' or 'necessary'.[93] The effect of such design features is that for those disputes where they have jurisdiction, tribunals determine where the precise balance between the competing interests protected by the relevant provisions lies.[94] The degree of discretion conferred upon adjudicators by some of these methods of review is highly controversial.[95] For example, what is widely known as proportionality balancing stricto sensu is the last stage of a structured three (or four)-stage proportionality analysis and asks whether the costs imposed

[89] See generally ibid 23–30.

[90] Ibid 22.

[91] Ibid 22, 327–28, 347.

[92] Ibid 23, 327–35 (arguing that a due regard obligation can achieve '[m]uch of what is sought from proportionality-based reasoning'); Russo (n 67) 4, 8–9, 16; Vadi (n 73) 135–36 (regarding reasonableness).

[93] See e.g. Olivier Corten, 'The Notion of "Reasonable" in International Law: Legal Discourse, Reason and Contradictions' (1999) 48 ICLQ 613, 614–16 (discussing the '"adaptability function" of the notion of reasonableness').

[94] For this point in relation to the law of the sea, see e.g. James Harrison, 'Safeguards against Excessive Enforcement Measures in the Exclusive Economic Zone – Law and Practice' in Henrik Ringbom (ed), *Jurisdiction over Ships: Post-UNCLOS Developments in the Law of the Sea* (Brill Nijhoff 2015) 218. The broader theoretical point is that such design features are an example of incomplete contracting and substantial delegation to adjudicators: see e.g. Joel P Trachtman, 'The Domain of WTO Dispute Resolution' (1999) 40 HILJ 333, 344ff.

[95] See e.g. José E Alvarez, 'Is Investor-State Arbitration "Public"?' (2016) 7 JIDS 534, 551–52.

by a measure are disproportionate to its benefits, having regard to the relative importance of the legally protected interest that the measure restricts and the permissible aim that is furthered by the measure.[96] The prospect of international tribunals engaging in proportionality balancing stricto sensu is highly controversial as it effectively involves them second-guessing the regulating State's choice of how to prioritise the competing values.[97]

In relation to the methods of review used by tribunals, this book suggests that there are underappreciated possibilities for comparative learning between the trade and investment contexts, where this debate is well established, and UNCLOS and ICJ adjudication, where this issue has only received scholarly attention more recently,[98] despite comparable problems and adjudicatory responses repeatedly arising in recent case law. Again, however, it will be demonstrated that differences in context remain important and shape how the issue of the method of review arises in different settings. Analysing this issue in wider comparative perspective is important because, across diverse settings, international tribunals are increasingly faced with balancing partially competing interests[99] and there is a need for legal techniques that can meet this challenge.[100]

The third challenge facing contemporary international tribunals analysed by this book concerns whether adjudicators, through their decisions, seek to contribute to broader processes of dispute resolution. Specifically, this part of the analysis considers whether adjudication is largely retrospective and seeks to dispose of a dispute, or whether adjudication also has a partly prospective focus and aims to provide the disputing parties guidance for their future interactions. This aspect of

[96] See e.g. Aharon Barak, *Proportionality: Constitutional Rights and Their Limitations* (CUP 2012) 340–44, 349–62; Joel P Trachtman, 'Trade and ... Problems, Cost-Benefit Analysis and Subsidiarity' (1998) 9 EJIL 32, 74; Henckels (n 73) 25–26.

[97] See e.g. Vadi (n 73) 65–67; Foster (n 10) 26–27, 324–25. The penultimate stage of proportionality analysis, known as necessity or least restrictive means testing, has sometimes been criticised for overly empowering adjudicators and restricting States' regulatory autonomy: e.g. Vadi (n 73) 66. However, it is typically tempered by requiring that any alternative measure must make an equivalent contribution to the State's regulatory aim and be reasonably available in terms of cost and technical feasibility.

[98] See e.g. Russo (n 67); James Harrison, 'Patrolling the Boundaries of Coastal State Enforcement Powers: The Interpretation and Application of UNCLOS Safeguards Relating to the Arrest of Foreign-Flagged Ships' (2017) 42 L'Observateur des Nations Unies 117; Pasquale De Sena and Lorenzo Acconciamessa, 'Balancing Test' in Hélène Ruiz-Fabri (ed), *Max Planck Encyclopedia of International Procedural Law* (OUP 2021).

[99] Shelton (n 35) 553.

[100] Henckels (n 75) 6.

the book builds on various strands of existing literature. As others have highlighted, in some circumstances international adjudication may be most effective in terms of dispute resolution where it clarifies key contested issues of law and fact and provides a framework in which the parties can resolve their dispute, for example through subsequent negotiation.[101] This aspect of the analysis is relevant to the role of tribunals in scrutinising State conduct for compliance with international norms, with many suggesting that adjudicators are, given their legal training, better equipped to judge the decision-making procedure a State has followed, such as which interests it has taken into account, rather than second-guessing the merits of an underlying decision.[102] Facilitative approaches to adjudication that involve a tribunal referring certain issues back to the parties are obviously more deferential than an approach in which the tribunal would itself decide the relevant issues.[103] Scholars focusing on particular regimes have also praised facilitative and procedurally focused forms of adjudicatory scrutiny in existing jurisprudence. For example, many have argued that certain early WTO Appellate Body decisions offer a desirable example of international adjudication imposing procedural guidelines on the disputing parties' interactions, such as requiring regulating States to consider affected foreign interests, but leaving the parties scope to resolve the underlying dispute themselves.[104] Law of the sea commentators have also praised the 'predominantly facilitative'[105] or 'conflict management role'[106] sometimes performed by ITLOS, whereby

[101] Anna Spain, 'Examining the International Judicial Function: International Courts as Dispute Resolvers' (2011) 34 Loy LA Int'l & Comp LR 5, 8–10, 28–31; Spain (n 26) 366, 377–78, 384–85; Lowe (n 13) 220–22; Vaughan Lowe, 'The Interplay between Negotiation and Litigation in International Dispute Settlement' in *Law of the Sea, Environmental Law, and Settlement of Disputes* (n 28) 244–47. See also Tom Ginsburg and Richard H McAdams, 'Adjudicating in Anarchy: An Expressive Theory of International Dispute Resolution' (2004) 45 William and Mary Law Review 1229.

[102] See e.g. Trachtman (n 80) 755–56, 784; Ioannidis (n 77) 109–11.

[103] See somewhat similarly Shirlow (n 69) 130–31, 138–39 (proposing the category of 'deference as deferral', which includes situations where an international adjudicator refers certain issues for determination by domestic authorities).

[104] See e.g. von Bogdandy and Venzke (n 10) 206; Sungjoon Cho, 'Of the World Trade Court's Burden' (2009) 20 EJIL 675, 717–20. Further literature cited in Chapter 2, n 301.

[105] Natalie Klein, *Dispute Settlement in the UN Convention on the Law of the Sea* (CUP 2005) 83–84.

[106] Robin Churchill, 'Some Reflections on the Operation of the Dispute Settlement System of the UN Convention on the Law of the Sea during Its First Decade' in David Freestone, Richard Barnes and David Ong (eds), *The Law of the Sea: Progress and Prospects* (OUP 2006) 411–12; Vaughan Lowe, 'The "Complementary Role" of ITLOS in the

the Tribunal has clarified the relevant legal framework and ordered the disputing parties to engage in further cooperation or environmental monitoring.

However, facilitative forms of adjudication have also been subject to significant criticisms. As we will see, an entirely substance-neutral form of adjudicatory scrutiny is an illusion, and even under more procedural forms of review adjudicators must make important normative choices, such as how far States must go in considering foreign interests or pursuing cooperative solutions.[107] The tendency of some tribunals to proceduralise disputes has also been criticised as undermining the aims of the substantive obligations in question, and thus, for example, not producing any improvement in environmental outcomes.[108]

The contribution of international tribunals as 'dispute resolvers'[109] is heavily influenced by their institutional architecture. For example, the prospective nature of WTO remedies, and the fact that findings of non-compliance by WTO adjudicators are typically followed by a process of diplomatic bargaining, means it makes particular sense to view adjudication in that regime as contributing to a broader process of dispute resolution. In contrast, we rarely see investment treaty arbitrators attempting to contribute to a broader process of dispute resolution, as opposed to tribunals aiming to dispose of the parties' dispute. This is due to several factors including that compensation is the dominant remedy used in investment treaty arbitration, and tribunals are constituted ad hoc and are not well placed to supervise post-adjudication cooperation between the parties. The commercial rather than diplomatic backgrounds of many participants in investment treaty arbitration, and the fact that in many instances the disputing parties will no longer have an ongoing

Development of Ocean Law' in Harry N Scheiber and Jin-Hyun Paik (eds), *Regions, Institutions, and Law of the Sea: Studies in Ocean Governance* (Martinus Nijhoff 2013) 30–34.

107 Andrew Lang, *World Trade Law after Neoliberalism: Reimagining the Global Economic Order* (OUP 2011) 345–47. See also Bradly J Condon, 'Does International Economic Law Impose a Duty to Negotiate?' (2018) 17 Chinese JIL 73, 102 (arguing that imposing an obligation to negotiate 'is an intrusive approach to dispute settlement').

108 Stephens (n 12) 100–02. See also the critique of proceduralising disputes in Martti Koskenniemi, 'Peaceful Settlement of Environmental Disputes' (1991) 60 Nordic JIL 73. Some have also questioned more fundamentally the utility of distinguishing between substance and procedure: see Benoit Mayer, 'The Pitfalls of Ineffective Conceptualization: The Case of the Distinction between Procedure and Substance' (2022) 33 EJIL 1307.

109 Spain (n 101).

relationship by the time of an award, further explain why we generally do not see investment treaty tribunals performing a partly facilitative, forward-looking role.

C. Issues of Case Selection

1. *What Constitutes an Environmental Case?*

This book uses the focus of environmental disputes to reflect on the functions of international adjudication and an important question is therefore how to define an environmental case. This book builds on the approach of existing international law contributions that have suggested it is preferable to focus on those disputes that have 'an environmental or natural resources component',[110] rather than focusing on the apparently environmental characteristics of the applicable law or institutional context.[111] As we will see throughout this book, disputes with an environmental component routinely arise under treaties and in institutions that might not be characterised as environmental and require one to understand a wide range of other international legal issues.[112] Specifically, this book focuses on cases involving adjudication of the obligations of States in disputes that include an environmental component, that is, cases where at least one of the issues at stake is a question of environmental protection or management.[113]

This, of course, still raises the question of what counts as an environmental issue or component within a case and generally international lawyers have not spent much time debating definitions of the environment.[114] At one level, the question might be answered intuitively based

[110] Sands (n 28) 315, 319.

[111] Alan Boyle and James Harrison, 'Judicial Settlement of International Environmental Disputes: Current Problems' (2013) 4 JIDS 245, 250; Hey (n 24) 4–5.

[112] Boyle and Harrison (n 111) 249; Hey (n 24) 6–9.

[113] This draws on the approach of Stephens (n 12) 346. See also Daniel Behn and Malcolm Langford, 'Trumping the Environment? An Empirical Perspective on the Legitimacy of Investment Treaty Arbitration' (2017) 18 JWIT 14, 17–19 (suggesting in an investor–State context to focus on disputes where a domestic environmental measure is challenged or the host State argues its measure is justified for environmental reasons).

[114] See e.g. the treatment of this issue in Philippe Sands and Jacqueline Peel, *Principles of International Environmental Law* (4th ed., CUP 2018) 14–15; Dupuy and Viñuales (n 22) 28–31; Alan Boyle and Catherine Redgwell, *Birnie, Boyle, and Redgwell's International Law and the Environment* (4th ed., CUP 2021) 5–7; Daniel Bodansky, *The Art and Craft of International Environmental Law* (Harvard UP 2010) 9–11. A more detailed treatment is provided by Romano (n 31) 15–24.

on experience in this area of law. For example, the *Iron Rhine* Tribunal noted that across international environmental law '"environment" is broadly referred to as including air, water, land, flora and fauna, natural ecosystems and sites, human health and safety, and climate'.[115] Similarly, Boyle and Harrison note that: 'Most of what we generally regard as "environmental" concerns pollution of air, freshwater and oceans; climate change; unsustainable use of natural resources; loss of biodiversity, ecosystems and habitat; and conservation of endangered species and natural heritage.'[116]

Understandings of the environment have 'expanded rapidly over the past several decades', shifting from compartmentalised to holistic approaches and increasingly incorporating social, cultural and economic factors.[117] Contemporary ecology suggests that the historically influential 'distinction between "nature" and "human" is untenable' because '[h]uman systems, such as economies, cultures, and polities, are subsystems nested within larger ecological and biogeochemical systems'.[118] Above all, the concept of the Anthropocene, developed in the natural sciences and employed in recent years in law and many other disciplines, suggests that the Earth has entered a new geological epoch 'in which humanity has become the dominant force of global environmental change' and 'human and natural forces are intermixed and inseparable'.[119] In this

[115] *In the Arbitration Regarding the Iron Rhine ("Ijzeren Rijn") Railway (Belgium v Netherlands)*, Award (24 May 2005), 140 ILR 130, [58].

[116] Boyle and Harrison (n 111) 250. Similarly: Dupuy and Viñuales (n 22) 31.

[117] Lee Godden and Jacqueline Peel, *Environmental Law: Scientific, Policy and Regulatory Dimensions* (OUP 2010) 15–27.

[118] Jonathan Baert Wiener, 'Law and the New Ecology: Evolution, Categories, and Consequences' (1995) 22 Ecology LQ 325, 349; Daniel B Botkin, *The Moon in the Nautilus Shell: Discordant Harmonies Reconsidered from Climate Change to Species Extinction, How Life Persists in an Ever-Changing World* (OUP 2012) 324–25. Noting the significance of this development: Romano (n 31) 17–20; Tuomas Kuokkanen, *International Law and the Environment: Variations on a Theme* (Brill 2002) 260–61.

[119] Tim Stephens, 'What Is the Point of International Environmental Law Scholarship in the Anthropocene?' in Ole W Pedersen (ed), *Perspectives on Environmental Law Scholarship: Essays on Purpose, Shape and Direction* (CUP 2018) 121–24; Louis J Kotzé, *Global Environmental Constitutionalism in the Anthropocene* (Hart 2016) 33–37; Sandrine Maljean-Dubois and others, 'Anthropocene', International Law Association White Paper 02, 2022, 11–12 www.ilaparis2023.org/wp-content/uploads/2022/08/ADI-ILA-anthropocene-EN-PLANCHES.pdf. See generally Jorge E Viñuales, 'The Organisation of the Anthropocene' (2018) 1 Brill Research Perspectives in International Legal Theory and Practice 1.

perspective, the ultimate unit of analysis is 'the planet as an interdependent integrated social-ecological system'.[120]

This expansion in understandings of the environment means that more cases will potentially qualify as having an environmental component, and it is appropriate to reject certain definitions that have previously been advanced. For example, writing in 1975, Bilder defined international environmental disputes as disagreements 'relating to the alteration, through human intervention, of natural environmental systems', seeking to focus on the natural rather than social environment.[121] Today it is far less certain that the sharp distinction between humans and nature within this definition can hold, given the developments just outlined.

Writing twenty-five years after Bilder, Romano defined an international environmental dispute as '[a] conflict of views or of interest between two or more States ... relating to an anthropogenic alteration of an ecosystem, having detrimental effect on human society and leading to environmental scarcity of natural resources.'[122] Part of Romano's definition, specifically the focus on potential or realised detrimental effects of human-induced alterations of ecosystems, captures much of what is at stake in international disputes with an environmental component. Yet today the inter-State limitation is not appropriate, for example given the massive number of investor–state arbitrations in recent years with an environmental or natural resources component,[123] and the substantial jurisprudence developed by regional human rights courts concerning the environment.[124] Romano's other restrictions – that the dispute concerns environmental scarcity as opposed to other types of scarcity, for example

[120] Frank Biermann, *Earth System Governance: World Politics in the Anthropocene* (MIT Press 2014) 16, 20; Louis J Kotzé and others, 'Earth System Law: Exploring New Frontiers in Legal Science' (2022) 11 Earth System Governance 100126; Maljean-Dubois and others (n 119) 12.

[121] Bilder (n 29) 153. Bilder included further limitations that are problematic, such as only focusing on inter-State disputes and excluding disputes concerning the management of natural resources: ibid. For a similar definition see Catherine A Cooper, 'The Management of International Environmental Disputes in the Context of Canada-United States Relations: A Survey and Evaluation of Techniques and Mechanisms' (1986) 24 Can YB Int'l L 247, 249.

[122] Romano (n 31) 29.

[123] For example, a recent UNCTAD study counted (up to the end of 2021) some 175 treaty-based investor–State cases that involved measures related to environmental protection: UNCTAD, 'Treaty-Based Investor–State Dispute Settlement Cases and Climate Action', IIA Issues Note No 4 (2022) 2.

[124] See n 134.

physical or socio-economic scarcity,[125] and that renewable, rather than non-renewable, resources are involved[126] – are also questionable. For example, a large number of investment treaty arbitrations in recent years have concerned non-renewable resources and questions around the host State's right to allocate the right to exploit such resources and liability for resulting environmental damage.[127]

In selecting the case law to be covered, this book has sought to avoid overly restrictive definitions. This reflects that environmental cases were selected as a focus precisely because they are representative of the highly varied nature of contemporary international adjudication and the professional versatility this demands of international lawyers. Nevertheless, certain restrictions have been imposed. For example, in recent years numerous disputes have arisen in WTO dispute settlement and investment treaty arbitration concerning State measures to incentivise renewable energy sources.[128] In the WTO context, such disputes have focused on the legality of subsidies and domestic content requirements.[129] In the investment treaty context, such disputes have focused on State liability for altering the incentives that apply to investments in the renewable energy sector, that is, obligations of regulatory stability and respecting the

[125] Romano (n 31) 28.

[126] Ibid 27–29. Romano acknowledges that non-renewable resources may lead to the degradation of renewable resources, which is his focus: ibid 27.

[127] See e.g. *Adel A Hamadi Al Tamimi v Oman*, ICSID Case No ARB/11/33, Award (3 November 2015); *Perenco Ecuador Ltd v Ecuador*, ICSID Case No ARB/08/6, Interim Decision on the Environmental Counterclaim (11 August 2015); *Burlington Resources Inc v Ecuador*, ICSID Case No ARB/08/5, Decision on Counterclaims (7 February 2017); *Occidental Petroleum Corporation & Ors v Ecuador*, ICSID Case No ARB/06/11, Award (5 October 2012); *Crystallex v Venezuela* (n 5); *Quiborax SA v Bolivia*, ICSID Case No ARB/06/2, Award (16 September 2015).

[128] See e.g. Daniel Behn and Ole Kristian Fauchald, 'Governments under Cross-Fire? Renewable Energy and International Economic Tribunals' (2015) 12 Manchester JIEL 117 (also highlighting relevant EU law issues); Henok Asmelash, 'The First Ten Years of WTO Jurisprudence on Renewable Energy Support Measures: Has the Dust Settled Yet?' (2022) 21 WTR 455; Alessandro Monti, *Promoting Renewable Energy: The Mutual Supportiveness of Climate and Trade Law* (Edward Elgar 2023) chs 5–6; Rahmi Kopar, *Stability and Legitimate Expectations in International Energy Investments* (Hart 2021).

[129] See e.g. Appellate Body Reports, *Canada – Certain Measures Affecting the Renewable Energy Generation Sector; Canada – Measures Relating to the Feed-in Tariff Program*, WT/DS412/AB/R, WT/DS426/AB/R, adopted 24 May 2013; Appellate Body Report, *India – Certain Measures Relating to Solar Cells and Solar Modules*, WT/DS456/AB/R and Add.1, adopted 14 October 2016; Panel Report, *United States – Certain Measures Relating to the Renewable Energy Sector*, WT/DS510/R and Add.1, circulated 27 June 2019.

legitimate expectations of investors under the fair and equitable treatment standard.[130] Overall, such renewable energy disputes, as they have arisen to date, have only incidentally raised environmental considerations, which, for example, have explained the rationale behind measures to incentivise particular types of energy supply.[131] This book does not place a primary focus on disputes concerning renewable energy incentives; however, such cases are discussed where they are particularly relevant to the themes analysed.

2. *The Adjudicatory Bodies Covered*

The adjudication settings covered by this book – adjudication in the WTO and under UNCLOS, ICJ litigation, and investment treaty arbitration – were selected because they are the key fora of global reach where environmental cases have been repeatedly litigated.[132] Compared to existing studies of international environmental adjudication, a key contribution of this book is to provide a state of the art treatment of treaty-based investor–State arbitration, which is analysed in a comparative manner alongside the key sites of inter-State adjudication that regularly hear environmental disputes.[133] A question that runs throughout this

[130] See cases discussed in Chapter 5, text at nn 140–156.

[131] See e.g. *India – Solar Cells* (n 129) [5.123]–[5.151] (consideration of India's argument that its domestic content requirements were necessary to secure compliance with domestic or international environmental laws); *Canada – Renewable Energy* (n 129) [5.186]–[5.190]; Behn and Langford (n 113) 18–19 (excluding renewable energy disputes from their definition of an environmental case); Boyle and Harrison (n 111) 249 fn 22 (arguing 'the simple fact that a trade or investment dispute relates to an environmental industry does not make it an environmental dispute if there are no questions of environmental law or policy' at issue). Contrast Jorge E Viñuales, 'Foreign Investment and the Environment in International Law: The Current State of Play' in Kate Miles (ed), *Research Handbook on Environment and Investment Law* (Edward Elgar 2019) 20 (including in his definition of investment disputes with an environmental component disputes concerning 'environmental markets' and highlighting the growth in disputes arising from 'energy transition policies').

[132] In future it is possible the International Criminal Court (ICC) may hear environmental cases. See generally Matthew Gillett, *Prosecuting Environmental Harm before the International Criminal Court* (CUP 2022). See also ICC Office of the Prosecutor (OTP), 'Policy Paper on Case Selection and Prioritisation' (15 September 2016) [41] (ICC OTP indicated that it would give particular consideration to prosecuting crimes within the Court's jurisdiction involving 'the destruction of the environment, the illegal exploitation of natural resources or the illegal dispossession of land').

[133] Due to its comparative focus, this book differs from the burgeoning literature that focuses specifically on the intersection of investment law and environmental issues:

book is the extent to which treaty-based investor–State arbitration is comparable to the three inter-State adjudication settings studied.

The key international tribunals that regularly hear environmental cases and are not considered by this book are regional human rights courts[134] and regional courts of economic integration.[135] This approach was adopted because such bodies are heavily tied to the specific regional human rights or regional integration contexts in which they operate and accordingly raise difficulties for comparative analysis that seeks to draw more general conclusions regarding the functions of international adjudication.[136] Where a tribunal is embedded within a strong regional integration or regional human rights project, this can provide a basis for adjudicators engaging in certain tasks, such as invalidating national-level measures, or weighing the importance of competing regulatory aims, which are much more controversial in regimes of global reach that do not enjoy any strong value-based consensus.[137]

e.g. Kate Miles (ed), *Research Handbook on Environment and Investment Law* (Edward Elgar 2019); Flavia Marisi, *Environmental Interests in Investment Arbitration: Challenges and Directions* (Kluwer Law International 2020); Jorge E Viñuales, *Foreign Investment and the Environment in International Law* (CUP 2012); Saverio Di Benedetto, *International Investment Law and the Environment* (Edward Elgar 2013).

134 For discussion of the case law of the various bodies, see e.g. Marie-Catherine Petersmann, *When Environmental Protection and Human Rights Collide: The Politics of Conflict Management by Regional Courts* (CUP 2022) 57–70; Shigeta (n 31) 68–115; Alan Boyle, 'Human Rights and the Environment: Where Next?' (2012) 23 EJIL 613; Sands and Peel (n 114) 819–27; Monica Feria-Tinta and Simon C Milnes, 'The Rise of Environmental Law in International Dispute Resolution: The Inter-American Court of Human Rights Issues a Landmark Advisory Opinion on the Environment and Human Rights' (2016) 27 Ybk IEL 64.

135 Regarding relevant European Court of Justice (ECJ) case law, see e.g. Ludwig Krämer, 'The Environment before the European Court of Justice' in Christina Voigt (ed), *International Judicial Practice on the Environment* (CUP 2019); Marie-Catherine Petersmann, 'When Environmental Protection and Human Rights Collide: Four Heuristics of Conflict Resolution' in Christina Voigt (ed), *International Judicial Practice on the Environment* (CUP 2019); Petersmann (n 134) 70–73; Shigeta (n 31) 137–84; Sands and Peel (n 114) 187–89, 883–87.

136 Similarly, Alter has argued that the ECJ and the European Court of Human Rights must be understood in light of unique contextual factors and thus present difficulties for comparative analysis: Alter (n 8) 106, 109. As Alter highlights, in some regions, such as Asia and the Pacific and the Middle East, there is little adjudication that occurs within regional human rights or regional integration frameworks: 87, 97–98, 110.

137 See e.g. ibid. 282–328 (analysing an 'international constitutional review' role whereby courts invalidate national measures and suggesting this function is explicitly given to some courts of regional integration, and in practice has also been exercised by certain regional human rights courts and international criminal courts).

This book also does not cover quasi-adjudicatory bodies that hear disputes with an environmental component. For example, it does not cover the large number of conferences of the parties and their non-compliance mechanisms developed under multilateral environmental agreements,[138] human rights treaty bodies and their individual complaint mechanisms,[139] or the inspection procedures established within multilateral development banks to enable review of projects.[140] As these bodies do not issue binding decisions, they do not meet a key criterion for being included within any definition of international tribunals and the related concept of international adjudication.[141] Furthermore, these bodies are sometimes designed to operate in a manner that is markedly different from adjudication, as in the context of many environmental non-compliance mechanisms.[142]

D. Methodological Insights from Comparative Law

This book seeks to *identify* and *explain* similarities and differences in how the three selected challenges are managed by adjudicators across the four contexts studied. These are, in short, the traditional aims of comparative law,[143] and it is instructive to consider methodological debates in comparative law insofar as they may offer insights into the challenges

138 See e.g. Meinhard Doelle, 'Non-compliance Procedures' in Lavanya Rajamani and Jacqueline Peel (eds), *The Oxford Handbook of International Environmental Law* (2nd ed., OUP 2021); Tullio Treves and others (eds), *Non-Compliance Procedures and Mechanisms and the Effectiveness of International Environmental Agreements* (TMC Asser Press 2008); Stephens (n 12) 81–89; Shigeta (n 31) 117–37.

139 For discussion of relevant contributions, see e.g. Petersmann (n 134) 73–75; Shigeta (n 31) 69–72.

140 See for overview and further references Sands and Peel (n 114) 176–77.

141 Cesare PR Romano, 'A Taxonomy of International Rule of Law Institutions' (2011) 2 JIDS 241, 253–61; Romano, Alter and Shany (n 6) 6, 8–9.

142 See e.g. Convention on Access to Information, Public Participation in Decision-Making and Access to Justice in Environmental Matters (1998) 2161 UNTS 447, art 15 (compliance mechanism intended to be 'non-confrontational, non-judicial and consultative'). Noting this is generally true of non-compliance mechanisms in environmental treaties: Cesare Pitea and Attila Tanzi, 'Non-compliance Mechanisms: Lessons Learned and the Way Forward' in Tullio Treves and others (ed), *Non-compliance Procedures and Mechanisms and the Effectiveness of International Environmental Agreements* (TMC Asser Press 2008) 569–70.

143 Jaakko Husa, 'Research Designs of Comparative Law – Methodology or Heuristics?' in Maurice Adams and Dirk Heirbaut (eds), *The Method and Culture of Comparative Law: Essays in Honour of Mark Van Hoecke* (Hart 2014) 53–54; Jaakko Husa, *Introduction to Comparative Law* (2nd ed., Hart 2023) 153.

of comparing different sites of international adjudication.[144] Historically, the dominant approach to comparative law has been functionalism, which focuses on functionally equivalent problems and legal solutions developed across different contexts.[145] According to functionalist approaches, the legal doctrines and institutions of different societies can be compared where they fulfil similar functions, and every legal system 'faces essentially the same problems, and solves these problems by quite different means though very often with similar results'.[146] Functionalism is the subject of substantial debate within comparative law scholarship, and key criticisms include that it 'exaggerates the extent to which different societies face similar problems', underemphasises the 'cultural, economic, political and social context within which legal rules exist', and cannot provide a basis for evaluating different legal solutions.[147] The major alternative to functionalism that exists in

[144] Note that this inquiry differs from the emerging field of 'comparative international law', which focuses on how international law is understood within different national and regional legal systems rather than on variations between different subfields of international law: see Anthea Roberts and others, 'Comparative International Law: Framing the Field' (2015) 109 AJIL 467, 469. Others have highlighted the relevance of comparative law for comparing different international legal regimes: e.g. Valentina Vadi, *Analogies in International Investment Law and Arbitration* (CUP 2015); Claire Buggenhoudt, *Common Interests in International Litigation: A Case Study on Natural Resource Exploitation Disputes* (Intersentia 2017) 28–29; Mads Andenas and Duncan Fairgrieve, 'Courts and Comparative Law: In Search of a Common Language for Open Legal Systems' in Mads Andenas and Duncan Fairgrieve (eds), *Courts and Comparative Law* (OUP 2015) 4–5, 9–11. Some comparative lawyers have also emphasised the need to broaden their field beyond national legal systems to include the study of transnational regimes: e.g. Mathias Reimann, 'Beyond National Systems: A Comparative Law for the International Age' (2001) 75 Tulane LR 1103, 1115–19; Annelise Riles, 'Wigmore's Treasure Box: Comparative Law in the Era of Information' (1999) 40 HILJ 221, 276–77.

[145] Ralf Michaels, 'The Functional Method of Comparative Law' in Mathias Reimann and Reinhard Zimmermann (eds), *The Oxford Handbook of Comparative Law* (2nd ed., OUP 2019) 347–48, 386–87; Christopher A Whytock, 'Legal Origins, Functionalism, and the Future of Comparative Law' [2009] Brigham Young ULR 1879, 1879; Konrad Zweigert and Hein Kötz, *Introduction to Comparative Law* (Tony Weir tr, OUP 1998) 34.

[146] Zweigert and Kötz (n 145) 34. Consider also: Michaels (n 145) 347–48, 374–76; Shirlow (n 69) 52–53; Catherine Valcke and Matthew Grellette, 'Three Functions of Function in Comparative Legal Studies' in *The Method and Culture of Comparative Law* (n 143) 101–11; A Esin Örücü, 'Methodology of Comparative Law' in Jan M Smits (ed), *Elgar Encyclopedia of Comparative Law* (2nd ed., Edward Elgar 2012) 561–63; Husa, *Introduction* (n 143) 122–24.

[147] Whytock (n 145) 1886–87, 1897–98; Michaels (n 145) 380–81, 385. Seminally: Günter Frankenberg, 'Critical Comparisons: Re-thinking Comparative Law' (1985) 26 HILJ 411, 412–40.

comparative law literature is cultural approaches, which emphasise that legal rules are heavily intertwined with their broader social, economic, and cultural context, and at their strongest suggest that different legal systems are not comparable.[148]

The perspective of this book is towards the functionalist end of the methodological spectrum,[149] as the common yardsticks that structure my comparison are three challenges facing international tribunals, namely managing change in applicable legal norms or relevant facts, scrutinising State conduct for compliance with international obligations, and contributing to broader processes of dispute resolution.[150] Much of my analysis focuses on the extent to which the problems faced, legal techniques used in response, and functions performed by tribunals are comparable across the contexts studied.[151] This book shares the implicitly functionalist view that comparative inquiry can make one aware of comparable challenges faced, and potentially useful legal techniques developed, in other contexts.[152] However, it is crucial to remember that even where international tribunals appear to face similar problems or develop similar solutions, differences persist reflecting the varied contexts in which tribunals operate and the numerous interrelated factors which shape their work. The challenge is partly one of managing 'scale change'[153] and differentiating

148 Vadi (n 144) 31–33; Mathias Reimann, 'The Progress and Failure of Comparative Law in the Second Half of the Twentieth Century' (2002) 50 Am. J. Comp. L. 671, 680–82; Riles (n 144) 240–49. Examples of cultural approaches include: Frankenberg (n 147) 441–55; Pierre Legrand, 'The Impossibility of Legal Transplants' (1997) 4 Maastricht J. Eur. & Comp. L. 111, 120–24. The risk of incommensurability due to contextual differences has also been highlighted by those who have compared different international legal regimes: e.g. Martins Paparinskis, 'Substantive Standards of Investment Protection under EU Law and International Investment Law' in Emmanuel Gaillard and Hélène Ruiz-Fabri (eds), *EU Law and International Investment Arbitration* (Juris 2018) 231–32.

149 Vadi (n 144) 30 (noting all approaches fit somewhere on a sliding scale from the wholly functionalist to the purely cultural).

150 In comparative law terms, such a common yardstick is referred to as a *tertium comparationis*: see e.g. Husa, *Introduction* (n 143) 154–58. For a sophisticated discussion of the potential for functional comparison of the problems facing international courts and tribunals, see Shirlow (n 69) 52–58.

151 See generally Michaels (n 145) 347–48, 371, 386–87.

152 For similar claims in an international law context, see e.g. William W Park and Thomas W Walsh, 'Review Essay: The Uses of Comparative Arbitration Law' (2008) 24 Arbitration International 615, 615; Vadi (n 144) 230.

153 Riles (n 144) 225, 253–53 (on the appropriate scale for analysis, and managing scale change, as a fundamental problem in comparativism).

between levels of analysis because legal regimes often appear similar at one level of analysis and different at another level of analysis.[154]

In order to address potential shortcomings of a functional approach, this book analyses in significant detail contextual factors relevant to understanding each of the adjudication settings studied.[155] Each chapter begins with an analysis of such factors, which include whether adjudication occurs within a wider regime with particular goals, the activity of other law-making processes within the regime, whether compulsory jurisdiction exists and which actors can access adjudication, the appointment arrangements for adjudicators, and the types of remedies typically utilised.[156] Attention to such contextual factors is in fact required by a functional approach as the functions of a court or tribunal may be unstated and implicit[157] and become clear through analysis of considerations such as the structure and procedure of a tribunal.[158] I attempt to explain my findings of similarity or difference regarding the case law analysed in light of such contextual considerations.

Clearly, focusing on other aspects of international adjudication may have produced different findings.[159] However, as justified above, the three challenges focused on in this book were selected because they capture key contemporary challenges facing international tribunals, and also serve as a useful proxy for developing a broader, comparative

[154] Michaels (n 145) 374.

[155] See Vicki C Jackson, 'Comparative Constitutional Law: Methodologies' in Michel Rosenfeld and András Sajó (eds), *The Oxford Handbook of Comparative Constitutional Law* (OUP 2012) 72 (suggesting a 'contextualized functionalism' is possible and 'requires a willingness to question whether functions, concepts, or doctrines that appear similar may in fact be quite different' and to pay attention to how, within each legal system compared, 'seemingly separate institutions or legal practices are connected to, and influenced by, others').

[156] Also highlighting the importance of such factors: Webb (n 45) 147–201; Jürgen Kurtz, 'The Merits and Limits of Comparativism: National Treatment in International Investment Law and the WTO' in Stephan W Schill (ed), *International Investment Law and Comparative Public Law* (OUP 2010) 252–55; Steven R Ratner, 'Regulatory Takings in Institutional Context: Beyond the Fear of Fragmented International Law' (2008) 102 AJIL 475, 485–87, 520–21.

[157] Michaels (n 145) 369–70. See also Jaakko Husa, 'Methodology of Comparative Law Today: From Paradoxes to Flexibility?' (2006) 58 Revue Internationale De Droit Comparé 1095, 1102–04 (emphasising that functional approaches require understanding the wider socio-legal context of rules and institutions).

[158] Yuval Shany, 'Effectiveness of International Adjudication: Assessing Functions and Performance' (2014) 108 ASIL Proceedings 113, 114; David D Caron, 'Towards a Political Theory of International Courts and Tribunals' (2006) 24 Berkeley JIL 401, 410.

[159] See Michaels (n 145) 377.

assessment of the functions of international adjudication. Functionalism is a constructive approach to law in that it involves developing hypotheses about the problems faced by legal systems and how they are responded to by legal institutions and doctrines. Accordingly, functional approaches, such as this study, should be judged according to their contribution to our understanding of the legal systems compared.[160]

E. An Overview of the Chapters to Come

Chapter 2 analyses the three selected challenges confronting international tribunals – change, review of State conduct, and dispute resolution – in WTO dispute settlement. It demonstrates that within the WTO's environmental case law, adjudicators have grappled with the question of potential change in applicable international legal norms, and, even more frequently, changes in relevant facts that affect what an applicable legal norm requires at a particular point in time. In the context of disputes under the Agreement on the Application of Sanitary and Phytosanitary Measures, WTO adjudicators have developed a highly structured approach to the issue of the standard of review that may foreseeably be drawn upon by adjudicators in other contexts also faced with 'fact-intensive environmental disputes'.[161] While this approach avoids WTO adjudicators themselves deciding on the correctness of contested scientific claims that are often raised by environmental disputes, it requires adjudicators to determine what counts as an adequate risk assessment process. The chapter analyses the elaborate form of necessity testing that has been developed by WTO adjudicators as a method of review, or balancing test, when scrutinising measures that pursue a permissible regulatory aim but also restrict a competing treaty-protected interest in trade liberalisation.[162] It argues that the WTO's necessity jurisprudence contains important lessons for other international tribunals. Finally, the chapter considers the contribution of certain early trade and environment disputes to the so-called 'chapeau jurisprudence' concerning the general exceptions contained in WTO covered agreements. As noted above, this case law has been interpreted

[160] Ibid 368–72, 386–87.

[161] Peel (n 85) 457–58.

[162] My wording here draws on Foster (n 10) 147, 152 (discussing the WTO 'necessity formula' as an 'elaborate' standard developed by adjudicators for judging the legality of States' regulatory measures).

by many commentators as a desirable example of a procedurally focused form of international adjudicatory scrutiny that pushes States to consider affected foreign interests.[163] In short, although the chapeau jurisprudence does not impose a free-standing obligation to cooperate, these cases highlight that WTO adjudication often contributes to a broader process of dispute settlement, including because of the system's prospectively focused system of remedies and strong diplomatic ethos.

Chapter 3 analyses the three selected challenges in UNCLOS adjudication, undertaken by ITLOS and arbitral tribunals. The chapter analyses significant examples of UNCLOS adjudicators incrementally adapting the Convention, given changes in wider international law, reflecting, inter alia, that the Convention includes various generic terms, obligations to protect the marine environment framed in general terms, and instructs adjudicators to apply other relevant international law. The standard of review is shown to be a key problem in the context of ITLOS' prompt release jurisdiction, which raises questions also seen in the other adjudication contexts studied, for example given the greater proximity of domestic authorities to local conditions. The chapter also demonstrates that UNCLOS adjudicators have increasingly employed balancing tests, such as necessity testing, that raise equivalent questions to such methods of review as seen in the other contexts considered, with some UNCLOS adjudicators even noting the parallel to WTO necessity testing. Finally, UNCLOS environmental adjudication provides repeated examples of tribunals attempting to contribute to broader processes of dispute resolution, for example by ordering the disputing parties to engage in further cooperation.

Chapter 4 turns to environmental litigation before the ICJ. The ICJ's responses to the three selected challenges are shaped by the Court's general and consent-dependent jurisdiction, which means that it adjudicates across highly varied legal contexts and is particularly sensitive to consent-based concerns. There are repeated examples of the ICJ incrementally updating aging treaties in light of wider developments in international law. In its environmental case law, the ICJ has often faced the question of how to balance two partially competing interests, both protected by the relevant legal regime, and how intensely to scrutinise domestic-level determinations that may have involved the application of specialist forms of non-legal expertise or an assessment of local circumstances. While the

[163] See n 104.

Court's approach to such questions is shaped by the particular context in which it adjudicates, the legal techniques used in scrutinising State conduct for compliance with international law display important functional similarities with those seen in the other contexts studied. The ICJ has often adjudicated with a partly prospective focus, seeking to facilitate future cooperation between the disputing parties.

Chapter 5 addresses investment treaty arbitration. Investment treaty tribunals, like the other international tribunals considered in this book, are often faced with determining whether applicable international legal norms have evolved. However, differently from the other contexts studied, investment treaty tribunals, by applying investment treaty norms in particular disputes, also play a crucial role in determining the permissible degree of change in host State regulation. In scrutinising State conduct for compliance with investment treaty obligations, arbitrators have endorsed many of the reasons for a limited degree of deference to domestic authorities also seen in the other contexts studied. Investment treaty tribunals have also employed methods of review encountered in the other contexts studied, with a growing number of tribunals engaging in the controversial step of proportionality balancing stricto sensu. In contrast to the other adjudication settings studied in this book, there are few examples of investment treaty tribunals performing a forward-looking, facilitative role and contributing to broader processes of dispute resolution. This reflects inter alia that in this context the disputing parties frequently do not have an ongoing relationship by the time of a final award and adjudication is widely understood as a retrospectively focused compensation mechanism, in contrast to the more diplomatic ethos of the inter-State adjudication mechanisms studied.

Chapter 6, which concludes the study, draws together and extends the insights gained from the comparative analysis undertaken. It analyses convergences and divergences in how the three selected challenges are managed across the four adjudication contexts studied and advances explanations for the trends identified. The chapter also reflects on the wider implications emerging from this book for our understanding of the functions of international adjudication in contemporary international law.

2

Adjudication in the World Trade Organization

This chapter concerns the dispute settlement system (DSS) of the World Trade Organization (WTO), which since its creation in 1995 has been the most active site of inter-State adjudication and has routinely heard disputes with an environmental component.[1] This chapter proceeds as follows. Section A analyses numerous features of institutional context relevant to understanding the role of adjudication in this regime. Section B considers how WTO adjudicators have managed the problem of potential changes in applicable legal norms or changes in relevant facts. Section C analyses how WTO adjudicators have approached the issues of the appropriate standard and method of review when scrutinising State conduct for compliance with applicable legal norms. Section D considers how WTO adjudicators have contributed to broader processes of dispute resolution in certain key environmental disputes. Section E consolidates the findings of this chapter by drawing a series of conclusions regarding how contextual features of WTO adjudication shape the practices analysed.

It is appropriate to justify the type of WTO disputes considered in interrogating these themes. To analyse the issue of the standard of review, I focus on disputes arising under the Agreement on the Application of Sanitary and Phytosanitary Measures (SPS Agreement).[2] While the issue of the standard review raises distinct issues under different WTO-covered agreements,[3] for present purposes focusing on the sanitary and phytosanitary (SPS) context is justified because the issue

[1] See e.g. Petros C Mavroidis, *The WTO Dispute Settlement System: How, Why and Where?* (Edward Elgar 2022) 95, 469; Peter Van den Bossche, 'The Demise of the WTO Appellate Body: Lessons for Governance of International Adjudication?', WTI Working Paper No 02/2021, 1–2.

[2] Agreement on the Application of Sanitary and Phytosanitary Measures, Marrakesh Agreement Establishing the World Trade Organisation, Annex 1A (1994) 1867 UNTS 493 ('WTO Agreement').

[3] See generally Claus-Dieter Ehlermann and Nicolas Lockhart, 'Standard of Review in WTO Law' (2004) 7 JIEL 491, 503–19.

has been given sustained attention in this setting, reflecting that more than other contexts, SPS cases have presented adjudicators with contested, factually complex scientific claims.[4] The SPS discourse, because it is comparatively well developed, has the potential to inform approaches to the standard of review in other contexts where international adjudicators also face 'fact-intensive environmental disputes'.[5]

In analysing the methods of review used in WTO environmental adjudication I consider disputes arising under the General Agreement on Tariffs and Trade (GATT),[6] the Agreement on Technical Barriers to Trade (TBT Agreement),[7] and the SPS Agreement.[8] This focus is appropriate because environmental cases have been frequently litigated in these contexts and WTO adjudicators have developed a distinctive necessity jurisprudence across these agreements to determine the legality of measures that pursue legitimate regulatory interests but also restrict treaty-protected interests in trade liberalisation. In analysing the contribution of WTO adjudicators as 'dispute resolvers' I focus on aspects of the case law developed under the 'chapeau test' that must be satisfied to rely upon the GATT Article XX general exceptions. Clearly, there are many other areas of WTO practice where adjudication contributes to broader processes of dispute resolution. However, this focus is justified because many commentators have suggested that certain aspects of the chapeau jurisprudence, as developed in prominent environmental cases such as *US – Gasoline*[9] and *US – Shrimp*,[10] represent a desirable, procedurally focused

[4] Lukasz Gruszczynski, 'Standard of Review of Health and Environmental Regulations by WTO Panels' in Geert Van Calster and Denise Prévost (eds), *Research Handbook on Environment, Health and the WTO* (Edward Elgar 2013) 732; Tracey Epps, 'Recent Developments in WTO Jurisprudence: Has the Appellate Body Resolved the Issue of an Appropriate Standard of Review in SPS Cases?' (2012) 62 University of Toronto Law Journal 201, 202.

[5] Jacqueline Peel, 'Of Apples and Oranges (and Hormones in Beef): Science and the Standard of Review in WTO Disputes under the SPS Agreement' (2012) 61 ICLQ 427, 457–58; Katalin Sulyok, *Science and Judicial Reasoning: The Legitimacy of International Environmental Adjudication* (CUP 2020) 178–79; Makane Moïse Mbengue and Rukmini Das, 'The ICJ's Engagement with Science: To Interpret or Not to Interpret?' (2015) 6 JIDS 568, 575–76.

[6] General Agreement on Tariffs and Trade (1994), WTO Agreement, Annex 1A (1994) 1867 UNTS 190.

[7] Agreement on Technical Barriers to Trade, WTO Agreement, Annex 1A (1994) 1868 UNTS 120.

[8] SPS Agreement (n 2).

[9] Appellate Body Report, *United States – Standards for Reformulated and Conventional Gasoline*, WT/DS2/AB/R, adopted 20 May 1996.

[10] Appellate Body Report, *United States – Import Prohibition of Certain Shrimp and Shrimp Products*, WT/DS58/AB/R, adopted 6 November 1998; Appellate Body Report, *United*

form of adjudicatory review, whereby adjudicators push regulating States to pursue cooperative solutions and consider affected foreign interests.

A. Institutional Context for WTO Dispute Settlement

1. *The Goals of the WTO DSS*

Article 3 of the Dispute Settlement Understanding (DSU) is the starting point for understanding the goals of the DSS.[11] One explicit goal, reflected in Article 3.2 of the DSU, is to provide 'security and predictability to the multilateral trading system'.[12] As Shlomo Agon notes, this ultimate goal can be broken into several more specific intermediate goals, namely providing coherent interpretations of WTO law, inducing compliance with WTO norms, resolving disputes, and curbing unilateral actions that could harm the security of the system.[13] One of the most important aims of the DSS, based on its negotiating history, is curbing unilateralism, and in particular preventing unilateral determinations of illegality or unilaterally imposed sanctions.[14] As outlined below, the DSS is notable for having a detailed and compulsory set of procedures for determining disputes over compliance.

Article 3.2 further provides that the DSS 'serves to preserve the rights and obligations of Members under the covered agreements, and to clarify the existing provisions of those agreements'.[15] WTO adjudicators play an important role in 'interpreting ambiguities and filling gaps in the agreements'.[16] However, the remaining parts of Article 3.2 regulate how this task is undertaken. Adjudicators are instructed to apply 'customary rules

States – Import Prohibition of Certain Shrimp and Shrimp Products – Recourse to Article 21.5 of the DSU by Malaysia, WT/DS58/AB/RW, adopted 21 November 2001.

11 Sivan Shlomo Agon, *International Adjudication on Trial: The Effectiveness of the WTO Dispute Settlement System* (OUP 2019) 62; Sivan Shlomo-Agon and Yuval Shany, 'The WTO Dispute Settlement System' in Yuval Shany, *Assessing the Effectiveness of International Courts* (OUP 2014) 191; Understanding on Rules and Procedures Governing the Settlement of Disputes, WTO Agreement, Annex 2 (1994) 1869 UNTS 401 ('DSU').

12 DSU art 3.2.

13 Shlomo Agon (n 11) 65.

14 See esp Petros C Mavroidis, 'Dispute Settlement in the WTO: Mind over Matter' in Kyle Bagwell and Robert W Staiger (eds), *Handbook of Commercial Policy*, vol 1A (North-Holland 2016); Shlomo Agon (n 11) 84–85.

15 DSU art 3.2.

16 Shlomo-Agon and Shany (n 11) 195; Shlomo Agon (n 11) 78–81.

of interpretation of public international law',[17] which is arguably an attempt to foreclose an expansive, teleological approach to interpretation.[18] More concretely, the final sentence of Article 3.2 states that '[r]-ecommendations and rulings of the DSB [(Dispute Settlement Body)] cannot add to or diminish the rights and obligations provided in the covered agreements'.[19] Relatedly, Article 3.9 provides that the provisions of the DSU 'are without prejudice to the rights of Members to seek authoritative interpretation of provisions of a covered agreement through decision-making under the WTO Agreement'.[20] The WTO Agreement provides that the Ministerial Conference and General Council, bodies consisting of representatives of all WTO members, 'have the exclusive authority to adopt interpretations' of the Agreement, by a three-fourths majority.[21] The Appellate Body (AB) has held that adopted panel and AB reports create 'legitimate expectations among WTO Members' and must be 'taken into account', but are not strictly binding beyond the parties to the dispute and do not constitute subsequent treaty practice.[22]

Another goal with strong support in Article 3 of the DSU is that of settling disputes.[23] Under Article 3.7 'the aim of the dispute settlement mechanism is to secure a positive solution to a dispute' and '[a] solution mutually acceptable to the parties to a dispute and consistent with the covered agreements is clearly to be preferred'.[24] Article 3.3 also refers to 'the prompt settlement of situations', and the DSS is notable, as compared to other international tribunals, for establishing explicit time frames for the duration of proceedings.[25] Given this strong basis in treaty

17 DSU art 3.2.

18 Jan Klabbers, 'On Rationalism in Politics: Interpretation of Treaties and the World Trade Organization' (2005) 74 Nordic JIL 405, 412; Armin von Bogdandy, 'Law and Politics in the WTO: Strategies to Cope with a Deficient Relationship' (2001) 5 Max Planck Ybk UN Law 609, 617.

19 DSU art 3.2. But see Klabbers (n 18) 413–14 (development of the law through interpretation is inevitable whatever 'the WTO tries to tell its Member[s]').

20 DSU art 3.9.

21 WTO Agreement art IX:2.

22 Appellate Body Report, *Japan – Taxes on Alcoholic Beverages*, WT/DS8/AB/R, WT/DS10/AB/R, WT/DS11/AB/R, adopted 1 November 1996, 13–14; *US – Shrimp (Art 21.5)* (n 10) [108]–[109]. See also Appellate Body Report, *United States – Final Anti-Dumping Measures on Stainless Steel from Mexico*, WT/DS344/AB/R, adopted 20 May 2008, [160]–[161].

23 See DSU arts 3.3, 3.4, 3.7; Shlomo Agon (n 11) 74–76.

24 DSU art 3.7.

25 See DSU arts 12.8–12.9, 17.5, 20. On the goal of ensuring prompt settlement of disputes see Shlomo Agon (n 11) 76–77.

text, WTO adjudicators have often highlighted that settling disputes is the primary aim of the DSS.[26] However, certain restrictions are placed on the goal of settling disputes, including that solutions agreed between the parties, and recommendations and rulings of the DSB, must be consistent with the covered agreements.[27]

Two further goals find some support in Article 3, although they are debated. The first is the goal of maintaining the balance of trade concessions between WTO members.[28] Article 3.3 states that:

> The prompt settlement of situations in which a Member considers that any benefits accruing to it directly or indirectly under the covered agreements are being impaired by measures taken by another Member is essential to the effective functioning of the WTO and the maintenance of a proper balance between the rights and obligations of Members.[29]

This goal reflects an idea from the GATT era, which has been carried forward into the WTO, that at the heart of the system lies not only the legal rights and obligations contained in the WTO agreements, but also a set of trade concessions exchanged between members at the time of entry, and this balance must be maintained.[30] This goal finds some support in the WTO system of remedies, under which, as explained below, as a last resort, when a measure found to be inconsistent with a covered agreement has not been brought into compliance, the complaining member can request authorisation to suspend the application of equivalent trade concessions.[31] A second contested goal of the DSS is inducing compliance with WTO norms.[32] Article 3.7 of the DSU states that 'in the absence of a mutually agreed solution, the first objective of the

[26] See e.g. Panel Report, *European Communities – Regime for the Importation, Sale and Distribution of Bananas, Complaint by Ecuador*, WT/DS27/R/ECU, adopted 25 September 1997, [7.32]; Appellate Body Report, *United States – Measure Affecting Imports of Woven Wool Shirts and Blouses from India*, WT/DS33/AB/R, adopted 23 May 1997, 18–19.

[27] See DSU, arts 3.4–3.5. On the potential tension between the goal of settling disputes and other goals of the DSS, such as clarifying the law for the benefit of the wider membership and ensuring compliance with WTO law, see John H Jackson, *Sovereignty, the WTO, and Changing Fundamentals of International Law* (CUP 2006) 146; Shlomo Agon (n 11) 73, 76–77.

[28] Shlomo-Agon and Shany (n 11) 193–94; Shlomo Agon (n 11) 65–66.

[29] DSU art 3.3.

[30] See e.g. Joost Pauwelyn, 'Enforcement and Countermeasures in the WTO: Rules Are Rules–Toward a More Collective Approach' (2000) 94 AJIL 335, 339–40.

[31] DSU arts 22.2, 22.4.

[32] See Shlomo-Agon and Shany (n 11) 195–96; Shlomo Agon (n 11) 71–73.

dispute settlement mechanism is usually to secure the withdrawal of measures which are found to be inconsistent with the covered agreements.[33] However, debates concerning WTO remedies have highlighted that there is considerable disagreement over whether the DSS has the aim of inducing compliance with WTO obligations, or continues to operate according to the more limited GATT logic of restoring the balance of trade concessions.[34]

The DSS should also be understood in light of the broader goals of the WTO, reflecting the 'regime support' function of international tribunals embedded within wider functional regimes.[35] The goals of the WTO include raising living standards, 'ensuring full employment and a large and steadily growing volume of real income and effective demand, and expanding the production of and trade in goods and services, while allowing for the optimal use of the world's resources in accordance with the objective of sustainable development', and protecting the environment.[36] Explicit recognition is given to the 'need for positive efforts designed to ensure that developing countries, and especially the least developed among them, secure a share in the growth in international trade commensurate with the needs of their economic development'.[37] Tariff reduction and the removal of other barriers to trade are framed as a means for contributing to the above-mentioned objectives.[38] The WTO Agreement also aims to 'develop an integrated, more viable and durable multilateral trading system',[39] and the DSS is recognised within key provisions of the DSU as central to the wider organisation.[40]

[33] DSU art 3.7.

[34] See e.g. Shlomo-Agon and Shany (n 11) 210–11 (succinct overview of the debate); Joost Pauwelyn, 'The Calculation and Design of Trade Retaliation in Context: What Is the Goal of Suspending WTO Obligations?' in Chad P Bown and Joost Pauwelyn (eds), *The Law, Economics and Politics of Retaliation in WTO Dispute Settlement* (CUP 2010) (reviewing the debate and arguing the mechanism of WTO retaliation has multiple goals, despite a gradual evolution from rebalancing concessions to rule compliance); David Palmeter and Stanimir A Alexandrov, '"Inducing Compliance" in WTO Dispute Settlement' in Daniel LM Kennedy and James D Southwick (eds), *The Political Economy of International Trade Law: Essays in Honor of Robert E. Hudec* (CUP 2002) (arguing the system does not aim to induce compliance but merely to rebalance concessions).

[35] Shlomo Agon (n 11) 67; Shlomo-Agon and Shany (n 11) 192.

[36] WTO Agreement, preamble.

[37] Ibid.

[38] Ibid.

[39] Ibid.

[40] See DSU art 3.2, 3.3. See also above text at n 14.

A related function of the DSS is to confer legitimacy on the WTO and its underlying norms from the perspective of both WTO members and external constituencies, for example by resolving disputes in an independent and principled manner rather than on the basis of the relative power of the members involved, providing detailed reasons for decisions, and addressing the concerns of civil society.[41] As Shlomo Agon has noted, this function is reflected in the practice of WTO adjudicators adding explanatory paragraphs to their rulings in controversial trade linkage disputes that are not crucial to the legal reasoning but address the concerns of external constituencies.[42]

2. *Other Institutional Features of WTO Dispute Settlement Relevant to This Study*

(a) From GATT to the WTO: The Shift to Compulsory Jurisdiction and the Creation of Wide-Ranging Appellate Jurisdiction

A crucial difference between the WTO DSS and its GATT predecessor is the shift from a consensus requirement under GATT to a 'reverse-consensus' model in the WTO. Whereas in the GATT it was possible for a member to block the establishment of a panel, in the WTO 'there is effectively a right to have a panel established',[43] since the DSB, composed of all WTO members,[44] can only block such establishment by consensus, which the complaining party can prevent.[45] Furthermore, whereas the GATT system required consensus for the adoption of panel reports or for authorisation to suspend concessions, in the WTO these decisions are subject to 'reverse consensus', meaning the relevant decision (e.g. adoption of a panel report) is taken unless there is a consensus not to do so, which a victorious member can prevent.[46] In short, the DSS is designed

[41] Shlomo-Agon and Shany (n 11) 193; Joseph HH Weiler, 'The Rule of Lawyers and the Ethos of Diplomats: Reflections on the Internal and External Legitimacy of WTO Dispute Settlement' (2001) 35 JWT 191, 204; Shlomo Agon (n 11) 68–71. Shlomo Agon highlights that this in turn requires the WTO DSS to sustain its own legitimacy, ibid 86–87.

[42] Sivan Shlomo-Agon, 'Clearing the Smoke: The Legitimation of Judicial Power at the WTO' (2015) 49 JWT 539, 583–85; Shlomo Agon (n 11) 121–24, 154–56.

[43] Jackson (n 27) 153.

[44] WTO Agreement art IV:2–3.

[45] DSU art 6.1.

[46] See DSU arts 16.4, 17.14, 22.6. Note that near the end of the GATT-era, in the 1989 Montreal Ministerial Conference, the GATT membership agreed to move to a position of reverse consensus: see Mavroidis (n 1) 96–97, 106.

to contain a system of compulsory jurisdiction, and operated in this way from 1995 until the demise of the AB in 2019, a development that will be explained shortly.[47] The creation of a standing AB was an innovation introduced in the shift from GATT to the WTO, essentially as a check on erroneous panel reports and as a quid pro quo for members losing the ability to block the adoption of panel reports.[48] Under the DSU, an appeal is permitted on 'issues of law covered in the panel report and legal interpretations developed by the panel'.[49] The breadth of this appeal mechanism is unusual in wider international law, where there is often no appeal mechanism, as in the ICJ or UNCLOS adjudication, or only challenge to adjudicatory decisions on narrow grounds, as in investment treaty arbitration.[50]

(b) WTO Dispute Settlement since 2019: The Demise of the AB and the Partial Undermining of Compulsory Jurisdiction

WTO dispute settlement has changed markedly in recent years due to the demise of the AB in December 2019 when it fell below the quorum of three members required to decide appeals. This development has also partly undermined the panel process, as, under the DSU, a panel report cannot be adopted if an appeal has been lodged.[51] Accordingly, a member that loses at the panel stage can lodge an appeal, despite there being no AB to hear the appeal, and thereby unilaterally prevent the panel report being adopted. Such 'appeals into the void' have occurred in relation to many although not all of the panel reports have been circulated since the AB's demise.[52]

[47] See also DSU art 23 (members must resolve their disputes concerning the covered agreements through the dispute settlement procedures established in the DSU, and cannot make unilateral determinations that a violation has occurred).

[48] See e.g. Peter Van den Bossche, 'From Afterthought to Centerpiece: The WTO Appellate Body and Its Rise to Prominence in the World Trading System' in Giorgio Sacerdoti, Alan Yanovich and Jan Bohanes (eds), *The WTO at Ten: The Contribution of the Dispute Settlement System* (CUP 2006) 292–94; Debra P Steger, 'The Founding of the Appellate Body' in Gabrielle Marceau (ed), *A History of Law and Lawyers in the GATT/WTO: The Development of the Rule of Law in the Multilateral Trading System* (CUP 2015) 447.

[49] DSU art 17.6.

[50] Jackson (n 1) 156. See generally Giorgio Sacerdoti, 'Appeal and Judicial Review in International Arbitration and Adjudication: The Case of the WTO Appellate Review' in Ernst-Ulrich Petersmann (ed), *International Trade Law and the GATT/WTO Dispute Settlement System* (Kluwer Law International 1997) 254–77.

[51] DSU art 16.4.

[52] For a list of 'appeals into the void' up to March 2022, see Mavroidis (n 1) 62.

Given the demise of the AB, a subset of WTO members have created an interim solution that applies between themselves, the 'Multi-Party Interim Appeal Arrangement' (MPIA). This is a procedural agreement that any WTO member can join by notifying the DSB.[53] Parties to the MPIA agree that while the AB is not functioning they will use arbitration under Article 25 of the DSU for any appeals between themselves.[54] The pool of ten MPIA arbitrators was constituted in July 2020, and there have already been numerous agreements between WTO members (including some non-parties to the MPIA) to resort to Article 25 arbitration for any appeals in particular disputes, and one appellate decision issued under the MPIA.[55] The MPIA is designed to maintain the core features of appellate review before the AB under the DSU, with three members of the pool of ten arbitrators, selected on the basis of randomised rotation, to hear disputes.[56]

The demise of the AB, due to the United States (US) blocking all attempts to (re)appoint AB members from August 2017 onwards, is well covered in existing literature and only a brief overview will be provided here.[57] The reasons cited by the US for blocking all AB appointments are numerous, long-standing, and some of them are shared by other WTO members. In summary, the US accused the AB of engaging in impermissible judicial law-making, developing a doctrine of precedent that lacks a basis in the DSU, and engaging in review of panels' fact-finding, despite the limitation of appeals to issues of law. The US also raised procedural concerns, including the AB having exceeded the 90-day time limit for appellate proceedings under the DSU without seeking the approval of the disputing parties, and the AB itself authorising members whose terms

[53] Multi-Party Interim Appeal Arrangement Pursuant to Article 25 of the DSU, JOB/DSB/1/Add.12, 30 April 2020, [12].

[54] See ibid [1], [9]–[10].

[55] For ongoing coverage of developments concerning the MPIA, see the dedicated part of the *International Law and Economic Policy Blog* https://ielp.worldtradelaw.net/dsu-25-interim-appeals/. The first appeal arbitration decision under the MPIA was *Colombia – Anti-Dumping Duties on Frozen Fries from Belgium, Germany and the Netherlands*, WT/DS591/ARB25, Award of the Arbitrators (21 December 2022).

[56] MPIA (n 53) [3]–[4], [6].

[57] See e.g. Chang-fa Lo, Jinji Nakagawa and Tsai-yu Lin (eds), *The Appellate Body of the WTO and Its Reform* (Springer 2020); 'Symposium: International Trade in the Trump Era' (2018) 44 The Yale Journal of International Law Online 1–103; 'Symposium: Can International Trade Law Recover?' (2019) 113 AJIL Unbound 38–66; 'Special Issue: Solving the WTO Dispute Settlement System Crisis' (2019) 20 JWIT 785–890; Robert Mcdougall, 'The Crisis in WTO Dispute Settlement: Fixing Birth Defects to Restore Balance' (2018) 52 JWT 867.

expired during an appeal to continue hear the appeal rather than seeking the authorisation of the DSB.[58] During 2018–19, numerous proposals for reforms to WTO dispute settlement were circulated by other WTO members in an attempt to address US concerns; however, none of these were ultimately adopted.[59] Since the demise of the AB, a large number of WTO members have continued to put on the agenda of each DSB meeting a proposal to initiate a process for appointing new AB members; however, this has been consistently blocked by the US.[60] The WTO's twelfth ministerial conference in June 2022 noted the 'challenges and concerns with respect to the dispute settlement system including those related to the Appellate Body' and committed 'to conduct discussions with the view to having a fully and well-functioning dispute settlement system accessible to all Members by 2024'.[61] At the time of writing in July 2023, informal discussions among WTO members regarding dispute settlement reform are ongoing, which are aimed at producing an outcome by the WTO's next ministerial conference in February 2024.[62] It is possible that significant reforms to WTO dispute settlement may occur in coming years.

(c) The WTO's 'Missing Legislator'[63]

Until the demise of the AB in 2019, the WTO combined an extremely active, and hierarchically unified, adjudicatory mechanism with little in the way of political procedures that could correct the decisions of adjudicators.[64] The provision in the WTO Agreement for authoritative interpretation by a three-fourths majority of members has not been used for various reasons, including that the General Council and Ministerial

[58] See e.g. Joshua Paine, 'The WTO's Dispute Settlement Body as a Voice Mechanism' (2019) 20 JWIT 820, 847–48 (with further references); United States Trade Representative, 'Report on the Appellate Body of the World Trade Organization', February 2020, https://ustr.gov/sites/default/files/Report_on_the_Appellate_Body_of_the_World_Trade_Organization.pdf.

[59] For an overview of these proposals, see e.g. Paine (n 58) 848–54; William J Davey, 'WTO Dispute Settlement: Crown Jewel or Costume Jewelry?' (2022) 21 WTR 291, 293–96.

[60] See e.g. WTO DSB, Minutes of Meeting of 19 September 2023, WT/DSB/M/483, 19 October 2023 [7.2]–[7.26].

[61] WTO MC12 Outcome Document, WT/MIN(22)/24, WT/L/1135, 22 June 2022, [4].

[62] See e.g. DSB, Minutes of Meeting of 28 July 2023, WT/DSB/M/482, 11 September 2023, [5.1]–[5.37].

[63] The term is borrowed from von Bogdandy (n 18) 651.

[64] See von Bogdandy (n 18) 616, 625, 633; Jackson (n 27) 159.

Conference operate via consensus.[65] Since the creation of the WTO in 1995, members have only managed to agree on two new multilateral agreements of limited scope: the Agreement on Trade Facilitation and the Agreement on Fisheries Subsidies, and certain sectorial or plurilateral agreements of limited scope.[66]

Given this context, during the twenty-five years of its operation de facto the AB authoritatively shaped the meaning of the covered agreements through its rulings, despite those rulings formally not being binding beyond the parties to the dispute nor constituting subsequent practice.[67] The relative significance of adjudication in the processes through which WTO law develops is likely to decline in future given the demise of the AB and the concerns aired in that episode (shared by members other than the US); the current ability to appeal panel reports into the void for non-MPIA members; an MPIA mechanism that is limited to a subset of WTO members and instructs arbitrators to address only 'those issues that are necessary for the resolution of the dispute' and

[65] See generally Claus-Dieter Ehlermann and Lothar Ehring, 'The Authoritative Interpretation under Article IX:2 of the Agreement Establishing the World Trade Organization: Current Law, Practice and Possible Improvements' (2005) 8 JIEL 803, 813–18. Other mechanisms for changing WTO law include amendment and waivers, which, unlike authoritative interpretations, have been used a handful of times, although they are also characterised by high voting thresholds and a preference to operate via consensus: see e.g. Peter Van den Bossche and Werner Zdouc, *The Law and Policy of the World Trade Organization: Texts, Cases and Materials* (5th ed, CUP 2021) 157–60; Hunter Nottage and Thomas Sebastian, 'Giving Legal Effect to the Results of WTO Trade Negotiations: An Analysis of the Methods of Changing WTO Law' (2006) 9 JIEL 989, 991–94, 1001–02. For a genealogy of the development of the principle of consensus decision-making in the GATT-era and its strengthening in the WTO-era, see Claerwen O'Hara, 'Consensus Decision-Making and Democratic Discourse in the General Agreement on Tariffs and Trade 1947 and World Trade Organisation' (2021) 9 London Review of International Law 37.

[66] Examples include several sectorial services agreements and the Information Technology Agreement, which eliminates tariffs on covered products. There are various legal means by which sectorial or plurilateral agreements can be brought within the WTO legal framework, including WTO members agreeing to modify their schedules on a coordinated basis. Since 2017, plurilateral negotiations open to all WTO members have been ongoing regarding several 'Joint Statement Initiatives' (JSIs) on various issues. While substantive agreement has been reached regarding two JSIs, on services domestic regulation and investment facilitation, the legal basis for incorporating the outcomes of JSIs into the WTO legal framework remains debated. See generally: Americo Beviglia Zampetti, Patrick Low and Petros C Mavroidis, 'Consensus Decision-Making and Legislative Inertia at the WTO: Can International Law Help?' (2022) 56 JWT 1; Mavroidis (n 1) 7, 68, 70–71; Van den Bossche and Zdouc (n 65) 97–98, 105–06.

[67] Weiler (n 41) 201.

that are raised by the parties;[68] and a notable decline since the mid-2000s in the number of requests for consultations that are being submitted by WTO members.[69]

Nevertheless, while the AB existed, its de facto authoritative role in interpreting WTO law led to certain dynamics that are worth noting. It became routine for appeals to be filed, not only by losing parties but also by successful complainants if the panel report contained undesirable reasoning.[70] A related aspect of WTO practice is the routinely exercised right of non-disputing members to participate as third parties, both at the panel stage and on appeal.[71] These practices reflect that rulings of WTO adjudicators have a wider significance for all members in shaping the evolving GATT/WTO *acquis*.[72]

(d) The Adjudicators in WTO Dispute Settlement

WTO panels consist of three members appointed on an ad hoc basis.[73] The WTO Secretariat proposes nominations to the disputing parties and while strictly the parties can only oppose nominations 'for compelling reasons',[74] in practice this operates as a right of veto.[75] Where the disputing parties cannot agree on panellists within twenty days of the establishment of a panel, the WTO Director-General can, when requested by a party, appoint the panellists.[76] Over time, disputing parties have increasingly been unable to agree on the panellists, leading to greater Director-General involvement in the appointment of panellists.[77] WTO insiders emphasise that the disputing parties are always consulted prior to candidates being proposed by the Secretariat, and even where the Director-General appoints the panel, the process remains

68 MPIA (n 53) [10].
69 See e.g. figures and discussion in Mavroidis (n 1) 146–49, 475–76.
70 Jackson (n 27) 156.
71 Third parties 'having a substantial interest in a matter' who notify the DSB have an opportunity to make submissions and be heard: DSU arts 10.2, 17.4.
72 Sungjoon Cho, *The Social Foundations of World Trade: Norms, Community and Constitution* (CUP 2014) 132–34. See cases cited above n 22.
73 See DSU art 8.5.
74 DSU art 8.6.
75 Joost Pauwelyn, 'The Rule of Law without the Rule of Lawyers? Why Investment Arbitrators Are from Mars, Trade Adjudicators from Venus' (2015) 109 AJIL 761, 784, fn 133.
76 DSU art 8.7.
77 Mavroidis (n 1) 421–22.

driven by the parties' preferences.[78] Individuals who are nationals of the parties to a dispute, or a third party, cannot serve as panellists without the agreement of the parties,[79] and this largely excludes nationals of States who are frequently parties to WTO disputes.[80] In contrast to investment arbitration in particular, but also inter-State arbitration and ad hoc judges in other international courts, there is no ability in the WTO for adjudicators to be appointed by one of the disputing parties.[81] The WTO Secretariat maintains an indicative list of potential panellists, to which members can add qualified persons,[82] but there is no requirement that panellists come from this list, and many do not.[83] The typical background of a WTO adjudicator is overwhelmingly someone with significant government experience and a law degree.[84] Unusually, while individual opinions are permitted in WTO adjudication, the DSU mandates that they are anonymised.[85] Compared to other international tribunals individual opinions are rare.[86]

Although it now only exists on paper, the AB is, under the DSU, composed of seven persons, three of whom serve on any one case,[87] in a system of rotation designed to ensure random selection.[88] Members of the AB are appointed by consensus of the DSB, composed of all WTO members, after a screening process where powerful WTO members have in prior episodes exercised particular influence.[89] The membership of the AB is required to be 'broadly representative' of the WTO

[78] Reto Malacrida, 'WTO Panel Composition: Searching Far and Wide for Administrators of World Trade Justice' in Gabrielle Marceau (ed), *A History of Law and Lawyers in the GATT/WTO: The Development of the Rule of Law in the Multilateral Trading System* (CUP 2015) 317.

[79] DSU art 8.3.

[80] Pauwelyn (n 75) 789.

[81] Ibid 787.

[82] DSU art 8.4; See also art 8.1 (regarding qualification requirements).

[83] Pauwelyn (n 75) 785.

[84] Ibid 772–74; Gregory Shaffer, Manfred Elsig and Sergio Puig, 'The Law and Politics of WTO Dispute Settlement' in Wayne Sandholtz and Christopher A Whytock (eds), *Handbook on the Politics of International Law* (Edward Elgar 2017) 285–86.

[85] DSU arts 14.3, 17.11; Jeffrey L Dunoff and Mark A Pollack, 'The Judicial Trilemma' (2017) 111 AJIL 225, 264.

[86] Dunoff and Pollack (n 85) 264–66. See WTO Appellate Body, Working Procedures, WT/AB/WP/6 (2010) r 3(2) (AB and its divisions to 'make every effort to take their decisions by consensus').

[87] DSU art 17.1.

[88] Working Procedures for Appellate Review (n 86) r 6(2).

[89] Shaffer, Elsig and Puig (n 84) 277–79; Manfred Elsig and Mark A Pollack, 'Agents, Trustees, and International Courts: The Politics of Judicial Appointment at The World

membership,[90] and, while the AB existed, major economies, such as the US, the European Union (EU), and China had 'a quasi-permanent seat'.[91] As explained above, the MPIA is a pool of ten arbitrators, composed by the parties to the MPIA by consensus, who are selected according to the same qualification criteria that apply to the AB.[92] There is to be an 'appropriate overall balance' in the pool of arbitrators, and regional diversity clearly informed the initial selection of arbitrators.[93]

It is also important to appreciate the influential role played by the WTO's Secretariat.[94] The Secretariat is given a role under the DSU in assisting panels on legal and other relevant matters and providing secretarial support.[95] The key point is that the Secretariat is permanent, and has much more accumulated expertise and time than panellists, who typically have other full-time jobs.[96] For example, the Secretariat prepares issues papers and drafts the initial opinion, a practice which also occurred in the AB while it existed.[97]

(e) Remedies in WTO Dispute Settlement

A final contextual feature relevant to understanding WTO adjudication is its system of remedies. In summary the process works as follows. Where WTO adjudicators conclude that a measure is inconsistent with a covered agreement, they must recommend that the losing member bring the measure 'into conformity'.[98] Adjudicators can 'suggest ways in which the Member concerned could implement the recommendations'[99] but

Trade Organization' (2014) 20 European Journal of International Relations 391, 393–94, 403–09.

90 DSU art 17.3.

91 Shaffer, Elsig and Puig (n 84) 278.

92 MPIA (n 53) [4] and annex 2.

93 MPIA (n 53) [4]. For the standing pool of arbitrators see JOB/DSB/1/Add.12/Suppl.5. In July 2022 the standing pool of arbitrators was renewed unchanged for a further two years: JOB/DSB/1/Add.12/Suppl.8.

94 See e.g. Joost Pauwelyn and Krzysztof Pelc, 'Who Guards the "Guardians of the System"? The Role of the Secretariat in WTO Dispute Settlement' (2022) 116 AJIL 534; Shaffer, Elsig and Puig (n 84) 287–91; Weiler (n 41) 205–06; Tommaso Soave, 'Who Controls WTO Dispute Settlement? Socio-Professional Practices and the Crisis of the Appellate Body' (2020) 29 Italian YBIL 13, 25–27.

95 See DSU art 27.1.

96 Shaffer, Elsig and Puig (n 84) 288; Pauwelyn and Pelc (n 94) 548.

97 See generally Pauwelyn and Pelc (n 94) 538–45; Soave (n 94) 26–27.

98 DSU art 19.1.

99 Ibid.

this power is non-binding and used reluctantly,[100] which is an important signal of deference towards the sovereignty retained by members.[101] As noted above, in the absence of an agreed solution the first objective of the DSS is to secure the withdrawal of measures found to be WTO inconsistent.[102] Compensation is to be 'resorted to only if the immediate withdrawal of the measure is impracticable and as a temporary measure', and the final, least preferred option is the suspension of trade concessions, which must be authorised by the DSB.[103]

Once a panel or the AB's rulings and recommendations are adopted by the DSB, a member has 'a reasonable period of time' in which to comply, a period which can be mutually agreed by the parties or be fixed by arbitration and should usually not exceed fifteen months.[104] After a reasonable period of time is set, the issue of the member's implementation of the ruling is placed on the DSB's agenda and the member concerned must provide reports on its implementation of the ruling.[105] Where there is disagreement regarding whether the losing member has complied with a ruling, either party can bring compliance proceedings before the original panel, which can be appealed.[106] If a member fails to bring a measure into compliance within the reasonable period of time, the victorious member may request that the losing member enter into negotiations to develop 'mutually acceptable compensation'.[107] Such compensation is voluntary[108] and only aims to compensate for future harm, until a DSB ruling is implemented.[109] If satisfactory compensation is not agreed, the victorious member can request authorisation from the DSB to suspend the application to the losing member 'of concessions or other obligations under the covered agreements',[110] which are to be 'equivalent to the level of nullification of impairment' suffered by the complaining party.[111] If the losing member objects to the level of retaliation proposed,

[100] See generally David Palmeter, Petros C Mavroidis and Niall Meagher, *Dispute Settlement in the World Trade Organization: Practice and Procedure* (3rd ed., CUP 2022) 512–17.
[101] Shlomo-Agon and Shany (n 11) 207–08.
[102] DSU art 3.7.
[103] DSU arts 3.7, 22.1.
[104] DSU art 21.3.
[105] See DSU art 21.6.
[106] DSU art 21.5.
[107] DSU art 22.2.
[108] DSU art 22.1.
[109] Chester Brown, *A Common Law of International Adjudication* (OUP 2007) 219.
[110] DSU art 22.2.
[111] DSU art 22.4.

an arbitrator can be appointed to determine the appropriate level of suspension of concessions and this decision is final.[112]

Plainly, under the above system, the parties retain a high degree of control over how their dispute is resolved after a finding of non-compliance is made.[113] The system is strikingly prospectively focused – being aimed primarily at bringing non-compliant measures into conformity, and arguably also restoring the balance of trade concessions where non-compliant measures are maintained after the reasonable period of time – rather than compensating for past damage.[114] In practice, diplomatic bargaining frequently occurs at multiple points in the above process. Disputes are often resolved through diplomatic negotiations, informed by the decisions of WTO adjudicators, and judicial decision-making 'simply serves to help the parties resolve their dispute'.[115] Furthermore, where domestic measures have been found WTO-inconsistent, including in high-profile trade linkage disputes, adjudicators have often focused their ruling on how the measure is administered, rather than the underlying policy or law. This gives members a relatively straightforward option for bringing the measure into compliance, for example through administrative changes at the level of the domestic executive, without abandoning the underlying policy objective.[116]

B. Balancing Stability and Change in the Environmental Case Law of the WTO

The section analyses how WTO adjudicators have addressed the problem of potential changes in applicable international legal norms or changes in

[112] DSU arts 22.6, 22.7.

[113] Brooks E Allen, 'The Use of Non-Pecuniary Remedies in WTO Dispute Settlement: Lessons for Arbitral Practitioners' in Michael E Schneider and Joachim Knoll (eds), *Performance as a Remedy: Non-Monetary Relief in International Arbitration* (Juris 2011) 289–90, 297.

[114] Brown (n 109) 220. See text above at nn 29–34.

[115] Gregory Shaffer, 'Developing Country Use of the WTO Dispute Settlement System: Why It Matters, the Barriers Posed' in James C Hartigan (ed), *Trade Disputes and the Dispute Settlement Understanding of the WTO: An Interdisciplinary Assessment* (Emerald Group Publishing 2009) 174; Pauwelyn (n 75) 802; Shlomo Agon (n 11) 177, 317 (highlighting the role of WTO dispute settlement rulings in perennial disputes of '(re)framing renegotiating environments and constructing focal points around which the parties can coordinate').

[116] Shaffer, Elsig and Puig (n 84) 304; Robert Howse, 'The World Trade Organization 20 Years On: Global Governance by Judiciary' (2016) 27 EJIL 9, 52; Shlomo Agon (n 11) 119, 156–58, 162–63.

relevant facts. Others have argued that the ability of WTO adjudicators to adapt the law incrementally, in the absence of new treaty law, treaty amendment, or authoritative interpretation, has been a key reason for the system's success,[117] and it is accordingly an excellent example for analysing this aspect of international adjudication.

1. *Managing Change in International Legal Norms*

A celebrated, but also often misunderstood, instance of WTO adjudicators addressing the problem of potential change in applicable legal norms is the AB's report in *US – Shrimp*.[118] The relevant part of the case concerned whether the challenged US measure – an import ban on shrimp harvested with fishing technology that could adversely affect sea turtles, unless the harvesting nation had in place measures comparable to those of the US to protect sea turtles – provisionally fell within the exception in GATT Article XX(g). This provision covers 'measures relating to the conservation of exhaustible natural resources'.[119] The AB rejected the argument, made by the complaining members, that the term 'exhaustible natural resources' only covered non-living natural resources and could not, in light of its drafting history, cover living resources.[120]

The AB began its analysis by noting that the words in question, although 'crafted more than 50 years ago ... must be read ... in the light of contemporary concerns of the community of nations about the protection and conservation of the environment.'[121] In order to support this position, which on its face threatens stability, the AB moved immediately to show its basis in existing law and in members' consent. First, it noted that the 'preamble attached to the *WTO Agreement* shows that the signatories to that Agreement of 1994, were fully aware of the importance and legitimacy of environmental protection as a goal of national and international policy', highlighting the explicit reference to 'the objective of sustainable development'.[122] Next, the AB reasoned that the term

[117] Robert Howse, 'Moving the WTO Forward-One Case at a Time' (2009) 42 Cornell ILJ 223, 223–24, 230–31; Alan Yanovich, 'The Evolving WTO Dispute Settlement System' in Yasuhei Taniguchi, Alan Yanovich and Jan Bohanes (eds), *The WTO in the Twenty-First Century: Dispute Settlement, Negotiations, and Regionalism in Asia* (CUP 2007) 248, 257.

[118] *US – Shrimp* (n 10).

[119] GATT art XX(g).

[120] See *US – Shrimp* (n 10) [127]–[128].

[121] Ibid [129].

[122] Ibid.

'natural resources' was a 'generic term ... [that] is not "static" in its content or reference but is rather "by definition, evolutionary"'.[123] Accordingly, it was 'pertinent to note that modern international conventions and declarations make frequent references to natural resources as embracing both living and non-living resources'.[124] Specifically, the AB referred inter alia to provisions of UNCLOS, the 1992 Convention on Biological Diversity (CBD), and Agenda 21, although as the AB itself noted, several of the disputing parties were not parties to these agreements.[125] For the AB, '[g]iven the recent acknowledgement ... of the importance of concerted bilateral or multilateral action to protect living natural resources', and the explicit reference to sustainable development in the preamble of the WTO Agreement, it was 'too late in the day' to interpret Article XX(g) 'as referring only to the conservation of exhaustible mineral or other non-living natural resources', as the complainants advocated.[126] The AB noted that its finding was 'in line with the principle of effectiveness in treaty interpretation'.[127] In determining whether the sea turtles at issue were 'exhaustible' natural resources, the AB further noted that all recognised species of sea turtles were listed in Appendix 1 of the Convention on International Trade in Endangered Species of Wild Fauna and Flora as species threatened with extinction.[128]

In summary, on the AB's approach, WTO members had agreed to a generic term whose precise content could evolve over time in light of relevant international law and policy on conservation.[129] A crucial piece of context for making sense of the interpretative approach adopted is that

[123] Ibid [130], partly quoting ICJ, *Legal Consequences for States of the Continued Presence of South Africa in Namibia (South West Africa) notwithstanding Security Council Resolution 276 (1970)*, Advisory Opinion, ICJ Rep 1971, p. 16, [53]. For another example, outside the environmental context, of WTO adjudicators concluding that a treaty term had a generic meaning, see Appellate Body Report, *China – Measures Affecting Trading Rights and Distribution Services for Certain Publications and Audiovisual Entertainment Products*, WT/DS363/AB/R, adopted 19 January 2010, [395]–[397].

[124] *US – Shrimp* (n 10) [130].

[125] Ibid [130] and fns 110–113.

[126] Ibid [131].

[127] Ibid.

[128] Ibid [132].

[129] See Sondre Torp Helmersen, 'The Evolutionary Treaty Interpretation by the WTO Appellate Body' in Georges Abi-Saab and others (eds), *Evolutionary Interpretation and International Law* (Hart 2019) 218–19 (suggesting the evolutionary interpretation in *US – Shrimp* concerned vagueness, understood as disagreement over what precisely the term encompassed, rather than ambiguity, in the sense of the term having more than one

the WTO was at the time facing intense legitimacy concerns regarding its responsiveness to environmental concerns.[130] The AB's references to evolutionary interpretation and various international environmental law instruments served an important legitimation function, particularly with constituencies external to the WTO, in demonstrating its openness to international law beyond the WTO.[131] However, strictly these references were not necessary for the AB to reach its conclusion, since, as it noted in passing, several GATT panels had previously held that living resources fell within Article XX(g).[132] Additionally, the AB did not accept that the drafting history of the provision demonstrated an intention to exclude living natural resources from Article XX(g),[133] and there is evidence that even in 1947, when the relevant words were drafted, the ordinary meaning of the term included living resources.[134] For these and other reasons, several commentators emphasise that the references to evolutionary interpretation were not necessary to resolve the case,[135] and doubt whether the AB's approach is correctly understood as an example of evolutive interpretation at all.[136]

The issue of potential change in applicable legal norms also arose in *EC – Biotech*, which concerned the legality of various measures adopted by the European Communities (EC) and some EC member States that affected the approval and marketing of certain biotechnology products in the EC.[137] The EC sought to have the Panel interpret the applicable WTO provisions in light of two external treaties, the CBD and its Biosafety Protocol,[138] and the precautionary principle, which it argued had

meaning). In the same volume, Graham Cook, 'The Illusion of "Evolutionary Interpretation" in WTO Dispute Settlement', 185 (similar).

130 Howse (n 116) 38–39. See generally Shlomo Agon (n 11) ch 5.

131 Ibid.

132 *US – Shrimp* (n 10) [131] citing *United States – Prohibition of Imports of Tuna and Tuna Products from Canada*, adopted 22 February 1982, BISD 29S/91, [4.9] and *Canada – Measures Affecting Exports of Unprocessed Herring and Salmon*, adopted 22 March 1988, BISD 35S/98, [4.4]. See also *United States – Restrictions on Imports of Tuna*, 16 June 1994, unadopted, DS29/R, [5.13].

133 *US – Shrimp* (n 10) [131], fn 114.

134 See Helmersen (n 129) 216; Julian Wyatt, *Intertemporal Linguistics in International Law: Beyond Contemporaneous and Evolutionary Treaty Interpretation* (Hart 2020) 177.

135 Helmersen (n 129) 216.

136 Wyatt (n 134) 174–79; Cook (n 129) 185–87.

137 For a description of the measures at issue see Panel Report, *European Communities – Measures Affecting the Approval and Marketing of Biotech Products*, WT/DS291/R, WT/DS292/R, WT/DS293/R, adopted 21 November 2006, [7.97]–[7.146].

138 Ibid [7.53]–[7.55]; Cartagena Protocol on Biosafety to the CBD (2000) 2226 UNTS 208.

'become a fully-fledged and general principle of international law'.[139] The Panel's approach strongly favoured the interest of treaty stability and legal certainty, suggesting that any other rule invoked needed to be applicable between all parties to the treaty under interpretation, that is, all WTO members.[140] As the CBD and Biosafety Protocol were not applicable between all WTO members, neither of them were applicable under Article 31(3)(c) of the Vienna Convention on the Law of Treaties (VCLT).[141] The effect of this interpretation is to give a veto power to WTO members who have not consented to the relevant non-WTO rules over the evolution of the WTO Agreement in light of such other rules.[142] The Panel's approach ensures a high degree of stability: WTO members will not be taken by surprise by interpretations of the WTO Agreement in light of other rules of international law that they have not consented to,[143] but WTO law, and similarly any other multilateral treaty with a large number of parties, is rendered static and isolated, unable to reflect important developments in wider international law.[144]

A somewhat more nuanced balance between stability and legal certainty, and change and responsiveness to broader legal developments, was struck by the AB in *EC – Hormones*, a case concerning an import ban of the EC on beef treated with certain types of growth hormones, where the EC argued that the relevant provisions of the SPS Agreement should be interpreted in accordance with the precautionary principle.[145] The AB began by finding that whether the precautionary principle had 'been widely accepted by Members as a principle of *general* or *customary international law* appears less than clear', and that 'at least outside the field of international environment law, [it] still awaits authoritative

[139] *EC – Biotech* (n 137) [7.77]–[7.79].

[140] See ibid [7.68], [7.70]–[7.72].

[141] Ibid [7.74]–[7.75]; VCLT (1969) 1155 UNTS 331, art 31(3)(c). The Panel also found that 'the legal status of the precautionary principle remains unsettled' and it was not necessary to take a position on this issue: [7.88]–[7.89].

[142] Margaret A Young, 'Regime Interaction in Creating, Implementing and Enforcing International Law' in Margaret A Young (ed), *Regime Interaction in International Law: Facing Fragmentation* (CUP 2012) 95–96.

[143] See *EC – Biotech* (n 137) [7.71].

[144] However, note that the Panel accepted that other relevant rules of international law may be used to inform the ordinary meaning of a term in the treaty under interpretation under VCLT art 31(1): ibid [7.92]–[7.95].

[145] Appellate Body Report, *European Communities – Measures Concerning Meat and Meat Products (Hormones)*, WT/DS26/AB/R, WT/DS48/AB/R, adopted 13 February 1998, [1]–[5], [121].

formulation'.[146] This move was plainly motivated by the AB's desire not 'to take a position' on this controversial question.[147] Yet despite not taking such a position, the AB held that the precautionary principle 'finds reflection in Article 5.7 of the SPS Agreement', and in the sixth recital of the preamble and Article 3.3, which 'recognize the right of Members to establish their own appropriate level of sanitary protection, which level may be higher (i.e., more cautious) than that implied in existing international standards'.[148] Further, the AB was able to find space for precautionary reasoning in its instruction that a panel, charged with scrutinising a Member's SPS measures, 'should, bear in mind that responsible, representative governments commonly act from perspectives of prudence and precaution where risks of irreversible, e.g. life-terminating, damage to human health are concerned'.[149] These statements are significant because prior to this interpretation, the precautionary principle was not explicitly mentioned in the relevant provisions of the SPS Agreement, whereas subsequently, such a reading is an established part of WTO jurisprudence.[150] Moreover, so as not to threaten legal certainty, the AB presented its interpretative findings, as in *US – Shrimp*, as already present within the treaty provisions WTO members had consented to. Conscious not to move too far away from those provisions, the AB noted that the precautionary principle did not justify 'SPS measures that are otherwise inconsistent with the obligations of Members set out in particular provisions of that Agreement' nor 'relieve a panel from the duty of applying the normal (ie. customary international law) principles of treaty interpretation'.[151] These comments are aimed at addressing members' interest in certainty over the content of their obligations under the SPS Agreement.

India – Solar Cells also raised an interesting issue of potential change in applicable international legal norms. In this case, India sought to justify domestic content requirements for the production of solar cells, which were held to violate relevant WTO disciplines, under the exception

146 Ibid [123] (emphasis in original).

147 Ibid [123]. Similarly: *EC – Biotech* (n 137) [7.88]–[7.89].

148 *EC – Hormones* (n 145) [124]. Note that the EC did not rely upon Article 5.7, rather the provision arose within debate over whether the precautionary principle could inform the interpretation of other provisions of the SPS Agreement: [120]–[121].

149 Ibid [124].

150 See e.g. Appellate Body Report, *United States – Continued Suspension of Obligations in the EC – Hormones Dispute*, WT/DS320/AB/R, adopted 14 November 2008, [680].

151 *EC – Hormones* (n 145) [124].

in GATT Article XX(j) for measures that are 'essential to the acquisition or distribution of products in general or local short supply'. The Panel accepted India's argument that the terms 'products in general or local short supply' were 'not static in their "content or reference", but are "sufficiently generic that what they apply to may change over time"'.[152] The terms were not limited to situations of short supply arising from war or natural disasters, as was foreseen when the provision was drafted, but could cover shortages arising from other causes.[153] The Panel also accepted that 'the types of measures that are "essential" to address situations of general or local short supply may need to be seen in the context of contemporary concerns of a country and the international community'.[154] These parts of the Panel's reasoning suggest that the meaning of Article XX(j) might evolve, for example given new concerns of the international community. However, the Panel ultimately held that the 'applicable legal standard for what it means to be a "product in general or local short supply"' had not changed over time. Furthermore, even if, as a consequence of globalisation and trade liberalisation the factual circumstances for invoking the provision no longer existed – a suggestion the Panel did not accept – 'it would not be open to a treaty interpreter to change the applicable legal standard'.[155]

Subsequently, the AB interpreted Article XX(j) in open-ended terms, explaining that the provision's application depends upon a range of factors that are clearly prone to change. These included the different levels of economic development of members, which were recognised as potentially relevant to whether products are in short supply in a particular market.[156] Again, however, rather than being a true instance of evolutionary interpretation, where a contemporaneous meaning of a treaty term was favoured over an original meaning,[157] this is another example of WTO adjudicators clarifying the content of treaty provisions that are framed in open-ended terms, meaning the factual circumstances that the provision applies to could change over time.

[152] Panel Report, *India – Certain Measures Relating to Solar Cells and Solar Modules*, WT/DS456/R, adopted 14 October 2016, [7.232], quoting *US – Shrimp* (n 10) [130].

[153] Ibid [7.232], [7.208]–[7.215].

[154] Ibid [7.232].

[155] Ibid [7.233], [7.229].

[156] Appellate Body Report, *India – Certain Measures Relating to Solar Cells and Solar Modules*, WT/DS456/AB/R, adopted 14 October 2016, [5.71]–[5.72].

[157] On this being the narrow or strict sense of evolutive interpretation see Wyatt (n 134) 87–89, 102–11.

2. *Managing Change in Relevant Facts*

This subsection considers cases where WTO adjudicators have faced the issue, already touched on above, that facts which affect the application of relevant treaty provisions may change over time. Strictly speaking, these are not instances of evolutive interpretation, where the meaning of a treaty term changes over time, but examples of evolutive application, where the meaning of the term remains constant but the facts to which it is applied change.[158] Even if one does not accept that treaty interpretation and application can be easily distinguished, the following cases can be understood as instances where the ordinary meaning of the relevant terms require an interpreter to take account of factual circumstances that may change, such as the state of scientific knowledge.[159]

In *US – Continued Suspension*,[160] the EC argued that it had brought its measures into compliance after the earlier *EC – Hormones* dispute, as it had conducted further scientific studies and was now applying one of its SPS measures, an import prohibition on the sale of meat treated with five of the hormones in question, on a provisional basis, as further scientific studies demonstrated some risk but did not make it possible to conduct a full risk assessment.[161] Accordingly, both the panel and AB in this case considered whether the EC's import ban was justified under Article 5.7 of the SPS Agreement, which permits the adoption of provisional SPS measures where relevant scientific evidence is 'insufficient' to conduct a full risk assessment.[162] For present purposes, what is notable is the consideration by the panel and the AB of how developments in relevant science (a factual change) could affect whether the evidence becomes 'insufficient' to conduct a full risk assessment, meaning that provisional SPS measures may be justified. The AB held that 'scientific progress may lead a WTO Member . . . to reconsider the risk assessment underlying an SPS measure' and either conduct a new risk assessment, or adopt provisional SPS measures where the 'scientific developments themselves do not permit the performance of a new risk assessment that is sufficiently

[158] See e.g. Helmersen (n 129) 162; Cook (n 129) 182–84.

[159] Eirik Bjorge, *The Evolutionary Interpretation of Treaties* (OUP 2014) 16–17, 129, 140–41.

[160] *US – Continued Suspension* (n 150).

[161] Ibid [10]–[12].

[162] SPS Agreement art 5.7. In contrast, where sufficient scientific evidence exists, members' SPS measures must be based on a risk assessment that is appropriate to the circumstances: art 5.1. See also arts 2.2, 5.2. On the relationship between these provisions, see e.g. ibid [674].

objective'.[163] Quoting the panel's observation that 'science continuously evolves', the AB held that scientific advances 'at the margins ... would not support the conclusion that previously sufficient evidence has become insufficient', however '[l]imiting the application of Article 5.7 to situations where scientific advances lead to a paradigm shift would be too inflexible an approach'.[164] Accordingly, the AB held that provisional SPS measures are permitted 'where new evidence from a qualified and respected source puts into question the relationship between the pre-existing body of scientific evidence and the conclusions regarding the risks'.[165] The panel was held to have erred in applying 'too inflexible' an approach, whereby it required that for the scientific evidence underlying a risk assessment to become insufficient 'there must be a *critical mass* of new evidence and/or information that calls into question the fundamental precepts of previous knowledge and evidence'.[166]

The issue of change in facts that would affect the application of the applicable international obligations also arose in *India – Agricultural Products,* which concerned a challenge by the US to an import ban by India on various agricultural products from countries reporting certain types of Avian Influenza.[167] Here the AB was interpreting the obligation to ensure SPS measures 'are adapted' to the SPS characteristics of the area from which a product originates under Article 6.1 of the SPS Agreement.[168] The AB held that this obligation 'is not static, but rather ongoing, requiring that SPS measures be adjusted over time so as to establish and maintain their continued suitability in respect of the

163 *US – Continued Suspension* (n 150) [701]. See also [695].

164 Ibid [703]. See also [702], [705]. Panel Report, *United States – Continued Suspension of Obligations in the EC – Hormones Dispute,* WT/DS320/R, adopted 14 November 2008, [7.645].

165 *US – Continued Suspension* (n 150) [703]. See also [725].

166 Ibid [705]–[707], [712]; Panel Report, *United States – Continued Suspension* (n 164) [7.648] (emphasis in original). A similar issue of changes in scientific evidence that require a regulating member to revisit a risk assessment has arisen in several cases under Articles 2.2 and 5.1 of the SPS Agreement, which require, inter alia that SPS measures are 'not maintained without sufficient scientific evidence' and are based on a risk assessment 'as appropriate to the circumstances'. These obligations have been found to have 'a continuing dimension': Panel Report, *United States – Measures Affecting the Importation of Animals, Meat and Other Animal Products from Argentina,* WT/DS447/R, adopted 31 August 2015, [7.336]–[7.347]; *EC – Biotech* (n 137) [7.3031]–[7.3034].

167 Appellate Body Report, *India – Measures Concerning the Importation of Certain Agricultural Products,* WT/DS430/AB/R, adopted 19 June 2015, [1.2]–[1.3], [4.1]–[4.13].

168 SPS Agreement art 6.1.

relevant SPS characteristics of the relevant areas'.[169] For example, adaptation of an SPS measure would be required 'if and when relevant SPS characteristics in relevant areas ... change ... [or if] an exporting Member objectively demonstrates the existence of a pest- or disease-free area'.[170] The AB further noted that 'compliance with the obligations in Articles 6.1 and 6.2 will be facilitated in circumstances where WTO Members put in place a regulatory scheme or structure that accommodates adaptation of SPS measures on an ongoing basis'.[171] This case, like *US – Continued Suspension*, is an example of WTO adjudicators recognising that because provisions of the SPS Agreement depend upon certain factual conditions (e.g. the SPS characteristics of an area), factual changes can affect what the relevant provisions require of a WTO member at any particular point in time.

Russia – Pigs also raised interesting questions regarding how factual changes would affect the application of relevant provisions of the SPS Agreement. This dispute concerned a challenge by the EU to an import ban by Russia on pig products from four EU member States – Estonia, Latvia, Lithuania, and Poland – and a separate, de facto import ban on pig products from the entire EU, due to an outbreak of African swine fever (ASF) in some EU member States beginning in 2014.[172] As the Panel noted, a challenge it faced was that it was adjudicating 'a complaint brought during the course of an active outbreak of a highly contagious disease ... when the situation continued to evolve rapidly'.[173] The Panel observed that:

> Temporal considerations play a role in the assessment of many of the European Union's claims under the SPS Agreement, given the need to examine the state of sufficiency of scientific evidence, available pertinent information, the adaptation of measures on an "ongoing basis" in cases involving regionalization under Article 6 and the existence of a

[169] *India – Agricultural Products* (n 167) [5.132]. See also [5.154]. Affirmed in Appellate Body Report, *Russian Federation – Measures on the Importation of Live Pigs, Pork and Other Pig Products from the European Union*, WT/DS475/AB/R, [5.33], [5.58]. Regarding the range of considerations that constitute the SPS characteristics to which a measure must be adapted, see also *US – Animals* (n 166) [7.642].

[170] *India – Agricultural Products* (n 167) [5.154].

[171] Ibid [5.138].

[172] Panel Report, *Russian Federation – Measures on the Importation of Live Pigs, Pork and Other Pig Products from the European Union*, WT/DS475/R, adopted 21 March 2017, [2.9].

[173] Ibid [7.965].

> "reasonable period of time" or any undue delays in respect of certain procedures.[174]

In the part of this case concerning the regionalisation obligations under Article 6 of the SPS Agreement, the Panel needed to determine whether the EU had objectively demonstrated to Russia that there were areas within the EU, and also within the four EU member States affected by outbreaks, which 'are, and *are likely to remain*' free of ASF disease, as required by Article 6.3 of the SPS Agreement.[175] Whether the EU had fulfilled this obligation was in turn relevant, although not dispositive, for determining whether Russia had adapted its measures to the SPS characteristics of the area from which products originate, as required by Article 6.1 of the SPS Agreement.[176] In terms of the appropriate time frame for its assessment, the Panel found that given the circumstances of the case it was permissible to consider evidence both pre- and post-dating the panel's establishment on 22 July 2014 – Russia having adopted its first import restrictions in January 2014 – up to a cut-off date of Russia's adoption of the last measures that fell within the panel's terms of reference (11 September 2014).[177]

The Panel found that the EU had objectively demonstrated to Russia by at least 7 February 2014 that there were areas in the EU, outside of the four affected States, that were free of ASF and likely to remain so, and Russia had failed to adapt its measures to the SPS characteristics of these areas.[178] In relation to the situation within the four affected States, the Panel found that the EU had provided Russia 'the necessary evidence to objectively demonstrate that, at any given point in time, there were ASF-free areas within each of the four affected EU member States'.[179] However, it was 'more difficult for the Panel to determine whether the information provided by the European Union was sufficient to objectively demonstrate that the disease-free areas within each of the four affected EU member States were "likely to remain" so', as required by

[174] Ibid [7.178].

[175] SPS Agreement art 6.3 (emphasis added).

[176] On the relationship between Article 6.1 and 6.3, see Appellate Body Report, *Russia – Pigs* (n 169) [5.97]–[5.100].

[177] Panel Report, *Russia – Pigs* (n 172) [7.176]. On the Panel's analysis of which measures fell within its terms of reference, see [7.154]–[7.166].

[178] Ibid [7.456], [7.477], [7.483]–[7.484], [8.1(d)(iv)-(v)].

[179] Ibid [7.963].

Article 6.3 of the SPS Agreement.[180] In this regard, the Panel highlighted that:

> we must make our ruling on the basis of the information that the European Union had provided to Russia as at [the cut-off date of] 11 September 2014. While both parties have provided information regarding subsequent cases of ASF within the four affected EU member States until the second half of 2015, neither party could have known, in September 2014, what the situation would be almost one year later.[181]

The Panel held that at least by 11 September 2014, the EU had provided Russia the necessary information to objectively demonstrate that there were ASF-free areas within three of the four affected member States (Estonia, Lithuania, and Poland), which were likely to remain ASF free.[182] In analysing whether Russia had had complied with the obligation to adapt its SPS measures to the SPS conditions of the affected member States, the Panel found it was appropriate to 'consider the most updated information on record in respect of the ASF outbreaks', despite the general cut-off date of 11 September 2014, given the '*ongoing nature of the obligation* to ensure adaptation' of SPS measures.[183] Having analysed information concerning outbreaks of ASF in the four affected member States until mid-2015, the Panel found that Russia had failed to recognise the ongoing existence of ASF-free areas within these States and had accordingly not adapted its measure, an outright import ban, to the SPS characteristics of these areas, as required by Article 6.1 of the SPS Agreement.[184] The Panel's conclusions on these issues were largely upheld on appeal.[185] Overall, the above analysis highlights that the application of the relevant treaty provisions depended on facts that were likely to change over time (e.g. the SPS characteristics of an area), and hence why temporal questions arose throughout the Panel's reasoning.

[180] Ibid [7.964].
[181] Ibid [7.965].
[182] Ibid [7.974], [7.976], [7.982], [7.985], [7.995], [7.1001]–[7.1004].
[183] Ibid [7.1014] (emphasis added).
[184] Ibid [7.1020], [7.1028].
[185] Appellate Body Report, *Russia – Pigs* (n 169) [5.88]. Part of the Panel's reasoning was modified, as in relation to the import ban on Latvian products, the Panel had not considered the implications of its finding that the EU had not objectively demonstrated to Russia that there were areas within Latvia that were likely to remain ASF free, as required by Article 6.3 of the SPS Agreement, for its analysis of whether Russia had adapted its SPS measures to the characteristics of those areas, as required by Article 6.1: [5.102]–[5.103], [5.108], [6.6]–[6.7].

C. The Standard and Method of Review in WTO Environmental Adjudication

1. *Standard of Review: The Approach Developed under the SPS Agreement*

(a) Background: The SPS Agreement and the Role of Science

This subsection addresses the issue of the standard of review by analysing how it has been managed by adjudicators in disputes under the SPS Agreement, reflecting that in this context WTO adjudicators have repeatedly been faced with contested, factually complex science-based claims.[186] As already touched on, the SPS Agreement gives a prominent role to scientific knowledge. While SPS measures that conform to international standards benefit from a presumption of compliance with the SPS and GATT Agreements,[187] measures which do not conform to international standards, either because none exist or a higher level of protection has been selected by a regulating member, must satisfy several requirements.[188] SPS measures must be 'applied only to the extent necessary to protect human, animal or plant life', be 'based on scientific principles', and 'not maintained without sufficient scientific evidence'.[189] They must also be 'based on' a risk assessment, as appropriate to the circumstances,[190] and in the assessment of risks members must take into account various factors including 'available scientific evidence'.[191] As noted above, provisional SPS measures are only permitted 'where relevant scientific evidence is insufficient'.[192] Adjudicating disputes under these provisions raises sharp legitimacy concerns because the WTO judiciary could potentially be 'turned into a science court' that would pronounce on scientific questions in the course of determining the legality of domestic regulations aimed at protecting human, animal, or plant life or health.[193]

186 See references cited above nn 4–5.
187 SPS Agreement art 3.2.
188 Ibid art 3.3.
189 Ibid art 2.2. See also art 3.3.
190 Ibid art 5.1.
191 Ibid arts 5.2–5.3.
192 Ibid art 5.7.
193 See e.g. Howse (n 116) 57, 59–60.

(b) The Approach Developed in SPS Case Law

The leading case regarding the standard of review under the SPS Agreement is *US – Continued Suspension*, which, as explained above, was a continuation of the *EC – Hormones* dispute.[194] This case involved extended argument over the scientific studies and risk assessments undertaken by the EC after it lost the initial dispute, and which it invoked to support its measures, which included a permanent import ban over cattle meat treated with one of the hormones in question. Specifically, the EC argued that in determining whether this measure complied with Article 5.1 of the SPS Agreement, which requires that SPS measures are 'based on a risk assessment', the panel had applied an incorrect, overly intrusive standard of review, whereby the panel sought to determine questions of scientific correctness regarding the risks involved.[195]

The AB emphasised that when reviewing the consistency of an SPS measure with the obligation under Article 5.1 that the measure is 'based on a risk assessment', a panel is not to substitute 'its own scientific judgement for that of the risk assessor' and conduct a de novo review. According to the AB 'the review power of a panel is not to determine whether the risk assessment undertaken by a WTO Member is correct, but rather to determine whether that risk assessment is supported by coherent reasoning and respectable scientific evidence and is, in this sense, objectively justifiable'.[196] The relevant background includes that on appeal in *EC – Hormones* the EC had argued that a '"deferential 'reasonableness standard" is applicable in "all highly complex factual situations, including the assessment of the risks to human health arising from toxins and contaminants"'.[197] The AB, after recalling that the standard of review under the SPS Agreement 'must reflect the balance established . . . between the jurisdictional competences conceded by the Members to the WTO and the jurisdictional competences retained by the Members', found that under Article 11 of the DSU the applicable

194 The EC, having lost the earlier *EC – Hormones* dispute, argued that it had brought its measures into compliance and thus the US and Canada had to cease the suspension of concessions. The EC had performed further scientific studies and new risk assessments after losing the initial case: *US – Continued Suspension* (n 150) [1], [10]–[12], [488]–[496].

195 *US – Continued Suspension* (n 150) [514].

196 Ibid [590].

197 *EC – Hormones* (n 145) [111]–[113].

standard of review is 'neither *de novo* review, as such, nor "total deference", but rather the "objective assessment of the facts"'.[198]

More concretely, in *US – Continued Suspension* the AB instructed panels to 'first, identify the scientific basis upon which the SPS measure was adopted'. The 'scientific basis need not reflect the majority view within the scientific community but may reflect divergent or minority views'.[199] Second, a panel must verify 'the scientific basis comes from a respected and qualified source', which requires that 'the views must be considered to be legitimate science according to the standards of the relevant scientific community'.[200] Third, a panel must 'assess whether the reasoning articulated on the basis of the relevant scientific evidence is objective and coherent', which involves reviewing 'whether the particular conclusions drawn by the Member assessing the risk find sufficient support in the scientific evidence relied upon'.[201] 'Finally, the panel must determine whether the results of the risk assessment "sufficiently warrant" the SPS measure at issue.'[202]

The Panel in *US – Continued Suspension* was faulted for having surveyed the scientific experts consulted in order to decide 'what it considered to be the best science rather than following the more limited exercise' just outlined.[203] While a Panel can utilise expert assistance to answer the four-step approach outlined above, a Panel should not seek to test 'whether the experts would have done a risk assessment in the same way and would have reached the same conclusions as the risk assessor'.[204] This reflects that a Panel's task is to review the member's risk assessment rather than to perform a risk assessment itself.[205]

On the above approach, panels are not to engage in de novo review of the scientific evidence on which a risk assessment is based. However, in *Australia – Apples*, where Australia's risk assessment was found to have an insufficiently close relationship to the underlying scientific evidence, the AB emphasised the distinction between 'scrutinizing the underlying scientific evidence ... [and] scrutinizing the reasoning of the risk assessor'. Specifically, the AB held that while:

198 Ibid [114]–[117]. See also [118]–[119].
199 *US – Continued Suspension* (n 150) [591]. See also ibid [194].
200 Ibid [591].
201 Ibid.
202 Ibid, see also [528].
203 Ibid [612], [598], [602].
204 Ibid [592].
205 Ibid [590], [592]. See also *US – Animals* (n 166) [7.321].

> a panel is not well suited to conduct scientific research and assessments itself, and should not substitute its judgement for that of a risk assessor ... [it] must be able to review whether the conclusions of the risk assessor are based on the scientific evidence relied upon, and are, accordingly, objective and coherent. Whether or not the requisite rational or objective relationship exists can only be ascertained through the examination of how the scientific evidence is used and relied upon to reach particular conclusions. In this respect, the reasoning employed by the risk assessor plays an important role in revealing whether or not such a relationship exists.[206]

This is an important aspect of the approach developed in the SPS case law. On the one hand, it reflects the tendency, which we will see is present in the other contexts studied in this book, for adjudicators to avoid de novo review of assessments based on scientific or other specialised expertise once they are satisfied that the input comes from a reputable source. On the other hand, the fact that WTO adjudicators must review the reasoning of a risk assessor to decide '[w]hether or not the requisite rational or objective relationship exists' between the scientific evidence, the conclusions drawn by the risk assessor and the SPS measures adopted,[207] shows that significant space is retained for international scrutiny over members' risk assessments and SPS measures. Through this approach, WTO adjudicators are, with the assistance of expert evidence, evaluating what counts as coherent reasoning within a risk assessment,[208] such that it will meet the standard of having a 'rational or objective' relationship with the underlying scientific evidence.[209] However, this is tempered by the fact that the question is not

[206] Appellate Body Report, *Australia – Measures Affecting the Importation of Apples from New Zealand*, WT/DS367/AB/R, adopted 17 December 2010, [225]. See generally [215], [220], [224]–[227]. See also Panel Report, *Costa Rica – Measures Concerning the Importation of Fresh Avocados from Mexico*, WT/DS524/R, adopted 31 May 2022, [7.448], [7.897]–[7.898].

[207] *Australia – Apples* (n 206) [225]–[227].

[208] *US – Continued Suspension* (n 150) [590], [592].

[209] *Australia – Apples* (n 206) [225]. Consider also Sulyok (n 5) 202–04, 209–11 (suggesting the focus in more recent SPS jurisprudence on the coherence of the reasoning of a risk assessor strikes an appropriate compromise between avoiding the need for adjudicators to determine issues of scientific correctness while ensuring meaningful scrutiny of members' SPS measures); Caroline E Foster, 'International Adjudication–Standard of Review and Burden of Proof: *Australia-Apples* and *Whaling in the Antarctic*' (2012) 21 RECIEL 80, 83 (arguing that such scrutiny is appropriate because otherwise international legal obligations would be undermined, and, in the context of the SPS agreement, disguised protection could go unaddressed). In her view, WTO panels have

whether the experts would have done a risk assessment in the same way as the regulating member and would have reached the same conclusions.[210]

There are two potential pitfalls that arise in this regard and are highly relevant to the wider problem of the standard of review in international adjudication. First, scrutinising the reasoning employed in a risk assessment involves many of the same difficulties that arise in scrutinising the underling scientific evidence, reflecting that both are questions relying on specialised expertise which adjudicators do not hold,[211] and accordingly there are difficulties in fully understanding and evaluating the (often conflicting) evidence of experts.[212] Second, if adjudicators decide upon the respective merits of rival risk assessment methodologies, this can bring them very close to engaging in de novo review of the relevant risk assessment, which, under the case law, is said to be impermissible.[213] On the other hand, the question of whether the reasoning of a risk assessor has a sufficient relationship with the underlying scientific evidence might be answered in a deferential way.[214] In this regard, some aspects of the approach developed by the AB reduce the scope for second-guessing the reasoning of national-level risk assessors. As we have seen, the AB has instructed panels to 'bear in mind that responsible, representative governments commonly act from perspectives of prudence and precaution where risks of irreversible, e.g. life-terminating, damage to human health are concerned', a statement which 'implies that an additional margin of discretion' is owed to members.[215] Furthermore, the relevant question is not merely risk 'ascertainable in a science laboratory operating under strictly controlled conditions, but also risk in

proven able to assess complex cases involving technical evidence: 85. Giulia Claudia Leonelli, *Transnational Narratives and Regulation of GMO Risks* (Hart 2021) ch 5, esp. 179, 224–26, 235, 238–39 (analysis suggesting that the SPS case law has in fact consistently involved WTO adjudicators engaging in de novo review of scientific evidence).

210 *US – Continued Suspension* (n 150) [592].

211 Gruszczynski (n 4) 755–56.

212 Ibid 743–46.

213 Ibid 755–56; Andrew Lang, *World Trade Law after Neoliberalism: Reimagining the Global Economic Order* (OUP 2011) 341. See also Catherine Button, *The Power to Protect: Trade, Health and Uncertainty in the WTO* (Hart 2004) 152–58, 190.

214 Gruszczynski (n 4) 756.

215 Ibid 741; *EC – Hormones* (n 145) [124].

human societies as they actually exist',[216] meaning the risks of abuse can be factored into a risk assessment.[217] While a risk assessment must assess the potential for the relevant risk may occur, the AB has accepted that a risk assessment does not have to be expressed in quantitative terms,[218] and '[w]here multiple factors may contribute to a particular risk, a risk assessor is not required to differentiate the individual contribution made by each factor'.[219]

Notwithstanding these moves to soften the intrusiveness of international scrutiny of national-level risk assessments and SPS measures, the above analysis shows that at a minimum, the approach developed in the SPS jurisprudence requires adjudicators, with the assistance of experts, to make important normative judgements about what amounts to an adequate risk assessment process in the circumstances.[220] The approach established in SPS case law is, in other words, hardly 'innocent of substantive implications',[221] even if it rightly seeks to avoid adjudicators themselves deciding on questions of scientific correctness, or themselves performing a risk assessment. In sum, the significance of the debate concerning the standard of review in this context is to highlight that while there are good reasons for adjudicators to avoid substitutionary de novo review of domestic-level determinations based on scientific or other specialised expertise, any meaningful form of international scrutiny requires adjudicators to take a stance on what counts as an adequate domestic decision-making process.[222]

2. *Methods of Review in WTO Adjudication: Necessity Testing as Developed in the GATT, TBT, and SPS Contexts*

Under the GATT, TBT, and SPS Agreements, necessity or least restrictive means testing has emerged as the dominant method of review for

216 *EC – Hormones* (n 145) [187].

217 *US – Continued Suspension* (n 150) [545]; *EC – Hormones* (n 145) [206].

218 See *US – Continued Suspension* (n 150) [569]; *EC – Hormones* (n 145) [186]–[187]; Panel Report, *Australia – Measures Affecting the Importation of Apples from New Zealand*, WT/DS367/R, adopted 17 December 2010, [7.441].

219 *US – Continued Suspension* (n 150) [562].

220 Jacqueline Peel, *Science and Risk Regulation in International Law* (CUP 2010) 354–55. See also Epps (n 4) 221–27 (supporting the approach in recent case law of a procedurally focused standard of review that focuses on the methodological rigour of a risk assessment rather than the ultimate conclusions reached).

221 Lang (n 213) 346.

222 Peel (n 220) 354–55.

scrutinising measures that pursue a legitimate policy aim but also restrict other treaty-protected interests in trade liberalisation. It is important to analyse this case law for the purposes of this book, because WTO necessity jurisprudence represents a distinctive and particularly elaborate method of review, or balancing test, which has been developed by international adjudicators. As explained in Chapter 1, both in the WTO context and more broadly, concerns have been raised regarding whether it is appropriate for international adjudicators to engage in proportionality balancing stricto sensu as it involves weighing the relative importance of the competing rights and interests.[223] As we will see, WTO necessity jurisprudence has largely avoided second-guessing the regulatory aims pursued by WTO members and instead focuses on scrutiny of the means employed by members to pursue their chosen regulatory ends.[224]

(a) Necessity Testing under GATT Article XX

Article XX of the GATT sets out a series of exceptions to the obligations contained in the Agreement given the importance of the domestic policy interests concerned.[225] In environmental cases to date, members have repeatedly sought to invoke the exceptions under Article XX covering measures (b) 'necessary to protect human, animal or plant life or health' and (g) 'relating to the conservation of exhaustible natural resources'.[226] A small number of cases with an environmental component have also involved Articles XX(a), covering measures 'necessary to protect public morals',[227] and XX(d), addressing measures 'necessary to secure compliance with laws or regulations which are not inconsistent' with the GATT.[228]

223 See Chapter 1, text at nn 95–97.

224 See e.g. Petros C Mavroidis, *The Regulation of International Trade*, vol 1 (MIT Press 2016) 436–37. Aspects of Section (C)(2) of this chapter draw on Joshua Paine, 'Autonomy to Set the Level of Regulatory Protection in International Investment Law' (2021) 70 ICLQ 696, 704–14.

225 *US – Shrimp* (n 10) [121].

226 GATT art XX.

227 Appellate Body Reports, *European Communities – Measures Prohibiting the Importation and Marketing of Seal Products*, WT/DS400/AB/R, WT/DS401/AB/R, adopted 18 June 2014.

228 Eg *India – Solar Cells* (n 152); Panel Report, *Indonesia – Measures Relating to Raw Materials*, WT/DS592/R, circulated 30 November 2022, appealed 8 December 2022. Equivalent exceptions to GATT art XX(a), (b) and (d) and are found in Article XIV(a)–(c) of the General Agreement on Trade in Services (GATS) and some of the case law cited in this subsection concerned the latter provisions.

In order for a measure to be justified under Article XX, it must first be shown to fall within one of the exceptions, and, second, it must fulfil the requirements of the 'chapeau' of Article XX.[229] At the first stage, the degree of connection required between the measure and the policy goal differs depending on the wording of the relevant Article XX exception.[230] The focus here is on the test that adjudicators have developed to determine whether a measure is 'necessary' in a large case law under Article XX(a), (b), and (d).[231] It is important to address this jurisprudence because, as Foster notes, the 'necessity formula' developed by the AB is an 'elaborate' balancing test that helps mediate between WTO members' collective interest in trade liberalisation and 'the general interest of all WTO Members in maintaining appropriate room to manoeuvre in non-economic policy spheres'.[232] As Foster further observes, the necessity jurisprudence has 'produce[d] an analytical standard that has demonstrated real staying power'.[233] It is also foreseeable that WTO necessity jurisprudence may be drawn upon by other international tribunals in future, in particular by investment treaty tribunals that are likely to face interpreting exceptions based on Article XX of the GATT, which have frequently been included in more recent investment treaties.[234] While GATT Article XX(g) has also been invoked in many environmental cases, the interpretation of the nexus it requires, that the measure be one 'relating to' the conservation of exhaustible natural resources, has been less controversial.[235]

[229] *US – Gasoline* (n 11) 22.

[230] Ibid 18.

[231] WTO adjudicators have interpreted this term in the same way under Article XX(a), (b), and (d), meaning the case law on Article XX(a) and (d) is also relevant, even if Article XX(b) is most obviously relevant for disputes with an environmental component. For argument that this interpretation is a mistake, see Gisele Kapterian, 'A Critique of the WTO Jurisprudence on "Necessity"' (2010) 59 ICLQ 89, 119.

[232] Caroline E Foster, *Global Regulatory Standards in Environmental and Health Disputes: Regulatory Coherence, Due Regard, and Due Diligence* (OUP 2021) 147, 152.

[233] Ibid 145, 152. See also Andrew D Mitchell and Elizabeth Sheargold, *Principles of International Trade and Investment Law* (Edward Elgar 2021) 111–12.

[234] Mitchell and Sheargold (n 233) 122–23.

[235] The term 'relating to' the conservation of exhaustible natural resources has been interpreted to require 'a close and genuine relationship of means and ends': *US – Shrimp* (n 10) [136]; Appellate Body Report, *China – Measures Related to the Exportation of Various Raw Materials*, WT/DS394/AB/R, WT/DS395/AB/R, WT/DS398/AB/R, adopted 22 February 2012, [355]; Appellate Body Report, *China – Measures Related to the Exportation of Rare Earths, Tungsten, and Molybdenum*, WT/DS431/AB/R, WT/DS432/AB/R, WT/DS433/AB/R, adopted 29 August 2014, [5.90], [5.95]–[5.96], [5.111]–[5.117].

Although the current necessity 'formula' was first developed in the *Korea – Beef* case concerning GATT Article XX(d) and measures to prevent deceptive practices,[236] for present purposes it is sufficient to begin with *Brazil – Retreaded Tyres*.[237] In this case Brazil sought to justify a ban on the importation of retreaded or used tyres under GATT Article XX(b) on the basis that the import ban would reduce the accumulation of waste tyres in Brazil, which, in turn, would reduce the risks to human, animal, and plant life and health posed by the accumulation of such waste.[238] The AB explained that:

> In order to determine whether a measure is "necessary" within the meaning of Article XX(b) . . . a panel must assess all the relevant factors, particularly the extent of the contribution to the achievement of a measure's objective and its trade restrictiveness, in the light of the importance of the interests or values at stake. If this analysis yields a preliminary conclusion that the measure is necessary, this result must be confirmed by comparing the measure with its possible alternatives, which may be less trade restrictive while providing an equivalent contribution to the achievement of the objective pursued.[239]

The AB stressed that it is for the complaining member to identify possible alternative less trade restrictive measures that the responding member could have taken, and a measure will only qualify as a 'genuine alternative' if it would achieve the responding members' '"desired level of protection with respect to the objective pursued"', and is '"reasonably available"', taking into account potential costs and technical difficulties.[240] The 'weighing and balancing' process, is, according to the AB, 'a holistic operation that involves putting all the variables of the equation together and evaluating them in relation to each other after having examined them individually, in order to reach an overall judgement'.[241]

236 See Appellate Body Report, *Korea – Measures Affecting Imports of Fresh, Chilled and Frozen Beef*, WT/DS161/AB/R, WT/DS169/AB/R, adopted 10 January 2001, esp. [161]–[166].

237 Appellate Body Report, *Brazil – Measures Affecting Imports of Retreaded Tyres*, WT/DS332/AB/R, adopted 17 December 2007.

238 See ibid [119], [135]–[136].

239 Ibid [156], similarly [178]. See also Appellate Body Report, *United States – Measures Affecting the Cross-Border Supply of Gambling and Betting Services*, WT/DS285/AB/R, adopted 20 April 2005, [305]–[307].

240 *Brazil – Retreaded Tyres* (n 237) [156], drawing on *US – Gambling* (n 239) [308]–[311].

241 *Brazil – Retreaded Tyres* (n 237) [182]; *EC – Seal Products* (n 227) [5.215].

With some minor variations, this test has been reaffirmed in subsequent jurisprudence.[242]

Significantly, within the necessity test developed under GATT Article XX, WTO adjudicators have not explicitly endorsed proportionality balancing stricto sensu, which would involve weighing the costs (in terms of trade restriction) and benefits of the measure, taking account of the relative importance of the non-trade policy objective pursued. Although the references to 'weighing and balancing' may at first glance resemble proportionality balancing stricto sensu, the 'weighing and balancing' is occurring as part of a multifaceted inquiry to determine if the measure is 'necessary' to achieve the regulating State's aim, or if a less trade restrictive alternative is reasonably available.[243] To the extent that the values pursued by a measure have been considered, this factor has been emphasised to ensure that measures pursuing important objectives, such as the protection of human health or life, are more easily found to be necessary.[244] This interpretation was foreshadowed as early as the *Korea – Beef*

242 See e.g. Appellate Body Report, *Colombia – Measures Relating to the Importation of Textiles, Apparel and Footwear*, WT/DS461/AB/R, adopted 22 June 2016, [5.70]–[5.75]. Note that in more recent case law, WTO adjudicators have held that prior to analysing the necessity of a measure, a panel must consider the 'design' of a measure to determine whether there is a relationship between the measure and the relevant policy aim invoked. In summary, this initial inquiry is not 'particularly demanding' and requires that the measure is 'not incapable' of contributing to the relevant policy aim – ie, it screens out measures that bear no relationship to the policy aim invoked: see *Colombia –Textiles* [5.67]–[5.70], [5.76]–[5.77].

243 Peter Van den Bossche, 'Looking for Proportionality in WTO Law' (2008) 35 Legal Issues of Economic Integration 283, 289–94; Donald H Regan, 'The Meaning of "Necessary" in GATT Article XX and GATS Article XIV: The Myth of Cost–Benefit Balancing' (2007) 6 WTR 347, 348–60; Andrew D Mitchell and Caroline Henckels, 'Variations on a Theme: Comparing the Concept of "Necessity" in International Investment Law and WTO Law' (2013) 14 Chicago Journal of International Law 93, 128–30, 135, 149–50; Ming Du, 'The Necessity Test in World Trade Law: What Now?' (2016) 15 Chinese JIL 817, 825–27, 835; Foster (n 232) 145, 148–49; David Sifonios, *Environmental Process and Production Methods (PPMs) in WTO Law* (Springer 2018) 197–99; Stefan Zleptnig, *Non-Economic Objectives in WTO Law* (Martinus Nijhoff 2010) 229, 244–47, 396; Contrast Filippo Fontanelli, 'Necessity Killed the GATT: Art XX GATT and the Misleading Rhetoric About "Weighing and Balancing"' (2012) 4 EJLS 39, 58, 65–66, 68; Alan O Sykes, 'The Least Restrictive Means' (2003) 70 The University of Chicago Law Review 625, 415–16.

244 See e.g. Van den Bossche (n 243) 290–91; Erich Vranes, *Trade and the Environment: Fundamental Issues in International Law, WTO Law, and Legal Theory* (OUP 2009) 274–76; Robert Howse and Elisabeth Türk, 'The WTO Impact on Internal Regulations: A Case Study of the *Canada–EC Asbestos* Dispute' in George A Bermann and Petros C Mavroidis (eds), *Trade and Human Health and Safety* (CUP 2006) 114–16; Du (n 243)

case, where, in the context of GATT Article XX(d), the AB noted that an interpreter could take account of 'the relative importance of the common interests or values' that a GATT-consistent law or regulation was intended to protect, as '[t]he more vital or important those common interests or values are, the easier it would be to accept as "necessary" a measure designed as an enforcement instrument'.[245] In subsequent cases, in undertaking the 'weighing and balancing' exercise, WTO adjudicators have repeatedly emphasised the importance of the values of protecting human life and health,[246] and protecting the environment.[247]

Nevertheless, arguably the references in the case law to the importance of the policy goal pursued 'reflects an unfortunate midpoint between a proportionality test and a necessity test that is truly deferential to the regulatory goals of WTO Members'.[248] A better approach may be to recognise the importance of all the regulatory aims recognised by GATT Article XX and to afford a general margin of appreciation to all domestic regulatory choices that fall within those provisions.[249] WTO adjudicators are not well placed to weigh the relative importance of different regulatory aims, as is involved in proportionality balancing stricto sensu, given they are international-level actors detached from democratically accountable domestic institutions.[250] Relatedly, WTO dispute settlement is not designed to impose a comprehensive normative vision on members, but to leave them free to pursue diverse regulatory goals.[251]

826–27. See also Regan (n 243) 352–53 (suggesting an additional degree of deference is appropriate for measures pursuing important interests because the harm of an improper invalidation in these cases is greater).

245 *Korea – Beef* (n 236) [162]; *Indonesia – Measures Relating to Raw Materials* (n 228) [7.250].

246 Appellate Body Report, *European Communities – Measures Affecting Asbestos and Asbestos-Containing Products*, WT/DS135/AB/R, adopted 5 April 2001, [172]; *Brazil – Retreaded Tyres* (n 237) [179].

247 *Brazil – Retreaded Tyres* (n 237) [179]; *Indonesia – Measures Relating to Raw Materials* (n 228) [7.254].

248 Benn McGrady, 'Necessity Exceptions in WTO Law: Retreaded Tyres, Regulatory Purpose and Cumulative Regulatory Measures' (2009) 12 JIEL 153, 162. Similarly, others note that there is a tension (and arguably a contradiction) between the AB including the importance of the relevant regulatory value within its necessity formula and the AB's consistent position that WTO members have the right to determine their own level of protection: Fontanelli (n 243) 54; Du (n 243) 825; Kapterian (n 231) 119.

249 McGrady (n 248) 163, 173.

250 See e.g. Kati Kulovesi, *The WTO Dispute Settlement System: Challenges of the Environment, Legitimacy and Fragmentation* (Kluwer Law International 2011) 190–96.

251 See e.g. Robert Howse, Joanna Langille and Katie Sykes, 'Pluralism in Practice: Moral Legislation and the Law of the WTO after *Seal Products*' (2015) 48 GWILR 81, 89–91;

The AB has also reduced the potential intrusiveness of necessity testing by holding that 'certain complex public health or environmental problems may be tackled only with a comprehensive policy comprising a multiplicity of interacting measures' and '[i]n the short term, it may prove difficult to isolate the contribution to public health or environmental objectives of one specific measure'.[252] Accordingly, in *Brazil – Retreaded Tyres*, the AB accepted that a measure may be shown to be necessary 'on the basis of a demonstration that the [measure] . . . is apt to produce a material contribution to its objective', including having regard to future projections based on sufficiently tested hypotheses.[253] These examples are significant because they show how necessity or least restrictive means testing can be softened to acknowledge the multifaceted policy challenges that are often at stake in environmental cases. As discussed below, these features of the necessity jurisprudence have been incorporated into the necessity jurisprudence developed under the TBT Agreement.[254]

While the above features of WTO necessity jurisprudence suggest it is a promising method of review developed by adjudicators to balance the competing interests protected by the relevant treaty provisions, certain criticisms should be noted. The approach of the panel and the AB in *Brazil – Retreaded Tyres* has been criticised for being overly deferential to Brazil in certain respects. For example, the Panel, in a finding upheld by the AB, accepted Brazil's submission that it had sought to reduce 'the risks to human, animal or plant life or health arising from the accumulation of waste tyres' 'to the maximum extent possible'.[255] However, the better view is that the level of protection that is pursued by a regulating member must be determined objectively by adjudicators rather than simply accepting a level of protection that is asserted by a responding

Kapterian (n 231) 92–93; Mavroidis (n 224) 420; Robert Howse and Joanna Langille, 'Continuity and Change in the World Trade Organization: Pluralism Past, Present, and Future' (2023) 117 AJIL 1, esp. 32–35.

252 *Brazil – Retreaded Tyres* (n 237) [151].

253 Ibid [150]–[151]. The AB also accepted that the contribution of a measure to the policy objective pursued can be assessed in quantitative or qualitative terms: ibid paras [145]–[146]; Affirmed in *EC – Seal Products* (n 227) [5.221]–[5.224]. See also *Indonesia – Measures Relating to Raw Materials* (n 228) [7.262]–[7.263].

254 See below text at nn 276–279.

255 Panel Report, *Brazil – Measures Affecting Imports of Retreaded Tyres*, WT/DS332/R, adopted 17 December 2007, [7.102], [7.108]; *Brazil – Retreaded Tyres* (n 237) [174].

member ex post.[256] Relatedly, Foster highlights that the degree to which both the panel and the AB were willing to accept Brazil's determinations regarding how the measure would contribute to the protection of human health was striking given that the measure only indirectly contributed to that aim, by reducing stockpiles of waste tyres.[257]

More generally, Bown and Trachtman argue that in its necessity jurisprudence generally, and in *Brazil – Retreaded Tyres* specifically, the AB has been 'unwilling to evaluate for itself, or to require a Panel to evaluate, in any but the most gross categories', the different factors that inform the weighing and balancing test. In their view, this failure to at least assess in magnitudes the relevant factors, such as a measure's degree of contribution to the relevant aim, means that the necessity test is too easy for States to satisfy and does not ensure that WTO members use the least trade restrictive means.[258]

(b) Necessity Testing under Article 2.2 of the TBT Agreement

In the case law concerning Article 2.2 of the TBT Agreement, WTO adjudicators have also developed a structured necessity or least restrictive means test as the established method of review and been careful to respect WTO members' choices of which policy aims to pursue. Article 2.2 requires that members' technical regulations do not create 'unnecessary obstacles to international trade' and are not 'more trade-restrictive than necessary to fulfil a legitimate objective, taking account of the risks non-fulfilment would create'.[259] Article 2.2 sets out a non-exhaustive list

[256] See e.g. McGrady (n 248) 156; Gabrielle Marceau and Joel P Trachtman, 'A Map of the World Trade Organization Law of Domestic Regulation of Goods: The Technical Barriers to Trade Agreement, the Sanitary and Phytosanitary Measures Agreement, and the General Agreement on Tariffs and Trade' (2014) 48 JWT 351, 386; Mitchell and Sheargold (n 233) 103–04; *US – Gambling* (n 239) [304].

[257] Foster (n 232) 156. See *Brazil – Retreaded Tyres* (n 237) [153]–[155]. For a similar criticism see Chad P Bown and Joel P Trachtman, '*Brazil – Measures Affecting Imports of Retreaded Tyres*: A Balancing Act' (2009) 8 WTR 85, 125–26.

[258] Bown and Trachtman (n 257) 88–89. Similarly: Joel P Trachtman, 'WTO Trade and Environment Jurisprudence: Avoiding Environmental Catastrophe' (2017) 58 HILJ 273, 292–94.

[259] TBT Agreement art 2.2. An earlier draft of Article 2.2 included a footnote stating that 'This provision is intended to ensure proportionality between regulations and the risks non-fulfilment of legitimate objectives would create', but this was not included in the final agreement: GATT Doc MTN.TNC/W/FA (20 December 1991) page G.3. Arguably, this supports the view that the provision does not permit proportionality balancing stricto sensu: Jan Neumann and Elisabeth Türk, 'Necessity Revisited: Proportionality in

of legitimate objectives, which are supplemented by the legitimate objectives listed in the sixth and seventh recital of the Agreement's preamble and potentially by legitimate objectives recognised by other covered agreements.[260] The sixth recital to the preamble of the TBT Agreement, which has been frequently emphasised by WTO adjudicators when interpreting Article 2.2, provides that:

> no country should be prevented from taking measures necessary to ensure the quality of its exports, or for the protection of human, animal or plant life or health, of the environment, or for the prevention of deceptive practices, at the levels it considers appropriate, subject to the requirement that they are not applied in a manner which would constitute a means of arbitrary or unjustifiable discrimination between countries where the same conditions prevail or a disguised restriction on international trade.

Article 2.2 of the TBT Agreement is said to be 'concerned with restrictions on international trade that exceed what is necessary to achieve the degree of contribution that a technical regulation makes to the achievement of a legitimate objective'.[261] In interpreting Article 2.2, the AB has drawn a parallel with the 'holistic weighing and balancing' test developed under GATT Article XX.[262] The assessment of necessity under Article 2.2 is said to involve a 'relational analysis of the trade-restrictiveness of the technical regulation, the degree of contribution that it makes to the achievement of a legitimate objective, and the risks non-fulfilment would create'.[263] As in the context of GATT Article XX, 'a comparison with reasonably available alternative measures is a conceptual tool for the purpose of ascertaining whether a challenged measure is more trade restrictive than necessary'.[264] Summarising this approach, the AB has suggested:

World Trade Organization Law after *Korea – Beef*, *EC – Asbestos* and *EC – Sardines*' (2003) 37 JWT 199, 221.

260 Appellate Body Report, *United States – Measures Concerning the Importation, Marketing and Sale of Tuna and Tuna Products*, WT/DS381/AB/R, adopted 13 June 2012, [313]; Appellate Body Reports, *United States – Certain Country of Origin Labelling (COOL) Requirements*, WT/DS384/AB/R, WT/DS386/AB/R, adopted 23 July 2012, [370]. The (non-exhaustive) legitimate objectives recognised in Article 2.2 are 'national security requirements; the prevention of deceptive practices; protection of human health or safety, animal or plant life or health, or the environment'.

261 *US – Tuna II* (n 260) [319].

262 Appellate Body Reports, *United States – Certain Country of Origin Labelling (COOL) Requirements – Recourse to Article 21.5 of the DSU by Canada and Mexico*, WT/DS384/AB/RW, WT/DS386/AB/RW, adopted 29 May 2015, [5.198], [5.203]–[5.204].

263 *US – Tuna II* (n 260) [318].

264 Ibid [320].

> A panel should begin by considering factors that include: (i) the degree of contribution made by the measure to the legitimate objective at issue; (ii) the trade-restrictiveness of the measure; and (iii) the nature of the risks at issue and the gravity of consequences that would arise from non-fulfilment of the objective(s) pursued by the Member through the measure. In most cases, a comparison of the challenged measure and possible alternative measures should be undertaken. In particular, it may be relevant for the purpose of this comparison to consider whether the proposed alternative is less trade restrictive, whether it would make an equivalent contribution to the relevant legitimate objective, taking account of the risks non-fulfilment would create, and whether it is reasonably available.[265]

In applying this test, WTO adjudicators have repeatedly emphasised that members are free to select which legitimate policy goals to pursue, and the level at which to pursue such aims, and have avoided a situation where adjudicators would second-guess the policy aims selected by members.[266] For example, in the *US – Tuna II* case, concerning the US' unilateral application of 'dolphin safe' labelling requirements to tuna sold on the US market, the AB overturned the panel's finding that the US measure was more trade restrictive than necessary, on the basis that the alternative measure advanced by Mexico would not contribute to the US policy objectives of ensuring consumer information and dolphin protection to the same degree as the impugned measure.[267] Similarly, in *US – Clove Cigarettes*, which concerned a ban by the US on many types of flavoured cigarettes to reduce youth smoking, the Panel rejected Indonesia's case under Article 2.2 as Indonesia had not demonstrated that its proposed alternative measures would achieve the same degree of contribution to the regulatory aim, and the proposed alternative measures involved a greater risk of non-fulfilment of that aim.[268] In the *US – COOL (21.5)* case, which concerned labelling requirements aimed at providing consumer information on the origin of meat products, but would apply equally to environmental labelling, the AB emphasised that

[265] Ibid (n 260) [322].

[266] In addition to the case law cited in the following paragraphs, consider Panel Report, *European Communities – Trade Description of Sardines*, WT/DS231/R, adopted 23 October 2002, [7.120] ('Article 2.2 and this preambular text affirm that it is up to the Members to decide which policy objectives they wish to pursue and the levels at which they wish to pursue them').

[267] *US – Tuna II* (n 260) [329]–[331].

[268] Panel Report, *United States – Measures Affecting the Production and Sale of Clove Cigarettes*, WT/DS406/R, adopted 24 April 2012, [7.423]–[7.424], [7.431].

any proposed alternative measure must achieve 'an *equivalent* degree of contribution to the relevant legitimate objective'.[269] As the AB noted, this interpretation 'comports with the principle reflected in the sixth preambular recital of the TBT Agreement – that a Member shall not be prevented from pursuing a legitimate objective "at the levels it considers appropriate"'.[270] Similarly, in the *Australia – Plain Packaging* cases, concerning Australia's tobacco plain packaging (TPP) measures, both the Panel and the AB at various points in their reasoning noted the need to respect Australia's right to determine its own level of protection – or degree in the reduction of smoking – through its full suite of tobacco control measures.[271]

In *US – COOL (21.5)*, the AB also held that that the phrase 'taking account of the risks non-fulfilment would create' in Article 2.2 cannot lessen the degree of contribution needed for an alternative measure to qualify as equivalent, as this could 'erode the principle that a member shall not be prevented from pursuing a legitimate objective "at the levels it considers appropriate"'.[272] Nevertheless the AB has accepted that 'the nature of the risks and the gravity of the consequences arising from the non-fulfilment of the technical regulation's objective' can inform the margin of appreciation enjoyed by a panel in assessing whether a proposed alternative measure would achieve an equivalent degree of contribution to the relevant objective.[273] This appears to suggest that where the risks of non-fulfilment of the technical regulation's objectives are grave, it will be more difficult to establish that a proposed alternative measure would make an equivalent contribution.[274] Notably, the AB has also

[269] *US – COOL (AB Art 21.5)* (n 262) [5.201] (emphasis in original).

[270] Ibid.

[271] Panel Reports, *Australia – Certain Measures Concerning Trademarks, Geographical Indications and other Plain Packaging Requirements Applicable to Tobacco Products and Packaging*, WT/DS435/R, WT/DS441/R, WT/DS458/R, WT/DS467/R, WT/DS458/R and WT/DS467/R adopted 27 August 2018, WT/DS435/R and WT/DS441/R adopted 29 June 2020, [7.1369], [7.1530], [7.1731]; Appellate Body Reports, *Australia – Certain Measures Concerning Trademarks, Geographical Indications and other Plain Packaging Requirements Applicable to Tobacco Products and Packaging*, WT/DS435/AB/R, WT/DS441/AB/R, adopted 29 June 2020, [6.502].

[272] *US – COOL (AB Art 21.5)* (n 262) [5.264]–[5.266].

[273] Ibid [5.215], [5.217]–[5.218], [5.254], [5.269].

[274] For a similar interpretation: Mitchell and Henckels (n 243) 144. See also *Australia – Tobacco Plain Packaging*, where, in its application of Article 2.2, the Panel emphasised the grave risks arising from non-fulfilment of the aim of reducing smoking in justifying its conclusion that the alternative measures proposed by the complainants would not make an equivalent contribution: Panel Reports, *Australia – Tobacco Plain Packaging* (n

rejected the argument that the relative importance of the objective pursued by a technical regulation – compared to other legitimate objectives – may be taken into account as part of assessing the 'risks non-fulfilment would create'.[275]

Importantly, within the necessity test developed under Article 2.2 of the TBT Agreement, WTO adjudicators have, as in the GATT Article XX jurisprudence considered above, recognised the long-term and multi-faceted nature of certain environmental or public health challenges, and the need for a range of complementary measures in response.[276] For example, in the *Australia – Plain Packaging* dispute, the AB accepted that in assessing whether the alternative measures, proposed by the claimants, to Australia's TPP measures made an equivalent contribution to Australia's aim of reducing smoking and thereby improving public health, it was relevant to consider any synergies between the impugned and proposed alternative measures and other measures Australia had in place, as part of a comprehensive policy to reduce tobacco use.[277] Similarly, in *US – Clove Cigarettes*, the Panel found that the alternative measures proposed by Indonesia were not true alternatives because, among other reasons, several of the alternatives were already being applied by the US, as part of its wider tobacco control policies.[278] The panel in *Australia – Plain Packaging* also noted that while its task was 'to assess the actual contribution of the measures to their objective [of reducing smoking] in light of the available evidence ... we must take due account of the possibility that the effects of certain measures may manifest themselves over a longer period of time and into the future'.[279]

Overall, the interpretations of Article 2.2 of the TBT Agreement to date have amounted to a necessity or least restrictive means test. There are few signs of WTO adjudicators themselves directly weighing the costs and benefits of a measure, in light of their own assessment of the relative

271), [7.1463], [7.1530]–[7.1531], [7.1614], [7.1683], [7.1715], [7.1722], [7.1725(d)]; Contrast Chris Downes, 'Worth Shopping Around? Defending Regulatory Autonomy under the SPS and TBT Agreements' (2015) 14 WTR 553, 567–72 (suggesting this aspect of Article 2.2 may provide a basis for proportionality balancing stricto sensu); Axel Desmedt, 'Proportionality in WTO Law' (2001) 4 JIEL 441, 459–60 (similar).

275 *US – COOL (AB Art 21.5)* (n 262) [5.276]–[5.279].

276 For a similar view of the case law see Foster (n 232) 166, 170.

277 Appellate Body Reports, *Australia – Tobacco Plain Packaging* (n 271) [6.502].

278 *US – Clove Cigarettes* (n 268) [7.425].

279 Panel Reports, *Australia – Tobacco Plain Packaging* (n 271) [7.938]–[7.940]. This part of the reasoning was upheld by the Appellate Body: see Appellate Body Reports, *Australia – Tobacco Plain Packaging* (n 271) [6.333]–[6.338].

importance of the competing values at stake, as would be involved in proportionality balancing stricto sensu.[280]

(c) Necessity Testing under SPS Agreement Article 5.6

WTO adjudicators have also developed a least restrictive means test under Article 5.6 of the SPS Agreement, which requires that SPS measures not be 'more trade-restrictive than required to achieve their appropriate level of . . . protection, taking into account technical and economic feasibility'.[281] The footnote to Article 5.6 adds that:

> a measure is not more trade-restrictive than required unless there is another measure, reasonably available taking into account technical and economic feasibility, that achieves the appropriate level of sanitary or phytosanitary protection and is significantly less restrictive to trade.[282]

Plainly, the text of the provision suggests that a least restrictive means test is the appropriate method of review.[283]

However, there are important differences between the necessity test developed under Article 5.6 of the SPS Agreement and the necessity jurisprudence under the GATT and TBT Agreements, considered above. The most important difference is that the benchmark that proposed alternative measures must meet under the SPS Agreement is the appropriate level of protection (ALOP) set by a member prior to adopting SPS

280 Similarly: Du (n 243) 840–42; Benedikt Pirker, *Proportionality Analysis and Models of Judicial Review: A Theoretical and Comparative Study* (Europa Law Publishing 2013) 321–22.

281 SPS Agreement, Art 5.6. The AB has noted that the more general provision of Article 2.2 – and specifically its requirement that SPS measures are 'applied only to the extent necessary to protect human, animal or plant life or health' – informs Article 5.6: see *Australia – Apples* (n 206) [339]–[340]. One arguable example of WTO adjudicators endorsing proportionality balancing stricto sensu under Article 2.2 of the SPS Agreement is *Japan – Apples*, where the Panel found that Japan's quarantine measure was 'clearly disproportionate to the risk identified on the basis of the scientific evidence available': Panel Report, *Japan – Measures Affecting the Importation of Apples*, WT/DS245/R, adopted 10 December 2003, [8.198], see also [8.181]. The AB upheld this interpretation, reasoning that the panel's reference to '"clear disproportion" . . . relates to the application in this case of the requirement of a "rational or objective relationship between an SPS measure and the scientific evidence"' in order for the measure not to be 'maintained without sufficient scientific evidence', as required by Article 2.2: Appellate Body Report, *Japan – Measures Affecting the Importation of Apples*, WT/DS245/AB/R, adopted 10 December 2003, [163]; Howse argues this is the only deviation from the AB's consistent rejection of proportionality balancing stricto sensu: Howse (n 116) 59, 62.

282 SPS Agreement, Art 5.6, fn 3.

283 Pirker (n 280) 324; Du (n 243) 845.

measures, rather than the level of protection actually achieved by the relevant measures.[284] This is significant because it allows the regulating member to set the level of protection it wishes to achieve ex ante and does not reduce it based on a balancing exercise taking into account factors such as the level of protection actually achieved by the measure adopted, the measure's trade restrictiveness, or the importance of the regulatory aim.[285] Thus, as others have noted, the necessity test under Article 5.6 of the SPS agreement is arguably more explicitly protective of regulatory autonomy than the necessity jurisprudence under other WTO agreements considered above.[286] As we have seen, the latter jurisprudence only requires alternative measures to achieve an equivalent contribution to the degree of contribution actually achieved by the impugned measure(s).[287]

The difference just noted reflects that the SPS agreement, uniquely, creates the metric of the ALOP 'which is taken to exist independently of the challenged measure' and used as a benchmark to determine whether the measure is more trade restrictive than necessary.[288] The idea here is that setting the ALOP 'is a *prerogative* of the Member concerned' and 'is an *objective*' determined ex ante, whereas an SPS measure 'is an *instrument* chosen to attain or implement that objective'.[289] Accordingly, the AB has held that WTO members have an implicit obligation to determine their ALOP with sufficient precision to enable the application of the SPS Agreement and if they do not do so the ALOP can be inferred 'on the basis of the level of protection reflected in the SPS measure actually applied'.[290]

Ordinarily, a panel adjudicating a claim under Article 5.6 is 'expected to accord weight to the respondent's articulation of its appropriate level of protection', particularly where it 'was specified in advance of the adoption of the SPS measure ... with sufficient precision, and where it

284 See Appellate Body Report, *Australia – Measures Affecting Importation of Salmon*, WT/DS18/AB/R, adopted 6 November 1998, [200]–[204]; *Australia – Apples* (n 206) [344]. Also noting this difference: Marceau and Trachtman (n 256) 382.

285 Du (n 243) 845; Marceau and Trachtman (n 256) 381.

286 See e.g. Du (n 243) 845; Joanne Scott, *The WTO Agreement on Sanitary and Phytosanitary Measures: A Commentary* (OUP 2009) 159–61; Mitchell and Sheargold (n 233) 110–11.

287 See above text at nn 239, 265–269.

288 Yury Rovnov, 'Appropriate Level of Protection: The Most Misconceived Notion of WTO Law' (2020) 31 EJIL 1343, 1344. The term is defined in Annex A of the SPS Agreement as '[t]he level of protection deemed appropriate by the Member establishing a sanitary or phytosanitary measure to protect human, animal or plant life or health': [5].

289 *Australia – Salmon* (n 284) [199]–[200] (emphasis in original).

290 Ibid [205]–[207].

has been consistently expressed by the responding Member'.[291] However, similar to the position noted above in relation to other WTO agreements, in the SPS context a panel does not have to completely defer to the respondent's characterisation of its ALOP and must determine this on the basis of the totality of the record.[292] To succeed with an Article 5.6 claim, a complainant has to advance scientific evidence to discharge its burden of establishing a prima facie case that its proposed alternative measure would meet the regulating member's ALOP.[293] If this is not shown, the proposed measure does not qualify as a true alternative.[294] Additionally, the complaining member must establish that the proposed alternative measure is reasonably available taking into account technical and economic feasibility and is significantly less trade restrictive than the contested measure.[295]

Overall, what is notable about the necessity jurisprudence developed under Article 5.6 of the SPS Agreement is that it is a least restrictive means test that avoids putting into question the regulatory objective, including the level of protection, selected by the regulating member ex ante, prior to adopting measures to achieve that objective. Nevertheless, certain difficulties with the approach under Article 5.6 should be noted. Despite the obligation to formulate the ALOP prior to adopting SPS measures, in practice WTO members often do not do so, or do not do so with sufficient precision, meaning the ALOP has to be induced, at least in part, from the SPS measures applied.[296] Arguably, this difficulty in applying Article 5.6 reflects the unsatisfactory formulation of the provision itself, which uses a benchmark, the ALOP, which is separate from

[291] *India – Agricultural Products* (n 167) [5.221].

[292] Ibid; Appellate Body Report, *Korea – Import Bans, and Testing and Certification Requirements for Radionuclides*, WT/DS495/AB/R, adopted 26 April 2019, [5.24], [5.34]; *Costa Rica – Avocados* (n 206) [7.155]–[7.156].

[293] *Australia – Apples* (n 206) [364]–[366].

[294] *Australia – Salmon* (n 284) [194].

[295] Ibid. See also Panel Report, *Japan – Measures Affecting the Importation of Apples – Recourse to Article 21.5 of the DSU by the United States*, WT/DS245/RW, adopted 20 July 2005, [8.171] (technical and economic feasibility to be assessed 'in the real world' including considering the risk of incorrect enforcement).

[296] See e.g. Hanna Schebesta and Dominique Sinopoli, 'The Potency of the SPS Agreement's Excessivity Test: The Impact of Article 5.6 on Trade Liberalization and the Regulatory Power of WTO Members to Take Sanitary and Phytosanitary Measures' (2018) 21 JIEL 123, 135–37; Rovnov (n 288) 1360–65 (finding that in practice both WTO panels, and WTO members themselves, have expressed the chosen ALOP in broad and imprecise qualitative formulations).

the level of protection achieved by the impugned measure.[297] Other difficulties are less specific to the SPS Agreement and can arise in least restrictive means testing generally, both under other WTO Agreements and beyond. For example, Schebesta and Sinopoli criticise the Article 5.6 jurisprudence on the basis that the 'reasonable availability' of alternative measures has been interpreted in a manner that does not take sufficient account of the capacity of the responding member to take the proposed alternative measures and the costs of doing so.[298] This point of wider relevance, beyond the SPS context, is that it is important to take factors such as the technical feasibility and costs of a proposed alternative measure into account so that only measures that are reasonably available to a regulating State qualify as genuine alternatives.

Schebesta and Sinopoli further criticise Article 5.6 and the resulting jurisprudence for not including within the balancing exercise the extent and importance of the regulatory benefits achieved by a measure, or the scale of the trade gains that would accrue from an alternative measure.[299] It is possible that including these factors in the balancing exercise could increase the regulatory space afforded to members in certain circumstances, for example if a measure with significant regulatory benefits (as compared to proposed alternatives) would be provided with an additional margin of appreciation. However, the cost–benefit analysis Schebesta and Sinopoli advocate risks opening up space for adjudicators to second-guess the regulatory aim chosen by a member. The current approach, by requiring that any alternative measure meets the ALOP set by the regulating member, avoids this.

D. The Contribution of WTO Adjudication to Broader Processes of Dispute Resolution: Examples from GATT Article XX Chapeau Jurisprudence

This section considers how WTO adjudicators have contributed to broader processes of dispute resolution by analysing one aspect of the case law developed in applying the 'chapeau test', or second step of justification that must be satisfied to invoke the GATT Article XX general

[297] Lukasz Gruszczynski, *Regulating Health and Environmental Risks under WTO Law: A Critical Analysis of the SPS Agreement* (OUP 2010) 249–50.
[298] Schebesta and Sinopoli (n 296) 132–33, 145.
[299] Ibid 144–45.

exceptions.[300] As noted above, this focus is justified because the relevant jurisprudence has been developed in prominent environmental disputes and has been interpreted by numerous commentators as a desirable example of international adjudicators ensuring that the disputing parties observe certain other-regarding procedural values without adjudicators themselves fully disposing of the contested issues.[301] For example, von Bogdandy and Venzke read this aspect of WTO practice as evidence that 'it may be advisable for international courts to refrain from the substantive interpretation of a contested norm and instead derive from it procedural guidelines that lead to a discursive handling of the conflict by the parties'. In their view such an approach 'pushes the parties to a conflict to resolve their dispute within a process under the guidance of international law and in the shadow of renewed judicial oversight'.[302] Similarly, Cho argues that WTO adjudicators should extend this line of jurisprudence, and 'encourage parties to continue deliberating and cooperating with each other until they reach a mutually acceptable regulatory solution', rather than 'weighing and balancing regulatory details of its own discretion'.[303] Plainly, these arguments envisage WTO adjudicators contributing to broader processes of dispute resolution by clarifying the legal framework and pushing regulating States to consider affected foreign interests and pursue cooperative solutions.

[300] On the chapeau jurisprudence, see generally Lorand Bartels, 'The Chapeau of the General Exceptions in the WTO GATT and GATS Agreements: A Reconstruction' (2015) 109 AJIL 95.

[301] In addition to the sources cited below, see Armin von Bogdandy, 'Legitimacy of International Economic Governance: Interpretative Approaches to WTO Law and the Prospects of Its Proceduralization' in Stefan Griller (ed), *International Economic Governance and Non-Economic Concerns: New Challenges for the International Legal Order* (Springer 2003) 126–33; Cho (n 72) 150–51, 156–60; Michael Ioannidis, 'A Procedural Approach to the Legitimacy of International Adjudication: Developing Standards of Participation in WTO Law' (2011) 12 German LJ 1175, 1175–76, 1195–200; Sivan Shlomo Agon and Eyal Benvenisti, 'The Law of Strangers: The Form and Substance of Other-Regarding International Adjudication' (2018) 68 University of Toronto Law Journal 598, 610–12, 619–21 (demonstrating that many other aspects of WTO jurisprudence also require WTO members to take into account the interests of affected foreigners); Maria Weimer, 'Reconciling Regulatory Space with External Accountability through WTO Adjudication – Trade, Environment and Development' (2017) 30 LJIL 901, 917–20.

[302] Armin von Bogdandy and Ingo Venzke, *In Whose Name? A Public Law Theory of International Adjudication* (OUP 2014) 206.

[303] Sungjoon Cho, 'Of the World Trade Court's Burden' (2009) 20 EJIL 675, 717–20.

Under the chapeau to Article XX, measures cannot be applied 'in a manner which would constitute a means of arbitrary or unjustifiable discrimination between countries where the same conditions prevail, or a disguised restriction on international trade'.[304] According to the AB, the chapeau is concerned with the 'manner in which the measure is applied' and operates to prevent abuse of the Article XX exceptions.[305] The AB has emphasised that Article XX 'must be applied reasonably, with due regard both to the legal duties of the party claiming the exception and the legal rights of the other parties concerned'.[306] Thus it has characterised applying the chapeau as involving:

> locating and marking out a line of equilibrium between the right of a Member to invoke an exception under Article XX and the rights of the other Members under varying substantive provisions . . . so that neither of the competing rights will cancel out the other . . . The location of the line of equilibrium . . . is not fixed and unchanging; the line moves as the kind and the shape of the measures at stake vary and as the facts making up specific cases differ.[307]

Turning to the instances of chapeau jurisprudence seen by commentators as a desirable adjudicatory approach, in *US – Gasoline* the US sought to justify the discrimination involved in its measure by highlighting the administrative difficulties that would be involved in allowing foreign gasoline refiners to establish a less onerous individual baseline under its domestic emissions legislation, as was permitted for domestic refiners.[308] The measure was held to fail the chapeau conditions because the US had not adequately pursued 'the possibility of entering into cooperative arrangements with the governments of Venezuela and Brazil or, if it had, not to the point where it encountered governments that were unwilling to cooperate'.[309] While the US had taken account of the costs

304 GATT art XX.

305 *US – Gasoline* (n 11) 22. See Bartels (n 300) 98–105 (critiquing many aspects of the existing chapeau jurisprudence, including that there is no distinction between the measure and its application).

306 *US – Gasoline* (n 11) 22; *US – Shrimp* (n 10) [156].

307 *US – Shrimp* (n 10) [159]. Consistently with this view, the AB has characterised the chapeau of Article XX as an 'expression of the principle of good faith', which encompasses the doctrine of *abus de droit*: [158]. Regarding this aspect of the reasoning, see Bartels (n 300) 102–04 (suggesting that the doctrine of abuse of rights concerns the Article XX exceptions as a whole, not the chapeau specifically).

308 *US – Gasoline* (n 11) 25–26.

309 Ibid 27 (also noting that the US had not pursued cooperative arrangements with foreign refiners).

involved for domestic refiners in deciding not to impose on them immediately a requirement of statutory baselines, there was 'nothing in the record to indicate that it did other than disregard that kind of consideration when it came to foreign refiners'.[310] This interpretation suggests that to apply a measure in a chapeau-compliant manner it is necessary to take account of the costs imposed on exporting members and in certain situations it may be necessary for a regulating member to explore the possibility of 'cooperative arrangements'.

The AB added significantly to such an approach in *US – Shrimp*. In this case, the US measure conditioned access to the US market on the use of 'turtle excluder devices' when harvesting shrimp.[311] The measure was found to be applied in a manner constituting 'unjustifiable discrimination' because it effectively required exporting members to adopt a regulatory program that was 'not merely *comparable*, but rather *essentially the same*,' as that applied to the US domestic industry, thus creating a 'rigid and unbending standard' for gaining certification for export to the US.[312] Part of the AB's reasoning was that other policies and measures that exporting countries had adopted to conserve sea turtles – the aim pursued by the US – were not taken into account.[313] It was:

> not acceptable ... for one WTO Member to use an economic embargo to *require* other Members to adopt essentially the same comprehensive regulatory program, to achieve a certain policy goal, as that in force within that Member's territory, *without* taking into consideration different conditions which may occur in the territories of those other Members.[314]

The US was faulted for failing to engage the appellees, and other exporting members, 'in serious, across-the-board negotiations with the objective of concluding bilateral or multilateral agreements for the protection and conservation of sea turtles', before enforcing its measure.[315] The fact that the US 'had negotiated seriously with some, but not with other Members (including the appellees)' – leading to the conclusion of one regional agreement to address the conservation aim pursued – was central to the finding of unjustifiable discrimination. It provided 'convincing demonstration that an alternative course of action was

[310] Ibid 28.
[311] See *US – Shrimp* (n 10) [2]–[6].
[312] Ibid [163] (emphasis in original).
[313] Ibid.
[314] Ibid [164] (emphasis in original). See also [165].
[315] Ibid [166].

reasonably open to the United States'.[316] The AB also emphasised that compared to fourteen countries that were offered a 'phase in' period of three years to comply with the US measure, other countries, including the appellees, had a four-month phase-in period, resulting in a heavier regulatory burden, and received less technology transfer assistance.[317]

In the subsequent compliance proceedings the AB clarified that in order to avoid 'arbitrary or unjustifiable discrimination' an importing member must engage in comparable negotiations with all exporting members, 'in the sense that comparable efforts are made, comparable resources are invested, and comparable energies are devoted to securing an international agreement', even if an agreement is secured with one group of countries but not another.[318] Understandably, the AB reasoned that the chapeau test could not require the US to conclude a multilateral agreement with all its trading partners.[319] The US was found to have engaged in 'serious good faith efforts' to negotiate an international agreement, meaning its measure was no longer applied in a manner that constituted arbitrary or unjustifiable discrimination.[320] The AB also found that the revised US measure allowed for certification on the basis that an exporting member engaged in conservation efforts of comparable effectiveness, and thus exhibited sufficient flexibility by taking into account the conditions prevailing in an exporting member's territory to avoid constituting arbitrary or unjustifiable discrimination.[321]

In *EC – Seal Products* the AB added to this line of jurisprudence. In its analysis of whether the EU's measures, which were a ban on the import of seal products with certain exceptions,[322] were applied in a manner that constituted arbitrary or unjustifiable discrimination, the AB emphasised

316 Ibid [171]–[172].

317 Ibid [173]–[176]. For criticism of these aspects of the reasoning, see Steve Charnovitz, 'The WTO's Environmental Progress' (2007) 10 JIEL 685, 704–05.

318 *US – Shrimp (Art 21.5)* (n 10) [122]. Note that in *US – Gambling* the AB refused to read an obligation to consult with other members into the test of whether a measure is necessary to protect public morals under GATS Article XIV(a): *US – Gambling* (n 239) [317]. While the Panel in this dispute had concluded that the US had not established that its measure was necessary, as it had not pursued the possibility of a negotiated outcome with Antigua, the AB reasoned that such an alternative measure was not reasonably available as 'consultations are by definition a process, the results of which are uncertain': [315]–[317].

319 *US – Shrimp (Art 21.5)* (n 10) [123].

320 Ibid [133]–[134].

321 Ibid [144]–[149].

322 See *EC – Seal Products* (n 227) [4.1]–[4.14].

that the EU had not made '"comparable efforts" to facilitate the access of the Canadian Inuit to the' exception for seal products resulting from traditional hunting by Inuit or other indigenous communities as it had for the Greenlandic Inuit, nor had the EU 'pursued cooperative arrangements' in this regard.[323] The AB also questioned whether the EU had taken into account the appropriateness of its regulatory regime for the conditions prevailing in exporting members, noting that setting up a 'recognised body', as required to benefit from the exception for indigenous hunting practices, 'may entail significant burdens in some instances'.[324] The AB also found that ambiguities in the criteria that had to be met to qualify for the exception and the broad discretion involved in its application 'could allow for abuse of the IC exception' and thus application in a manner that constituted arbitrary or unjustifiable discrimination.[325]

Clearly, the above jurisprudence demonstrates a concern for ensuring that regulating States have considered the interests of affected foreigners and have observed certain due process guarantees. However, as others have highlighted, WTO adjudicators have not held that the chapeau imposes a free-standing obligation to negotiate. Rather, such factors have been used as part of determining whether there was arbitrary or unjustifiable discrimination, which is the focus of the inquiry.[326] For example, in *US – Shrimp* a key aspect of the AB's finding of unjustifiable discrimination was that the US had not negotiated as seriously with, and thus treated equally, the complaining members as compared to other States in the Western hemisphere.[327] It is also important to emphasise that the

[323] Ibid [5.337].

[324] Ibid.

[325] Ibid [5.324]–[5.328].

[326] See Sifonios (n 243) 222–27; Bradly J Condon, 'Does International Economic Law Impose a Duty to Negotiate?' (2018) 17 Chinese JIL 73, 82, 89; Bradly J Condon, *Environmental Sovereignty and the WTO: Trade Sanctions and International Law* (Transnational Publishers 2006) 115–19, 123 (obligation to negotiate under the chapeau of Article XX depends on the factual context of the case and must be linked to the issue of discrimination); Robert Howse, 'The Appellate Body Rulings in the *Shrimp/Turtle* Case: A New Legal Baseline for the Trade and Environment Debate' (2002) 27 Columbia JEL 491, 505–09; Bartels (n 300) 122–23. Consistently with this suggestion, later WTO case law has interpreted this early chapeau jurisprudence as being concerned with the rationale that is advanced to explain any discrimination in the application of a measure, and whether that rationale can be reconciled with, or is rationally related to, the objective that has been found to provisionally justify a measure under a paragraph of Article XX: see e.g. *Brazil – Retreaded Tyres* (n 237) [225]–[227]; *EC – Seal Products* (n 227) [5.303]–[5.306].

[327] Sifonios (n 243) 222; Howse (n 326) 506–07.

chapeau only prevents *arbitrary or unjustifiable* discrimination *between countries where the same conditions prevail*, meaning that some forms of unilateralism and differentiation between WTO members are permitted, so long as the discrimination is rationally related to the policy objective pursuant to which a measure has been provisionally justified.[328] Overall, the Article XX chapeau jurisprudence is clear that a failure to negotiate equally with different exporting members will violate the chapeau and that regulating members must have regard to conditions prevailing in exporting members' territories. It is not clear, however, that the jurisprudence imposes any independent requirement to seek negotiated rather than unilateral solutions before imposing a trade-restrictive measure.[329]

Furthermore, while the chapeau test is more focused on '"how" a given measure should be applied, rather than "what" the measure should be',[330] there are some important qualifications to bear in mind regarding the seemingly procedural and other-regarding form of adjudicatory scrutiny emerging from this jurisprudence. As was noted above in considering debates over the standard of review in the SPS context, the idea of an entirely procedural, or substance-neutral, form of adjudicatory scrutiny is illusory, because difficult normative choices must still be made about what counts as an acceptable domestic-level process.[331] In the context of the chapeau jurisprudence such choices concern which interests deserve participation rights, or how far WTO adjudicators should go in encouraging cooperative solutions and requiring regulating members to consider affected foreign interests.[332] There is also some risk that 'processes can be manipulated to give the appearance of consideration of affected foreigners without in any way modifying a predetermined

328 Condon, 'Does International Economic Law Impose a Duty to Negotiate?' (n 326) 100–01; Trachtman (n 258) 300. Above n 326. Consistently with this view, the AB has held that the 'conditions' prevailing in different countries that are relevant for the purposes of the chapeau analysis are those 'relating to the particular policy objective under the applicable subparagraph' that is relied upon: *EC – Seal Products* (n 227) [5.299]–[5.301].

329 See above n 326; Sifonios (n 243) 224, 227, 231–32. Sifonios suggests that a failure to engage in negotiations prior to enacting a unilateral trade measure could in some circumstances amount to a 'disguised restriction on international trade' and thus violate the chapeau: 238–41.

330 Cho (n 303) 719.

331 See above text at nn 220–221.

332 Lang (n 213) 345–47. See also Sifonios (n 243) 239–41 (suggesting that adjudicators should scrutinise negotiation efforts in a formal manner and apply a deferential standard of review).

outcome'.[333] However, this risk is not unique to this aspect of WTO practice, or even international adjudication, but one that can arise whenever an international decision-maker seeks to ensure that domestic authorities observe certain other-regarding procedural values.

Nevertheless, despite these caveats, commentators are correct to highlight that the jurisprudence just considered contains promising signs of international adjudication acting as a mechanism that pushes regulating States to consider the interests of affected foreigners and pursue cooperative solutions. The idea of a prospectively focused style of international adjudicatory scrutiny, which lays down certain conditions that a regulating State must observe, fits particularly well with the context of WTO dispute settlement, where members have an opportunity to bring their practices into compliance after adjudication, as occurred in *US – Shrimp*.

E. Conclusion

Focusing on disputes with an environmental component, this chapter has considered how WTO adjudicators have experienced and responded to the three cross-cutting challenges traced throughout this book: managing change in legal norms or facts, scrutinising State conduct for compliance with international obligations, and contributing to broader processes of dispute settlement. In numerous respects the above analysis demonstrates that the practices reviewed are heavily shaped by contextual features specific to WTO dispute settlement. Yet the analysis also provides insights into wider challenges facing international adjudication more generally and certain legal techniques that are potentially transferable to other contexts.

Throughout the disputes considered above, the relevant treaty texts clearly shaped how the three challenges focused on by this book arose and were managed by adjudicators. For example, the cases concerning how factual changes affect members' obligations under the SPS Agreement reflect that provisions of that Agreement rely on factual matters that may change, such as the state of scientific knowledge or the SPS conditions prevailing in the territory of an exporting member. The use of least restrictive means testing across the GATT, TBT, and SPS Agreements is supported by the relevant treaty provisions which require measures to be 'necessary' or 'not more trade restrictive than

[333] Gregory Shaffer and Joel P Trachtman, 'Interpretation and Institutional Choice at the WTO' (2011) 52 Va JIL 103, 151–52.

necessary'.[334] Nevertheless, the more detailed formulations developed by WTO adjudicators go well beyond what is explicitly contained in the relevant treaty provisions. As Foster has argued, the 'necessity formula' that has been developed is an example of the significant law clarification role performed by WTO adjudicators, given the need for 'a more fine-grained' approach for judging the legality of members' regulatory measures and reconciling the competing interests of trade liberalisation and regulatory autonomy embodied in the relevant legal provisions.[335]

Institutional features of WTO adjudication also shape many of the practices observed in this chapter. The practice across the GATT, TBT, and SPS Agreements of employing a form of least restrictive means testing, rather than proportionality balancing stricto sensu, suggests that WTO adjudicators have generally respected members' choices of which regulatory goals, and levels of protection, to pursue.[336] This in turn reflects that the WTO is an organisation characterised by value-pluralism among its members and does not have a mandate to pursue a deeper normative vision that would involve international adjudicators themselves weighing the importance of different regulatory aims.[337] The use of a least restrictive means test, rather than proportionality balancing stricto sensu, should also be understood against the background that many of these cases have raised the sensitive question of scrutiny of domestic measures aimed at protecting environmental or human health interests. WTO dispute settlement has a need, as part of legitimating the wider organisation, to demonstrate that it is consistent with high levels of protection of such interests.[338]

The idea that adjudicators might contribute to broader processes of dispute resolution by clarifying the legal framework applicable to the parties' ongoing interactions fits well with the institutional features of WTO dispute settlement. As was highlighted, in this regime remedies are prospectively focused and adjudication is typically followed by a diplomatic bargaining process, in which adjudicators' decisions act as one reference point and members get an opportunity to redesign non-compliant measures.[339] The diplomatic ethos of the organisation, evident

[334] See above text at nn 226, 259, 281.
[335] Foster (n 232) 147, 152–53, 139–41.
[336] Howse (n 116) 53, 61–62.
[337] See above text at n 251.
[338] See above text at nn 41–42.
[339] See above text at nn 113–116.

in the significant diplomatic control retained over adjudication and the dominance of legally trained diplomats as adjudicators,[340] is also relevant here. Future chapters will show that meaningful comparisons can be drawn between the GATT Article XX chapeau jurisprudence considered above and developments in UNCLOS and ICJ adjudication. In those contexts, adjudication has often clarified the obligations of States to consider affected foreign interests and required the disputing parties to engage in post-adjudication negotiation or cooperation.[341]

The cases concerning potential change in international legal norms reflect that with the negotiating processes of the multilateral trade regime having been largely stalled since the conclusion of the Uruguay Round agreements, adjudication has been one mechanism for adjusting WTO law incrementally, including for incorporating concerns from other regimes.[342] *US – Shrimp* and, to a lesser degree, *EC – Hormones* are important examples of WTO adjudicators finding room for norms of international environmental law within WTO agreements against the background of major legitimacy concerns regarding the WTO's responsiveness to environmental considerations at the time the disputes were decided. As Condon has argued, a potential advantage of treaty provisions that use open-ended terms, such as GATT Article XX(b) and (g), is that they provide an opening for an interpreter to consider relevant rules of international law, or scientific knowledge regarding environmental risks, as they have evolved at the time of interpretation.[343] Nevertheless, there is an obvious risk that 'judicial decision making will alter members' obligations in a way that was not intended',[344] and the explicit instruction in the DSU that adjudication cannot add to or diminish the rights of members under the covered agreements is clearly felt by WTO adjudicators. A good example is the Panel's refusal in *EC – Biotech* to take account of external norms in a way that would arguably alter members' WTO obligations without their consent.

Other aspects of the WTO adjudicatory practices considered in this chapter can provide inspiration for international tribunals operating in

[340] Pauwelyn (n 75) 802.

[341] See Foster (n 232) 327–31 (noting the functional similarity between the chapeau case law requiring consideration of affected foreign interests and obligations of due regard in the law of the sea).

[342] See e.g. Gregory Messenger, *The Development of World Trade Organization Law: Examining Change in International Law* (OUP 2016) 61–62, 64–67. Above n 117.

[343] Condon, *Environmental Sovereignty and the WTO* (n 326) 9–10, 38–39.

[344] Ibid 40.

adjudication of their disputes.[13] However, the principle has to be appreciated in light of a number of other provisions of Part XV that limit the applicability of the 'Compulsory Procedures Entailing Binding Decisions' in Section 2. Nothing in Part XV undermines the right of States Parties to agree to settle disputes concerning UNCLOS by peaceful means of their own choice.[14] Furthermore, two provisions in the Convention envisage that the parties may agree to exclude the application of the Part XV procedures and are often invoked by reluctant respondents to claim that the compulsory, binding procedures under Part XV do not apply. First, Article 281 provides that where the parties to a dispute concerning UNCLOS 'have agreed to seek settlement of the dispute by a peaceful means of their own choice', the Part XV procedures 'only apply where no settlement has been reached by recourse to' the parties' chosen means and 'the agreement between the parties does not exclude any further procedure'.[15] Second, Article 282 provides that if the parties to an UNCLOS dispute have agreed that such a dispute 'shall, at the request of any party to the dispute, be submitted to a procedure that entails a binding decision, that procedure shall apply in lieu of the procedures provided for in this Part, unless the parties to the dispute otherwise agree'.[16]

Furthermore, significant limitations and exceptions to the applicability of the compulsory and binding procedures in Section 2 are established by Section 3 of Part XV.[17] Article 297 establishes generally applicable

Convention' (art 288(1)) but also 'any dispute concerning the interpretation or application of an international agreement related to the purposes of this Convention, which is submitted to it in accordance with the agreement' (art 288(2)). See also UNCLOS Annex VI, arts 21–22. There are several multilateral agreements on particular aspects of the law of the sea concluded since the entry into force of UNCLOS that use the dispute settlement system created by Part XV of UNCLOS rather than creating new adjudicatory bodies. See generally Tullio Treves, 'A System for Law of the Sea Dispute Settlement' in Freestone, Barnes and Ong (eds) (n 6) 417–32. Notably, all three implementing agreements concluded under UNCLOS, including the Agreement under the United Nations Convention on the Law of the Sea on the Conservation and Sustainable Use of Marine Biological Diversity of Areas beyond National Jurisdiction that was concluded in 2023, use the dispute settlement system created by Part XV of UNCLOS, although with some alterations: see Alex G Oude Elferink and others, 'Compulsory Jurisdiction as the DNA of LOSC Dispute Settlement: An Evolutionary Path' (2023) 38 IJMCL 185, 193–200.

13 Klein (n 3) 2, 349.

14 UNCLOS art 280.

15 UNCLOS art 281.

16 UNCLOS art 282.

17 For detailed treatment of these provisions see e.g. Klein (n 3) chs 3–4.

limitations, which remove many matters concerning the rights of coastal States within their EEZs from compulsory jurisdiction.[18] In summary:

- Disputes regarding the exercise by a coastal State of its sovereign rights or jurisdiction pursuant to UNCLOS are subject to the Section 2 procedures where the dispute concerns freedoms and rights of navigation, overflight or laying of submarine cables and pipelines, or other internationally lawful uses of the sea.[19]
- Claims alleging that the coastal State has contravened international rules and standards for the protection of the marine environment established by UNCLOS, or a competent international organisation under UNCLOS, are also subject to the Section 2 procedures.[20]
- For disputes over marine scientific research, disputes concerning the exercise by the coastal State of its discretionary powers within its EEZ or continental shelf are largely excluded from Section 2,[21] although there is provision for non-binding conciliation.[22] Marine scientific research on the high seas is subject to compulsory dispute resolution.[23]
- For fisheries disputes, there is a major exception for disputes relating to a coastal State's sovereign rights over living resources in its EEZ,[24] which are only subject to a limited form of non-binding conciliation.[25] In contrast, high seas fisheries disputes are subject to binding dispute settlement.[26]

Article 298 also enables States Parties at any time to declare in writing that they do not accept one or more of the Section 2 procedures for any of the following categories of dispute::

- Disputes concerning maritime boundary delimitations, or historic bays or titles, although where such a declaration is made there is provision for the dispute to be submitted to non-binding conciliation at the request of any party to the dispute;[27]

18 Churchill (n 6) 407.
19 UNCLOS art 297(1)(a)–(b).
20 UNCLOS art 297(1)(c).
21 UNCLOS arts 297(2)(a), 246, 253.
22 UNCLOS art 297(2)(b), Annex V, Section 2.
23 Boyle (n 7) 42–43.
24 UNCLOS art 297(3)(a).
25 UNCLOS art 297(3)(b)(c), Annex V, Section 2.
26 Boyle (n 7) 42–43.
27 UNCLOS art 298(1)(a).

- Disputes concerning military activities and disputes concerning some categories of law enforcement activities;[28]
- Disputes in respect of which the UN Security Council is exercising its functions under the UN Charter.[29]

Currently, a minority of UNCLOS parties have made declarations under Article 298.[30] As explained below, these generally applicable and optional exclusions reflect that in some areas of the Convention, because of the sensitivity of the interests at stake, States were not willing to accept compulsory binding dispute resolution.

2. *Choice of Dispute Settlement Procedures*

For those disputes where the compulsory, binding dispute settlement procedures in Section 2 apply, States are free to choose, by means of a prior declaration, between: (a) ITLOS, created under Annex VI; (b) the ICJ; (c) arbitration under Annex VII; or (d) for particular categories of dispute, special arbitration under Annex VIII.[31] Where a party has not made a declaration, or the parties' declarations do not match, Annex VII arbitration applies unless the parties otherwise agree.[32] Only a small fraction of UNCLOS parties have made declarations under Article 287,[33] meaning that arbitration by an Annex VII Tribunal has emerged as the default mechanism for disputes where the compulsory, binding procedures apply.[34] To date, fifteen Annex VII tribunals have been constituted, and ITLOS has registered thirty-two cases, although of the latter ten were prompt release cases (a limited form of jurisdiction discussed below) and eight were cases where ITLOS only decided on a request for provisional measures as an Annex VII tribunal had jurisdiction over the case. While the ICJ sometimes hears law of the sea cases (primarily concerning maritime boundary delimitation), it has not yet been seised pursuant to Part XV of UNCLOS. Similarly, special

28 See UNCLOS art 298(1)(b).
29 See UNCLOS art 298(1)(c).
30 The declarations are available online through the UN Treaties Collection. Such declarations operate on the principle of reciprocity: UNCLOS art 298(3).
31 UNCLOS art 287(1).
32 UNCLOS art 287(3), (5).
33 The declarations are available online through the UN Treaties Collection.
34 Churchill (n 6) 397.

arbitration under Annex VIII has not been used. Accordingly, these two potential fora for UNCLOS dispute settlement are not discussed further.

3. *The Adjudicators in UNCLOS Dispute Settlement*

ITLOS is composed of twenty-one members, appointed for renewable terms of nine years,[35] who must inter alia have recognised competence in the law of the sea.[36] No two members of ITLOS can be nationals of the same State,[37] and at least three members must come from each geographical grouping established in the UN.[38] The exact geographical distribution of seats among the UN regional groupings is governed by a decision of the States Parties to UNCLOS, and evolved somewhat in 2011 to introduce one 'floating seat' at the expense of one of the seats previously allocated to the Group of Western European and Other States.[39] As in the ICJ, on whose Statute ITLOS is modelled, members with the nationality of one of the parties to a dispute are permitted to participate (unless otherwise conflicted),[40] and where the Tribunal does not include a member with the nationality of the parties, the non-represented party or parties are able to nominate ad hoc judges.[41] Also following the ICJ model, members have a right to append a separate opinion,[42] and judgments record the votes of members on each operative provision of the Tribunal's judgment.[43] The result of these arrangements is that ITLOS has a bench that is more diverse than most international tribunals, which generally features a substantial amount of internal debate in the form of separate or dissenting opinions.

ITLOS can also form a special chamber upon the disputing parties' request, the composition of which is determined by the Tribunal with the approval of the parties.[44] As the parties can effectively agree on the

[35] UNCLOS Annex VI, art 5(1).

[36] UNCLOS Annex VI, art 2(1)–(2).

[37] UNCLOS Annex VI, art 3(1).

[38] UNCLOS Annex VI, art 3(2).

[39] Kriangsak Kittichaisaree, *The International Tribunal for the Law of the Sea* (OUP 2021) 28–29; P Chandrasekhara Rao and Philippe Gautier, *The International Tribunal for the Law of the Sea: Law, Practice and Procedure* (Edward Elgar 2018) [2.028]–[2.029].

[40] UNCLOS Annex VI, art 17(1).

[41] UNCLOS Annex VI, art 17(2)–(3).

[42] UNCLOS Annex VI, art 30(3); ITLOS, Rules of the Tribunal, art 125(2).

[43] ITLOS, Rules of the Tribunal, art 125(1)(l). See also Resolution on the Internal Judicial Practice of the Tribunal, ITLOS/10, 27 April 2005.

[44] UNCLOS Annex VI, art 15(2). ITLOS has also formed certain other chambers, pursuant to Article 15 of its Statute, which litigants are yet to utilise: <www.itlos.org/en/main/the-tribunal/chambers/>.

constitution of such a chamber, there is little difference, in terms of control over composition, with the option of Annex VII arbitration.[45] ITLOS also has a Seabed Disputes Chamber, composed of eleven members.[46] This Chamber has jurisdiction over disputes with respect to activities in the International Seabed Area, which is regulated under Part XI of UNCLOS and a 1994 implementing agreement.[47] The Seabed Disputes Chamber can give advisory opinions when requested by the Assembly or Council of the International Seabed Authority on legal questions within their scope of activities and has so far given one advisory opinion that will be discussed below.[48]

ITLOS has also held that as the full tribunal it has the power to give advisory opinions where it is authorised to do so by another agreement that confers jurisdiction on the Tribunal.[49] Among other requirements, the other international agreement must be 'related to the purposes of the Convention [and] specifically' provide for the submission to the Tribunal of requests for advisory opinions.[50] ITLOS as the full Tribunal has given one advisory opinion in 2015 concerning IUU fishing, which will be discussed below, and a second request for an advisory opinion concerning climate change, based on the jurisdiction granted in another agreement, is currently pending.[51]

Arbitral tribunals constituted under Annex VII consist of five members, with each party able to appoint one member, who may be its national, and the other three members – including the president of the tribunal – being nationals of third States, appointed by agreement.[52] Where the parties cannot agree on the jointly appointed arbitrators or the President, or a respondent does not exercise its right to appoint an arbitrator, a party can request the appointing authority to

45 Alan Boyle, 'UNCLOS Dispute Settlement and the Uses and Abuses of Part XV' (2014) 47 Revue Belge de Droit International 182, 190–92.

46 See UNCLOS Annex VI, arts 14, 35.

47 Agreement Relating to the Implementation of Part XI of the United Nations Convention on the Law of the Sea of 10 December 1982 (1994) 1836 UNTS 3. Regarding the jurisdiction of the Seabed Disputes Chamber see UNCLOS arts 187–91.

48 See UNCLOS arts 191, 159(10).

49 ITLOS Statute art 21; *Request for Advisory Opinion Submitted by the Sub-Regional Fisheries Commission*, Advisory Opinion, 2 April 2015, ITLOS Reports 2015, p. 4, [56], [58] ('*ITLOS 2015 Advisory Opinion*').

50 ITLOS, Rules of the Tribunal, art 138(1). See further *ITLOS 2015 Advisory Opinion* (n 49) [59]–[68]; Yoshifumi Tanaka, *The International Law of the Sea* (3rd ed., CUP 2019) 529–30.

51 See above nn 10 and 49.

52 UNCLOS Annex VII, art 3(a)–(d).

make the necessary appointments, who is, unless otherwise agreed, the President of ITLOS.[53] In practice, current or former judges of ITLOS have increasingly been appointed to Annex VII Tribunals, meaning there is a strong similarity in terms of composition to a chamber of ITLOS.[54] The involvement of current or prior ITLOS judges helps explain why there is little detectable difference between the interpretative approach of Annex VII Tribunals and ITLOS.[55] Early concerns that were raised over the potential for inconsistent interpretations between the different dispute settlement fora available under UNCLOS have not materialised.[56]

4. *Provisional Measures in UNCLOS Adjudication*

It is appropriate to explain briefly the basis for provisional measures in this regime as provisional measures are often requested from ITLOS prior to an arbitral tribunal, which has jurisdiction over the case, being constituted. In such circumstances, ITLOS has the power to grant provisional measures under Article 290(5) 'if it considers that *prima facie* the tribunal which is to be constituted would have jurisdiction and that the urgency of the situation so requires'.[57] This power must be understood in light of the grounds on which any UNCLOS court or tribunal can grant provisional measures under Article 290(1), specifically that in addition to prima facie jurisdiction being shown, provisional measures can be granted where 'appropriate ... to preserve the respective rights of the parties to the dispute or to prevent serious harm to the marine environment, pending the final decision'.[58] On one view, compared with a normal grant of provisional measures under Article 290(1), it is more difficult to obtain provisional measures under Article 290(5), pending the constitution of an arbitral tribunal, as the requirement of urgency is

[53] UNCLOS Annex VII, art 3(c)–(e). A list of arbitrators is maintained by the UN Secretary General, to which all States Parties can nominate four individuals: art 2(1). While arbitrators chosen by the parties are only 'preferably' to come from the list, appointments made by the appointing authority must come from the list: art 3(b)–(e).

[54] Roland Holst (n 3) 141; Alan Boyle, 'The Tribunal and the Rule of Law' in ITLOS (ed), *The Contribution of the International Tribunal for the Law of the Sea to the Rule of Law: 1996–2016* (Brill Nijhoff 2018) 200–01.

[55] Lan Ngoc Nguyen, *The Development of the Law of the Sea by UNCLOS Dispute Settlement Bodies* (CUP 2023) 295–97; Boyle (n 54) 200–01; Caroline E Foster, *Global Regulatory Standards in Environmental and Health Disputes: Regulatory Coherence, Due Regard, and Due Diligence* (OUP 2021) 54.

[56] Eg Roland Holst (n 3) 141, 245; Boyle (n 54) 199.

[57] UNCLOS art 290(5).

[58] See *MOX Plant (Ireland v United Kingdom)*, Provisional Measures, Order of 3 December 2001, ITLOS Reports 2001, p. 95, Sep. Op. Mensah.

stricter. Under Article 290(5) it must be shown that there is a risk of irreparable prejudice to the rights of the parties or serious harm to the marine environment in the period up until the Annex VII tribunal is constituted and in a position to modify, revoke, or affirm those measures,[59] rather than in the period until the determination of the merits.[60]

5. *Prompt Release Procedure*

ITLOS also has a limited,[61] independent, and unique[62] form of compulsory jurisdiction under Article 292, which applies in situations where one State Party has detained a vessel flagged in another State Party and it is alleged that the detaining State has not complied with provisions of the Convention regarding prompt release of vessels and their crew upon posting of a reasonable bond.[63] In such circumstances, the flag State can make an application or authorise a private party to make an application on its behalf.[64] ITLOS then has the task of determining whether the allegation made by the applicant, that the detaining State has not complied with a provision of the Convention for prompt release of vessels or crew upon the posting of a reasonable bond, is well founded.[65] If ITLOS determines that the applicant's allegation of non-compliance is well-founded, ITLOS must 'determine the amount, nature and form of the bond'.[66] When this bond is posted, the detaining State must comply promptly with the decision of ITLOS concerning release of the vessel or crew.[67]

The context for this aspect of UNCLOS dispute settlement is that the prompt release procedure was intended as one mechanism to prevent coastal States abusing their enforcement powers in the newly established

[59] *Land Reclamation in and around the Straits of Johor (Malaysia v Singapore)*, Provisional Measures, Order of 8 October 2003, ITLOS Reports 2003, p. 10, [68].

[60] *Southern Bluefin Tuna Cases (New Zealand v Japan; Australia v Japan)*, Provisional Measures, Order of 27 August 1999, ITLOS Reports 1999, p. 280, Sep. Op. Treves [3]–[4]; *"Enrica Lexie" (Italy v India)*, Provisional Measures, Order of 24 August 2015, ITLOS Reports 2015, p. 182, Diss. Op. Heidar [6]–[13]; *MOX Plant* (n 58) Sep. Op. Mensah. See further Tanaka (n 50) 524–25.

[61] The UNCLOS court or tribunal 'shall deal only with the question of release' and its determination is 'without prejudice to the merits of any case' brought at the domestic level against the detained vessel or crew: UNCLOS art 292(3).

[62] *"Camouco"* (n 11) Dec Laing. See also Sep. Op. Nelson.

[63] UNCLOS art 292(1).

[64] UNCLOS art 292(2).

[65] ITLOS, Rules of the Tribunal, art 113(1).

[66] ITLOS, Rules of the Tribunal, art 113(2).

[67] UNCLOS art 292(4).

EEZ to the detriment of flag States' interest in freedom of navigation.[68] There are two key areas of the Convention that refer to prompt release of vessels and hence are covered by this procedure. First, UNCLOS permits coastal States in the exercise of their sovereign rights to conserve and manage living resources in the EEZ to take measures to enforce their laws adopted in conformity with the Convention, including boarding, arrest and judicial proceedings,[69] and provides for the prompt release of arrested vessels and crew upon the posting of a reasonable bond.[70] In practice, this has meant ITLOS has heard numerous prompt release cases concerning vessels detained for violating the fisheries laws of coastal States, often in the context of coastal States attempting to combat the major conservation problem of IUU fishing. Second, Part XII of the Convention, dealing with protection and preservation of the marine environment, also permits detention of vessels in certain instances relating to pollution from vessels and provides for prompt release,[71] however these provisions have not yet been litigated.[72]

6. *Debating the Purposes of UNCLOS Dispute Settlement*

The purposes of the dispute settlement system contained in Part XV of UNCLOS must be understood in light of the wider goals of the Convention as Part XV is 'an integral part and an essential element of

[68] See text below n 182.
[69] UNCLOS art 73(1).
[70] UNCLOS art 73(2).
[71] UNCLOS arts 220(6)–(7), 226(1)(c). Article 226(1)(b) also arguably comes within the prompt release procedure: Yoshifumi Tanaka, 'Prompt Release in the United Nations Convention on the Law of the Sea: Some Reflections on the ITLOS Jurisprudence' (2004) 51 Netherlands ILR 237, 245. There is debate over exactly which provisions of UNCLOS fall within the prompt release procedure. ITLOS has observed that Article 73(2), Article 220(6)–(7), and 'at least to a certain extent, article 226, paragraph 1(c)' fall within the prompt release procedure, but left open the question of whether other provisions could also be subject to the prompt release procedure: *M/V 'SAIGA' (Saint Vincent and the Grenadines v Guinea)*, Prompt Release, Judgment, ITLOS Reports 1997, p. 16, [52]–[53], [73]. Some dissenting judgments outlined strong reasons regarding why the prompt release procedure should only apply to provisions of the Convention that explicitly refer to prompt release on the posting of a reasonable bond: Diss. Op. Park, Nelson, Chandrasekhara Rao, Vukas and Ndiaye [23]–[25]; Diss. Op. Wolfrum and Yamamoto [15]–[19]. See further Tanaka, ibid 241–48.
[72] For analysis, see eg James Harrison, 'Safeguards against Excessive Enforcement Measures in the Exclusive Economic Zone – Law and Practice' in Henrik Ringbom (ed), *Jurisdiction over Ships: Post-UNCLOS Developments in the Law of the Sea* (Brill Nijhoff 2015) 236–38.

the Convention'.[73] UNCLOS was intended to be a comprehensive 'legal order for the seas' that would, inter alia, promote 'peaceful uses of the seas and oceans, the equitable and efficient utilization of their resources, the conservation of their living resources, and the study, protection and preservation of the marine environment'.[74] Key aspects of Part XV clearly further goals of the wider regime, such as the power of tribunals to grant provisional measures to 'prevent serious harm to the marine environment',[75] or the unique mechanism for prompt release of detained vessels that prevents undue impingement on the regime's value of freedom of navigation.[76] Yet two goals, are, above all, repeated throughout discussions of the aims of UNCLOS dispute settlement. First, the dispute settlement system is said to have the purpose of maintaining and adapting the bargain contained in the Convention over time, by providing authoritative mechanisms for resolving disputes regarding its interpretation and application and some degree of international control over its implementation by States Parties.[77] For example, the first President of the diplomatic conference suggested during negotiations that:

> The provision of effective dispute settlement procedures is essential for stabilizing and maintaining the compromises necessary for the attainment of agreement on a convention. Dispute settlement procedures will be the pivot upon which the delicate equilibrium of the compromise must be balanced. Otherwise the compromise will disintegrate rapidly and permanently.[78]

This aim of maintaining and adapting the compromises contained in the Convention can be broken down into several more concrete functions of

[73] *South China Sea Arbitration (Philippines v China)*, Award on Jurisdiction and Admissibility (2015) 170 ILR 22, [2], [224].

[74] UNCLOS preamble.

[75] UNCLOS arts 290(1), 290(5).

[76] Trevisanut (n 11) 307 (discussing the 'regime maintenance' function of the prompt release procedure by 'protecting the balance between the interests of flag states/the fishing industry and the sovereign rights the LOSC has granted to coastal states'). See also below text at nn 182–185.

[77] Boyle (n 7) 38–39; Shabtai Rosenne and Louis B Sohn (eds), *United Nations Convention on the Law of the Sea 1982: A Commentary*, vol 5 (Martinus Nijhoff 1989) 7–8; AO Adede, *The System for Settlement of Disputes under the UN Convention on the Law of the Sea* (Martinus Nijhoff 1987) 241. See also Roland Holst (n 3) 284–85.

[78] Hamilton Shirley Amerasinghe, 'Memorandum by the President of the Conference on Document A/CONF.62/WP.9' in *Official Records of the Third United Nations Conference on the Law of the Sea*, vol V (United Nations) 122, UN Doc A/CONF.62/WP.9/Add.1.

UNCLOS dispute settlement.[79] One key function in this regard is the treaty interpretation function performed by Part XV tribunals in those disputes where they have jurisdiction.[80] As Klein and Parlett have argued, the decisions of Part XV tribunals have various broader consequences, beyond their binding effect for the disputing parties, including by establishing authoritative reference points that may be drawn upon by later tribunals and that may influence State practice, for example if other States Parties to UNCLOS, not parties to the case, take the judgment into account 'in their internal decision-making and policies or in interactions with other States'.[81] In short, beyond their implications for the particular dispute at hand, the decisions of UNCLOS tribunals may have implications for 'future conduct of all stakeholders in ocean governance . . . [and] for the public order of the oceans'.[82] Put differently, as Nguyen has argued, UNCLOS Part XV tribunals are correctly understood as performing a 'governance function', whereby 'they become the institutional guardians of the UNCLOS legal regime' issuing decisions that go beyond merely settling the disputes between the parties before them to 'provide normative guidance to States in implementing the Convention' and '"endorse" and protect the legal order that has been set up by the Convention'.[83] As Roland Holst has suggested, this prospectively focused governance function is particularly apparent in UNCLOS tribunals' interpretation and application of open-ended balancing principles that often appear in the Convention – eg provisions based on standards such as 'reasonableness' or 'due regard' – as it is foreseeable that 'the criteria that courts and tribunals develop for how these balancing principles are to be applied will have implications for future applications of those principles'.[84] A related function of UNCLOS tribunals that is directly linked to the broad aim of maintaining the sensitive bargain contained in the Convention is the function of determining

[79] Consider also the approach of Klein and Parlett, who argue that '[t]he core function for any UNCLOS judge . . . is the settlement of disputes' and identify multiple 'tasks' that must be performed to fulfil this function, including 'settling the procedure, treaty interpretation, fact-finding, deciding on claims and, where warranted, assessing remedies': Klein and Parlett (n 4) 22–36.

[80] Ibid 25.

[81] Ibid 32–33.

[82] Ibid 39–40.

[83] Nguyen (n 55) 285–87.

[84] Rozemarijn J Roland Holst, 'Reflections on the Governance Function of Compulsory Dispute Settlement in the Legal Order for the Ocean' (2023) 38 IJMCL 283, 293, 297.

State compliance with the Convention in those disputes that are submitted to Part XV dispute settlement where jurisdiction exists. Klein and Parlett term this function, correctly, as an enforcement role of Part XV tribunals, whereby such tribunals determine whether UNCLOS has been violated and award appropriate remedies.[85]

Nevertheless, in considering the role of international adjudication in maintaining, clarifying, and adapting the bargain contained in UNCLOS, it is important to remember that as, outlined above, the range of disputes subject to compulsory, binding dispute settlement under the Convention is carefully limited.[86] Mandatory adjudication was seen as necessary to maintain and adapt the bargain contained in some areas of the Convention, such as the compromise struck between coastal State and flag State interests within the newly created EEZ, which represented a major extension of coastal State jurisdiction and created the risk of abuse of enforcement powers.[87] Yet, as noted above, in other areas compulsory international scrutiny of State conduct was deliberately excluded given the sensitivity of the interests at stake, such as for disputes concerning fisheries or scientific research in the EEZ,[88] or the optional exclusion for maritime boundary delimitation.[89]

A second broad purpose of UNCLOS dispute settlement is to provide peaceful means of dispute settlement, which was intended to reduce the role of political, economic, and military pressure in resolving disputes.[90] These ideas find some support in UNCLOS' preamble, which refers to the Convention as contributing to international peace, security, and cooperation.[91] In this vein, the final president of the diplomatic conference, reflecting at the time of the Convention's conclusion on the achievements of some thirteen years of negotiations, noted that 'the world community's interest in the peaceful settlement of disputes and the prevention of force in the settlement of disputes between States have been advanced by the mandatory system of dispute settlement in the Convention'.[92] As we have

[85] Klein and Parlett (n 4) 30 (noting in delimitation cases this function involves determining 'where the boundary lies consistent with UNCLOS'), 9–10.

[86] Oda (n 9) 863; Klein (n 3) 28, 348.

[87] Boyle (n 7) 46–47; Klein (n 3) 353–54.

[88] Noyes (n 6) 687.

[89] Klein (n 3) 28, 53, 355–58; Boyle (n 7) 42.

[90] Klein (n 3) 25; Rosenne and Sohn (n 77) 7–8; Adede (n 77) 241; Karaman (n 7) 5.

[91] See UNCLOS preamble.

[92] TTB Koh, 'Statement by the President' in *Official Records of the Third United Nations Conference on the Law of the Sea*, vol XVII (United Nations) 13, UN Doc A/CONF.62/SR.185.

seen in Chapter 1, peaceful dispute settlement is a generic function of international courts, so it is not surprising that UNCLOS tribunals fulfil this role.[93] There is a strong case that the dispute settlement system of UNCLOS, with its significant element of compulsory jurisdiction, has contributed to reducing the relevance of power politics in ocean affairs and deterring 'unilateral attempts to extend coastal State jurisdiction'.[94]

Amongst law of the sea lawyers one can distinguish between a 'substantive ... regime building conception' of UNCLOS whereby the 'Convention stands at the heart of the public order of the oceans, and compulsory jurisdiction is integral to that public order', and a more consent-oriented 'procedural model' whereby the 'Convention is to be implemented by political arrangements that translate its general principles into precise legal measures, and compulsory jurisdiction is ancillary to the system of political institutions established to implement those principles'.[95] Those favouring the first narrative emphasise that, by becoming party to UNCLOS, States automatically consent to the adjudication of 'most disputes concerning its interpretation and application'.[96] Compulsory binding dispute settlement, as we have seen, is said to be necessary to maintain and adapt the bargain contained in the Convention over time, and to ensure that a rule-oriented system, centred on the Convention, is not overwhelmed by power politics. Yet as noted above, a competing, more qualified perspective correctly highlights that the system of compulsory jurisdiction in UNCLOS is carefully limited to some areas and not others.[97]

It is useful to note these contrasting views regarding the purposes of UNCLOS dispute settlement because they sometimes animate UNCLOS adjudication. For example, in the *Southern Bluefin Tuna* (SBT) case,

[93] See Chapter 1(B) text at nn 39–43.

[94] Eg Boyle (n 54) 195–97.

[95] Oxman (n 10) 279. See also Yoshifumi Tanaka, 'Reflections on the Philippines/China Arbitration Award on Jurisdiction and Admissibility' (2016) 15 LPICT 305, 323–24; Klein and Parlett (n 4) 8–9, 371; Philip Allott, '*Mare Nostrum*: A New International Law of the Sea' (1992) 86 AJIL 764 esp. 783–87 (interpreting UNCLOS 'as much more ... a public law system than ... a contractual arrangement', which represents a shift from traditional inter-State diplomacy to a system that constitutes an international public interest and hinting at implications of these views for understandings of the role of Part XV courts or tribunals).

[96] Bernard H Oxman, 'Courts and Tribunals: The ICJ, ITLOS, and Arbitral Tribunals' in Donald R Rothwell and others (eds), *The Oxford Handbook of the Law of the Sea* (OUP 2015) 415.

[97] See above n 9.

where an Annex VII Tribunal controversially held that the dispute settlement provision in a regional fisheries agreement between the parties operated to exclude implicitly the UNCLOS dispute resolution procedures (pursuant to Article 281 of the Convention), the majority supported this finding by emphasising that 'UNCLOS falls significantly short of establishing a truly comprehensive regime of compulsory jurisdiction'.[98] This reflects the limited 'procedural model' conception of UNCLOS. In contrast, Judge Keith, dissenting, in holding that jurisdiction was not excluded, recounted the familiar narrative of UNCLOS establishing a default rule of compulsory binding dispute settlement,[99] which is read as a decisive shift away from States' traditional freedom not to submit their disputes to adjudication.[100] More recently, the Tribunal in the *South China Sea Arbitration*, in overruling the *SBT* majority and holding that Article 281 requires the parties to exclude explicitly the further use of UNCLOS Part XV dispute resolution procedures,[101] emphasised that UNCLOS is 'a system whereby compulsory dispute resolution is the default rule', which is central to the Convention's object and purpose as 'a comprehensive agreement'.[102] Again, this is the substantive, regime-building conception of UNCLOS.

B. Balancing Stability and Change in UNCLOS Adjudication

This section analyses how UNCLOS adjudicators have managed the problem of changes in applicable international legal norms or changes in relevant facts that affect the application of such norms. Before turning to how this issue has been addressed in case law, it is worth noting several features of UNCLOS that make the Convention potentially able to adapt to new legal and factual developments.[103] First, UNCLOS is a framework

98 *SBT Award* (n 4) [60]–[62].

99 Ibid Sep. Op. Keith [19]–[22].

100 Ibid [23]–[29].

101 *Philippines v China (Jurisdiction)* (n 67) [223].

102 Ibid [224]–[225].

103 See generally Roland Holst (n 3); Richard Barnes, 'The Continuing Vitality of UNCLOS' in Jill Barrett and Richard Barnes (eds), *Law of the Sea: UNCLOS as a Living Treaty* (BIICL 2016) 478–84; Tomas Heidar, 'Introduction: How Does the Law of the Sea Adapt to New Knowledge and Changing Circumstances?' in Tomas Heidar (ed), *New Knowledge and Changing Circumstances in the Law of the Sea* (Brill Nijhoff 2020) 1–12; Bernard H Oxman, 'Tools for Change: The Amendment Procedure' in *Proceedings of the Twentieth Anniversary Commemoration of the Opening for Signature of the United Nations Convention on the Law of the Sea* (UN 2003) 199–204. Some aspects of Sections B and C of this chapter were previously published

treaty in the sense that in many areas it establishes broad principles and foresees that these will be implemented though more specific norms elaborated elsewhere.[104] Two or more States Parties can conclude inter se agreements modifying or suspending the provisions of the Convention between themselves, provided 'that such agreements do not relate to a provision derogation from which is incompatible with the effective execution of the object and purpose' of UNCLOS nor 'affect the application of the basic principles embodied' in it.[105] Some provisions of the Convention also expressly foresee that States may conclude subsequent agreements to implement the principles and objectives of UNCLOS, for example those contained in Part XII on marine environmental protection.[106] Second, in some areas, particularly Part XII concerning marine environmental protection, the provisions of UNCLOS contain so-called 'rules of reference', which are based on phrasing such as 'generally accepted international rules and standards'.[107] Such rules of reference create a 'degree of dynamism' because the external standards referred to may change over time, without any amendment of UNCLOS.[108] Indeed,

in Joshua Paine, 'The Judicial Dimension of Regime Interaction beyond Systemic Integration' in Seline Trevisanut, Nikolaos Giannopoulos and Rozemarijn Roland Holst (eds), *Regime Interaction in Ocean Governance: Problems, Theories and Methods* (Brill Nijhoff 2020), however the material has been significantly further developed here.

104 See eg Robin Churchill, 'The 1982 United Nations Convention on the Law of the Sea' in Donald R Rothwell and others (eds), *The Oxford Handbook of the Law of the Sea* (OUP 2015) 29–31; Alan Boyle, 'Further Development of the 1982 Convention on the Law of the Sea: Mechanisms for Change' in Freestone, Barnes and Ong (eds) (n 6) 41–42, 52–53, 61–62.

105 Additionally, inter se agreements cannot 'affect the enjoyment by other States Parties of their rights or the performance of their obligations' under UNCLOS: UNCLOS art 311 (3). For discussion, see eg Roland Holst (n 3) 113–17.

106 UNCLOS art 237 provides that Part XII is 'without prejudice . . . to agreements which may be concluded in furtherance of the general principles set forth in this Convention' but that 'Specific obligations assumed by States under special conventions, with respect to the protection and preservation of the marine environment, should be carried out in a manner consistent with the general principles and objectives of this Convention'. See also art 311(5).

107 On rules of reference, see eg James Harrison, *Making the Law of the Sea: A Study in the Development of International Law* (CUP 2011) 165–79; Bernard H Oxman, 'The Duty to Respect Generally Accepted International Standards' (1991) 24 NYUJ Int'l L. & Pol. 109, 121–39; Roland Holst (n 3) 150–66; Lan Ngoc Nguyen, 'Expanding the Environmental Regulatory Scope of UNCLOS through the Rule of Reference: Potentials and Limits' (2021) 52 ODIL 419.

108 Harrison (n 107) 171; Roland Holst (n 3) 150–51, 156; Jill Barrett, 'The UN Convention on the Law of the Sea: A "Living" Treaty?' in Jill Barrett and Richard Barnes (eds), *Law of the Sea: UNCLOS as a Living Treaty* (BIICL 2016) 22. UNCLOS at times refers to

some commentators suggest that the term 'generally accepted rules and standards' is itself an evolutionary term, whose meaning is capable of changing over time.[109] The object and purpose of UNCLOS, including that it was intended to 'settle ... all issues relating to the law of the sea' and establish a 'legal order for the seas and oceans',[110] also provides some support for a rebuttable presumption that the parties, when using generic terms, intended for these to be capable of evolving over time.[111] More specifically, a number of terms used throughout UNCLOS have been suggested to have an evolutionary meaning, including 'pollution', 'protection of the marine environment', 'conservation of living resources', and 'natural resources'.[112] Even if these terms are not strictly generic terms in the sense that their meaning is tied to a body of international law that may evolve, many provisions of UNCLOS are phrased in a sufficiently open-ended manner that they may be capable of incorporating subsequent factual developments.[113] For example, UNCLOS often uses terms such as 'reasonable' or 'necessary' that are inherently influenced by the particular context in which they are applied and that give adjudicators a key role in striking the precise balance between the competing interests at stake.[114] Finally UNCLOS often refers to rules of general international law, and the applicable law provision for Part XV tribunals instructs tribunals to apply 'other rules of international law not

'competent international organizations' without specifying particular organisations that are competent to adopt such standards. In contrast, where UNCLOS uses 'competent international organization' in the singular this is generally understood to be an exclusive reference to the International Maritime Organization. Additionally, such international rules and standards can be produced through diplomatic conferences. See eg Harrison ibid 171; Roland Holst ibid 155.

109 Boyle (n 104) 46; Catherine Redgwell, 'Treaty Evolution, Adaptation and Change: Is the LOSC "Enough" to Address Climate Change Impacts on the Marine Environment?' (2019) 34 IJMCL 440, 448–50; Irina Buga, *Modification of Treaties by Subsequent Practice* (OUP 2018) 191.

110 UNCLOS preamble.

111 *Navigational Rights* (n 12) para 66; Barnes (n 103) 480–81; Roland Holst (n 3) 197–99.

112 Buga (n 109) 191; Boyle (n 104) 46; Barrett (n 108) 25.

113 See Chapter 1 text at nn 64–65. See also James Harrison, *Saving the Oceans through Law: The International Legal Framework for the Protection of the Marine Environment* (OUP 2017) 30–31 (discussing how the terms 'rare' and 'fragile' ecosystems and habitats of 'depleted, threatened, or endangered' in UNCLOS art 194(5) are 'inherently flexible and they must be understood by reference to scientific information concerning the State of the marine environment. The scope of this obligation may thus vary over time').

114 See below text at nn 309–311.

incompatible with this Convention'.[115] Thus, Part XV Tribunals have recognised that in order to interpret and apply provisions of UNCLOS they may need to have regard to 'foundational or secondary rules of general international law' and other primary rules of international law when interpreting and applying 'broadly worded or general provisions' of the Convention.[116]

1. *Managing Change in International Legal Norms*

A first significant example of UNCLOS adjudicators interpreting the Convention in a manner that is highly responsive to changes in wider international law is the merits award in the *South China Sea Arbitration*.[117] In interpreting China's obligations under Part XII of UNCLOS concerning marine environmental protection, the Tribunal informed the content of the relevant obligations by having regard to the wider 'corpus of international law relating to the environment' much of which had emerged since the conclusion of UNCLOS.[118] The Tribunal reasoned that the content of the general obligation to protect and preserve the marine environment under Article 192 of UNCLOS had to be 'informed by the other provisions of Part XII and other applicable rules of international law'.[119] In interpreting the obligation in Article 192 of UNCLOS and the obligation in Article 194(5) to take measures 'necessary to protect and preserve rare or fragile ecosystems as well as the habitat of depleted, threatened or endangered species', the Tribunal had regard to the Convention on Biological Diversity to inform the meaning

[115] UNCLOS art 293(1); Boyle (n 104) 43. Note, however, that the jurisdiction of Part XV tribunals is ordinarily limited to disputes 'concerning the interpretation or application of this Convention': UNCLOS art 288(1). On the relationship between jurisdiction and applicable law see generally Roland Holst (n 3) 201–08; *The Arctic Sunrise (Netherlands v Russia)*, Award on the Merits (2015) 171 ILR 1, [188]–[192].

[116] *Arctic Sunrise*, Merits (n 115) [190]–[191]; *Duzgit Integrity Arbitration* (*Malta v São Tomé and Príncipe*), Award (2016) 173 ILR 95, [208].

[117] Similarly: Yoshifumi Tanaka, *The South China Sea Arbitration: Toward an International Legal Order in the Oceans* (Hart 2019) 135; Chie Kojima, 'South China Sea Arbitration and the Protection of the Marine Environment: Evolution of UNCLOS Part XII through Interpretation and the Duty to Cooperate' (2015) 21 Asian Yearbook of International Law 166; Makane Moïse Mbengue, 'The South China Sea Arbitration: Innovations in Marine Environmental Fact-Finding and Due Diligence Obligations' (2016) 110 AJIL Unbound 285, 286.

[118] *South China Sea Arbitration (Philippines v China)*, Award (2016) 170 ILR 180, [941] and generally [940]–[948], [984]–[990].

[119] Ibid [941]–[942].

of the term 'ecosystem',[120] and to the appendices of the Convention on International Trade in Endangered Species of Wild Fauna and Flora to determine that the species at issue were 'depleted, threatened or endangered species'.[121] The reference to these external instruments for the purposes of interpreting and applying UNCLOS was justifiable because both China and the Philippines were parties to the agreements invoked,[122] and, as the Tribunal noted in its Award on Jurisdiction and Admissibility, such instruments could be considered pursuant to the instruction under Article 293(1) of UNCLOS to apply 'other relevant rules of international law not incompatible with' UNCLOS and Article 31 (3)(c) of the VCLT.[123] As Kojima suggests, this aspect of the award demonstrates how the content of UNCLOS can effectively 'be updated or revised over time' through interaction with other treaty regimes.[124]

[120] Ibid [945]; Convention on Biological Diversity (1992) 1760 UNTS 79.

[121] *South China Sea*, Award (n 118) [956]–[957]; Convention on International Trade in Endangered Species of Wild Fauna and Flora (1973) 993 UNTS 243. Schatz criticises this aspect of the award, on the basis that Article 192 of UNCLOS only contains a very limited obligation and Article 194 is limited to issues of marine pollution: Valentin Schatz, 'Fishing for Interpretation: The ITLOS Advisory Opinion on Flag State Responsibility for Illegal Fishing in the EEZ' (2016) 47 ODIL 327, 333–34. Note, however, that another Annex VII Tribunal has also held that Article 194(5) is not limited to issues of marine pollution, and many commentators also take this view: *Chagos Marine Protected Area (Republic of Mauritius v United Kingdom)*, Award (2015) 162 ILR 1, [538], [320]; Detlef Czybulka, 'Article 194' in Alexander Proelss (ed), *United Nations Convention on the Law of the Sea: A Commentary* (CH Beck 2017) [1], [30]–[31]; Harrison (n 113) 29–31. Furthermore, the obligation in Article 192 of UNCLOS must be interpreted in light of the wider body of international environmental law that has emerged in recent decades: Maria Gavouneli, 'Protection Standards for the Marine Environment: Updating Part XII of the Law of the Sea Convention?' in Stephen Minas and H Jordan Diamond (eds), *Stress Testing the Law of the Sea: Dispute Resolution, Disasters & Emerging Challenges* (Brill Nijhoff 2018) 261–62, 266.

[122] *South China Sea*, Award (n 118) [956]. Within debates over Article 31(3)(c) of the VCLT, it is a common view that at least all the parties to the dispute, if not all parties to the treaty under interpretation, must be party to the external rule relied upon. For discussion of this debate, suggesting that the term 'parties' should have a flexible meaning depending on the application of a multifaceted 'proximity criterion', see eg Panos Merkouris, *Article 31(3)(c) VCLT and the Principle of Systemic Integration: Normative Shadows in Plato's Cave* (Brill Nijhoff 2015) 22–24, 92–93, 95–100. See also discussion in Kojima (n 117) 174.

[123] *South China Sea*, Award on Jurisdiction (n 73) [176]. Note that the Tribunal referred to Article 31(3) of the VCLT. The Tribunal did not specify the sub-paragraph of Article 31 (3) on which it relied, but as Nguyen notes, Article 31(3)(c) provides the most tenable basis: Nguyen (n 55) 161–62.

[124] Kojima (n 117) 173. See also Nguyen (n 55) 162; Klein and Parlett (n 4) 347–48 (arguing that the Tribunal was wrong to limit 'depleted, threatened or endangered species' in Article 194(5) of UNCLOS to those species listed in CITES).

The *South China Sea* Tribunal held that the general obligation to 'protect and preserve the marine environment' under Article 192 of UNCLOS:

> extends both to 'protection of the marine environment from future damage and preservation' in the sense of maintaining or improving its present condition ... [and] thus entails the positive obligation to take active measures to protect and preserve the marine environment, and by logical implication, entails the negative obligation not to degrade the marine environment.[125]

Importantly, drawing on the environmental jurisprudence of the ICJ, ITLOS, and inter-State arbitral tribunals, the Tribunal read various due diligence obligations into Articles 192 and 194, including the 'obligation of a flag State to ensure its fishing vessels not be involved in activities which will undermine a flag State's responsibilities under the Convention in respect of the conservation of living resources and the obligation to protect and preserve the marine environment'.[126] This obligation to ensure required '"due diligence" in the sense of a flag State not only adopting appropriate rules and measures, but also a "certain level of vigilance in their enforcement and the exercise of administrative control"'.[127] For the Tribunal, 'read against the background of other applicable international law', 'the general obligation to "protect and preserve the marine environment" in Article 192 includes a due diligence obligation to prevent the harvesting of species that are recognised internationally as being at risk of extinction and requiring international protection'.[128] Interpreting Article 192 in the context of Article 194(5), the Tribunal held that 'in addition to preventing the direct harvesting of species recognised internationally as being threatened with extinction, Article 192 extends to the prevention of harms that would affect depleted, threatened, or endangered species indirectly through the destruction of their habitat'.[129] China was found to have violated these obligations through its lack of due diligence and toleration of such activities by vessels flying its flag.[130] As Tanaka has highlighted, by reading various

[125] *South China Sea*, Award (n 118) [941].
[126] Ibid [941], [944].
[127] Ibid [944], quoting *ITLOS 2015 Advisory Opinion* (n 49) [131], in turn quoting *Pulp Mills on the River Uruguay (Argentina v Uruguay)* (Judgment) [2010] ICJ Rep 14, [197].
[128] *South China Sea*, Award (n 118) [956], [959].
[129] Ibid [959].
[130] Ibid [961]–[966]. See also [975] (China was not shown to have exercised a lack of due diligence regarding the use of explosives or cyanide by vessels flying its flag), [983]

due diligence obligations into UNCLOS, these aspects of the *South China Sea* Award enable the precise standard (eg under Article 192) to evolve, because a due diligence obligation inherently depends on factual conditions (eg regarding environmental knowledge and technology) at the time the obligation is applied.[131]

Regarding China's construction activities in the South China Sea, the Tribunal interpreted the duty to cooperate for the protection of the marine environment, based in the relevant provisions of UNCLOS, in light of case law from ITLOS and the ICJ concerning the duty to cooperate, both as an obligation under UNCLOS and under general international law.[132] There was 'no convincing evidence of China attempting to cooperate or coordinate with the other States bordering the South China Sea' and hence it was found to have breached the relevant provisions of UNCLOS.[133] Finally, the Tribunal informed the content of the obligation to perform and communicate an environmental impact assessment (EIA) under Article 206 of UNCLOS by having regard to international case law concerning the obligation to carry out an EIA under customary international law.[134] For example, in finding that China had failed to communicate an EIA, as required by Article 206 of UNCLOS, the Tribunal noted inter alia that the statements of China that the Tribunal was able to identify were 'far less comprehensive than EIAs reviewed by other international courts and tribunals'.[135] Although the Tribunal did not further explain what was meant by this standard of 'comprehensiveness',[136] its approach, referring to EIAs scrutinised by

(China was found to have violated Articles 192, 194(1) and 195(5) through its construction activities).

131 Tanaka (n 117) 135, Yoshifumi Tanaka, 'Obligation to Conduct an Environmental Impact Assessment (EIA) in International Adjudication: Interaction between Law and Time' (2021) 90 Nordic JIL 86, 94.

132 *South China Sea*, Award (n 118) [946], [984]–[986], citing inter alia *MOX Plant* (n 58) [82].

133 Ibid [984]–[986], [993], [1203(B)(13)(b)]. See the criticism by Scanlon and Beckman of this aspect of the award. They argue that the Tribunal paid insufficient attention to the wording of the provisions of UNCLOS that China was found to have breached (Articles 197 and 123), which, they highlight, cannot be equated with a general duty to cooperate in the context of transboundary harm: Zoe Scanlon and Robert Beckman, 'Assessing Environmental Impact and the Duty to Cooperate: Environmental Aspects of the Philippines v China Award' (2018) 3 Asia-Pacific Journal of Ocean Law and Policy 5, 19–29.

134 *South China Sea*, Award (n 118) [947]–[948], [997]–[991].

135 Ibid [989]–[990].

136 Mbengue (n 117) 286–87.

other international courts and tribunals, suggests 'the existence of a certain international standard that an EIA should meet under international law, despite the absence of explicit requirements in Article 206 of UNCLOS'.[137] Overall, the *South China Sea* Award is a striking example of adjudicators interpreting UNCLOS in a manner that is highly responsive to subsequent developments in international law. The Award added 'substance to the bare bones' obligations found in Part XII of UNCLOS.[138] It is a prime example of how UNCLOS adjudicators have repeatedly engaged in a form of 'contextual and systemic interpretation', which construes the relevant provisions in their wider legal context and in light of the object and purpose of UNCLOS.[139]

The issue of change in applicable international legal norms, given relevant developments in wider international law, also arose repeatedly in the 2011 Advisory Opinion of ITLOS' Seabed Disputes Chamber concerning *Responsibilities and Obligations of States Sponsoring Persons and Entities with respect to Activities in the Area.*[140] For example, the Chamber held that in addition to the precautionary approach being a direct obligation of sponsoring States under the Nodules Regulations and Sulphides Regulations, adopted by the International Seabed Authority, it was also applicable more generally as an 'integral part' of sponsoring States' due diligence obligation.[141] Here the Chamber supported its interpretation by referring to earlier remarks of ITLOS in the *SBT* cases, considered below, which implicitly hinted at '[t]he link between an obligation of due diligence and the precautionary approach', as well a 'trend towards making this approach part of customary international law'.[142] In light of this trend, while the standard clause for exploration contracts in the Nodules Regulations did not refer to the precautionary approach – unlike the standard contractual clause in the Sulphides

[137] Kojima (n 117) 177. Another significant analysis of the Tribunal's findings regarding China's obligation to conduct and communicate an EIA under Articles 205 and 206 of UNCLOS is provided by Scanlon and Beckman who consider the drafting history of the relevant provisions: Scanlon and Beckman (n 133) 11–18.

[138] Gavouneli (n 121) 260–61, 265–66.

[139] Roland Holst (n 3) 311–12.

[140] *Responsibilities and Obligations of States Sponsoring Persons and Entities with respect to Activities in the Area*, Advisory Opinion, 1 February 2011, ITLOS Reports 2011, p. 10.

[141] Ibid [125]–[127], [131]. On the general due diligence obligation of sponsoring States see generally [99]–[120].

[142] Ibid [132], [135], citing *SBT Order* (n 60) [77]–[80] and *Pulp Mills* (n 127) [164] (regarding a precautionary approach being relevant to the interpretation of another instrument).

Regulations – nevertheless, States, under their general due diligence obligation, had to take measures to oblige sponsored entities to adopt a precautionary approach.[143] Similarly, the Chamber reasoned that while sponsoring States had a direct obligation under the Regulations to undertake an EIA, this obligation extended 'beyond the scope of application of specific provisions of the Regulations', being a 'relevant factor for meeting the sponsoring State's due diligence obligation'.[144] In this regard, the Chamber noted that the obligation to conduct an EIA was an obligation under customary international law, applying by analogy the ICJ's statement from the preceding year in the *Pulp Mills* case.[145]

The question of potential change in applicable legal norms also arose when the Chamber considered the obligation to apply 'best environmental practices', which was provided for in the Sulphides Regulations but not the Nodules Regulations, where the standard contractual clause referred to the less demanding standard of 'best technology'. The Chamber reasoned that:

> The adoption of higher standards in the more recent Sulphides Regulations would seem to indicate that, in light of the advancement in scientific knowledge, States of the Authority have become convinced of the need for sponsoring States to apply "best environmental practices" in general terms so that they may be seen to have become enshrined in the sponsoring States' obligation of due diligence.[146]

In light of this conclusion concerning the content of sponsoring States' general obligation of due diligence, and '[i]n the absence of a specific reason to the contrary . . . the Nodules Regulations should be interpreted in light of the development of the law, as evidenced by the subsequent adoption of the Sulphides Regulations'.[147] Again, the fundamental question being addressed here was whether the applicable legal standards could evolve in light of relevant developments in international law. The Chamber's decision strongly favours evolution in relevant legal norms, for example by inferring from a later instrument the parties' intent as to the present meaning of an earlier instrument. The Chamber was able to rely on a recent ICJ judgment (*Pulp Mills*) to support its view of the content of States' customary international law obligations concerning due

143 *Seabed AO* (n 140) [133]–[134].
144 Ibid [142], [150].
145 Ibid [145], [147]–[148], citing *Pulp Mills* (n 127) [204].
146 Ibid [136].
147 Ibid [137].

diligence and the obligation to perform an EIA. The advisory context of the decision, where there is not the same emphasis on State consent as in contentious cases, arguably also helps explain the approach adopted.[148]

Another important instance of ITLOS addressing the issue of potential change in international legal norms is the Tribunal's 2015 advisory opinion in the *Request for an Advisory Opinion submitted by the Sub-Regional Fisheries Commission* (SRFC). The context of this case was that the SRFC, a regional fisheries management organisation composed of several West African States, had requested an advisory opinion from ITLOS on four questions concerning the problem of IUU fishing. The first question, which is the focus of the following analysis, was '[w]hat are the obligations of the flag State in cases where IUU fishing activities are conducted within the Exclusive Economic Zone' of members States of the SRFC.[149] The Tribunal noted that while 'the primary responsibility for taking the necessary measures to prevent, deter and eliminate IUU fishing rests with the coastal State' this did not 'release other States from their obligations'.[150] The Tribunal then engaged in a lengthy analysis of the obligations of flag States in relation to IUU fishing activities occurring in the EEZs of the SRFC member States that proceeded from first principles and read a range of obligations into UNCLOS 'that were not readily clear to all from the text'.[151]

As 'the issue of flag State responsibility for IUU fishing activities is not directly addressed in the Convention', ITLOS approached this issue by considering the 'general obligations of States under the Convention with regard to the conservation and management of marine living resources and . . . specific obligations of flag States in the exclusive economic zone

[148] See generally Nguyen (n 55) 269 (on advisory proceedings being 'more likely to give international courts and tribunals leeway to develop the law').

[149] *ITLOS 2015 Advisory Opinion* (n 49) [2]. See also [87]–[88] regarding how the Tribunal construed the scope of this question.

[150] Ibid [106], [108].

[151] Foster (n 55) 114–15. See also Klein and Parlett (n 4) 313. ITLOS' answer to the fourth question posed – which concerned the rights and obligations of the coastal State in ensuring the sustainable management of shared stocks or stocks of common interest – also added significant detail to the relevant provisions of UNCLOS. Among other contributions, ITLOS interpreted obligations imposed by UNCLOS to cooperate or seek to agree on measures for the sustainable management of shared stocks to 'entail corresponding rights' ([205]) and held that, despite its jurisdiction in this case being limited to the EEZs of SRFC Member States, these obligations extended to non-member States of the SRFC ([215]–[218]). Note that some judges suggested that this part of the Advisory Opinion did not go far enough in elucidating the relevant obligations to cooperate (Sep. Op. Paik [34]–[39]) or was mistaken about the relevant law (Sep. Op. Nidaye [9]–[37]).

of the coastal State'.[152] Turning first to the obligation of the flag State to 'effectively exercise its jurisdiction and control in administrative, technical and social matters over ships flying its flag' under Article 94(1) of UNCLOS, ITLOS held that the measures listed in the subsequent paragraphs of this provision were 'only indicative, not exhaustive'.[153] For ITLOS it followed from Article 94 that:

> as far as fishing activities are concerned, the flag State, in fulfilment of its responsibility to exercise effective jurisdiction and control in administrative matters, must adopt the necessary administrative measures to ensure that fishing vessels flying its flag are not involved in activities which will undermine the flag State's responsibilities under the Convention in respect of the conservation and management of marine living resources.[154]

The next step in ITLOS' reasoning was to refer to the general obligation of States Parties to protect and preserve the marine environment under UNCLOS which included as an 'integral element' the conservation of living resources, from which it concluded that 'the flag State is under an obligation to ensure compliance by vessels flying its flag with the relevant conservation measures concerning living resources enacted by the coastal State for its exclusive economic zone'.[155] Further relevant provisions of UNCLOS included the obligation of the flag State, in exercising its rights in the EEZ, to have due regard to the rights and duties of the coastal State and to comply with the laws and regulations adopted by the coastal State in accordance with the Convention (Article 58(3)), and the obligation of nationals of other States fishing in the EEZ to comply with conservation measures and other terms and conditions established in the coastal State's laws and regulations (Article 62(4)). Reading these obligations together, ITLOS reached the conclusion that 'flag States are obliged to take the necessary measures to ensure that their nationals and vessels flying their flag are not engaged in IUU fishing activities'.[156] This amounted to a '"responsibility to ensure", which was a "due diligence obligation" to take all necessary measures to ensure compliance and to prevent IUU fishing by fishing vessels flying its flag'.[157]

152 *ITLOS 2015 Advisory Opinion* (n 49) [109]–[110].
153 Ibid [116]–[117].
154 Ibid [119].
155 Ibid [120], citing *SBT Order* (n 60) [70].
156 *ITLOS 2015 Advisory Opinion* (n 49) [124].
157 Ibid [125]–[129]. See also [130]–[139] where the Tribunal further articulated the content of this due diligence obligation.

A criticism of the Tribunal's reasoning developed by some commentators is that the provisions of UNCLOS cited do not explicitly provide for such a due diligence obligation of flag States, nor do they provide sufficient support for the conclusions drawn by the Tribunal.[158] For example, Gao and Schatz both develop this line of criticism, inter alia raising doubts as to whether Article 94, concerning flag States' duties, extends to fisheries, or whether the 'very basic obligation' in Article 192, concerning protection of the marine environment, can provide a basis for a due diligence obligation of flag States in relation to the conservation of marine living resources.[159] While these criticisms have some purchase, as Foster has noted, it was arguably 'the content of the various provisions together', as well as the pressing nature of the problem of IUU fishing that the case presented, which generated ITLOS' conclusion about the obligations of flag States.[160] The advisory nature of the case perhaps also helps explain ITLOS' willingness to develop the law through interpretation.[161]

Judge Paik's separate opinion sheds further light on the issues concerning potential change in applicable legal norms that ITLOS faced in this case. Judge Paik's essential concern was that in addressing the first question posed, 'the Tribunal should have paid more attention to significant legal developments related to flag State responsibility concerning fisheries conservation and management that have taken place since the adoption of UNCLOS.[162] He noted that '[e]specially in the 1990s and onwards, a steady stream of treaties and other legal instruments have been adopted in response to growing international concern over IUU fishing'. While 'some of those instruments are voluntary in nature and not legally binding' Judge Paik emphasised that 'the post-UNCLOS normative developments as a whole . . . are relevant to the present case as they could give useful guidance as to the state and direction of international fisheries law' concerning flag State responsibility in relation to IUU fishing in foreign EEZs.[163]

158 Jianjun Gao, 'The ITLOS Advisory Opinion for the SRFC' (2015) 14 Chinese JIL 735, 749–54; Schatz (n 121) 330–34, 338–39.

159 Schatz (n 121) 332–34; Gao (n 158) 751–52.

160 Foster (n 55) 117.

161 See above n 148.

162 *ITLOS 2015 Advisory Opinion* (n 49) Sep. Op. Paik [1]–[5]. See also R Rajesh Babu, 'State Responsibility for Illegal, Unreported and Unrelated Fishing and Sustainable Fisheries in the EEZ: Some Reflections on the ITLOS Advisory Opinion of 2015' (2015) 55 Indian JIL 239, 263–64.

163 *ITLOS 2015 Advisory Opinion* (n 49) Sep. Op. Paik [5]. See also the discussion of post-UNCLOS fisheries agreements that ITLOS might have drawn upon in interpreting the relevant obligations under UNCLOS in Lan Ngoc Nguyen, 'Jurisdiction and Applicable

In relation to the general duties of flag States under Article 94 of UNCLOS, Judge Paik noted that:

> [o]ver time … flag State jurisdiction and control have evolved to cope with new issues, reflecting the changing needs of society and the new demands of the time. In interpreting article 94 of the Convention, it is important to take into account this evolving, open-ended context of the duties of the flag Sate.[164]

Regarding the question of 'what are the necessary measures to be taken by the flag State' to fulfil its obligation of due diligence to ensure vessels flying its flag do not engage in IUU fishing in the EEZ of SRFC Member States, Judge Paik criticised the majority for focusing on the text of UNCLOS and giving 'scant attention' to relevant developments that had occurred since the adoption of the Convention and could provide guidance on such 'necessary measures'.[165] Specifically, Judge Paik suggested that the 'rule of reference' concerning flag State duties regarding safety at sea in Article 94(5) of UNCLOS, as well as 'that the rule of reference employed in Part XII of the Convention in general … can be extended and applied by analogy to give effective content to the general yet rather vague obligations of the flag State in respect of IUU fishing'.[166] Judge Paik also adopted an expansive view of how rules of reference within UNCLOS may be interpreted, noting that:

> [While] there is no agreed definition of 'generally accepted' … it is evident that such regulations, procedures or practices need not be customary law or treaties of general acceptance.… In my view, regulations, procedures or practices established in international legal instruments that are accepted by a sufficient number of States may be regarded as being generally accepted. It may also be relevant that those regulations, procedures or practices are consistently upheld by a series of legal instruments.[167]

In summary, for Judge Paik, post-UNCLOS legal developments concerning flag State responsibility for IUU fishing could be 'indicative of' 'generally accepted international regulations, procedures and practices' and thus would inform the content of flag States' obligations under

Law in the Settlement of Marine Environmental Disputes under UNCLOS' (2021) 9 Korean J. Int. Comp. Law 337, 346–48; Nguyen (n 55) 97–98, 157–58.

164 *ITLOS 2015 Advisory Opinion* (n 49) Sep. Op. Paik [11].

165 Ibid [20]–[22].

166 Ibid [23]–[24]. Contrast Schatz (n 121) 336–37 (arguing that the drafters of UNCLOS deliberately did not create a rule of reference in Article 94(5) for fisheries obligations).

167 *ITLOS 2015 Advisory Opinion* (n 49) Sep. Op. Paik [26].

UNCLOS – which contained rules of reference – even if the subsequent legal developments were not directly binding.[168] Judge Paik's expansive approach to the rules of reference contained in UNCLOS would make the Convention highly responsive to subsequent legal and regulatory developments concerning IUU fishing.

The question of potential change in applicable legal norms also arose in the *SBT* cases at the provisional measures stage before ITLOS, which will be discussed further in Section D. In short, this dispute involved an attempt by Australia and New Zealand to halt a unilateral 'experimental fishing program' pursued by Japan and to limit Japan to the catch allocated to it within the Commission for the Conservation of Southern Bluefin Tuna.[169] For present purposes, what is relevant is that Australia and New Zealand argued that the provisions of UNCLOS they invoked had to be interpreted in light of the precautionary principle.[170] As Judge Laing noted, while the Tribunal's Order did not explicitly refer to the precautionary principle, its remarks were 'pregnant with meaning', and in practice did adopt a precautionary approach in prescribing provisional measures.[171] Specifically, while the Tribunal acknowledged that there was 'scientific uncertainty regarding measures to be taken to conserve the stock of southern bluefin tuna' and that it could not 'conclusively assess the scientific evidence presented by the parties', nevertheless 'measures should be taken as a matter of urgency to preserve the rights of the parties and to avert further deterioration of the southern bluefin tuna stock'.[172] As Judge Treves noted, because the decision occurred in a provisional measures context, where there is a need to preserve the rights at issue until the merits are decided, arguably a precautionary approach

[168] Ibid [27]. See also [28]. For an assessment of Judge Paik's attempt to extend the concept of rules of reference to the fisheries context, which suggests that there are difficulties with this approach, see Nguyen (n 107) 439–41.

[169] A longer explanation of the context of the case is provided below, text at nn 268–271.

[170] See Australia's Request for Provisional Measures, [1], [25], and New Zealand's Request for Provisional Measures, [1], [25].

[171] *SBT Order* (n 60) Sep. Op. Laing [13], [19], and generally [12]–[19]; Sep. Op. Shearer. Commentators have also viewed the order in this way: eg David Freestone, 'Caution or Precaution: "A Rose By Any Other Name…"?' (1999) 10 Ybk IEL 25, 29, 32; Tim Stephens, *International Courts and Environmental Protection* (CUP 2009) 225–26; Nguyen (n 55) 183; Simon Marr, 'The Southern Bluefin Tuna Cases: The Precautionary Approach and Conservation and Management of Fish Resources' (2000) 11 EJIL 815, 827.

[172] *SBT Order* (n 60) [77]–[80] (also noting that 'the parties should in the circumstances act with prudence and caution to ensure that effective conservation measures are taken to prevent serious harm to the stock of southern bluefin tuna').

could be justified as 'inherent in the very notion of provisional measures'.[173] In their separate opinions, Judges Treves, Laing, and Shearer also supported the Tribunal's interpretation by referring to a 1995 implementing agreement under UNCLOS, the Fish Stocks Agreement,[174] which adopts a precautionary approach, and at the time of the Order was signed but not ratified by the disputing parties.[175] Here, the judges were attempting to justify why the Tribunal's approach of interpreting the relevant provisions of UNCLOS in light of a precautionary approach did not impermissibly undermine legal certainty.[176]

2. *Managing Change in Relevant Facts*

UNCLOS adjudicators have also faced the related question of how changes in relevant facts may affect the application of legal norms, an issue that also often arises in the other adjudication contexts studied in this book. For example, in its *2011 Advisory Opinion*, discussed above, ITLOS' Seabed Disputes Advisory Chamber noted that, as regards the measures to be adopted by sponsoring States to fulfil their due diligence obligation, 'measures considered sufficiently diligent at a certain moment may become not diligent enough in light, for instance, of new scientific or technological knowledge',[177] meaning 'such measures should be kept under review so as to ensure that they meet current standards'.[178] Here, while the content of the relevant legal obligation remained constant, requiring States to exercise due diligence, applying the norm depended upon certain factual matters that were liable to change over time, such as the state of scientific or technical knowledge.[179]

173 Ibid Sep. Op. Treves [9]. See also [8] (holding that the requirement of urgency for provisional measures was only satisfied in light of a precautionary approach).

174 Agreement for the Implementation of the Provisions of the United Nations Convention on the Law of the Sea of 10 December 1982 Relating to the Conservation and Management of Straddling Fish Stocks and Highly Migratory Fish Stocks (1995) 2167 UNTS 3.

175 *SBT Order* (n 60) Sep. Op. Treves [10]–[11]; Sep. Op. Laing [20]; Sep. Op. Shearer.

176 Also reading the decision as allowing the fisheries provisions of UNCLOS to evolve in light of the precautionary principle: eg Boyle (n 104) 51; Buga (n 109) 336.

177 *Seabed AO* (n 140) [117]. The due diligence obligation of sponsoring States was reflected in several relevant provisions of UNCLOS that the Chamber had to apply: see generally [99]–[102], [107]–[120].

178 Ibid [222].

179 For similar recognition that what a due diligence obligation requires of States can evolve in light of scientific or technological developments, see eg International Law Commission, 'Draft Articles on Prevention of Transboundary Harm from Hazardous

C. The Standard and Method of Review in UNCLOS Adjudication

1. *Standard of Review in ITLOS' Prompt Release Case Law*

ITLOS' prompt release jurisdiction has given rise to significant debate concerning the appropriate standard or intensity of international adjudicatory review, given the impact on States' ability to take measures that pursue legitimate regulatory goals endorsed by UNCLOS and other international regimes, such as measures for the conservation and management of living resources in the EEZ. As outlined above, the treaty context is that for those provisions of UNCLOS that provide for the prompt release of detained vessels and their crews on the posting of a reasonable bond, the question of the reasonableness of the bond set by the detaining State is subject to international judicial scrutiny.[180] In short, an issue that was previously within the discretion of coastal States – the reasonableness of a bond regarding certain fisheries and marine pollution offences – is subject to international supervision.[181]

The background to the creation of the prompt release procedure is that it was recognised when negotiating UNCLOS that the establishment of the EEZ constituted a major extension of coastal State jurisdiction and that the power of coastal States to take enforcement measures raised the risk of abuse to the detriment of flag State interests.[182] Accordingly, ITLOS has recognised that Articles 73 and 292 establish a 'balance of interests' between the interests of coastal States, in ensuring compliance

Activities' [2001] II ILC Ybk 148, 154, commentary to art 3, para 11; Nele Matz-Lück and Erik Van Doorn, 'Due Diligence Obligations and the Protection of the Marine Environment' (2017) 42 L'Observateur des Nations Unies 177, 190–91.

180 See above text at nn 61–72. On the notion of a reasonable bond being an international one, determined by ITLOS, see *"Camouco"* (n 11) Diss. Op. Treves [4]; Dec. Laing; Sep. Op. Nelson.

181 Klein (n 3) 117; Seline Trevisanut, 'The Exercise of Administrative Functions by ITLOS: A Comment on Prompt Release Cases' in Nerina Boschiero and others (eds), *International Courts and the Development of International Law: Essays in Honour of Tullio Treves* (TMC Asser Press 2013) 317 ('in prompt release cases, ITLOS is . . . asked to control and evaluate the discretional exercise of sovereign rights by the coastal State').

182 See eg Rosemary Rayfuse, 'Standard of Review in the International Tribunal for the Law of the Sea' in Lukasz Gruszczynski and Wouter Werner (eds), *Deference in International Courts and Tribunals* (OUP 2014) 339–40; David Heywood Anderson, 'Prompt Release of Vessels and Crews' in Rüdiger Wolfrum (ed), *Max Planck Encyclopedia of International Law* (OUP 2008) [3]; Rosenne and Sohn (n 77) 67. There is a variety of other ways, beyond the prompt release procedure, that UNCLOS places limits on the enforcement powers of coastal States within the EEZ and thus strikes a balance with the competing interest of flag States in freedom of navigation. See eg Harrison (n 72).

with their laws and regulations, and flag States, in securing the prompt release of their vessels and crews, which is to serve as 'the guiding criterion for the Tribunal in its assessment of the reasonableness of the bond'.[183] The point of the prompt release procedure is to ensure that coastal States observe the requirement of setting reasonable bonds.[184] As Vice-President Nelson has noted: '[t]he notion of reasonableness is here used to curb the arbitrary exercise of the discretionary power granted to coastal States'.[185]

The 'need for judicial restraint at the international level',[186] given the direct impact of ITLOS' prompt release jurisdiction on national-level law enforcement procedures,[187] has been highlighted on multiple occasions by individual ITLOS judges. In the *Camouco* case, Judge Wolfrum emphasised that in exercising this form of jurisdiction, the international tribunal 'must not unnecessarily impinge upon the enforcement rights of the coastal State', including as the Convention, in providing for prompt release, is explicit that the judgment of the international tribunal is 'without prejudice to the merits of any case before the appropriate domestic forum'.[188] Judge Wolfrum highlighted that 'coastal States enjoy considerable discretion' in establishing and implementing laws for the conservation and management of living resources within the EEZ[189] and '[t]hese discretionary powers or margin of appreciation on the side of the coastal State limit the powers of the Tribunal on deciding whether a bond set by national authorities was reasonable or not'.[190] In their dissenting opinions, both Judges Anderson and Wolfrum suggested that the Tribunal should have taken inspiration from the 'margin of appreciation' doctrine developed by the European Court of Human Rights.[191] Similarly, in the *Volga* case Judge Cot held that:

> [t]he margin of appreciation applies both to the measures taken by the coastal State under article 73, paragraph 1, of the Convention and to the

[183] *The 'Monte Confurco' Case (Seychelles v France)*, Prompt Release, Judgment, ITLOS Reports 2000, p. 86, [70]–[72]; Affirmed in *"Volga" (Russian Federation v Australia)*, Prompt Release, Judgment, ITLOS Reports 2002, p. 10, [65].

[184] *Monte Confurco* (n 183) [73].

[185] Ibid Sep. Op. Nelson.

[186] *"Camouco"* (n 11) Diss. Op. Anderson.

[187] Trevisanut (n 135) 312.

[188] *"Camouco"* (n 11) Diss. Op. Wolfrum [8]; UNCLOS art 292(3).

[189] Ibid [11]–[12].

[190] Ibid [11]. See also [5]–[6].

[191] See *"Camouco"* (n 11) Diss. Op. Wolfrum [14]; Diss. Op. Anderson.

> amount of the bond referred to in paragraph 2 of that article. Provided that the bond is not "unreasonable", the Tribunal does not have to substitute its discretion for that of the coastal State. It has no intention of being an appellate forum against a decision of a national court ... nor is it the hierarchical superior of an administrative or government authority.[192]

When determining the appropriate standard of review in the context of prompt release proceedings, ITLOS has been faced with the question of how to scrutinise coastal State measures that pursue legitimate regulatory aims (eg the conservation of marine living resources) which are endorsed by UNCLOS and other relevant international regimes. UNCLOS itself does not lay out any criteria for determining the reasonableness of the bond in prompt release proceedings, and ITLOS has outlined a number of non-exhaustive relevant factors, including 'the gravity of the alleged offences, the penalties imposed or imposable under the laws of the detaining State, the value of the detained vessel and of the cargo seized, the amount of the bond imposed by the detaining State and its form'.[193] The issue of coastal States' regulatory autonomy came to a head in the *Volga* case, where Australia argued that the problem of IUU fishing in the Southern Ocean and resulting international concern, as evidenced through measures taken under the Convention on the Conservation of Antarctic Marine Living Resources (CCAMLR), justified its measures.[194] The Tribunal briefly acknowledged these 'international concerns' before finding that '[i]t is by reference to' the penalties applicable under the domestic laws of the detaining State 'that the Tribunal may evaluate the gravity of the alleged offences'.[195]

An alternative approach giving greater weight to the wider multilateral context for Australia's measures was outlined by several judges in separate or dissenting opinions. Judge Cot emphasised that Australia's measures 'should be seen within the context of a concerted effort within the FAO [Food and Agriculture Organization] and CCAMLR' to combat IUU fishing, and this context widened Australia's 'scope for action'.[196] Similarly, Judge Anderson emphasised that the 'duty of the coastal State

192 *Volga* (n 137) Sep. Op. Cot [22]. See also [14]–[18]. Judge Anderson also noted in passing 'the "margin of appreciation" to be accorded to domestic courts and domestic authorities': *Volga*, Diss. Op. Anderson [23].

193 *"Camouco"* (n 11) [67]; *Monte Confurco* (n 183) [76]; *"Hoshinmaru" (Japan v Russian Federation)*, Prompt Release, Judgment, ITLOS Reports 2005–2007, p. 18, [82].

194 *Volga* (n 137) para 66.

195 Ibid [68]–[69]. Affirmed in *"Juno Trader" (Saint Vincent and the Grenadines v Guinea-Bissau)*, Prompt Release, Judgment, ITLOS Reports 2004, p. 17, [87], [89].

196 *Volga* (n 137) Sep. Op. Judge Cot [12], and generally [2]–[12].

to ensure the conservation of the living resources of the EEZ' under Article 61 of UNCLOS, 'as well as the obligations of Contracting Parties to CCAMLR to protect the Antarctic ecosystem', were relevant factors that had to be considered in determining the reasonableness of a bond.[197] Judge ad hoc Shearer also suggested that:

> If deterrence is to be achieved, national courts must take into account the gravity not only of the particular offence but also of the effects of offences generally on the conservation efforts of the international community.. . . The Tribunal, and other international courts and tribunals, should be fully aware, and supportive, of these aims.[198]

This is the argument, also seen in other adjudication contexts studied in this book, that where a measure is taken by a regulating State pursuant to another international regime, or is consistent with internationally recognised practices, this can inform the standard of review to be applied.[199] The majority's narrow approach to the factors relevant to assessing the reasonableness of bonds was likely based on a view regarding the limited scope of the prompt release procedure and its purpose of securing the release of a vessel and crew in a timely manner. Yet as the individual opinions suggested, the majority approach in *Volga* placed insufficient emphasis on the wider multilateral conservation context for coastal State measures,[200] and resulted in an overly intrusive form of adjudicatory scrutiny. Subsequently, in a more recent prompt release case, the *Hoshinmaru*, ITLOS was willing to take account of a wider range of factors in assessing the reasonableness of a bond, emphasising the right of the coastal State (Russia) to conserve and manage the living resources

197 Ibid Diss. Op. Anderson [2]. Similarly: *"Camouco"* (n 11) Diss. Op. Anderson.

198 *Volga* (n 137) Diss. Op. Shearer [11]. See also [13].

199 See eg *Chemtura Corporation (formerly Crompton Corporation) v Canada*, UNCITRAL Award (2 August 2010), [135]–[138] (Tribunal emphasised that Canada's measure was taken pursuant to its international obligations and international concern regarding the relevant substance, not in bad faith). Discussed below Chapter 5(C)(1) text at nn 193–198. Harrison highlights that an UNCLOS tribunal's interpretation of the 'grounds of review' and the appropriate intensity of review could be informed a wider framework of applicable international norms, beyond UNCLOS itself, including relevant norms of international human rights law that may restrict a coastal State's enforcement powers: James Harrison, 'Patrolling the Boundaries of Coastal State Enforcement Powers: The Interpretation and Application of UNCLOS Safeguards Relating to the Arrest of Foreign-Flagged Ships' (2017) 42 L'Observateur des Nations Unies 117, 140–42.

200 Klein (n 3) 111–12; Rosemary Rayfuse, 'The Future of Compulsory Dispute Settlement under the Law of the Sea Convention' (2005) 36 VUWLR 683, 692–93.

in its EEZ, including through cooperation with the flag State (Japan) via the Russian–Japanese Commission on Fisheries.[201]

2. *Methods of Review in UNCLOS Adjudication*

In scrutinising State measures for compliance with UNCLOS, adjudicators have repeatedly faced the issue of balancing competing interests, both protected by the relevant legal regime, and have used methods of review that are shaped by the relevant context but also exhibit significant similarities to the methods of review seen in the other adjudication settings studied in this book. While the methods of review are not fully settled in the UNCLOS context, adjudicators have utilised variants of reasonableness-based tests, necessity testing, and proportionality balancing stricto sensu in scrutinising State measures that pursue a protected aim (eg combatting IUU fishing) but also undermine other protected interests, such as freedom of navigation.[202] In the prompt release setting, ITLOS as a whole has held that 'the amount of the bond should be proportionate to the gravity of the alleged offences'.[203] More concretely, Judge Cot has noted the obligation of a coastal State 'to ensure that its conduct is proportional to the aim being legally pursued, account being taken of the rights and freedoms granted to others or acknowledged under international law'.[204] Judge Laing has also suggested that the notion of a 'reasonable' bond must be interpreted in light of all 'pertinent international legal principles', including 'environmental and conservation concerns' and competing 'economic, humanitarian and other concerns' recognised by UNCLOS.[205] For Judge Laing, 'the Tribunal's articulation of the very multi-faceted concept of reasonableness should, as relevant, be patently and fully grounded in such synonymous notions as proportionality, balance, fairness, moderateness, consistency,

201 See *"Hoshinmaru"* (n 193) [85], [98]–[99]. For discussion see Nguyen (n 55) 32–34; Klein and Parlett (n 4) 328.

202 See generally Harrison (n 199); Camille Goodman, 'Rights, Obligations, Prohibitions: A Practical Guide to Understanding Judicial Decisions on Coastal State Jurisdiction over Living Resources in the Exclusive Economic Zone' (2018) 33 IJMCL 558; Erietta Scalieri, 'Discretionary Power of Coastal States and the Control of Its Compliance with International Law by International Tribunals' in Angela Del Vecchio and Roberto Virzo (eds), *Interpretations of the United Nations Convention on the Law of the Sea by International Courts and Tribunals* (Springer 2019) 353–58.

203 *"Hoshinmaru"* (n 193) [88]; See also *"Juno Trader"* (n 195) [89].

204 *Volga* (n 137) Sep. Op. Cot [21].

205 *Monte Confurco* (n 183) Diss. Op. Laing [6], see also [7]–[8].

suitability, tolerableness and absence of excessiveness'.[206] Interestingly, Judge Laing noted the potential for drawing inspiration from the form of necessity testing developed in GATT Article XX jurisprudence when scrutinising the power of the coastal State to take measures 'necessary' to ensure compliance with its laws and policies concerning conservation and management of living resources in the EEZ.[207]

The discourse on the appropriate standard and method of review in the context of scrutinising coastal State measures adopted pursuant to UNCLOS was developed considerably by ITLOS' 2014 judgment in the *M/V 'Virginia G'* case.[208] This case concerned the confiscation by Guinea-Bissau of a vessel engaged in 'bunkering' or refuelling fishing vessels in its EEZ, but was not a prompt release case and thus not confined to the question of the reasonableness of a bond set by the coastal State. ITLOS began by finding that coastal States have the power to regulate bunkering of foreign vessels fishing in the EEZ, as part of their right to conserve and manage living resources in the EEZ.[209] In applying Article 73(1) of the Convention, which entitles coastal States to take measures 'necessary to ensure compliance with' such laws, ITLOS held that one of the enforcement measures taken by Guinea-Bissau pursuant to its legislation – confiscation – was in the circumstances neither necessary nor reasonable and thus violated the provision.[210] After recalling the explicit requirement in Article 73(2) of the Convention that bonds set by a coastal State must be reasonable, ITLOS extended this concept, holding that 'the principle of reasonableness applies generally to enforcement measures under article 73 of' UNCLOS, and 'in applying enforcement measures due regard must be paid to the particular circumstances of the case and the gravity of the violation'.[211] Some nine judges

206 *Monte Confurco* (n 183) Diss. Op. Laing [9].

207 Ibid Diss. Op. Laing [3] and fn 2, referring to UNCLOS art 73(1).

208 *M/V 'Virginia G' (Panama/Guinea-Bissau)*, Judgment, ITLOS Reports 2014, p. 4.

209 Ibid [217], [223].

210 Ibid [265]–[271].

211 Ibid para 270. Both a dissenting judgment and commentators have suggested that the Tribunal was unjustified in importing a requirement of reasonableness into the entirety of Article 73 and should have confined itself to assessing the necessity of the relevant measures. These perspectives suggest that there is a material difference between the standards of necessity under Article 73(1) and reasonableness under Article 73(2) and that the former provision leaves a greater margin of discretion to coastal States: see *M/V 'Virginia G'*, Diss. Op. Sérvulo Correia, [17]–[18], [20]–[21]; Zoe Scanlon, 'Upsetting the Balance? The Legality of Vessel Confiscation under the LOSC after the *M/V Virginia G* Case' (2018) 33 IJMCL 166, 179–80; Nguyen (n 55) 26.

dissented from the finding that Guinea-Bissau's confiscation measure was not necessary and thus violated Article 73(1) of UNCLOS. These judges criticised the majority for having engaged an inappropriately intrusive form of adjudicatory scrutiny.

A joint dissenting opinion of six judges held that 'international tribunals should exercise judicial restraint in dealing with the coastal State's discretionary powers under article 73, paragraph 1, of the Convention', since 'national courts or authorities are better placed to appreciate all the relevant considerations of law and fact . . . Hence, they should be given a broad "margin of appreciation"'.[212] They accused the majority of overstepping its limited role of 'judicial review' and functioning 'as an appellate authority substituting its judgment for that of the local authority'.[213] These judges emphasised that but for the limitation on the coastal State's enforcement powers under UNCLOS Article 73(1), the issue would have rested entirely within the discretion of the coastal State, and the provision's reference to the coastal State's 'sovereign rights' to manage living resources in the EEZ warranted deference.[214] The idea that national-level decision-makers may be 'better placed to appreciate all the relevant considerations of law and fact' is a standard justification for affording national-level decision-makers a degree of deference seen in all of the adjudication contexts considered in this book.[215] Judge ad hoc Sérvulo Correia, dissenting, also suggested the Tribunal had engaged in an inappropriately intrusive form of scrutiny, and judicial deference was warranted unless it was 'manifest or absolutely clear that a less intrusive or onerous measure would have been equally suitable and effective in attaining the legal aim'.[216] His suggested approach constitutes a necessity or least restrictive means test, where one only accepts a proposed alternative measure as a true alternative if it would be equally effective in achieving the relevant regulatory aim.[217]

Judge Paik, while agreeing with the majority that Guinea-Bissau's confiscation measure was not 'necessary' in the circumstances, placed the issue in a wider comparative perspective, noting that 'necessity is

[212] Ibid Joint Diss. Op. Hoffmann, Marotta Rangel, Chandrasekhara Rao, Kateka, Gao and Bouguetaia [50].

[213] Ibid [54]–[55].

[214] Ibid [49]–[52]. See also Diss. Op. Nidaye [163], [169]–[170]; Diss. Op Jesus, [19]–[22]; Dec. Gao [16]–[21]. Similarly: Harrison (n 72) 221.

[215] This is drawn together in the conclusion, below text at nn 307–308.

[216] *M/V 'Virginia G'* (n 208) Diss. Op. Sérvulo Correia [20]–[21].

[217] Ibid [18]–[19].

employed in a great number of areas of international law to address the relationship between an objective a State intends to seek and the means the State chooses to achieve that objective'.[218] Specifically, as Judge Paik noted,

> the notion of necessity attempts to balance two conflicting interests at play: namely, preserving the freedom of a State to achieve the objective it seeks through means of its choosing, and restraining the State from choosing means that would unduly infringe the protected rights or interests of another entity.[219]

In terms reminiscent of WTO necessity testing, Judge Paik suggested that:

> the Tribunal should consider both the extent to which the measure contributes to the achievement of the objective sought and the degree to which the measure encroaches upon the protected rights of other States. The greater the contribution and the less the encroachment, the more likely the measure will be considered to be necessary.[220]

He further suggested that in assessing the necessity of a measure, the Tribunal should also consider 'the relative importance of those interests to the respective State or States' and 'the availability of other measures (equally effective and less onerous)'.[221] Judge Paik's approach arguably endorses proportionality balancing stricto sensu, given his consideration of the relative importance of the relevant interests to the respective States. While Judge Paik took into account 'the vital importance to Guinea-Bissau of protecting living resources in its EEZ', given it was a poor country highly dependent on fishing activities facing the problem of IUU fishing, he also included within his balancing exercise the importance to flag States of freedom of navigation in the EEZ.[222] Ultimately, Judge Paik found that several aspects of the circumstances in which Guinea-Bissau's confiscation measure had been imposed suggested that the measure was not 'necessary'.[223]

Subsequently, UNCLOS adjudicators further developed the methods of review, or balancing tests, to be used when scrutinising State conduct

[218] *M/V 'Virginia G'* (n 208) Sep. Op. Paik [9]. See also [14].
[219] Ibid [9].
[220] Ibid [25].
[221] Ibid [24], [29].
[222] Ibid [31]–[34].
[223] Ibid [35]–[38].

for compliance with the Convention in the merits award in the *Arctic Sunrise* case. This case concerned Russia's boarding, seizure, and detention of a Netherlands-flagged vessel, chartered by Greenpeace, from which Greenpeace attempted to conduct a protest on an offshore oil production platform in Russia's EEZ.[224] This occurred as part of a broader 'save the Arctic' campaign conducted by Greenpeace, which sought to achieve a ban on offshore oil drilling and fishing in Arctic waters.[225] Besides concerning an environmental protest, the case had another environmental aspect: in considering the potential legal bases for Russia's measures, the Tribunal considered whether Russia, as the coastal State, could have taken its measures pursuant to provisions of UNCLOS concerning protection of the marine environment.[226] The Netherlands, as the flag State of the ship, alleged that Russia's measures breached various provisions of UNCLOS, mainly focusing upon freedom of navigation and the coastal State's obligation, within the EEZ, to have due regard to the rights of other States.[227] An important contribution of principle made by the award is its finding that measures taken by the coastal State to prevent interference with its sovereign rights for exploration and exploitation of non-living resources in the EEZ are subject to the requirements of 'reasonableness, necessity and proportionality'.[228] Ultimately the Tribunal did not proceed to scrutinise whether Russia's measures satisfied these criteria as it found that Russia's measures lacked any permissible legal basis under UNCLOS.[229] Nevertheless, the award makes clear that even if Russia's measures had been found to pursue a legitimate aim recognised by UNCLOS, they would have been subject to scrutiny in terms of 'reasonableness, necessity and proportionality'.[230] More generally, the *Arctic Sunrise* award highlighted the need to balance the right to protest at sea, as an internationally lawful use of the sea related to freedom of navigation, with the rights and duties of the coastal State in the EEZ.[231]

[224] For the facts of the dispute, see generally *Arctic Sunrise*, Merits (n 115) [70]–[139].

[225] Ibid [77].

[226] See ibid [286]–[297], [307]–[313]. The background was that Russia had alluded to the fact that the actions of Greenpeace in conducting the protest could have exposed the Arctic to serious environmental risks: [287], [292].

[227] Ibid [140].

[228] Ibid [324], [326], see also [222]. Foster highlights that this aspect of the award may have been a response to the Netherlands' arguments: Foster (n 55) 67.

[229] *Arctic Sunrise*, Merits (n 115) [333].

[230] Ibid [222], [326].

[231] Ibid [227]–[230].

For example, the Tribunal identified a number of 'legitimate interests of coastal States', based on preventing interferences with the exercise of their sovereign rights in the EEZ, which could justify curtailing the right of protest at sea.[232] Immediately afterwards, the Tribunal stressed that 'the coastal State should tolerate some level of nuisance through civilian protest' as part of the obligation to have due regard to the rights of other States, including the right of protest at sea.[233] On the facts, it was conclusive for the Tribunal that at the time the *Arctic Sunrise* was boarded by Russian forces it 'was no longer engaged in actions that could potentially interfere with the exercise by Russia of its sovereign rights as a coastal State'.[234]

The 2016 Award in the *Duzgit Integrity Arbitration* extended the reasoning of *Arctic Sunrise* Award concerning the applicable methods of review in the UNCLOS context, holding more generally that: '[t]he exercise of enforcement powers by a (coastal) State in situations where the State derives these powers from provisions of the Convention' is subject to the requirement of reasonableness, which 'encompasses the principles of necessity and proportionality'.[235] Specifically, the Tribunal applied these principles in scrutinising São Tomé's exercise of its right, as the coastal State, to take enforcement measures in its archipelagic waters against an unauthorised transfer of cargo.[236] The Tribunal found that some of São Tomé's enforcement measures, in 'detaining the vessel, requesting the Master to come onshore to explain the circumstances' and requiring the payment of a fine were 'well within . . . its law enforcement jurisdiction and must be given deference'.[237] However, the other penalties imposed by São Tomé were, in combination, found to be 'unreasonable and disproportionate' and thus violate São Tomé's

232 Ibid [327].

233 Ibid [328].

234 Ibid [329]–[330], [332]. Foster thus suggests that the case turned upon a 'capability test', in short, that 'Russia's action was not capable of preventing an interference with Russia's sovereign rights, as there was no threat to these rights at the time the action was taken': Foster (n 55) 66, 63.

235 *Duzgit Integrity Arbitration* (n 116) [209] ('These principles do not only apply in cases where States resort to force, but to all measures of law enforcement'). The *Duzgit Integrity Arbitration* had a limited environmental component, as Malta claimed that some of the enforcement measures taken by São Tomé, specifically selling the oil on board the ship and forcing a further ship-to-ship transfer to be conducted, had violated several provisions of UNCLOS concerning protection of the marine environment. These claims were rejected: see [278]–[293].

236 Ibid [254], [234]–[236].

237 Ibid [255].

obligations as a coastal State, having regard to the nature of the original offence and São Tomé's interest in ensuring respect for its sovereignty.[238] Judge Kateka, dissenting, while accepting the basic approach of applying the standards of reasonableness, necessity, and proportionality to coastal State enforcement measures in archipelagic waters, suggested that greater deference should have been afforded to São Tomé's measures, given the importance of the interest of ensuring respect for coastal State laws, and the 'broad margin of appreciation' enjoyed by coastal States.[239]

This section has demonstrated that the appropriate standard and method of review are significant issues in UNCLOS case law and that the resulting debates bear many similarities to how these issues arise in the other adjudication settings studied in this book.

D. The Contribution of UNCLOS Adjudicators to Broader Processes of Dispute Resolution

This section demonstrates that UNCLOS adjudicators, and particularly ITLOS, have repeatedly performed a 'predominantly facilitative',[240] or 'conflict management role',[241] whereby they have clarified the legal framework applicable to the parties' relationship and ordered the parties to engage in further negotiation or cooperation.[242] These developments are significant because they suggest that international adjudication can complement broader processes of dispute resolution. A prime example of this facilitative, conflict management role is ITLOS' 2003 provisional measures order in the *Land Reclamation* case between Malaysia and Singapore. Essentially, this dispute arose out of Malaysia's concerns about land reclamation activities undertaken by Singapore in the Straits of Johor. The dispute involved concerns by Malaysia about the environmental impacts of Singapore's works and Singapore's failure to consult

[238] Ibid [256]–[261].
[239] *Duzgit Integrity Arbitration* (n 116) Diss. Op. Kateka [9]–[28].
[240] See Klein (n 3) 83–84.
[241] Churchill (n 6) 411–12.
[242] Vaughan Lowe, 'The "Complementary Role" of ITLOS in the Development of Ocean Law' in Harry N Scheiber and Jin-Hyun Paik (eds), *Regions, Institutions, and Law of the Sea: Studies in Ocean Governance* (Martinus Nijhoff 2013) 30–36; Vaughan Lowe, 'The Interplay between Negotiation and Litigation in International Dispute Settlement' in Tafsir Malick Ndiaye and Rüdiger Wolfrum (eds), *Law of the Sea, Environmental Law, and Settlement of Disputes: Liber Amicorum Judge Thomas A. Mensah* (Martinus Nijhoff 2007) 242–44.

with Malaysia (which is the focus here), as well as an unresolved dispute between the parties concerning maritime boundaries.[243] Malaysia had presented Singapore with a request for the establishment of an Annex VII arbitral tribunal in July 2003 and also requested that Singapore agree to certain provisional measures. After Singapore refused to suspend its land reclamation works, as requested by Malaysia, Malaysia filed a request for provisional measures with ITLOS in September 2003.[244]

Before ITLOS, Malaysia sought orders that Singapore suspend its land reclamation activities, provide Malaysia with full information regarding its planned works, allow Malaysia to comment on the project's impact, and negotiate with Malaysia regarding unresolved issues.[245] The Tribunal recalled the fundamental and enforceable nature of the duty to cooperate under the Convention and general international law,[246] and variously found that Singapore had not assessed the impact of its works on Malaysian waters,[247] there had been insufficient cooperation between the parties prior to the initiation of Annex VII proceedings,[248] and it could not be excluded that 'the land reclamation works may have adverse effects on the marine environment'.[249] Given the potential impact of Singapore's works on the marine environment, 'prudence and caution require[d] that Malaysia and Singapore establish mechanisms for exchanging information and assessing the risks or effects of land reclamation works and devising ways to deal with them'.[250] While the Tribunal did not order that the works be halted (as Malaysia had requested), it ordered the parties to establish an independent group of experts to conduct within twelve months a study on the effects of Singapore's works and potential mitigation measures, and to regularly exchange information and assess the risks or effects of Singapore's activities.[251] The Tribunal's order must be understood in light of assurances offered by Singapore during the hearing, which included that Singapore accepted

[243] See Malaysia's Request for Provisional Measures [5]; Cheong Koon Hean, Tommy Koh and Lionel Yee, *Malaysia & Singapore the Land Reclamation Case: From Dispute to Settlement* (Straits Times Press 2013) 22–29.

[244] See Malaysia's Request for Provisional Measures [9]–[11]; Koon Hean, Koh and Yee (n 243) 29–30, 35–39.

[245] *Land Reclamation* (n 59) [23].

[246] Ibid [92]; Similarly: Joint Dec. Hossain and Oxman; Sep. Op. Lucky [12], [14]–[16].

[247] *Land Reclamation* (n 59) [95].

[248] Ibid [97]. See also Sep. Op. Lucky [14].

[249] *Land Reclamation* (n 59) [96].

[250] Ibid [99].

[251] Ibid [106(1)(a)–(b)].

Malaysia's proposal for the establishment of an independent scientific study on terms agreed by the parties and that Singapore would not undertake irreversible action in the area of primary concern to Malaysia before the completion of the joint study.[252] Indeed, due to the extent of the assurances that Singapore had offered during the oral hearing, some judges suggested that the Tribunal should not have ordered provisional measures.[253] Overall, the *Land Reclamation* case provides a striking example of ITLOS performing a facilitative, conflict management role, whereby the Tribunal clarified the legal framework governing the parties' future interactions and ordered them to engage in further cooperation.[254] Shortly after ITLOS' order, the parties engaged in negotiations and agreed the framework for the joint study by December 2003.[255] Subsequently, the independent group of experts submitted a unanimous report to the parties in November 2004, and on 9 January 2005, the day before a scheduled appearance before the Annex VII tribunal to discuss the joint report, the representatives of the parties reached an in-principle agreement to settle the dispute.[256] The settlement agreement was signed by the parties in April 2005 and incorporated into an agreed award of the Annex VII Tribunal.[257]

ITLOS also ordered the disputing parties to engage in further cooperation in its 2001 Provisional Measures Order in the *MOX Plant* case. This case arose from a wider dispute between Ireland and the UK concerning the latter's authorisation of a Mixed Oxide Plant ('MOX Plant') for the

[252] See ibid [76]–[80], [84]–[88].

[253] See ibid Dec. Nelson, [4]–[6]; Dec. Anderson, [3]–[5].

[254] For similar assessments see Lowe, 'The "Complementary Role" of ITLOS in the Development of Ocean Law' (n 242) 30, 36; Tommy Koh and Jolene Lin, 'The Land Reclamation Case: Thoughts and Reflections' (2006) 10 Singapore YBIL 1, 4. Note also that the oral hearing appears to have assisted the parties to narrow the issues in dispute. While Malaysia initially sought an order that Singapore suspend all land reclamation activities in the vicinity of the States' maritime boundary or areas claimed by Malaysia, Malaysia indicated during the hearing that it was one of the areas at issue that was of particular concern and that Malaysia's concerns could be significantly reduced if Singapore provided a formal undertaking regarding that area: *Land Reclamation* (n 59) [23(a)], [83]–[85]; Philippe Gautier, 'The International Tribunal for the Law of the Sea: Activities in 2003' (2004) 3 Chinese JIL 241, 263–64.

[255] Koon Hean, Koh and Yee (n 243) 78.

[256] Koh and Lin (n 254) 5.

[257] *Case Concerning Land Reclamation by Singapore in and around the Straits of Johor (Malaysia v Singapore)*, Decision of 1 September 2005, XXVII RIAA 133. For a detailed account of the work of the joint group of experts, and the subsequent negotiations that resolved the dispute, see Koon Hean, Koh and Yee (n 243) esp. 78–119.

reprocessing of spent nuclear fuels at Sellafield in the UK, which borders the Irish Sea.[258] Before ITLOS, Ireland sought various provisional measures in relation to the MOX Plant authorised by the UK, including that the UK suspend its authorisation of the plant, or otherwise prevent the plant's operation, and ensure that there were no movements within UK waters of radioactive materials associated with the MOX Plant.[259] The case involved significant disagreement over scientific evidence, with the UK contending that Ireland had failed to provide proof to demonstrate a risk of serious harm to the marine environment or of irreparable prejudice to the rights of Ireland, and Ireland invoking the precautionary principle to reverse the burden of proof and to inform the urgency requirement under Article 290(5).[260] After holding that Ireland had not met the urgency requirement, the Tribunal immediately noted that 'the duty to cooperate is a fundamental principle in the prevention of pollution of the marine environment under Part XII of the Convention and general international law and that rights arise therefrom which the Tribunal may consider appropriate to preserve under article 290 of the Convention'.[261] Accordingly, relying on its power to prescribe provisional measures different to those requested, the Tribunal stated that 'prudence and caution require that Ireland and the United Kingdom cooperate in exchanging information concerning risks or effects of the operation of the MOX plant and in devising ways to deal with them'.[262]

258 The wider dispute produced litigation before three other international tribunals. In June 2001, Ireland instituted arbitration under the 1992 Convention for the Protection of the Marine Environment of the North-East Atlantic, with that tribunal rendering an award in July 2003: *Dispute Concerning Access to Information under Article 9 of the OSPAR Convention (Ireland v United Kingdom)*, Final Award (2003) 126 ILR 334. Ireland instituted proceedings under UNCLOS in October 2001 and the Annex VII Tribunal with jurisdiction over the dispute was constituted in February 2002. In July 2003 it suspended its proceedings, after numerous European Community (EC) law issues arose, essentially concerning the parties' competence, as EC members, to bring proceedings before an UNCLOS tribunal: *MOX Plant Case (Ireland v United Kingdom)*, Order No 3 (2003) 126 ILR 310, [20]–[30]. In 2003 the European Commission instituted proceedings against Ireland before the European Court of Justice, alleging that Ireland had breached various EC law obligations by instituting the UNCLOS proceedings. These allegations were upheld by the ECJ's judgment: *Commission v Ireland*, Case C-459/03, Judgment of 30 May 2006, [2006] ECR I-04635. Subsequently Ireland withdrew its claim before the UNCLOS arbitral tribunal: see the Tribunal's Order No 6, 6 June 2008 <https://pca-cpa.org/en/cases/100/>.

259 See *MOX (ITLOS)* (n 58) [29].

260 Ibid [71]–[75].

261 Ibid [81]–[82].

262 Ibid [83]–[84].

The parties were ordered to enter into consultations to exchange further information on possible consequences of the plant for the Irish Sea, monitor risks or effects of the operation of the plant for the Irish Sea, and devise measures to prevent pollution of the marine environment.[263]

As Judge Treves highlighted, in effect 'the Tribunal drew a distinction between the substantive right invoked by Ireland not be polluted . . . and rights of a procedural character relating to cooperation and information'.[264] The same distinction between substance and procedure is evident in the Separate Opinion of Judge Wolfrum, who rejected Ireland's reliance on the precautionary principle, given that it would have required the Tribunal to evaluate in a summary way evidence regarding the potential impact of the MOX Plant on radioactivity in the Irish Sea – an issue that was to be addressed by the Annex VII Tribunal at the merits stage – without being in a position to assess the relevant evidence. Nevertheless, he supported the alternative orders made by ITLOS, which were 'in keeping with the overriding nature of the obligation to cooperate'.[265] My analysis of aspects of GATT Article XX chapeau jurisprudence in the previous chapter suggests that the sharp distinction between substance and procedure introduced by these two judges should be approached cautiously. As was highlighted in the WTO context, while adjudicators can order regulating States to consider affected foreign interests or to cooperate, there is no avoiding difficult normative decisions about which interests deserve procedural rights and to what extent regulating States should pursue cooperative (rather than unilateral) solutions.[266]

ITLOS' provisional measures order in the *SBT* case, discussed above, is also a significant example of an international tribunal performing 'a

[263] Ibid [89(1)]. Some judges criticised this aspect of the order, as in their view there was no potential for irreparable prejudice to the procedural rights invoked by Ireland in the period before the constitution of the Annex VII Tribunal: Sep. Op. Mensah; Sep. Op. Anderson. See also Vaughan Lowe and Robin Churchill, 'The International Tribunal for the Law of the Sea: Survey for 2001' (2002) 17 IJMCL 463, 483. ITLOS also ordered the Parties to submit a report regarding compliance with the provisional measures within two weeks of the Order: [86], [89(2)]. Before the Annex VII Tribunal, Ireland requested further provisional measures, requiring additional forms of cooperation and provision of information by the UK. This was refused, although the Tribunal did make a recommendation to the parties: *MOX Plant*, Order No 3 (n 258) [32]–[33], [64]–[67] and operative part [4].

[264] *MOX (ITLOS)* (n 58) Sep. Op. Treves [7].

[265] Ibid Sep. Op. Wolfrum.

[266] See Andrew Lang, *World Trade Law after Neoliberalism: Reimagining the Global Economic Order* (OUP 2011) 345–47.

facilitative, problem-solving approach'.[267] This dispute involved a disagreement in the 1990s between Australia and New Zealand on the one hand, and Japan on the other, about the 'total allowable catch' (TAC) for southern bluefin tuna within the framework of the Convention for the Conservation of Southern Bluefin Tuna (CCSBT), which at the time consisted of these three States.[268] Essentially, Japan had sought an increase in the TAC and agreement on an 'experimental fishing program', however these proposals were not agreed within the Commission created under CCSBT, which was unable to agree on an annual TAC in 1998. From 1998 onwards, Japan unilaterally proceeded with an experimental fishing program.[269] Subsequently, in June 1999, Australia and New Zealand instituted Annex VII proceedings against Japan and sought provisional measures from ITLOS, pending the constitution of the arbitral tribunal. Before ITLOS, Australia and New Zealand sought orders inter alia that Japan immediately cease its unilateral experimental fishing program and limit its catch to the national allocation last agreed within the CCSBT Commission, taking into account the fish taken as part of the unilateral program.[270] On the other hand, Japan, in addition to asking ITLOS to deny the request for provisional measures, requested that if ITLOS were to determine it appropriate to grant provisional measures, it should order the parties to engage in negotiations for six months to reach consensus on the issues dividing them, with any outstanding disagreements at the end of that period to be resolved by a panel of independent scientists.[271]

In substance ITLOS agreed to four of the five provisional measures requested by Australia and New Zealand, inter alia ordering all three States to limit their annual catches to their national allocations within the last agreed TAC and to refrain from conducting any experimental fishing program unless this was agreed by the other parties or the experimental catch was counted within the relevant national allocation.[272] However, it

[267] Douglas M Johnston, 'Fishery Diplomacy and Science and the Judicial Function' (2000) 10 Ybk IEL 33, 38–39.
[268] *SBT Order* (n 60) 23–24.
[269] *SBT Award* (n 4) [24]–[26].
[270] *SBT Order* (n 60) [34].
[271] Ibid [35].
[272] Cf *SBT Order* (n 60) [90(1)(a)–(d)] with the provisional measures finally requested by Australia and New Zealand ([34]). Notably, ITLOS did not explicitly endorse the third provisional measure requested, namely 'that the parties act consistently with the precautionary principle in fishing for SBT pending a final settlement of the dispute'.

is two further provisional measures ordered by ITLOS that are particularly noteworthy for present purposes. Firstly, ITLOS ordered that Australia, New Zealand, and Japan 'should resume negotiations without delay with a view to reaching agreement on measures for the conservation and management of southern bluefin tuna'.[273] Second, it ordered that these three States 'should make further efforts to reach agreement with other States and fishing entities engaged in fishing for southern bluefin tuna, with a view to ensuring conservation and promoting the objective of optimum utilization of the stock'.[274] The parties were also ordered to submit a report to ITLOS on compliance with these measures within just under six weeks of the order.[275] ITLOS' provisional measures order appears to have had a positive effect in prompting the parties to re-engage in further negotiations within the CCSBT Commission in late 1999 and early 2000.[276] However, a negotiated solution to the dispute was only reached in the following years, with the three States, within the CCSBT Commission, variously establishing a process to rely on the advice of independent scientists (rather than national scientific advisers), broadening the CCSBT to include other relevant fishing States, and eventually agreeing upon a TAC and national allocations.[277] Nevertheless, not all members of ITLOS welcomed its facilitative approach in this case. Judge ad hoc Shearer suggested that the Tribunal should have made an order that Japan was prima facie in breach of its international obligations in conducting its unilateral experimental fishing program. He noted:

> the Tribunal, in its prescription of measures in this case, has behaved less as a court of law and more as an agency of diplomacy. While diplomacy, and a disposition to assist the parties in resolving their dispute amicably, have their proper place in the judicial settlement of international disputes, the Tribunal should not shrink from the consequences of proven facts.[278]

[273] *SBT Order* (n 60) [90(1)(e)].

[274] Ibid [90(1)(f)].

[275] Ibid [88], [90(2)].

[276] See Bill Mansfield, 'Compulsory Dispute Settlement after the Southern Bluefin Tuna Award' in Alex G Oude Elferink, and Donald R Rothwell (eds), *Oceans Management in the 21st Century: Institutional Frameworks and Responses* (Martinus Nijhoff 2004) 259, 265.

[277] For discussion of developments after the ITLOS order and arbitral award, see eg Tim Stephens, 'The Limits of International Adjudication in International Environmental Law: Another Perspective on the Southern Bluefin Tuna Case' (2004) 19 IJMCL 177, 183–86; Ibid 259–66.

[278] *SBT Order* (n 60) Sep. Op Shearer.

This hints at some of the main critiques of international tribunals adopting a facilitative approach to dispute settlement, including that such approaches may lead to courts or tribunals abdicating their adjudicatory role and to international norms not being fully enforced.[279]

The subsequent award of the Annex VII Tribunal in the *SBT* case also contains notable statements by the Tribunal in which it attempted to contribute to the wider process of resolving this dispute, even though it concluded, controversially, that it lacked jurisdiction because the parties had agreed through the dispute settlement provision in the CCSBT to opt out of the compulsory binding procedures contained in Section 2 of Part XV of UNCLOS. Specifically, after revoking the provisional measures ordered by ITLOS (given the finding that it lacked jurisdiction), the Tribunal included five final paragraphs in its award that addressed the parties' future relationship.[280] The Tribunal noted that:

> revocation of the Order prescribing provisional measures does not mean that the Parties may disregard the effects of that Order or their own decisions made in conformity with it. The Order and those decisions – and the recourse to ITLOS that gave rise to them – as well as the consequential proceedings before this Tribunal, have had an impact: not merely in the suspension of Japan's unilateral experimental fishing program during the period that the Order was in force, but on the perspectives and actions of the Parties.[281]

The next two paragraphs recorded statements of the representatives of the parties during the hearing that essentially recognised the more cooperative approach that had been taken within the Commission since the ITLOS order, and their willingness to engage in further negotiations. The Tribunal observed that: '[a]n agreement on the principle of having an experimental fishing program and on the tonnage of that program appears to be within reach. The possibility of renewed negotiations on other elements of their differences is real'.[282] The Tribunal further highlighted that despite the parties' failure to agree to submit the dispute to arbitration pursuant to Article 16 of the CCSBT, they remained under an obligation to continue to seek to resolve the dispute via the variety of peaceful means set out in that provision. The Tribunal noted that if the

279 See eg the criticisms in Stephens (n 277) 188, 194; Rayfuse (n 200) 708–09.

280 *SBT Award* (n 4) [67]–[71].

281 Ibid [67].

282 Ibid [68].

parties were to resort to the third-party procedures listed in the CCSBT, '[t]heir content and modus operandi can be refined and developed by the Parties to meet their specific needs', and provided examples of a potentially flexible, partly diplomatic configuration.[283] These final paragraphs of the arbitral award have been correctly viewed as the Tribunal performing a facilitative and forward-looking role, including by commentators involved in the proceedings.[284] As Mansfield, one of New Zealand's counsel, summarises: 'both the ITLOS and the Arbitral Tribunal saw their roles as going beyond consideration of the legal issues and the formal relief sought, and pointing the parties in the right direction to resolve their underlying difficulties'.[285]

ITLOS has also performed a facilitative, conflict management role in more recent disputes with an environmental component. For example, in *Ghana v Côte d'Ivoire*, a case concerning disputed maritime areas that involved questions of potential marine environmental harm from resource exploration and exploitation activities, a Special Chamber of ITLOS, in a 2015 provisional measures order, repeated ITLOS' prior statements concerning the obligation to cooperate to prevent harm to the marine environment,[286] and ordered the parties to 'cooperate to that end'.[287] The Chamber appears to have understood its role as one of managing the parties' conflict: Ghana was ordered to ensure that no new drilling occurred in the disputed area, to prevent confidential information being used to the detriment of Côte d'Ivoire, and to conduct continuous monitoring of all activities undertaken by Ghana or with its authorisation in the disputed area to prevent serious environmental harm.[288] Yet the Chamber also refused Côte d'Ivoire's request that Ghana suspend ongoing activities where drilling had already taken

[283] Ibid [70].

[284] See Mansfield (n 276) 265–66.

[285] Ibid 265.

[286] *Delimitation of the maritime boundary in the Atlantic Ocean (Ghana/Côte d'Ivoire)*, Provisional Measures, Order of 25 April 2015, ITLOS Reports 2015, p. 146, [73].

[287] Ibid [108(1)(d)]. See also [108(1)(e)].

[288] Ibid [108(1)(a)–(c)]. Similarly to other provisional measures cases before ITLOS, the Tribunal ordered the parties to report back to the Tribunal on steps taken to comply with the order within one month: ibid [105], [108(2)] and ITLOS, Rules of the Tribunal, art 95(1). In the subsequent merits award, the Special Chamber found that Ghana had not violated the provisional measures ordered, as alleged by Côte d'Ivoire: *Delimitation of the maritime boundary in the Atlantic Ocean (Ghana/Côte d'Ivoire)*, Judgment, ITLOS Reports 2017, p. 4, [648]–[658].

place, reasoning that this would unduly burden Ghana and could endanger the marine environment.[289]

My claim that UNCLOS adjudicators have repeatedly played a facilitative, conflict management role whereby they have sought to clarify the legal framework governing the parties' future interactions is also supported by certain aspects of the 2015 award in the *Chagos Marine Protected Area* arbitration. However, due to the polarised nature of the underlying dispute, which concerns the UK's continuing unlawful presence in the Chagos Archipelago,[290] the 2015 arbitral award appears to have had little effect on the subsequent relationship between the UK and Mauritius. In terms of a facilitative mode of adjudication, what is of interest is the part of the arbitral award where the Tribunal explained why the UK, in unilaterally declaring a marine protected area (MPA) in 2010, had violated its obligation under UNCLOS to have due regard for Mauritius' rights or to consult with Mauritius.[291] The Tribunal noted that:

> the extent of the regard required by the Convention will depend upon the nature of the rights held by Mauritius, their importance, the extent of the anticipated impairment, the nature and importance of the activities contemplated by the United Kingdom, and the availability of alternative approaches. In the majority of cases, this assessment will necessarily involve at least some consultation with the rights-holding State.[292]

Considering the manner in which the MPA had been proclaimed, and the significant effects on Mauritius' interests,[293] the Tribunal emphasised that UK had failed to properly consult with Mauritius, or balance its own

[289] *Ghana/Côte d'Ivoire*, Provisional Measures (n 286) [99]–[101]. For criticism of this aspect of the Tribunal's Order see Yoshifumi Tanaka, 'Unilateral Exploration and Exploitation of Natural Resources in Disputed Areas: A Note on the *Ghana/Côte d'Ivoire* Order of 25 April 2015 before the Special Chamber of ITLOS' (2015) 46 ODIL 315, 324–25.

[290] See *Legal Consequences of the Separation of the Chagos Archipelago from Mauritius in 1965*, Advisory Opinion, ICJ Rep [2019] 95, esp. [177], [182], [183(4)]. On the relationship between the ICJ advisory opinion and the subsequent General Assembly resolution (73/295), which set a deadline of six months for the UK to withdraw from the Chagos that was not complied with, *see Delimitation of the maritime boundary in the Indian Ocean (Mauritius/Maldives)*, Preliminary Objections, Judgment, ITLOS Reports 2020–2021, p. 17, [226]–[229]. See also [243]–[247] on the legal status of the Chagos Archipelago after these developments.

[291] See *Chagos MPA* (n 121) [520], [540].

[292] Ibid [519].

[293] See ibid [521]–[522].

rights and interests with those of Mauritius.[294] The Tribunal, in an approach with similarities to the decisions of WTO adjudicators in cases such as *US – Shrimp*, *US – Gasoline*, and *EC – Seals*,[295] contrasted the consultative approach adopted by the UK towards the United States (US), another State with rights and interests in the area, which served as a 'yardstick' for measuring the regard owed to Mauritius.[296] While the Tribunal did not exclude that environmental considerations could potentially justify the infringement of Mauritius' fishing rights in the territorial sea, this would have required 'significant engagement with Mauritius to explain the need for the measure and to explore less restrictive alternatives'.[297] The Tribunal concluded by emphasising that it had:

> taken no view on the substantive quality or nature of the MPA or on the importance of environmental protection. The Tribunal's concern has been with the manner in which the MPA was established, rather than its substance. It is now open to the Parties to enter into the negotiations that the Tribunal would have expected prior to the proclamation of the MPA, with a view to achieving a mutually satisfactory arrangement for protecting the marine environment.[298]

In short, this aspect of the award envisaged adjudication, having clarified the legal framework applying to the parties' relationship, operating in a complementary manner with future negotiations between the parties. Although there were negotiations between the UK and Mauritius concerning the implementation of the arbitral award in 2015 and 2016, these ceased in November 2016.[299] Notably, in late 2016 the UK also (reportedly without consulting Mauritius) permitted its agreement with the US, granting the US use of the Chagos Archipelago, to continue in force for a further twenty years by not pursuing an option to terminate it unilaterally within two years of the end of the initial period of validity of fifty

[294] Ibid [534]–[535].

[295] Discussed above Chapter 2(D), text at nn 308–329.

[296] See *Chagos MPA* (n 121) [528], [535].

[297] Ibid [541]. For subsequent application of due regard obligations in the EEZ, adopting the *Chagos* Award's interpretation of the content of these obligations and emphasising the balancing function of due regard, see *The 'Enrica Lexie' Incident (Italy v India)*, PCA Case No 2015-28, Award, 21 May 2020, [973]–[978], and Joint Diss. Op. Rao and Robinson [16]–[19].

[298] See *Chagos MPA* (n 121) [544].

[299] *Legal Consequences of the Separation of the Chagos Archipelago* (n 290), Written Statement of the United Kingdom, 15 February 2018, [6.18]–[6.20].

years, which fell on 30 December 2016.[300] Thus, despite these aspects of the arbitral award that envisaged the arbitration contributing to future negotiations, overall it appears to have had limited impact on subsequent interactions between the UK and Mauritius.[301]

The *South China Sea Arbitration* is another instance where adjudication was unlikely to play a facilitative role given the polarised nature of the dispute, with China not participating in the arbitration, although the Tribunal appears to have understood its role as clarifying the legal obligations applicable to the parties' future relationship. Interestingly for present purposes, the Philippines sought a prospectively focused declaration that China respect the rights and freedoms of the Philippines under UNCLOS, comply with its obligations under the Convention (including those concerning protection of the marine environment), and exercise its rights in the South China Sea with due regard to those of the Philippines, but the Tribunal refused to make such an order.[302] Essentially, the Tribunal took the view that such an order would not add anything to the award, which had already clarified the rights and obligations of the parties.[303] For the Tribunal, the purpose of dispute resolution was 'to clarify the Parties' respective rights and obligations and thereby to facilitate their future relations in accordance with the general obligations of good faith that both governments unequivocally recognise' and this had already been achieved.[304] Yet, the polarised setting of this dispute – with China not participating in the proceedings nor recognising the subsequent award – made it unlikely that the Tribunal would be able to perform a conflict management role.[305] Such a role is far more likely to emerge in cases where there is a degree of common ground

[300] *Legal Consequences of the Separation of the Chagos Archipelago* (n 290), Written Statement of Mauritius, 1 April 2018, vol I, [3.98]–[3.99], [4.22].

[301] In November 2022 the UK Government announced it would enter into negotiations with Mauritius to resolve the wider dispute over the status of the Chagos Archipelago. The 2015 arbitral award of the UNCLOS tribunal does not appear to have been central to this subsequent development, which came after the 2019 Advisory Opinion of the ICJ and the subsequent General Assembly Resolution that both squarely addressed the illegality of the UK's ongoing presence in the Archipelago (see above n 290). See eg Philip Loft, 'British Indian Ocean Territory: UK to Negotiate Sovereignty 2022/23', House of Commons Library Research Briefing, 22 November 2022, 22–26.

[302] *South China Sea*, Award (n 118) [1182]–[1201].

[303] Ibid [1195], [1199], [1201].

[304] Ibid [1198]–[1200].

[305] See also Justine Bendel, *Litigating the Environment: Process and Procedure before International Courts and Tribunals* (Edward Elgar 2023) 42. Subsequent studies focused on the question of compliance suggest that in practice the award was not entirely

between the parties and a willingness to resolve the underlying dispute (eg the *Land Reclamation* or *SBT* cases). Furthermore, unlike in cases where there was a possibility of improving ongoing environmental risk management through requiring cooperation between the parties (eg *Land Reclamation* or *Mox Plant*), in this case there was little scope for future environmental remediation with the Tribunal noting: 'In practical terms, neither this decision nor any action that either Party may take in response can undo the permanent damage that has been done to the coral reef habitats of the South China Sea.'[306]

E. Conclusion

Using the focus on environmental disputes, this chapter has analysed how the three cross-cutting challenges focused on by this book – change in law or facts, review of State conduct for compliance with international law, and contributing to broader processes of dispute resolution – arise in UNCLOS adjudication and are responded to by adjudicators. The adjudicatory practices considered in this chapter are clearly influenced by the particular context and constraints within which UNCLOS adjudicators operate. Yet the practices analysed also provide insights into broader challenges facing international adjudication and legal responses with relevance beyond this context.

It is sometimes suggested that the prompt release procedure 'is unique in international adjudication', in that it is a final rather than interlocutory proceeding, limited to the specific question of the reasonableness of the bond set by the coastal State pursuant to enforcement powers recognised by the Convention.[307] However, this mechanism raises familiar questions concerning the appropriate standard and method of review. Fundamentally what is at issue is an international discipline – the requirement to set reasonable bonds – which acts as a check on the enforcement powers of coastal States within the EEZ and ensures that the interests of flag States, also protected by the Convention, are taken into account. Both in the prompt release context and in other more wide-ranging cases discussed above, the rationales cited by UNCLOS adjudicators as supporting some degree of deference – such as that coastal

ignored by China: Hao Duy Phan, 'International Courts and State Compliance: An Investigation of the Law of the Sea Cases' (2019) 50 ODIL 70, 81–82.

306 *South China Sea*, Award (n 118) [1178].

307 *"Camouco"* (n 11) Dec. Laing, 44.

States may have greater familiarity with relevant facts and considerations of local law, or that coastal States were pursuing legitimate regulatory aims recognised by UNCLOS and other applicable international regimes – are standard reasons for deference. Similar arguments have been advanced in debates over the standard of review in the other adjudication contexts considered in this book, particularly the trade and investment contexts, but also, as we will see, in some aspects of the ICJ's case law. In short, while the regulatory autonomy at issue in the UNCLOS case law is a particular type of regulatory autonomy – for example concerning coastal States' sovereign rights to take measures to conserve and manage living resources in the EEZ – the case law considered above should be analysed alongside other contexts where international tribunals scrutinise States' exercise of regulatory powers for conformity with international law. As Harrison has suggested: 'disputes about the meaning of UNCLOS safeguards on the exercise of coastal State enforcement power fit into a broader model of international law that seeks to' protect 'one actor from the abuse of discretionary power wielded by another actor'.[308]

The wording of relevant provisions of UNCLOS clearly informed the methods of review that have been used by adjudicators to balance competing interests. For example, the requirements in the Convention that bonds set by coastal States for prompt release be 'reasonable',[309] and that a coastal State may only take enforcement measures which are 'necessary' to secure compliance with its laws regarding living resources in the EEZ,[310] clearly lay the ground for some form of balancing exercise. When combined with the design feature of compulsory jurisdiction such indeterminate standards have meant that courts and tribunals have played a prominent role in striking the precise balance between the competing interests at stake in specific disputes.[311] The balancing techniques developed in the UNCLOS case law reviewed above exhibit important similarities with those seen in the other contexts studied in this book. In the UNCLOS case law considered above, which covers both prompt release context and more wide-ranging cases, adjudicators have

[308] Harrison (n 199) 125–26. Similar: Scalieri (n 202) 349–62, 379.
[309] UNCLOS art 73(2).
[310] Ibid art 73(1).
[311] Harrison (n 72) 218; Erik Franckx, '"Reasonable Bond" in the Practice of the International Tribunal for the Law of the Sea' (2002) 32 Calif WILJ 303, 309; Harrison (n 199) 118; Goodman (n 202) 559–60.

variously recognised that either a reasonableness-based test, a necessity or least restrictive means test, or proportionality balancing stricto sensu might be applied when scrutinising the exercise of enforcement powers of a State under UNCLOS. A valid criticism that has been raised by some commentators and separate or dissenting opinions has been that the content of such balancing tests, and the standard or intensity of review with which they are to be applied, has not been sufficiently clarified and there has been a tendency to treat tests that are understood as distinct in other contexts (eg reasonableness, necessity, or proportionality stricto sensu) as interchangeable.[312] While approaches to these issues from other settings cannot simply be transplanted into the UNCLOS context,[313] there are aspects of the case law on the method or standard of review from the other international adjudication settings studied that might provide inspiration for UNCLOS adjudicators. For example, certain practices developed in WTO necessity jurisprudence, such as only treating a measure as a genuine alternative where it would clearly make an equivalent contribution to the regulating State's chosen regulatory aim, or was reasonably available in terms of cost, are clearly relevant to the UNCLOS context.[314] Likewise, some of the criticisms of proportionality balancing stricto sensu that have been developed in the other adjudication contexts studied are relevant to the UNCLOS debates considered in this chapter. These criticisms include that unlike a necessity or least restrictive means test, proportionality balancing stricto sensu gives adjudicators a role in evaluating the relative importance of the regulatory aim pursued by a State and that it confers undue discretion on adjudicators. Such critiques were raised in some of the separate or dissenting opinions considered above, which accused the majority of overly intruding upon the regulatory autonomy of coastal States.[315] Overall, the UNCLOS case law analysed in this chapter is a sometimes-overlooked site of treaty-based adjudication where, as in the other contexts studied in this book, variations on proportionality analysis are emerging as an established technique for balancing competing legally protected interests.

The idea of a prospectively focused and facilitative form of adjudication has particular traction in the UNCLOS context. In part this

[312] See e.g. Harrison (n 199) 138; Nguyen (n 55) 23–24, 248.
[313] See *M/V 'Virginia G'* (n 208) Sep. Op. Paik [14].
[314] See above text at n 217.
[315] See e.g. the dissenting opinions in *M/V 'Virginia G'* and *Duzgit Integrity Arbitration*, discussed above text at nn 212–216 and 239.

reflects that UNCLOS contains numerous provisions that provide a basis for an obligation to cooperate, including regarding protection and preservation of the marine environment,[316] although this textual basis has been built upon by the case law considered above. The fundamental nature of the obligation to cooperate under UNCLOS provided a basis for the proactive, conflict management role performed by ITLOS in cases such as *Land Reclamation*, *MOX Plant*, *SBT*, and *Ghana v Côte d'Ivoire*. The fact that these were all provisional measures decisions is an important contextual consideration. In a provisional measures setting a facilitative and prospectively focused form of adjudicatory review is arguably particularly appropriate given the aim is to preserve the rights at issues, pending a decision on the merits.[317] However, the idea that adjudication might perform the role of clarifying the parties' legal obligations and facilitating their future interactions is not limited to the provisional measures context. For example, in *Chagos*, the Tribunal, while holding that the UK had not sufficiently consulted with Mauritius prior to declaring a MPA, emphasised that it had not taken a view on the substantive environmental protection issues involved and that it was for the parties to negotiate on such matters after the award.[318] Similarly, the *South China Sea* Tribunal understood its role as clarifying the parties' obligations in order 'to facilitate their future relations'.[319] However, the polarised nature of these two disputes, and the lack of common ground between the parties, meant that such a facilitative mode of adjudication was unlikely to be effective.

UNCLOS as a treaty is particularly open to being affected by subsequent changes in international law, given that it is a major regulatory treaty concluded for an indefinite duration, contains numerous terms of a generic or open-ended nature, often refers to rules of general international law or international standards developed elsewhere, and, in certain areas, anticipates the conclusion of subsequent regional agreements.[320] As many of the obligations concerning protection of the

[316] See e.g. UNCLOS arts 117–18, 123, 197–201.

[317] On a related point, see Neil Craik, 'The Duty to Cooperate in International Environmental Law: Constraining State Discretion through Due Respect' (2019) 30 Ybk IEL 22, 29.

[318] See above text at n 298.

[319] See above n 304.

[320] See generally Boyle (n 104) 41–55; Irina Buga, 'Between Stability and Change in the Law of the Sea Convention: Subsequent Practice, Treaty Modification, and Regime

marine environment contained in UNCLOS are framed in general terms, there is clearly potential for States' compliance with such obligations to be informed by current environmental norms and standards.[321] Given Part XII of the Convention is subject to the compulsory binding procedures contained in Part XV, a significant opening is established for Part XV courts and tribunals to contribute to the development of this aspect of the Convention.[322] The fact that UNCLOS courts and tribunals are instructed, as matter of applicable law, to apply 'other rules of international law not incompatible with this Convention'[323] also provides a basis for drawing on environmental norms that have emerged since the conclusion of UNCLOS. The relative openness of UNCLOS to subsequent developments in international law was evident in many of the cases considered above, including the precautionary approach applied by ITLOS in the *SBT* order, the evolutionary interpretation of several applicable legal norms in the *2011 Advisory Opinion*, and the *South China Sea* Tribunal's use of the wider 'corpus of international law concerning the environment' to inform the meaning of obligations in Part XII of UNCLOS.[324] As Matz-Lück and Van Doorn have highlighted, while due diligence is not explicitly mentioned in the text of UNCLOS, in many of the cases due diligence was used by adjudicators as a yardstick for evaluating States' compliance with obligations under the Convention, and whether States had exercised the required diligence was informed by taking account of more recently emerged environmental principles (eg the obligation to conduct an EIA, the precautionary approach). Thus, due diligence appears to operate as something of a 'gateway to enrich the obligations established under' UNCLOS with more recent environmental norms.[325] The broader point is that the jurisprudence of Part XV courts and tribunals has added significant 'normative depth' and specificity to the environmental obligations contained in Part XII of UNCLOS,

Interaction' in Donald R Rothwell and others (eds), *The Oxford Handbook of the Law of the Sea* (OUP 2015). Further references cited above n 103.

321 See e.g. UNCLOS arts 192, 194, 197, 204, 206–12. See also Klein and Parlett (n 4) 353.

322 It is noteworthy that it has repeatedly been held that Part XII of the Convention and the compulsory binding procedures in Part XV are not limited to disputes concerning marine pollution: *Chagos MPA* (n 121) [320]–[322]; *South China Sea*, Award (n 118) [945].

323 UNCLOS art 293(1).

324 *South China Sea*, Award (n 118) [941].

325 Matz-Lück and Van Doorn (n 179) 178–80; 191–94.

contributing to a process of 'evolutive transformation'.[326] The jurisprudence reviewed above provides significant evidence of UNCLOS courts and tribunals, as Roland Holst puts it, engaging in 'a contextual and systemic approach to interpretation; linking rights to corresponding obligations that are informed by the object and purpose of the Convention at large, its overall balance of interests, and sometimes also relevant obligations under general international law'.[327] This is not to say that the concerns of legal stability or State consent were ignored in the above case law, rather it generally reflects an attempt by adjudicators to draw the full consequences from the obligations States have agreed to, and to ensure that the Convention will be able to effectively respond to contemporary regulatory challenges.[328]

[326] Gavouneli (n 121) 261, 266, generally 258–66; Alexander Proelss, 'The Contribution of the ITLOS to Strengthening the Regime for the Protection of the Marine Environment' in Angela Del Vecchio and Roberto Virzo (eds), *Interpretations of the United Nations Convention on the Law of the Sea by International Courts and Tribunals* (Springer 2019) 104–05; Nguyen (n 55) 192.

[327] Roland Holst (n 3) 311–12. Similarly: Foster (n 55) 89, 114–15, 129–30, 290–92.

[328] Ibid.

4

International Court of Justice Litigation

This chapter analyses the three selected challenges facing international tribunals traced throughout this book – managing change, reviewing State conduct for compliance with international law, and dispute resolution – in relation to the environmental case law of the International Court of Justice (ICJ). The ICJ has since the 1970s heard a significant number of cases with an environmental component, and such cases have been a regular feature of the Court's docket since the mid-1990s.[1] This chapter explores how the adjudicatory practices of the ICJ are shaped by the particular contextual features of ICJ litigation. For example, the Court's analysis of environmental disputes is shaped by its general subject matter jurisdiction and its lack of any compulsory jurisdiction,

[1] For discussion of various phases in the ICJ's environmental case law see Malgosia Fitzmaurice, 'The International Court of Justice and International Environmental Law' in Christian J Tams and James Sloan (eds), *The Development of International Law by the International Court of Justice* (OUP 2013); Jorge E Viñuales, 'The Contribution of the International Court of Justice to the Development of International Environmental Law: A Contemporary Assessment' (2008) 32 Fordham ILJ 232. In addition to the cases discussed below, there are a few cases that had an environmental component and were not decided on the merits, either because they were settled beforehand or as the Court found there was no jurisdiction. See especially *Case Concerning Aerial Herbicide Spraying (Ecuador v Colombia)*, Application Instituting Proceedings, 31 March 2008, esp. [37]–[38] (case partly concerned liability for damage to human health and the environment resulting from herbicide spraying and was settled by agreement: see *Aerial Herbicide Spraying (Ecuador v Colombia)*, Order of 13 September 2013, ICJ Rep [2013] 278). See also *Fisheries Jurisdiction (Spain v Canada)*, Jurisdiction of the Court, Judgment, ICJ Rep [1998] 432 (case concerned unilateral fisheries conservation measures taken by Canada and the Court held there was no jurisdiction). *Certain Phosphate Lands in Nauru (Nauru v Australia)*, Preliminary Objections, Judgment, ICJ Rep [1992] 240 (Nauru's claims concerned inter alia alleged breaches of the principle of permanent sovereignty over natural resources and responsibility for the rehabilitation of land damaged by phosphate mining: see Memorial of Nauru, 20 March 1990, [415]–[419], [488]–[489]). After the Court upheld jurisdiction, the case was settled by agreement: see Agreement between Australia and the Republic of Nauru for the Settlement of the Case in the International Court of Justice concerning Certain Phosphate Lands in Nauru [1993] 32 ILM 1474.

which means that it adjudicates across a wide range of different legal contexts and is particularly sensitive to consent-based concerns. However, as we will see, the ICJ is also adept at formulating parts of its legal reasoning in generalisable terms that are potentially transferable to other contexts. Furthermore, given the Court's immense semantic authority, its decisions are frequently drawn upon in subsequent legal discourse, including by other international tribunals. Accordingly, analysing the ICJ's practices in relation to the three cross-cutting challenges considered throughout this book is an important step in the overall inquiry into how international tribunals might discharge their functions given the demands being placed upon them and the limitations of their roles.

This chapter proceeds as follows. Section A analyses various contextual features relevant to understanding this adjudication setting, in order to provide a stronger basis for the comparative analysis undertaken. Section B considers how the ICJ has managed the problem of change in applicable legal norms or change in relevant facts. We will see that the ICJ has repeatedly updated aging treaty frameworks in light of developments in international law, but concerns have also been raised about this practice potentially undermining legal certainty and State consent. Section C considers how the issues of the standard and method of review have arisen and been addressed in the ICJ's environmental case law. Section D demonstrates that within the ICJ's environmental case law there are repeated examples of the Court adjudicating with a partly prospective focus, seeking to provide guidance to facilitate the parties' interactions after adjudication. Section E draws together and extends the findings of the analysis undertaken.

A. Institutional Context for ICJ Litigation

1. *The Lack of Compulsory Jurisdiction*

A crucial difference in institutional context between the ICJ and the other adjudication mechanisms studied in this book is the manner in which States consent to adjudicative jurisdiction. In the other contexts studied, States, as part of joining the relevant regime-creating treaty (eg UNCLOS, the WTO Agreement) agree in advance to adjudicate certain categories of disputes. In contrast, insofar as contentious cases are concerned, the ICJ does not have any form of such so-called 'compulsory jurisdiction'.[2] While the ICJ is the 'principal judicial organ of the United Nations',[3] and all members of the UN are automatically parties to its Statute,[4] its contentious jurisdiction always requires an additional act of consent by the relevant States.[5]

There are essentially three ways in which State consent to the contentious jurisdiction of the Court can arise. First, the parties can agree after a dispute has arisen to submit it to the Court.[6] While the parties will typically jointly submit a written agreement to the Court, there are no strict requirements as to form so long as the agreement of the parties is established.[7] Accordingly, those rare situations where a State has unilaterally commenced litigation and the respondent State has subsequently agreed to submit to the Court's jurisdiction are properly characterised as a variant of this first situation, consent coming after the dispute has arisen.[8] Second, treaties may contain a compromissory clause in which the treaty parties agree prospectively to submit a certain class of disputes – typically disputes concerning the interpretation and application of the agreement – to the ICJ.[9] In practice many treaties do not confer jurisdiction on the ICJ and such clauses are only rarely being included in

[2] Christian Tomuschat, 'Article 36' in Andreas Zimmermann and others (eds), *The Statute of the International Court of Justice: A Commentary* (3rd ed., OUP 2019) [145]; Pieter Kooijmans, 'The ICJ in the 21st Century: Judicial Restraint, Judicial Activism, or Proactive Judicial Policy' (2007) 56 ICLQ 741, 743, 747 (ICJ 'handicapped by the principle of consent'); Sara McLaughlin Mitchell and Andrew P Owsiak, 'The International Court of Justice' in Robert M Howard and Kirk A Randazzo (eds), *Routledge Handbook of Judicial Behavior* (Routledge 2018) 446. This use of the term 'compulsory jurisdiction' to refer to courts and tribunals where the relevant regime-creating treaty involves some degree of advance consent to adjudication should be distinguished from the optional clause system under Article 36(2) of the ICJ's Statute, discussed below text at nn 11–14, which is occasionally also referred to as amounting to 'compulsory jurisdiction'.

[3] UN Charter art 92.

[4] Ibid art 93(1).

[5] Tomuschat (n 2) [19]. This is despite Article 36(1) of the Court's Statute referring to 'matters specifically provided for in the Charter of the United Nations': Statute of the International Court of Justice (1945) 33 UNTS 993, art 36(1) ('ICJ Statute'): see Tomuschat (n 2) [47].

[6] ICJ Statute art 36(1).

[7] Malcolm N Shaw, *Rosenne's Law and Practice of the International Court: 1920–2015* (5th ed., Brill Nijhoff 2016) 579–81; Tomuschat (n 2) 743–46.

[8] Known as *forum prorogatum*. For outline of the instances where this has arisen see Tomuschat (n 2) 743–44.

[9] ICJ Statute art 36(1).

new treaties.[10] Third, States can 'at any time unilaterally declare that they recognise as compulsory *ipso facto* and without special agreement, in relation to any other State accepting the same obligation, the jurisdiction of the Court'.[11] Such declarations are typically made conditionally, subject to 'reservations' whereby States exclude certain categories of disputes from their acceptance of compulsory jurisdiction.[12] Currently, 74 States have made optional clause declarations[13] out of 193 UN member States, and since the Court's founding 'the relative proportion of UN membership accepting compulsory jurisdiction has shrunk considerably'.[14]

In short, the Court's contentious jurisdiction is thoroughly consensual and follows 'the logic of *realpolitik*'.[15] This has implications for the Court's work and results in certain differences between the ICJ and the other international tribunals considered in this book. First, because it is often difficult to find a basis for ICJ jurisdiction, and as the Court's jurisdiction is not subject matter limited, its cases are far more varied than the other tribunals studied in terms of the areas of law concerned.[16] While in some areas the ICJ does hear repeated cases concerning the same subject matter – for example maritime boundary delimitation – overall, compared to the other tribunals studied in this book, it has far fewer opportunities to hear similar types of disputes on a repeated basis. While this diversity of the ICJ's caseload most obviously concerns the subject matter of the disputes it hears, there is also significant diversity in the legal basis on which the dispute is brought and the Court is empowered to adjudicate (eg between cases brought under a compromissory clause, focusing on the interpretation and application of a particular treaty, as compared to cases focusing on customary international law). Second, because its contentious jurisdiction always depends on an additional act of consent, the ICJ faces, arguably more

[10] Rotem Giladi and Yuval Shany, 'The International Court of Justice' in Yuval Shany, *Assessing the Effectiveness of International Courts* (OUP 2014) 170; Gary Born, 'A New Generation of International Adjudication' (2012) 61 Duke LJ 775, 861–63. A full list of treaties with such a compromissory clause is available on the Court's website.

[11] ICJ Statute art 36(2).

[12] ICJ Statute art 36(3). See generally Tomuschat (n 2) 759–75.

[13] See the list on the Court's website <www.icj-cij.org/declarations>.

[14] See Giladi and Shany (n 10) 170–71 (with relevant figures).

[15] Tomuschat (n 2) 719–20, 728.

[16] Karen J Alter, 'The International Court of Justice in Comparison: Understanding the Court's Limited Influence' (2021) 21 MJIL 676, 682, 689; Christian Djeffal, *Static and Evolutive Treaty Interpretation: A Functional Reconstruction* (CUP 2015) 215; Shaw (n 7) 31.

than the other bodies considered in this book, the constant threat that States will not in future grant it jurisdiction over their disputes.[17] This leads to a bias towards emphasising State consent, particularly on jurisdictional issues.[18] Consent-based considerations feature in the other international adjudication contexts studied too, and those institutions are also sensitive to securing a future caseload; however, the ICJ's jurisdictional situation means that this consideration becomes particularly pressing.

In addition to its contentious jurisdiction, the ICJ also has an advisory jurisdiction pursuant to which the UN General Assembly or the Security Council may request an advisory opinion 'on any legal question'.[19] Other UN organs and agencies can also be authorised by the General Assembly to request advisory opinions from the ICJ 'on legal questions arising within the scope of their activities'.[20] In recent decades, the Court has averaged a small handful of advisory proceedings per decade. In terms of cases with an environmental component, at the time of writing advisory proceedings are ongoing in a wide-ranging request by the General Assembly concerning the international obligations of States to protect the environment in the context of climate change.[21] In the 1990s, two advisory opinions requested by the General Assembly and World Health Organization in relation to the legality of the threat or use of nuclear weapons also raised significant environmental issues.[22]

[17] See e.g. Gleider I Hernández, 'International Judicial Lawmaking' in Catherine Brölmann and Yannick Radi (eds), *Research Handbook on the Theory and Practice of International Lawmaking* (Edward Elgar 2016) 204.

[18] Gleider I Hernández, *The International Court of Justice and the Judicial Function* (OUP 2014) 47–50 (on jurisdictional issues), 288 (more generally); Armin von Bogdandy and Ingo Venzke, *In Whose Name? A Public Law Theory of International Adjudication* (OUP 2014) 41; Hersch Lauterpacht, *The Development of International Law by the International Court* (rev. ed., Stevens & Sons 1958) 91, 95. As Hernández highlights, this bias towards State consent is also explained by other factors besides the Court's jurisdictional situation, such as the backgrounds of judges, who are frequently former government legal advisers, and the role of States in the process by which judges are elected: 137–40.

[19] UN Charter art 96(1). On the ICJ's advisory jurisdiction, see generally, eg, Mahasen M Aljaghoub, *The Advisory Function of the International Court of Justice 1946–2005* (Springer 2006).

[20] UN Charter art 96(2). For a list of UN organs and agencies that have been authorised to request advisory opinions see <www.icj-cij.org/organs-agencies-authorized>.

[21] *Obligations of States in respect of Climate Change*, Request for Advisory Opinion, 12 April 2023.

[22] *Legality of the Threat or Use of Nuclear Weapons*, Advisory Opinion, ICJ Rep [1996] 226, [27]–[33]. See also Diss. Op. Weeramantry, ICJ Rep [1996] 429, esp. 454–56, 463–64, 506; Diss. Op. Koroma, ICJ Rep [1996] 556, 578. The Court refused the request for an advisory opinion made by the World Health Organization: see *Legality of the Use by a State of*

2. The Goals of the ICJ

The starting point for understanding the aims of the ICJ is Article 38(1) of the Court's Statute, which states that the Court's 'function is to decide in accordance with international law such disputes as are submitted to it'.[23] The goal of settling disputes in accordance with international law is also supported at a high level of generality by several provisions of the UN Charter,[24] which are relevant to the aims of the ICJ because the Court's Statute is an 'integral part' of the Charter and the Court the 'principal judicial organ' of the wider organisation.[25] The Court itself has stated that its function is to decide the issues in dispute between the parties in accordance with relevant rules of international law.[26] As we have seen in Chapter 1, peaceful dispute settlement is a generic goal common to international courts.[27] Similarly, another generic function of international tribunals that we have encountered throughout in this book, namely assessing state compliance with international law, is also performed by the ICJ.[28]

Despite this not being a goal reflected in the Court's constitutive documents,[29] there is little doubt that the Court, by deciding cases, also contributes to the clarification and development of international law, and the debate is really over the degree to which this occurs.[30] The Court itself has noted, as might be expected of a judicial body, that 'it states the existing law and does not legislate. This is so even if, in stating and applying the law, the Court necessarily has to specify its scope and

Nuclear Weapons in Armed Conflict, Advisory Opinion, ICJ Rep [1996] 66, esp. [1], [21]–[26], [31]–[32]. See also Diss. Op. Weeramantry, ICJ Rep [1996] 101, esp. 111, 140–45; Diss. Op. Koroma, ICJ Rep [1996] 172, esp. 175–76, 215–18.

23 ICJ Statute art 38(1).

24 UN Charter arts 1(1), 2(3), 36(3). See discussion in Giladi and Shany (n 10) 164–66.

25 Ibid art 92.

26 See e.g. *LaGrand (Germany v United States of America)*, Judgment, ICJ Rep [2001] 466, [52]; *Nuclear Tests (New Zealand v France)*, Judgment, ICJ Rep [1974] 457, [58], [60]; *Northern Cameroons (Cameroon v United Kingdom)*, Preliminary Objections, Judgment, ICJ Rep [1963] 15, 33–34.

27 See Chapter 1, n 36 and text at nn 39–41.

28 Giladi and Shany (n 10) 164 ('obtaining the conformity of judicial settlements with international law as an ICJ goal').

29 Giladi and Shany (n 10) 168.

30 See especially Lauterpacht (n 18) 3–5, 70–71 (suggesting while the Court had not made a significant contribution to maintaining international peace it had 'made a tangible contribution to the development and clarification' of international law). See also Giladi and Shany (n 10) 185–86.

sometimes note its general trend.'[31] Amongst commentators it is possible to identify two broad views about the degree to which the Court has the purpose of contributing to the development of international law. One school of thought stresses that, at least in contentious cases, the Court is engaged in deciding the dispute presented to it, with its primary audience being the parties to the case and any development of the law being a secondary and ancillary matter.[32] Another view, while accepting that the Court has the primary function of deciding the disputes presented to it, foregrounds to a greater degree the Court's secondary and important function of contributing, through its decisions, to the development of international law.[33]

This book supports the latter view. Given the immense semantic authority which the Court enjoys and the degree to which its judgments are closely followed and deferred to by other actors,[34] including other international tribunals,[35] the ICJ '"cannot avoid contributing"' to the clarification and development of international law by deciding

[31] *Legality of the Threat or Use of Nuclear Weapons* (n 22) [18].

[32] See e.g. Iain Scobbie, '"All Right, Mr. DeMille, I'm Ready for My Close-up": Some Critical Reflections on Professor Cassese's "The International Court of Justice: It is High Time to Restyle the Respected Old Lady"' (2012) 23 EJIL 1071, 1087 (ICJ 'principally a transactional court'); Francesco Messineo, 'The Functions of the International Court of Justice: Tending to the Law While Settling Disputes?' in Avidan Kent, Nikos Skoutaris and Jamie Trinidad (eds), *The Future of International Courts: Regional, Institutional and Procedural Challenges* (Routledge 2019) esp. 116–21; Stephan Wittich, 'The Judicial Functions of the International Court of Justice' in Isabelle Buffard and others (eds), *International Law between Universalism and Fragmentation: Festschrift in Honour of Gerhard Hafner* (Martinus Nijhoff 2008) 994–96; Robert Y Jennings, 'The Judicial Function and the Rule of Law in International Relations' in Robert Y Jennings, *Collected Writings of Sir Robert Jennings*, vol 1 (Kluwer Law International 1998) 483–84; Alter (n 16) 691, 697; Franklin Berman, 'The International Court of Justice as an "Agent" of Legal Development' in Christian J Tams and James Sloan (eds), *The Development of International Law by the International Court of Justice* (OUP 2013) 11–12.

[33] See especially Lauterpacht (n 18) 70–71, 42–43, 21–22. See also Charles De Visscher, *Theory and Reality in Public International Law* (PE Corbett tr, rev. ed., Princeton University Press 1968) 390; Tom Ginsburg, 'The Institutional Context of the International Court of Justice' in Carlos Espósito and Kate Parlett (eds), *The Cambridge Companion to the International Court of Justice* (CUP 2023) 91–92, 99.

[34] Hernández (n 18) 5; DP O'Connell, *International Law*, vol 1 (2nd ed., Stevens & Sons 1970) 32 (statements of the law by the ICJ 'are accorded in writings a truly astonishing deference').

[35] See e.g. Alain Pellet, 'The Case Law of the ICJ in Investment Arbitration' (2013) 28 ICSID Review 223; James Crawford, Freya Baetens and Rose Cameron, 'Functions of the International Court of Justice' in Carlos Espósito and Kate Parlett (eds), *The Cambridge Companion to the International Court of Justice* (CUP 2023) 36–37.

cases.[36] As Hernández has argued, a full account of the Court's contribution in this regard needs to include, beyond its clarification and development of particular norms, its influence in shaping the very terms of international legal discourse and what counts as acceptable argumentation.[37] We will see below that although the ICJ typically adjudicates in a particular legal context, it has often managed to couch part of its reasoning in more generalisable terms that can be drawn upon in subsequent legal discourse. Nevertheless, the Court is ultimately only one actor in wider processes of law-development. Its influence varies across issue areas, and depends on multiple factors, many of which are beyond its control, such as how often cases in an issue area are submitted to it, whether competing law-developing agencies operate within the area, and whether the area of law is already codified.[38]

The ICJ does not have a 'regime support' function in the same sense as the other tribunals considered in this book (particularly ITLOS or while it was operating the WTO Appellate Body), as it is not created by, and embedded within, a particular functionally oriented regime.[39] However, the ICJ does sometimes perform such a 'regime support' function in other weaker senses. At a relatively specific level the Court may have a particular role within the treaty or legal regime applicable to a dispute. For example, we will see below that in the *Whaling* case, where the dispute was primarily governed by the International Convention for the Regulation of Whaling ('Whaling Convention'),[40] there was significant debate over the Court's role within the wider regime created by the Convention.[41] More generally, given the Court's status as 'principal judicial organ' of the UN and its general jurisdiction, some commentators view the Court as having the function of supporting and legitimating the wider normative regime of international law.[42] Consistently with this view, we will see below that in the context of greater

[36] Giladi and Shany (n 10) 168 (quoting an anonymous interview with an ICJ judge). See also 182–83. See also Joan E Donoghue, 'The Role of the World Court Today' (2012) 47 Georgia Law Review 181, 197–98.

[37] Hernández (n 18) 5, 88–93.

[38] Christian J Tams, 'The ICJ as a "Law-Formative Agency": Summary and Synthesis' in Tams and Sloan (eds), *Development* (n 1) 391–96.

[39] On the definition of regimes see Chapter 1, n 12.

[40] (1946) 161 UNTS 74.

[41] *Whaling in the Antarctic (Australia v Japan, New Zealand intervening)*, Judgment, ICJ Rep [2014] 226.

[42] Giladi and Shany (n 10) 166–67, 185–88; Rotem Giladi and Yuval Shany, 'Assessing the Effectiveness of the International Court of Justice' in Carlos Espósito and Kate Parlett

specialisation of different branches of international law, the ICJ has played an informal role in providing guidance on general concepts of international law and 'mainstreaming' specialised regimes into the wider body of general international law.[43] In relation to its advisory jurisdiction, outlined above, the ICJ can also be said to have a 'regime support' role within the UN as an international organisation, although it is not a central role.[44] Nevertheless, while the ICJ can be said to have 'regime support' role in these looser senses, it is important to emphasise the distinction, in terms of institutional context, with the tribunals studied in other chapters, which are all created for the purposes of deciding disputes in regimes with particular goals.

3. *The Judges in ICJ Litigation*

The ICJ consists of fifteen members, each of a different nationality.[45] Judges who hold the nationality of one of the parties are permitted to participate in cases involving that party (unless otherwise conflicted).[46] Where the Court does not include a national of a party, the non-represented party or parties can nominate a judge ad hoc.[47] Members of the Court are elected by separate votes of the UN General Assembly and Security Council,[48] from a list of nominations created by national groups in the Permanent Court of Arbitration (PCA).[49] Members are required to be 'persons of high moral character' and possess the qualifications required for appointment to the highest judicial offices in their countries or be 'juristconsults of recognized competence in international law'.[50] In addition to such qualifications, electors are to bear in mind that

(eds), *The Cambridge Companion to the International Court of Justice* (CUP 2023) 107, 119.

43 See e.g. Fitzmaurice (n 1) 373–74; Tams (n 38) 383–84; Viñuales (n 1); Mads Andenas, 'Reassertion and Transformation: From Fragmentation to Convergence in International Law' (2015) 36 Georgetown JIL 685; Andrew Lang, 'The Role of the International Court of Justice in a Context of Fragmentation' (2013) 62 ICLQ 777.

44 Giladi and Shany (n 10) 166–67; Ginsburg (n 33) 96–99.

45 ICJ Statute art 3(1).

46 ICJ Statute art 31(1).

47 See ICJ Statute arts 31(2)–(6).

48 See ICJ Statute arts 8, 10, 11, 12.

49 ICJ Statute art 4(1). A national group in the PCA is made up of four persons nominated by each member State of the PCA: Convention for the Pacific Settlement of International Disputes (1907) art 44. See also ICJ Statute art 4(2); Shaw (n 7) 373–77.

50 ICJ Statute art 2.

the Court as a whole includes 'representation of the main forms of civilization and of the principal legal systems of the world'.[51] Until 2017, there was an informal convention that a seat was always given to each of the five permanent members of the Security Council.[52] Furthermore, within the electing institutions, an informal convention exists that the seats on the Court are divided up according to the regional groupings that are used within the UN, which are based on the distribution of non-permanent seats on the Security Council.[53] Judges are elected for terms of nine years, and can be re-elected.[54] As might be expected, the appointment process is highly political and this extends to decisions over the re-election of sitting ICJ judges.[55] Nevertheless, it must be remembered that judges are elected and serve in an individual capacity, not as representatives of the nominating State.[56] The Court has tended to be composed of former diplomats and politicians with a legal background, former legal advisers to foreign ministries, practitioners from the international bar, and, to a lesser degree, international law academics or former national judges.[57] Thus the Court's bench is, on the whole, sensitive to States' interests and sovereignty-based concerns.[58] The Court drafts its judgments through a multi-stage, highly collective process, which involves all members of the Court,[59] and judges have a right to give an individual opinion whether or not they dissent.[60] The option to

[51] ICJ Statute art 9.

[52] Bardo Fassbender, 'Article 9' in Andreas Zimmermann and others (eds), *The Statute of the International Court of Justice: A Commentary* (3rd ed., OUP 2019) [20]; Shaw (n 7) 393–95.

[53] See e.g. Fassbender (n 52) [22]–[25]; Ruth Mackenzie and others, *Selecting International Judges: Principle, Process, and Politics* (OUP 2010) 28–29.

[54] ICJ Statute art 13(1).

[55] See e.g. Giladi and Shany (n 10) 172–73; Ksenia Polonskaya, 'Selecting Candidates to the Bench of the World Court: (Inevitable) Politicization and Its Consequences' (2020) 33 LJIL 409.

[56] ICJ Statute art 2; Hugh Thirlway, *The International Court of Justice* (OUP 2016) 10–11.

[57] Robert Kolb, *The Elgar Companion to the International Court of Justice* (Edward Elgar 2014) 108–09. See also ch 7. For the biographies of current members see the Court's website.

[58] Giladi and Shany (n 10) 173; Hernández (n 18) 288, 137–40.

[59] This is governed by the Resolution concerning the Internal Judicial Practice of the Court (1976). See generally Hernández (n 18) 104–06; Jeffrey L Dunoff and Mark A Pollack, 'International Judicial Practices: Opening the "Black Box" of International Courts' (2018) 40 Mich. J. Int'l L. 47, 81–85; Kenneth Keith, 'The Role of an ICJ Judge' in Carlos Espósito and Kate Parlett (eds), *The Cambridge Companion to the International Court of Justice* (CUP 2023) 59–62.

[60] ICJ Statute art 57; ICJ Rules of Court art 95(2).

do so is heavily used and leads to a diversity of views in most cases.[61] While the collective judgment of the Court carries greater weight, individual opinions are important for fully understanding the choices that the Court has made.[62]

B. Balancing Stability and Change in the ICJ's Environmental Case Law

This section analyses how the ICJ has experienced and responded to the challenge of balancing the competing interests of stability and change when interpreting and applying applicable international legal norms. As explained in Chapter 1, this is a pressing problem facing international tribunals because in many areas treaty-making has stagnated and yet a large number of disputes continue to be litigated, meaning demands for change are often directed at adjudicators.[63] The ICJ has frequently been confronted with this challenge because it often adjudicates over dated treaties given its general and consent-dependent jurisdiction. Accordingly, the Court's case law is an important resource for understanding the role of international adjudication in incrementally adapting international law to new demands.[64]

1. *Managing Change in International Legal Norms*

The challenge of balancing the competing demands of ensuring legal certainty through interpretation and allowing legal norms to evolve, given relevant developments in international law, was a key issue in the *Whaling* case. This case involved a dispute over whether whaling research permits granted by Japan were covered by the exception in Article VIII(1) of the Whaling Convention, which enables whaling 'for

[61] See e.g. Rainer Hofmann and Linda Karl, 'Article 57' in Andreas Zimmermann and others (eds), *The Statute of the International Court of Justice: A Commentary* (3rd ed., OUP 2019) [35] (finding that up to November 2018 the ICJ had made 383 decisions – including all judgments, advisory opinions, and orders – which produced 1,432 individual opinions).

[62] Hernández (n 18) 96–97, 112–13.

[63] See Chapter 1, text at nn 55–58.

[64] Cf Lauterpacht (n 18) 14 (Court's prior decisions as 'a repository of legal experience'). Sections B(1) and C(2)(a) of this chapter draw to a limited extent on Joshua Paine, 'The Judicial Dimension of Regime Interaction beyond Systemic Integration' in Seline Trevisanut, Nikolaos Giannopoulos and Rozemarijn Roland Holst (eds), *Regime Interaction in Ocean Governance: Problems, Theories and Methods* (Brill Nijhoff 2020).

purposes of scientific research'.[65] Australia, and New Zealand intervening, argued that the treaty provision only authorised the granting of special permits to kill whales where non-lethal methods were not available, and supported this view by relying on various resolutions and guidelines adopted by the International Whaling Commission (IWC), arguing these constituted subsequent agreement between the treaty parties or subsequent practice.[66] The Court found that 'Australia and New Zealand overstate the legal significance of the recommendatory resolutions and Guidelines on which they rely', including because many of the resolutions had been adopted without the support of all parties to the Convention, and in particular Japan, and thus could not constitute subsequent agreement or practice.[67] This finding operates to ensure treaty stability and legal certainty by affirming that subsequent agreement and subsequent practice require the consent, either explicit or implicit, of all treaty parties.[68] Nevertheless, the Court permitted a degree of evolution in the relevant treaty regime by finding that the treaty parties had an obligation 'to co-operate with the IWC and the Scientific Committee and thus should give due regard to' the non-binding recommendations of these bodies.[69] This obligation was then emphasised in the Court's subsequent reasoning as to why Japan's program, given its lack of consideration of the feasibility of non-lethal methods, was not covered by the treaty exception.[70]

65 Whaling Convention art VIII(1).

66 *Whaling* (n 41) [78]–[81].

67 Ibid [83].

68 On the restricted and consensual nature of subsequent practice, see eg Laurence Boisson de Chazournes, 'Subsequent Practice, Practices, and "Family-Resemblance": Towards Embedding Subsequent Practice in Its Operative Milieu' in Georg Nolte (ed), *Treaties and Subsequent Practice* (OUP 2013) 53–56; International Law Commission (ILC), Draft Conclusions on Subsequent Agreements and Subsequent Practice in relation to the Interpretation of Treaties with Commentaries, [2018] II(2) ILC Ybk 25, 63, Conclusion 10 and commentary [1]–[3].

69 *Whaling* (n 41) [83]. Note that several judges held that the Court should have made additional findings concerning Japan's failure to cooperate meaningfully with the IWC and its Scientific Committee: see Sep. Op. Sebutinde [15]–[20]; Sep. Op. Charlesworth [11]–[17]; Sep. Op Bhandari [7]–[18].

70 See *Whaling* (n 41) [137], [144]; Hamamoto suggests that the obligation to give due regard to IWC recommendations only applied to those resolutions adopted by consensus, noting that the requirement to consider the feasibility of non-lethal methods, emphasised in the Court's later scrutiny of Japan's program, was contained in resolutions adopted by consensus. In contrast a resolution which was not adopted by consensus, and which only permitted lethal methods where non-lethal alternatives were not available, was noted by the Court in considering the subsequent practice issue (judgment [78]) but was not

The suggestion that these interpretative questions involved managing a tension between ensuring legal certainty and allowing the relevant legal framework to evolve, given relevant developments in international law, is strongly supported by several of the individual opinions rendered. Specifically, several judges suggested that the Court had, through its interpretation of the obligation to give due regard to IWC resolutions, impermissibly allowed the Convention regime to evolve and undermined legal certainty for parties to the Convention. Judge Abraham noted that the obligation to 'give due regard' to IWC recommendations 'cannot have the effect . . . of transforming those recommendations into binding decisions'.[71] Similarly, Judge Greenwood emphasised that because the Convention already contained a process enabling the IWC to adopt binding amendments to its Schedule,[72] there was 'less of a case for treating [non-binding] recommendations as having significant effects on the basis of an evolutionary interpretation', which could allow changes lacking sufficient support for an amendment 'to be introduced through the back door'.[73] Judge Owada also criticised Australia and New Zealand's argument that the Whaling Convention had evolved towards greater emphasis on conservation as 'tantamount to an attempt to change the rules of the game as provided for in the Convention',[74] emphasising that the Convention was 'not malleable . . . according to changes in the surrounding socio-economic environments'.[75] The concern for ensuring legal certainty through interpretation is clear in all these remarks.

In contrast, several other judges emphasised that the regime established by the Whaling Convention had evolved in the direction of conservation and this narrowed the scope of the exception for scientific whaling. For example, Judge Xue noted that while the treaty exception

endorsed in its analysis of the availability of non-lethal alternatives (judgment [137]): Shotaro Hamamoto, 'From the Requirement of Reasonableness to a "Comply and Explain" Rule: The Standard of Review in the Whaling Judgment' in Malgosia Fitzmaurice and Dai Tamada (eds), *Whaling in the Antarctic: Significance and Implications of the ICJ Judgment* (Brill Nijhoff 2016) 43–44. While this is a plausible reading of the Judgment, it is problematic to suggest that those resolutions adopted by a large majority have no relevance to the obligation of due regard. Contrast *Whaling* (n 41) Sep. Op. Charlesworth [4], [13].

71 Ibid Diss. Op. Abraham [38] (translation by registry).

72 Regarding the institutional framework created by the Convention, see *Whaling* (n 41) [45]–[47].

73 Ibid Sep. Op. Greenwood [7], [5].

74 Ibid Diss. Op. Owada [16].

75 Ibid [12].

formally remained intact, a number of developments within the Convention regime meant that it had evolved in the direction of conservation and thus it was 'hard to claim that' the scope of the exception 'stays the same as before'.[76] Similarly, Judge Yusuf favoured evolution of the relevant treaty, holding that developments within the Convention regime, in particular the moratorium on commercial whaling, meant the balance within the Convention had 'clearly shifted ... in favour of more conservation and less exploitation'.[77] He suggested that given these developments, and developments in wider international environmental law, the Court should have asked whether Japan's conduct frustrated the object and purpose of the Convention.[78] Plainly, this view allows greater evolution in the legal framework in light of relevant developments in international law.

Both parties had in their pleadings addressed the relevance of broader international environmental law for interpreting the exception in the Whaling Convention.[79] Such references to wider international law, including the precautionary principle, are notable for their complete absence from the majority judgment.[80] This may reflect that the Court was conscious of the role of the IWC as a body empowered to update the Convention over time.[81] However, there is a stark contrast with the individual opinions of some judges who would have allowed far greater evolution of the treaty exception in light of subsequent developments in relevant international law. For example, Judge ad hoc Charlesworth held that 'treaties dealing with the environment should be interpreted wherever possible in light of the precautionary approach, regardless of the

[76] Ibid Sep. Op. Xue [12].

[77] Ibid Diss. Op. Yusuf [25]–[26].

[78] Ibid [26].

[79] For Australia's arguments regarding the relevance of other international environmental law for interpreting the Whaling Convention, see Memorial of Australia, 9 May 2011, vol I, [4.81]–[4.91] and CR 2013/7, [48]–[58] (Boisson de Chazournes). For Japan's position, see Counter-Memorial of Japan, 9 March 2012, vol I, [6.15]–[6.30], [9.33]–[9.36] and CR 2013/13, [23]–[53] (Boyle). In its application instituting proceedings, Australia made independent claims that Japan had violated certain other international environmental treaties besides the Whaling Convention, but these claims were dropped by the time of Australia's memorial: see *Whaling in the Antarctic (Australia v Japan)*, Application Instituting Proceedings, 31 May 2010, [38].

[80] Similarly: Margaret A Young and Sebastián Rioseco Sullivan, 'Evolution through the Duty to Cooperate: Implications of the *Whaling* Case at the International Court of Justice' (2015) 16 MJIL 311, 313, 326–27.

[81] See the point made by Judge Greenwood: above text at n 73.

date of their adoption'.[82] This required, in terms of interpreting the scope of the exception for scientific whaling, that lethal methods 'be indispensable to the purposes of scientific research' and non-lethal methods 'be used wherever possible'.[83] Similarly, Judge Cançado Trindade held that the Whaling Convention had to be interpreted in light of other international instruments relevant to the conservation and management of marine mammals which followed 'a conservation-oriented approach and the precautionary principle', and this warranted a narrow interpretation of the scientific whaling exception.[84] These interpretations favour legal change by narrowing the exception in the Whaling Convention, in light of the emergence of the precautionary principle as a principle of international law, to a greater degree than the majority judgment. While these approaches might be argued to undermine legal certainty by enabling the content of the treaty exception to evolve without the agreement of all parties to the Convention, there is a strong argument that agreement amongst all treaty parties is an inappropriate threshold because it effectively gives each party to a widely ratified multilateral treaty a veto over its evolution.[85]

In the *Pulp Mills* case, which concerned Uruguay's authorisation and construction of two pulp mills on the River Uruguay and their environmental effects, the Court was also squarely faced with the question of how the parties' obligations under the 1975 Statute of the River Uruguay, on which the Court's jurisdiction was based, might be affected by changes in other relevant international legal norms. Argentina claimed that the 1975 Statute had to be interpreted in light of other relevant rules of international law, particularly those concerning watercourses and the environment, to ensure its interpretation continued to evolve with changes in environmental standards,[86] a proposition the Court accepted.[87] Argentina further argued that certain provisions of the 1975 Statute had the effect of incorporating into the Statute the parties' obligations under other multilateral environmental treaties, some of which post-dated the Statute, and the Court could adjudicate on compliance with those treaties

82 *Whaling* (n 41) Sep. Op. Charlesworth [9].

83 Ibid [10].

84 Ibid Sep. Op. Cançado Trindade [57]–[59].

85 Margaret A Young, 'Regime Interaction in Creating, Implementing and Enforcing International Law' in Margaret A Young (ed), *Regime Interaction in International Law: Facing Fragmentation* (CUP 2012) 95–96.

86 *Pulp Mills on the River Uruguay (Argentina v Uruguay)* (Judgment) [2010] ICJ Rep 14, [55].

87 Ibid [65]–[66].

also.[88] The Court's rejection of the latter argument is unsurprising and operates to protect legal certainty: the relevant provisions of the Statute did not, on their face, actually incorporate the other international obligations,[89] and the parties' consent to jurisdiction was limited to disputes concerning the interpretation and application of the 1975 Statute.[90]

Nevertheless, the Court responded in other ways to the need for the obligations under the Statute to evolve with changes in environmental standards. For example, the Court accepted that 'a precautionary approach may be relevant in the interpretation and application of the provisions of the Statute'.[91] Importantly, the Court also held that the parties' obligation under the 1975 Statute 'to protect and preserve the aquatic environment' had an evolutionary character, and had to be interpreted in light of the obligation to undertake an environmental impact assessment where proposed industrial activities pose a risk of significant transboundary harm, which could 'now be considered a requirement under general international law'.[92] What the Court did through these steps was to balance the interest of legal certainty – specifically by not asserting jurisdiction over the other treaties where such consent had not been given – with the interest of allowing the 1975 Statute to evolve, by holding that it contained an evolutionary term, whose meaning could evolve in light of relevant developments in international law. Again, what we see is that given the relatively underdeveloped processes for law adjustment on the international plane, international tribunals often face the question of how to interpret applicable legal norms in a manner that takes account of relevant developments in wider international law without unduly undermining legal certainty.

Gabčikovo-Nagymaros is another significant example of the Court managing the challenge of taking account of subsequent developments in international law in interpreting an aging treaty while nevertheless attempting to ensure a sufficient degree of legal certainty. Here, one of Hungary's arguments as to why its termination of a 1977 treaty for the joint construction of a hydroelectric project was lawful was that subsequent developments in international environmental law precluded the

88 Ibid [53], [56].

89 Rather the Statute created an independent obligation for the parties to exercise their regulatory powers to protect and preserve the aquatic environment 'in accordance with applicable international agreements': see ibid [61]–[63].

90 Ibid [48].

91 Ibid [164].

92 Ibid [204].

performance of the treaty.[93] In response, drawing on relatively general treaty wording that was clearly open to such an interpretation, the Court emphasised that several provisions of the treaty permitted, and indeed required, the parties to take new environmental norms into account in their implementation of the treaty.[94] Importantly, this interpretation allowed the Court to favour treaty stability by rejecting Hungary's various arguments that the relevant treaty had been terminated without appearing backwards in terms of the environmental standards applied.[95]

Several individual opinions support the suggestion that the Court was, through this approach, navigating a delicate balance between allowing the applicable legal norms to evolve, given relevant developments in international law, and ensuring legal certainty for the treaty parties. For example, Judge Bedjaoui attempted to limit the consequences of the evolutionary interpretation undertaken by the Court, emphasising that, in general, treaties are to be interpreted consistent with the parties' intention at the time of conclusion[96] and a State in no way '*incurs evolutionary and indeterminate duties*'.[97] For him, 'there is good reason to protect the autonomy of the will', and thus, barring a basis in specific treaty language, such as the use of vague terms whose meaning is based on the general law, an evolutionary interpretive approach is not appropriate.[98] The contrast with Judge Weeramantry's approach is stark: for him the issue was not one of respecting State consent and treaty stability,

[93] This was one of five arguments advanced by Hungary to support the lawfulness of its purported termination of the treaty: *Gabčikovo-Nagymaros (Hungary/Slovakia)*, Judgment, ICJ Rep [1997] 7, [92]–[97].

[94] Ibid [112], [140]. The provisions of the 1977 treaty emphasised by the Court were Articles 15 and 19. Article 15 required the parties 'shall ensure, by the means specified in the joint contractual plan, that the quality of the water in the Danube is not impaired as a result of the construction and operation of the System of Locks', and Article 19 required '[t]he Contracting Parties shall, through the means specified in the joint contractual plan, ensure compliance with the obligations for the protection of nature arising in connection with the construction and operation of the System of Locks': ibid [18].

[95] *Gabčikovo-Nagymaros* (n 93) [103]–[104], [112] and generally [92]–[115]; Sep. Op. Bedjaoui [18] ('This is the first major case brought before the Court in which there is such a sensitive ecological background that it has moved to centre stage, threatening to divert attention from treaty law. International public opinion would not have understood had the Court disregarded the new law, whose application was called for by Hungary.' Translation by registry); Fitzmaurice (n 1) 368 (decision ultimately prioritises treaty stability and State responsibility over environmental concerns).

[96] *Gabčikovo-Nagymaros* (n 93) Sep. Op. Bedjaoui [14].

[97] Ibid (emphasis in original).

[98] Ibid [17]–[18].

but rather consistency with the present normative order. Since environmental treaties affect human rights, they 'cannot be applied in such a manner as to constitute a denial of human rights as understood at the time of their application', even if such standards have evolved since the treaty's conclusion.[99] In short, Judge Bedjaoui's interpretation achieved a reconciliation that heavily favours certainty for the treaty parties, whereas Judge Weeramantry placed priority on the interest of consistency of treaty obligations with the contemporary legal order. The two interpretations reflect fundamentally different views regarding the role of international tribunals in incrementally adapting treaty obligations.

The adjudicatory technique of allowing the applicable law to evolve by construing a treaty term as having an evolutionary meaning, and thus permitting change, while nevertheless claiming to respect the treaty parties' intent, was on full display in the Court's 2009 judgment in the *Dispute regarding Navigational and Related Rights.*[100] In this case, the parties were in dispute as to their respective rights under a dated bilateral river treaty, including regarding the scope of Costa Rica's right of free navigation under the treaty, which was subject to Nicaragua's right to regulate for environmental and other purposes. In justifying an evolutive interpretation of the term 'commerce', so as to allow Costa Rica's right of free navigation to cover new activities, such as the transport of persons for profit, the Court spent significant time explaining why its approach gave effect to, and thus implicitly did not override, the treaty parties' intent. After first acknowledging that there are situations where respecting the parties' common intention will require that a term be given its original meaning,[101] the Court noted:

> On the other hand, there are situations in which the parties' intent upon conclusion of the treaty was, or may be presumed to have been, to give the terms used ... a meaning or content capable of evolving, not one fixed once and for all, so as to make allowance for, among other things, developments in international law. In such instances it is indeed in order to respect the parties' common intention at the time the treaty was concluded, not to depart from it, that account should be taken of the meaning acquired by the terms in question upon each occasion on which the treaty is to be applied.[102]

[99] *Gabčikovo-Nagymaros* (n 93) Sep. Op. Weeramantry 114–15.
[100] *Dispute regarding Navigational and Related Rights (Costa Rica v Nicaragua)*, Judgment, ICJ Rep [2009] 213.
[101] Ibid [63].
[102] Ibid [64].

The question facing the Court was squarely one of change, namely that the commercial transport of passengers on the river had become more common since the treaty was concluded.[103] The Court reconciled the change its interpretation permitted with the need to ensure legal certainty by suggesting that its solution respected the treaty parties' common intention. In this respect, it noted that 'commerce' was 'a generic term referring to a class of activity', and that the treaty was entered into 'for an unlimited duration'.[104] In contrast, in their individual opinions, several judges accused the Court of failing to respect the treaty parties' intent, and thus, implicitly, of undermining legal certainty through its interpretation.[105] Notably, in another part of the judgment, concerning Nicaragua's power as sovereign to regulate in those areas of the river where Cost Rica had a right of navigation under the treaty, the Court also held that the legitimate public purposes that could be pursued by such regulation could have evolved since the conclusion of the treaty some 150 years ago '*in ways that could never have been anticipated by the Parties at the time*: protecting the environment is a notable example'.[106]

2. *Managing Change in Relevant Facts*

The ICJ has repeatedly faced the problem of dealing with changes in facts that affect the application of relevant legal norms. A good example is the 1999 judgment in the *Case concerning Kasikili/Sedudu Island* where the Court was charged with determining a boundary and the legal status of an island, partly on the basis of a nineteenth-century treaty that referred to the 'main channel' of the River Chobe without defining this term.[107] As Judge Weeramantry highlighted, the case had an environmental component because the area concerned was of ecological importance

[103] Ibid [58].

[104] Ibid [66]–[70]. Commentators have also suggested that the intention of the treaty parties or their 'time-will' is the key to determining whether an evolutive interpretation is justified: see e.g. Panos Merkouris, '(Inter)Temporal Considerations in the Interpretative Process of the VCLT: Do Treaties Endure, Perdure or Exdure?' (2014) 45 Netherlands YBIL 121, 143–44.

[105] *Navigational Rights* (n 100) Sep. Op. Skotnikov [4]–[7]; Dec. Guillame [15].

[106] *Navigational Rights* (n 100) [85], [89] (emphasis added). For another recent application of evolutionary interpretation, albeit in a dissenting opinion, where the approach was not endorsed by the Court, see *Alleged Violations of Sovereign Rights and Maritime Spaces in the Caribbean Sea (Nicaragua v Colombia)*, Judgment, ICJ Rep [2022] 266, Diss. Op. McRae [39]–[48].

[107] *Kasikili/Sedudu Island (Botswana/Namibia)*, Judgment, ICJ Rep [1999] 1045, [17]–[27].

and the Court could have regard to the need to preserve this resource in undertaking its task.[108] Importantly for present purposes, the Court held that it could take into account contemporary scientific knowledge '[i]n order to illuminate the meaning of' the treaty term agreed in 1890.[109] The tension between taking into account the contemporary scientific knowledge, while ensuring a degree of continuity in the legal concept being applied, was highlighted by Judge Higgins. She emphasised that the Court was applying 'a somewhat general term, decided upon by the parties in 1890 to a geographic and hydrographic situation much better understood today', which was distinguishable from a generic legal term that would itself evolve over time.[110] She stressed that:

> we must never lose sight of the fact that we are seeking to give flesh to the intention of the parties, expressed in generalized terms in 1890. We must trace a thread back to this point of departure.. . . our task is to decide what general idea the parties had in mind, and then make reality of that general idea through the use of contemporary knowledge.[111]

In contrast, Judge Weeramantry suggested that given the age of the treaty 'modern scientific criteria are not the indicia appropriate for determining what was commonly understood to be the main channel', the parties having had, in 1890, a non-technical understanding of this term.[112] The underlying question that the judges were grappling with is one seen in all of the adjudication settings studied in this book, namely how changes in relevant facts affect the application of a legal norm despite the content of the norm remaining constant. Clearly the relevant treaty term, referring to the 'main channel', was open to being affected by subsequent developments in technical knowledge. In many of the environmental cases studied, in taking account of changing factual circumstances, there will not be the same difficulty in tracing a thread back to the treaty parties' original intent. For example, when treaty drafters include in agreements terms such as 'due diligence' or 'best available technology', they no doubt recognise that the application of such terms will depend upon the state of relevant facts, such as scientific knowledge or technical capacity, at the time when the term is applied.[113]

[108] Ibid Diss. Op. Weeramantry [80]–[93], [103]–[119]. See also [4]–[6].
[109] *Kasikili/Sedudu* (n 61) [20].
[110] Ibid Dec. Higgins [1]–[3].
[111] Ibid [4].
[112] Ibid Diss. Op. Weeramantry [67]–[69], [29].
[113] See Chapter 6, text at nn 36–37.

A final example that raised both the question of change in relevant legal norms and change in relevant facts was the unique situation faced by the Court in 1995 in determining New Zealand's *Request for an Examination of the Situation*,[114] pursuant to a paragraph of the Court's 1974 *Nuclear Tests* judgment,[115] which concerned the legality of French atmospheric nuclear testing in the South Pacific, given, among other reasons, its environmental effects.[116] The context was that the 1974 judgment had found New Zealand's case against France without object in light of unilateral declarations by France that it would cease atmospheric nuclear testing and move to underground testing.[117] However, it further provided 'that if the basis of this Judgment were to be affected, the Applicant could request an examination of the situation in accordance with the provisions of the Statute', in a context where France had subsequently removed the jurisdictional consent enabling the proceedings,[118] meaning no new case could be instituted. Importantly, New Zealand's argument in 1995, in seeking to rely on this provision, was that the 'basis of the Judgment' had been 'affected' in light of subsequent developments in fact and law. New Zealand argued that by 1995 knowledge regarding the risks of underground nuclear testing had evolved and the assumption made in the 1974 judgment that underground testing was safe was erroneous, meaning 'the basis of the Judgment had been affected by virtue of changes in the factual situation'.[119] New Zealand sought to support its case through scientific evidence that had emerged in the period between 1974 and 1995.[120] New Zealand also argued that developments in international environmental law since 1974 had affected the basis of the judgment.[121]

In finding that the basis of the 1974 judgment concerned atmospheric nuclear testing, and accordingly had not been affected, the Court held that it could not take into account New Zealand's arguments concerning

[114] *Request for an Examination of the Situation in Accordance with Paragraph 63 of the Court's Judgment of 20 December 1974 in the Nuclear Tests (New Zealand v France) Case*, Order, ICJ Rep [1995] 288.

[115] *Nuclear Tests* (n 23) [63].

[116] See eg New Zealand's application instituting proceedings: *Nuclear Tests (New Zealand v France)* ICJ Pleadings, vol II, 8, [25]–[28].

[117] *Nuclear Tests* (n 23) [45]–[62], [65].

[118] Ibid [63].

[119] *Request for an Examination* (n 104) [32]–[33].

[120] See the discussion of this evidence in ibid Diss. Op. Weeramantry 348–58.

[121] *Request for an Examination* (n 104) [34].

the consequences of French underground nuclear testing since 1974, nor developments since then in international law.[122] In contrast, several dissenting judgments, which found that the basis of the 1974 judgment had been affected, developed an approach under which the Court's task was much less backwards looking and static, albeit at the risk of being seen to assert jurisdiction where the 1974 judgment provided no basis for it.[123] For example, Judge ad hoc Palmer suggested that in the majority approach: 'The law appears as some disembodied construct that is far removed from the concerns of the real world. The law is frozen in time, nothing beyond 1974 has any relevance or importance in interpreting paragraph 63, except a resumption of atmospheric testing.'[124] Similarly, Judge Weeramantry emphasised that: 'A court, faced with a science-oriented problem of present and future damage in 1995, cannot resolve it by ignoring the knowledge acquired between 1974 and 1995, and by applying to the problem in hand the knowledge of 1974. That would be an exercise in unreality.'[125] For Judge Weeramantry, '[i]f what seemed safe in 1974 now reveals its hazards in a manner not known or expected then, there is a responsibility lying upon the Court to take note of this change in the fundamental assumptions underlying its Judgment of 1974'.[126] In contrast, Judge Shahabuddeen made a strong consent-based point against allowing New Zealand's request, specifically that the Court could not have, through the proviso in the 1974 judgment, vested itself with jurisdiction over acts which post-dated France's termination of jurisdiction in that year.[127]

Ultimately, it is perhaps unsurprising that faced with interpreting the 1974 judgment the Court construed the provision enabling an examination of the situation narrowly, as this was the only possible basis for jurisdiction in 1995, and the Court, given its characteristics, is particularly sensitive to consent-based concerns on jurisdictional issues.[128] The above analysis demonstrates that the underlying functional question

[122] Ibid [62]–[63].

[123] See also ibid Diss. Op. Koroma, 378–79.

[124] Ibid Diss. Op. Palmer [96]. See also [77].

[125] Ibid Diss. Op. Weeramantry 340.

[126] Ibid 329.

[127] Ibid Sep. Op. Shahabuddeen 315.

[128] Judge ad hoc Palmer noted that the majority decision followed in a tradition of caution by the ICJ based on considerations of jurisdictional consent: ibid Diss. Op. Palmer [104]–[105]. Similarly: Malgosia Fitzmaurice, 'International Protection of the Environment' (2001) 293 RdC 9, 376. See above n 18.

facing the Court was how subsequent developments in facts, such as changes in scientific knowledge, or developments in international environmental norms, could affect the basis of the 1974 judgment. These questions arose sharply in this case given the immense expansion of international environmental law since the 1974 judgment,[129] and the potential for the factual assumptions underpinning the judgment to be affected by subsequent developments in scientific knowledge regarding the risks of underground nuclear testing. While the strictly consensual basis of the ICJ's jurisdiction clearly shaped how the Court responded to these questions, the case is also illustrative of the broader challenge facing international tribunals of responding to factual and legal change.

C. The Standard and Method of Review in ICJ Environmental Case Law

This section analyses how the problems of the appropriate standard and method of review have arisen in the ICJ's environmental case law, demonstrating that while the way these issues arise is shaped by contextual features of the Court's work, the underlying challenges and adjudicatory responses bear important similarities with those seen in the other adjudication settings studied in this book.

1. *Standard of Review in ICJ Environmental Case Law*

The problem of the intensity of an international tribunal's scrutiny of determinations made by domestic authorities and the consequent allocation of decision-making authority is a key problem that arises in ICJ litigation. While the terminology of a 'standard of review' is not entrenched in this context, the underlying functional problem is strongly present in relevant case law. As we will see below, the ICJ has already drawn to some degree on the approach developed by WTO adjudicators to the standard of review in SPS cases. However, the treaty context in which the ICJ operates may be quite different and typically varies between cases.

The question of the appropriate standard of review received explicit attention in the *Whaling* case, where Australia, ultimately successfully, argued that permits granted by Japan were not covered by the exception

[129] See ibid Diss. Op. Palmer [77].

in Article VIII(1) of the Whaling Convention, which allows whaling 'for purposes of scientific research'.[130] In order to determine whether Japan's program was 'for the purposes of' scientific research,[131] the Court asked 'whether in the use of lethal methods, the programme's design and implementation are reasonable in relation to achieving its stated objectives', adding that the 'standard of review is an objective one'.[132] The relevant background here included that Japan had argued that the Court should approach the standard of review in a similar way to the approach developed in SPS cases in the WTO context. Specifically, Japan argued that the Court should limit its review to whether a reasonable State could regard Japan's program as constituting scientific research and avoid being drawn into debate over the scientific merits of the program.[133]

The ICJ emphasised that it was not its role to 'pass judgment on the scientific merit or importance of' the scientific objectives of a whaling program, '[n]or . . . to decide whether the design and implementation of a programme are the best possible means of achieving its stated objectives'.[134] Nevertheless, the Court's analysis of a series of factors, drawn from the parties' arguments,[135] to concretise its test of whether the design and implementation of Japan's program was reasonable in relation to its stated objectives, suggests a standard of review that was far from affording Japan complete deference on the underlying determinations concerned.[136] For example, regarding Japan's decision to use lethal

[130] Whaling Convention art VIII(1).

[131] The Court first asked whether Japan's program 'involves scientific research', which it answered affirmatively in a few paragraphs: *Whaling* (n 41) [86], [127]. Australia had advanced criteria to inform the meaning of 'scientific research' under the Convention and the Court rejected these and avoided offering an alternative definition: [70]–[86].

[132] Ibid [67], see also [88].

[133] See CR 2013/22, [19]–[20], [31] (Lowe); Counter-Memorial of Japan (n 79) [9.7], [9.16]–[9.17]. For further background regarding how the issue of the 'standard of review' arose over the course of the written and oral pleadings see Hamamoto (n 63) 39–42; Caroline E Foster, *Global Regulatory Standards in Environmental and Health Disputes: Regulatory Coherence, Due Regard, and Due Diligence* (OUP 2021) 76–78.

[134] *Whaling* (n 41) [88]. Similarly [69]. The majority did not engage with the issue of achieving an appropriate institutional balance under the Convention vis-à-vis the Scientific Committee: Guillaume Gros, 'The ICJ's Handling of Science in the Whaling in the Antarctic Case: A Whale of a Case?' (2015) 6 JIDS 578, 604.

[135] See *Whaling* (n 41) [88].

[136] In addition to endorsing the terminology 'standard of review', the *Whaling* judgment may be significant for the Court's focus on the design and implementation of the State measure concerned. Potentially, this offers a method of reviewing State measures that is independent of the regulating State's motivations: see Caroline E Foster, 'Methodologies

methods in its research program, the Court emphasised Japan's failure to explain why it had not considered the use of non-lethal means to achieve its research objectives.[137] Then, in reviewing the scale of lethal methods used, the Court stated that while it was not seeking 'to second-guess the scientific judgments made by individual scientists or Japan', it would examine whether, on the evidence, Japan had 'demonstrated a reasonable basis' for the sample sizes selected in light of the program's stated research objectives,[138] and raised numerous doubts in this regard,[139] ultimately finding that the selected sample sizes were not reasonable.[140] Finally, the Court reasoned that the gap between Japan's target sample sizes and the actual take of whales suggested 'that the target sample sizes are larger than are reasonable in relation to achieving' the stated research objectives.[141]

Several dissenting opinions criticised the Court for having, through the above analysis, employed an inappropriately intense form of scrutiny and pronounced on matters that, under the relevant treaty regime, initially fell within Japan's discretion as the regulating State, subject to evaluation by the Scientific Committee of the IWC.[142] For example, Judge Owada, dissenting, submitted that the Court was wrong to include within the scope of its review matters concerning the design and implementation of Japan's whaling program,[143] when, under the Whaling Convention, such matters were 'primarily left to the discretionary decision of the granting Government' and only subject to review by the Scientific Committee.[144] By expanding the scope of its review in this way, Judge Owada submitted that the majority had wrongly conducted a de novo review of Japan's program,[145] and taken a position on contested issues of scientific

and Motivations: Was Japan's Whaling Programme for Purposes of Scientific Research' in Fitzmaurice and Tamada (eds), *Whaling in the Antarctic* (n 70) 36–37.

137 See *Whaling* (n 41) [141]–[144].

138 Ibid [185], similarly [172].

139 Ibid [181], [188]–[189], [198].

140 Ibid [224]–[225].

141 Ibid [212], generally [209]–[212].

142 Under Paragraph 30 of the Schedule to the Whaling Convention there is a process established whereby States are obliged to provide proposed permits for scientific whaling to the IWC before they are issued in order to allow a sub-body, the Scientific Committee, to review and comment upon them.

143 *Whaling* (n 41) Diss. Op. Owada [32].

144 Ibid [19]–[21], [38].

145 Ibid [38].

merit.[146] For him, under the Convention, the Court's role was limited to ensuring that a State was acting in good faith and observing the established procedures.[147] While the concept of reasonableness could assist in checking that a decision was not '"arbitrary" or "patently out of bounds"', besides such situations, the Court should not have substituted its own discretion for that of the regulating State.[148] Similarly, in their dissenting opinions, Judges Abraham and Yusuf accused the Court of impermissibly assessing the scientific merit of Japan's program and pronouncing on matters that were, under the Convention regime, subject to review by the Scientific Committee.[149]

Yet the approach of the majority judgment does not differ radically from the legal techniques used in similar contexts by the other international tribunals considered in this book, which also often stressed that they were not well placed to engage in substitutionary de novo review of determinations involving the application of specialised forms of non-legal expertise that they did not hold.[150] Similarly to the approach seen in the other tribunals studied in this book, the ICJ took the view that it was not well placed to scrutinise the scientific merit of the underlying determinations, or whether the means chosen by the regulating State to achieve its goals were the best possible ones available, but, on the other hand, Japan's reliance on the scientific whaling exception had to be subject to a degree of independent scrutiny. Through its analysis, the ICJ made a series of important choices that defined what would count as

[146] Ibid [25], [38].
[147] Ibid [21], [28].
[148] Ibid [39]–[40].
[149] See ibid Diss. Op. Abraham [33]–[36], [38]; Diss. Op. Yusuf [17], [44], [61].
[150] Cf case law discussed in Chapters 2(1)(b) and 5(C)(1). Gros argues that the WTO Appellate Body's approach from the SPS context was transposed very inexactly, since while the established WTO approach focuses on the decision-making process involved in the regulating member's risk assessment, in *Whaling* the ICJ did not focus on the decision-making process surrounding Japan's decision to issue the relevant permits, but on whaling program itself: Gros (n 134) 602–03, 606, 608–09. While it is correct that the established WTO approach is largely focused on the member's risk assessment process, panels are required to determine, as a final step, whether the results of a risk assessment 'sufficiently warrant' the SPS measure concerned: Appellate Body Report, *United States – Continued Suspension of Obligations in the EC – Hormones Dispute*, WT/DS320/AB/R, adopted 14 November 2008, [591]. Nevertheless, the criticism that the ICJ's analysis should have focused on Japan's decision to grant the special permits under Article VIII, rather than the program itself, is well founded and was noted by several judges: *Whaling* (n 41) Sep. Op. Xue [12]; Diss. Op. Yusuf [12]–[13], [17]; Dec. Keith [8].

an adequate decision-making process for issuing a permit for scientific whaling.

The question of the appropriate standard of review, and the consequent allocation of powers between international adjudicators and domestic authorities, has also been raised by recent ICJ cases concerning the obligation of States to conduct an environmental impact assessment (EIA) in the context of activities that pose a risk of significant transboundary harm. As noted above, in *Pulp Mills* the Court interpreted an applicable treaty obligation:

> in accordance with a practice which in recent years has gained so much acceptance among States that it may now be considered a requirement under general international law to undertake an environmental impact assessment where there is a risk that the proposed industrial activity may have a significant adverse impact in a transboundary context, in particular, on a shared resource.[151]

The Court further stated that:

> it is for each State to determine in its domestic legislation or in the authorization process for the project, the specific content of the environmental impact assessment required in each case, having regard to the nature and magnitude of the proposed development and its likely adverse impact on the environment as well as to the need to exercise due diligence in conducting such an assessment.[152]

This statement has often been 'interpreted as meaning that the environmental impact assessment obligation has no independent content and that there is simply a *renvoi* to domestic law'.[153] However, the dominant view that has emerged in recent ICJ case law and commentary is that the appropriate standard of review is not one of complete deference to the national level.[154] Several judges in individual opinions appended to the 2015 merits judgment in the *Certain Activities* and *Construction of a Road* cases emphasised that while domestic authorities are left a certain

[151] *Pulp Mills* (n 86) [204].

[152] Ibid [205]. Affirmed in *Certain Activities Carried Out by Nicaragua in the Border Area (Costa Rica v Nicaragua) and Construction of a Road in Costa Rica along the San Juan River (Nicaragua v Costa Rica)*, Judgment, ICJ Rep [2015] 665, [104].

[153] *Certain Activities/Construction of a Road* (n 152) Sep. Op. Dugard [18].

[154] See also Alan Boyle, 'Developments in the International Law of Environmental Impact Assessments and Their Relation to the Espoo Convention' (2011) 20 RECIEL 227, 229 (drawing on the International Law Commission's work in this area and arguing there is international oversight of domestic-level EIAs).

level of discretion – reflecting that they are better placed to determine the precise details of an EIA – a degree of international scrutiny is retained through the requirement that the assessment be conducted in accordance with the standard of 'due diligence' in the prevailing circumstances.[155] Again, this is the functional question of the intensity with which international adjudicators should scrutinise the conduct of national-level decision-makers and the consequent impact on the allocation of decision-making power. The significant deference afforded to national authorities is arguably appropriate, given their greater familiarity with local circumstances that will inform the content of an EIA, compared to detached international adjudicators. However, the fact that the obligation to conduct an EIA is subject to a variable, fact-specific standard of due diligence in the circumstances shows that space for international scrutiny is maintained. Future decisions by international adjudicators in scrutinising domestic-level EIAs may further clarify what counts as an acceptable domestic decision-making process in this area.

2. *Methods of Review in ICJ Environmental Case Law*

In the environmental case law reviewed, there are important functional similarities between the methods of review used by the ICJ and those employed in the other adjudication contexts studied considered in this book, although the methods of review are shaped by the particular

155 *Certain Activities/Construction of a Road* (n 152) Sep. Op. Donoghue [15]; Sep. Op. Dugard [18]. Judge Bhandari also outlined minimum international standards for conducting an EIA: Sep. Op. Bhandari [41]–[46]. The precise relationship between States' obligation to exercise due diligence to prevent significant transboundary harm and the obligation to conduct an EIA is debated. In *Certain Activities/Construction of a Road* (n 152) some judges emphasised that the obligation to conduct an EIA is not free-standing but arises from States' general due diligence obligation: Donoghue (n 36) [13]; Sep. Op. Owada [18], [20]–[21]. Contrast Dugard, ibid [9]–[11], [17] (conducting an EIA is an independent obligation). See further Neil Craik, 'The Duty to Cooperate in the Customary Law of Environmental Impact Assessment' (2020) 69 ICLQ 239 (arguing that the obligation to conduct an EIA should be understood as part of the obligation to cooperate, rather than as part of the obligation of due diligence in relation to potential transboundary harm); Tamar Meshel, 'Unmasking the Substance Behind the Process: Why the Duty to Cooperate in International Water Law Is Really a Substantive Principle' (2019) 47 Denver JILP 29 (similar); Jutta Brunnée, 'Procedure and Substance in International Environmental Law' (2020) 405 RdC 81, 149–50 (procedural requirements such as conducting an EIA have an independent existence in customary international law and are also part of the obligation to exercise due diligence in the face of risks of significant transboundary harm).

contexts in which the ICJ adjudicates. Section 2(a) will demonstrate that while the terminology of necessity testing is not entrenched in the ICJ case law reviewed, the Court has at times used a test of reasonableness, developed from the specific treaty framework concerned, which involves asking whether an alternative measure, less restrictive of other legally protected interests, could have been employed. Section 2(b) suggests that there are only very limited signs of the ICJ employing proportionality balancing stricto sensu in its case law.

(a) Necessity or Least Restrictive Means Testing in the ICJ

Although the terminology of necessity testing is not entrenched in the ICJ's case law, the Court has repeatedly used a test of reasonableness developed from the specific treaty or legal context concerned. This test often involves asking whether there were alternative measures, less restrictive of other legally protected interests, which the regulating State could have employed, as would be involved in a necessity/least restrictive means test. Again, the *Whaling* case is instructive. As noted above, the factors used by the Court in formulating its test of whether a whaling program's design and implementation were reasonable in relation to the stated scientific objectives included 'decisions regarding the use of lethal methods' and 'the scale of the programme's use of lethal sampling'.[156] In a crucial part of its analysis, the Court highlighted several reasons why Japan's research plan should have included greater analysis of the feasibility of using non-lethal methods to achieve its research objectives.[157] These included that Japan had claimed that it did not use lethal methods more than was necessary to achieve its research objectives, but non-lethal methods were not practical in some circumstances or 'would involve "unrealistic" amounts of time and expense'.[158] The Court also noted that as Australia's experts had 'referred to significant advances in a wide range of non-lethal research techniques over the past 20 years', these should have been analysed in the design of Japan's program. Additionally, as discussed above, Japan was under a duty to give due regard to IWC resolutions and guidelines, which called 'upon States parties to take into account whether research objectives can be achieved using non-lethal methods'.[159]

[156] *Whaling* (n 41) [88].
[157] Ibid [137]–[144].
[158] Ibid [129], [137].
[159] Ibid [137].

The ensuing analysis strongly resembles least restrictive means testing, with the Court highlighting Japan's failure to make greater 'use of non-lethal methods in order to reduce or eliminate the need for lethal sampling',[160] and failure to compare the relative costs of a program that more extensively used non-lethal alternatives.[161] As scientific research was the protected aim under the relevant treaty provision, the Court, just as least restrictive means testing would suggest, held that lethal sampling could not be used on a greater scale than was reasonable for achieving the program's stated scientific objectives, for example for the extraneous purpose of funding research.[162] At one point the Court even noted Japan's failure to refute the view of one of Australia's experts that Japan's program could attain 'nearly the same level of accuracy' as that sought with a smaller lethal take.[163] While the Court did not use the label of necessity or least restrictive means testing, functionally the method of review employed operated in a very similar way, balancing the interest protected by the scientific whaling exception with the partially competing protected interest of conservation by ensuring that Japan could not use lethal methods on a greater scale than was required to achieve its scientific objectives.[164]

A reasonableness test developed from the relevant treaty framework that operated very similarly to least restrictive means testing was also employed in the 2009 judgment in the *Dispute regarding Navigational and Related Rights*. In this case the Court scrutinised various Nicaraguan regulations concerning use of the River San Juan, which were challenged by Costa Rica as an unreasonable restriction on its right of free navigation under the applicable treaty, and defended by Nicaragua, which enjoyed sovereignty over the river, as serving other legitimate purposes under the treaty such as environmental protection, law enforcement, and navigational safety.[165] At the start of this part of its analysis, the Court

[160] Ibid [144], similarly [141].
[161] Ibid [143].
[162] Ibid [94], [142].
[163] Ibid [190].
[164] The point that the Court's analysis effectively involved necessity testing, a variant of proportionality analysis, has been recognised by other commentators: see eg Asier Garrido-Muñoz, 'Managing Uncertainty: The International Court of Justice, "Objective Reasonableness" and the Judicial Function' (2017) 30 LJIL 457, 467–71; Enzo Cannizzaro, 'Proportionality and Margin of Appreciation in the *Whaling* Case: Reconciling Antithetical Doctrines?' (2016) 27 EJIL 1061, 1062–64, 1068–69.
[165] Several of the Nicaraguan regulations were found to be justified: *Navigational Rights* (n 100) [88]–[89], [104], [109], [118], [141].

held that Nicaragua's power to regulate Costa Rica's exercise of its right of free navigation under the applicable treaty was 'not unlimited, being tempered by the rights and obligations of the Parties'.[166] More specifically, the Court, drawing on the parties' arguments, set out various requirements that a regulation would have to satisfy to comply with the treaty, including that the regulation must not render impossible or substantially impede the exercise of the treaty right of free navigation, 'must have a legitimate purpose', 'must not be discriminatory', and 'must not be unreasonable, which means that its negative impact on the exercise of the right in question must not be manifestly excessive when measured against the protection afforded to the purpose invoked'.[167] In setting out the 'factual context' for its assessment of Nicaragua's regulations, the Court also noted that:

> a court examining the reasonableness of a regulation must recognize that the regulator, in this case the State with sovereignty over the river, has the primary responsibility for assessing the need for regulation and for choosing, on the basis of its knowledge of the situation, the measure that it deems most appropriate to meet that need. It will not be enough in a challenge to a regulation simply to assert in a general way that it is unreasonable. Concrete and specific facts will be required to persuade a court to come to that conclusion.[168]

In applying this test to the Nicaraguan measures contested by Costa Rica, the Court reasoned that for some of Nicaragua's measures Costa Rica had not demonstrated that the alternative measures it proposed were sufficient to achieve the regulatory aims pursued by Nicaragua,[169] or were practical in terms of cost and effectiveness.[170] Again, while this reasonableness test does not have the established structure of necessity testing as developed in WTO jurisprudence, functionally it is operating in a similar way,[171] and the resulting 'formula has the potential for broader adoption and evolution'.[172] Through the test it set out, the Court

[166] *Navigational Rights* (n 100) [87].

[167] *Navigational Rights* (n 100) [87]. See also [86]. On the origins of the test enunciated in the parties' pleadings see also Foster (n 133) 84. This approach to assessing the reasonableness of a measure has been largely reaffirmed in a different legal context in *Certain Iranian Assets (Islamic Republic of Iran v United States of America)*, Judgment, 30 March 2023, [147]–[149] and generally [144]–[157].

[168] *Navigational Rights* (n 100) [101], [98]. Affirmed in *Certain Iranian Assets* (n 167) [146].

[169] *Navigational Rights* (n 100) [106].

[170] Ibid [128].

[171] See similarly Muñoz (n 164) 469.

[172] Foster (n 133) 58, 84.

balanced Nicaragua's right to regulate for legitimate purposes, as sovereign over the river, against Costa Rica's partially competing right of free navigation under the applicable treaty, including by assessing whether the alternative measures proposed by the complaining party would secure the legitimate regulatory aims pursued by the respondent State and were practically available. Like many of the adjudicatory decisions reviewed in other chapters of this book, the ICJ was careful not to conclude without strong evidence that alternative measures proposed by the complaining party were reasonably available, reflecting that an overly strict form of necessity testing can undermine States' legitimate regulatory autonomy.

Necessity testing and the consideration of potential alternative less restrictive measures also featured briefly in *Gabčikovo-Nagymaros* given Hungary's reliance on necessity as a circumstance precluding wrongfulness under customary international law. In explaining why Hungary had not established this excuse, the Court emphasised that even if Hungary faced serious ecological risks, as it claimed, it had alternative measures available, other than abandoning the agreed works, for responding to such risks, even if the alternative measures envisaged by the Court would have been more costly.[173] The Court's stance on the availability of alternative measures reflects that in the law of State responsibility necessity can only be invoked as a circumstance precluding wrongfulness where the relevant act (involving non-compliance with a State's international obligation) is the only means of safeguarding an essential interest of State against a grave and imminent peril.[174] Yet despite this particular context, which informed the strictness of the necessity test applied, the method of review operated to mediate between two legally protected, partly competing interests, specifically Czechoslovakia's interest in Hungary performing the agreed works under the applicable treaty and Hungary's interest in being able to safeguard an essential ecological interest of State.

(b) Proportionality Balancing Stricto Sensu in ICJ Environmental Case Law

In the ICJ cases reviewed, there are only very limited signs of the ICJ engaging in proportionality balancing stricto sensu where beyond

[173] *Gabčikovo-Nagymaros* (n 93) [55]–[57].

[174] See ILC, 'Draft Articles on the Responsibility of States for Internationally Wrongful Acts with Commentaries' [2001] II(2) ILC Ybk 31, art 25(1)(a) and [15] of commentary; James Crawford, *State Responsibility: The General Part* (CUP 2013) 311–12.

checking whether a measure was the least restrictive means available to achieve a legitimate regulatory aim, adjudicators proceed to balance in an open-ended manner the relative importance of the competing legally protected interests at stake. In *Navigational Rights*, as noted in the last subsection, the Court, in stating the criteria it would apply to determine if Nicaragua's regulations complied with the treaty, suggested a final step whereby a regulation 'must not be unreasonable, which means that its negative impact on the exercise of the right in question must not be manifestly excessive when measured against the protection afforded to the purpose invoked'.[175] On its face, this formulation may be read as permitting proportionality balancing stricto sensu since it contemplates weighing the negative impact on the right affected (e.g. freedom of navigation) against the protection a measure affords to the permissible regulatory purpose pursued and possibly ruling the measure 'manifestly excessive' even where it was the only, or the only reasonably available, way to secure the relevant regulatory aim.[176] Yet, when one considers the scrutiny applied to the contested Nicaraguan regulations, as demonstrated in the last subsection, key parts of the Court's analysis resemble necessity testing rather than proportionality balancing stricto sensu, with the Court holding that the proposed alternative measures did not qualify as true alternatives because they would not secure the relevant regulatory aims,[177] or were not practically available in terms of cost or effectiveness.[178] Furthermore, to some degree the applicable treaty regime provided a pre-existing balance between the parties' competing interests that the Court could apply to resolve some of the disagreements concerning the contested Nicaraguan regulations, without itself engaging in an open-ended balancing exercise.[179] Accordingly, despite the test formulated by the Court in this case seeming to contemplate proportionality balancing stricto sensu, the method of review actually applied in scrutinising Nicaragua's regulations resembled least restrictive means testing.

Gabčíkovo-Nagymaros is a clear example of the ICJ engaging in a true balancing of the competing interests at stake; however, this occurred in the context of the law of countermeasures where such balancing is well

[175] *Navigational Rights* (n 100) [87(5)]. Affirmed and applied in *Certain Iranian Assets* (n 167) [149], [156]–[157].

[176] Also reading it as potentially permitting proportionality balancing stricto sensu: Henckels (n 119) 161.

[177] *Navigational Rights* (n 100) [106].

[178] Ibid [128].

[179] See e.g. ibid [114]–[124].

accepted. The Court held that Czechoslovakia's unilateral implementation of a variant of the original project, after Hungary's internationally wrongful suspension and termination of its part of the agreed works, 'was not a lawful countermeasure because it was not proportionate',[180] given it involved Czechoslovakia 'unilaterally assuming control of a shared resource, and thereby depriving Hungary of its right to an equitable and reasonable share of the' watercourse concerned.[181] This use of proportionality balancing stricto sensu reflects the specific context of the law of countermeasures, where it is accepted that the relative importance of the rights protected by the primary rules at issue is one of the factors to be weighed in determining whether a countermeasure is commensurate with the injury suffered due to the initial internationally wrongful act.[182] The case does not support the idea that proportionality balancing stricto sensu is emerging as a generally applicable method of review in the ICJ.

D. The Contribution of the ICJ to Broader Processes of Dispute Resolution

In the environmental cases reviewed there are repeated examples of the ICJ undertaking a prospectively focused and facilitative style of adjudication that aims to encourage future cooperation between the parties and provide guidance on the applicable legal framework, while leaving the parties some room to resolve their dispute and similar disputes that may arise between them in future. These practices are significant because they provide evidence of international adjudication contributing to wider processes of dispute resolution and complementing other means of dispute settlement, such as post-adjudication negotiation between the parties.[183]

The ICJ's judgments in the *Fisheries Jurisdiction* cases[184]– which concerned Iceland's unilateral extension of its exclusive fisheries zone

180 *Gabčikovo-Nagymaros* (n 93) [87].

181 Ibid [85]. On this aspect of the judgment see further Afshin Akhtarkhavari, *Global Governance of the Environment: Environmental Principles and Change in International Law and Politics* (Edward Elgar 2011) 133–39.

182 ILC, Articles on State Responsibility (n 174) art 51 and commentary to art 51, [6]–[7]; *Gabčikovo-Nagymaros* (n 93) [85]; Crawford (n 174) 697–99.

183 See also the analysis of this aspect of the ICJ's environmental jurisprudence in Akhtarkhavari (n 181) 116–26.

184 *Fisheries Jurisdiction* (*United Kingdom v Iceland*), Merits, Judgment ICJ Rep [1974] 3; *Fisheries Jurisdiction* (*Federal Republic of Germany v Iceland*), Merits, Judgment, ICJ Rep [1974] 175.

and the processes through which conservation measures for the relevant fish stocks should be taken – are a prime example of the Court placing the parties under an obligation to cooperate and allowing them scope to resolve their dispute. In these cases, the Court noted that '[t]he most appropriate method for the solution of the dispute is clearly that of negotiation', given that resolving the contested issues required 'detailed scientific knowledge of the fishing grounds' and 'the relevant information and expertise would be mainly in the possession of the Parties'.[185] While the Court set out a number of principles that the parties' negotiations had to take into account, including the need to pay due regard to the interests of third States, the resolution of the dispute was left for the parties.[186] This approach reflected that the Court found that the parties had an:

> obligation to keep under review the fishery resources in the disputed waters and to examine together, in the light of scientific and other available information, the measures required for the conservation and development, and equitable exploitation, of those resources, taking into account any international agreement in force between them.[187]

In short, these cases are an example of the Court clarifying the applicable legal framework and passing parts of the dispute back to the parties for further negotiation.[188] However, it should be noted that the dispute was not actually resolved through negotiations between the parties, as contemplated by the Court, but through wider developments at the diplomatic level, specifically with the establishment of the Exclusive Economic Zone as part of the conclusion of UNCLOS.[189]

185 Ibid (UK) [73] ('The Court would, for this reason, meet with difficulties if it were itself to attempt to lay down a precise scheme for an equitable adjustment of the rights involved.'). Ibid (FRG) [65].

186 Ibid (UK) [79(3)–(4)]; Ibid (FRG) [77(3)–(4)]. See also *Fisheries Jurisdiction* (*UK*), Dec. Singh 41–42 (supporting the Court's approach including as the issues concerned 'best lend themselves to settlement by negotiation'); Sep. Op. De Castro 103–04 (similar); Sep. Op. Dillard 67–71 (supporting the Court's role in providing guidelines to facilitate negotiations in disputes regarding shared resources). Criticising these aspects of the Judgment: Diss. Op. Gros [17], [27]–[34]; Diss Op. Petrén 159–60.

187 *Fisheries Jurisdiction* (*UK*) (n 184) [72], [79(4)(e)]. The Court also reasoned that the concept of preferential rights, recognised in the Judgment, implicitly required negotiations between the parties: [74], [62]. Similarly: *Fisheries Jurisdiction (FRG)* (n 184) [64], [66], [54].

188 The suggestion that this is how the Court saw its role in this dispute is confirmed by *Fisheries Jurisdiction (UK)* (n 184) [75], [78]; *Fisheries Jurisdiction (FRG)* (n 184) [67], [69].

189 Regarding developments after the Judgment, see eg Cesare PR Romano, *The Peaceful Settlement of International Environmental Disputes: A Pragmatic Approach* (Kluwer Law International 2000) 170–73.

Gabčikovo-Nagymaros is another prominent example of a partly prospectively focused and facilitative style of adjudication being undertaken by the ICJ. In the prospective part of the judgment the Court held that the parties were under a legal obligation to negotiate regarding how the treaty's objectives could be fulfilled going forward, taking into account current environmental standards.[190] This must be understood in light of the fact that the agreement submitting the case to the Court provided that once the judgment was given, the parties would negotiate on the modalities for its execution.[191] Yet it is significant in terms of the approach to adjudication emerging from the judgment that the Court's guidance was largely at the level of broad principle rather than specifics. In short, having made the major finding that the treaty remained in force, and was able to incorporate contemporary environmental standards, it was for the parties to negotiate to bring the project as it had been implemented within that regime.[192] Interestingly, in the part of the judgment addressing the legal consequences of the internationally wrongful acts that the ICJ found had been committed by both parties, while the Court found that both Hungary and Slovakia were under an obligation to pay compensation to each other, it suggested 'that the issue of compensation could satisfactorily be resolved in the framework of an overall settlement if each of the Parties were to renounce or cancel all financial claims and counter-claims'.[193] The Court also suggested that the parties could 'profit from the assistance and expertise of a third party'.[194] All of these aspects of the judgment highlight that the ICJ employed a partly prospective and facilitative approach to adjudicating the case, drawing on the basis provided in the agreement submitting the dispute

[190] *Gabčikovo-Nagymaros* (n 93) [139]–[142], [155(2)(B)]. Judge Bedjaoui highlighted that the obligation to negotiate in good faith flowed from general international law concerning the environment and watercourses, not just the treaty: Sep. Op. Bedjaoui [69].

[191] Special Agreement art 5(2), cited in *Gabčikovo-Nagymaros* (n 93) p. 12. See also art 2(2) of the Special Agreement: 'The Court is also requested to determine the legal consequences . . . arising from its Judgment'.

[192] *Gabčikovo-Nagymaros* (n 93) [144]–[147]. It is worth noting in this regard that the Court avoided engaging in detail with the extensive scientific evidence that had been presented by both parties: see [54], [140]. Stephen Stec, 'Do Two Wrongs Make a Right? Adjudicating Sustainable Development in the Danube Dam Case' (1999) 29 Golden Gate University Law Review 317, 377–80.

[193] *Gabčikovo-Nagymaros* (n 93) [153]. See also [155(1)(D)].

[194] Ibid [143].

to the Court, in which the parties had clearly envisaged the need for subsequent negotiations to resolve the dispute.[195]

As is well known, the *Gabčikovo-Nagymaros* judgment has not resolved the parties' dispute, despite repeated negotiations between the parties over some twenty years.[196] While there are a range of wider political factors, independent of the Court's judgment, which explain the failure to resolve the dispute,[197] the case also highlights the potential pitfalls of a facilitative approach to adjudication, namely that if a judgment is too open ended it may not give the parties sufficient guidance to resolve their dispute.[198] This risk is significant and must be remembered. Nevertheless, *Gabčikovo-Nagymaros* remains a striking example of a facilitative and prospectively focused mode of adjudication, which attempts to assist the disputing parties to rebuild their relationship.[199]

[195] Consider also Pieter HF Bekker, 'Gabcikovo-Nagymaros Project (Hungary/Slovakia), Judgement' (1998) 92 AJIL 273, 277–78; Loris Marotti and Paolo Palchetti, 'Of Restoring Compliance, Lex Specialis and Intersecting Wrongs: The Question of "Remedies" in *Gabčikovo-Nagymaros*' in Serena Forlati, Makane Moïse Mbengue and Brian McGarry (eds), *The Gabčíkovo-Nagymaros Judgment and Its Contribution to the Development of International Law* (Brill Nijhoff 2020) 155, 159.

[196] Regarding developments since the Judgment, see especially Boldizsár Nagy, 'The ICJ Judgment in the Gabčíkovo-Nagymaros Project Case and Its Aftermath: Success or Failure?' in Hélène Ruiz Fabri and others (eds), *A Bridge Over Troubled Waters: Dispute Resolution in the Law of International Watercourses and the Law of the Sea* (Brill Nijhoff 2021) 40–53.

[197] On these wider factors, see generally ibid 40–53, 55–56; Gábor Baranyai and Gábor Bartus, 'Anatomy of a Deadlock: A Systemic Analysis of Why the Gabčíkovo–Nagymaros Dam Dispute Is Still Unresolved' (2016) 18 Water Policy 39, 45–48.

[198] Criticising the judgment on such grounds, eg Laurence Boisson de Chazournes and Antonella Angelini, 'After "The Court Rose": The Rise of Diplomatic Means to Implement the Pronouncements of the International Court of Justice' (2012) 11 LPICT 1, 21; Christine Gray, 'Remedies' in Cesare PR Romano, Karen J Alter and Yuval Shany (eds), *The Oxford Handbook of International Adjudication* (OUP 2013) 877–78; Baranyai and Bartus (n 197) 45–48.

[199] Kooijmans (n 2) 749. Address by Judge Stephen M Schwebel, President of the ICJ, to the UN General Assembly, 27 October 1997 <www.icj-cij.org/public/files/press-releases/9/3009.pdf>. Other examples of the ICJ performing such a role, from beyond a strictly environmental context, also exist. See eg *Obligation to Negotiate Access to the Pacific Ocean (Bolivia v Chile)*, Judgment, ICJ Rep [2018] 507, [176], and in the same case, Dec. Yusuf [8]–[11], and Diss. Op. Daudet [57]–[58]. Another example is *Passage through the Great Belt (Finland v Denmark)*, Provisional Measures, Order of 29 July 1991, ICJ Rep [1991] 12, [33]–[35] where although the Court declined to indicate provisional measures, it noted that 'pending a decision of the Court on the merits, any negotiation between the Parties with a view to achieving a direct and friendly settlement is to be welcomed'. See also Sep. Op. Broms, ICJ Rep [1991] 37, 38–39; Dec. Tarrasov, 23–24. Contrast Sep. Op. Oda, 26–27.

The ICJ's 2015 judgment in the *Certain Activities* and *Construction of a Road* cases, between Costa Rica and Nicaragua, also provides significant evidence of the Court providing guidance on the legal obligations applicable to the parties' relationship and emphasising the need for future cooperation.[200] In the *Construction of a Road* case, the Court found that Costa Rica, in constructing a road close to Nicaragua's territory, had not fulfilled its obligation to perform an EIA, given the risk of significant transboundary harm posed by the project.[201] Significantly, the Court noted that for any further works in the area, 'Costa Rica remains under an obligation to prepare an appropriate environmental impact assessment . . . should they carry a risk of significant transboundary harm.'[202] The Court also noted 'Nicaragua's commitment, made in the course of the oral proceedings, that it will co-operate with Costa Rica in assessing the impact of such works' and highlighted in this regard that 'if the circumstances so require, Costa Rica will have to consult in good faith with Nicaragua . . . to determine the appropriate measures to prevent significant transboundary harm or minimize the risk thereof'.[203] In considering the situation going forward, as part of deciding on the remedies requested, the Court also noted that:

> Costa Rica has begun mitigation works in order to reduce the adverse effects of the construction of the road on the environment. It expects that Costa Rica will continue to pursue these efforts in keeping with its due diligence obligation to monitor the effects of the project on the environment. It further reiterates the value of ongoing co-operation between the Parties in the performance of their respective obligations in connection with the San Juan River.[204]

200 *Certain Activities/Construction of a Road* (n 152).

201 Ibid [153]–[162].

202 Ibid [173].

203 Ibid. This reflected the position under general international law that where an 'environmental impact assessment confirms that there is a risk of significant transboundary harm, the State planning to undertake the activity is required . . . to notify and consult in good faith with the potentially affected State, where that is necessary to determine the appropriate measures to prevent or mitigate that risk': [104]. The Court did not examine Costa Rica's failure to notify and consult with Nicaragua, reasoning that Costa Rica had not complied with the prior obligation to conduct an EIA: [168]. Judge Donoghue criticised the Court's formulation of the obligation to notify and consult neighbouring States as too restrictive, noting such an obligation could arise at other stages, before an EIA was completed, and could include matters besides risk mitigation: Sep. Op. Donoghue [21]–[24].

204 *Certain Activities/Construction of a Road* (n 152) [228].

In the *Certain Activities* case brought by Costa Rica, while the Court found that Nicaragua had not breached any procedural obligations owed to Costa Rica as a neighbouring State, it concluded this part of its analysis by noting Nicaragua's commitment to perform a new EIA before any substantial expansion of its dredging program, including to assess the risk of transboundary harm and to 'notify, and consult with, Costa Rica'.[205] Additionally, in relation to the compensation that the Court found Costa Rica was owed, for material damage resulting from Nicaragua's violations of Costa Rica's territorial sovereignty, the Court directed the parties to engage in negotiations to agree the amount of compensation, and provided that if no agreement was reached within twelve months either party could request the Court to determine the amount of compensation.[206] All of these aspects of the case provide evidence of the ICJ adjudicating with a partly prospective focus and clarifying the legal obligations of the parties in an effort to facilitate their future interactions.

In the *Pulp Mills* case, the Court also emphasised the duty of the parties to cooperate prospectively, after it explained at length how the cooperative mechanism established by the relevant bilateral river treaty operated and why Uruguay had breached the procedural obligations owed.[207] Specifically, after concluding that Argentina had not proved that Uruguay had breached the treaty obligation to protect and preserve the aquatic environment and to prevent pollution,[208] the Court added a paragraph concerning the parties' ongoing monitoring obligations, which arose from the obligation to cooperate through the bilateral river commission established.[209] The Court concluded its judgment by again highlighting the ongoing duty of the parties to cooperate through the

205 Ibid [112].

206 Ibid [142], [229(5)(a)–(b)]. Subsequently, after the parties were unable to agree, the Court determined the amount of compensation owed to Costa Rica in a 2018 judgment: *Certain Activities Carried Out by Nicaragua in the Border Area (Costa Rica v Nicaragua)*, Compensation, Judgment, ICJ Rep [2018] 15.

207 *Pulp Mills* (n 86) [80]–[158]. The Court found that Uruguay breached its procedural obligations to cooperate imposed by the treaty: [143]–[149], but not its substantive obligations under the treaty: [169]–[265]. In deciding on earlier requests for provisional measures, the Court also emphasised the need for cooperation between the parties under the relevant bilateral river treaty: see *Pulp Mills on the River Uruguay (Argentina v Uruguay)*, Provisional Measures, Order of 13 July 2006, ICJ Rep [2006] 113, [81]–[84]; *Pulp Mills on the River Uruguay (Argentina v Uruguay)*, Provisional Measures, Order of 23 January 2007, ICJ Rep [2007] 3, [53].

208 *Pulp Mills* (n 86) [190], [265]. See further [190]–[265].

209 Ibid [266].

treaty framework established.[210] Within a few months of the judgment, the two parties had agreed, through the bilateral river commission created by the treaty, to establish a joint environmental monitoring program.[211] It appears that the existence of a standing institutional mechanism that could be utilised after the Court's judgment may have affected the role played by the Court within a wider process of dispute resolution.

Conversely, there are cases where the ICJ arguably could have made a greater contribution to ongoing processes of dispute resolution and did not do so. One example is the Court's 2022 judgment in *Dispute Over the Status and Use of the Waters of the Silala*, a dispute between Chile and Bolivia over a transboundary watercourse that had significant environmental components, concerning, among other issues, obligations to prevent transboundary environmental harm.[212] The Court found that four out of five of Chile's claims and two out of three of Bolivia's counter-claims were without object because, interpreting the parties' submissions, the Court held that the parties agreed in substance on these claims and counter-claims, meaning there was no need for a declaratory judgment recording points on which the parties agreed.[213] In contrast, several judges who rendered individual opinions viewed the Court's approach as unsatisfactory because it failed to provide sufficient legal certainty that could be beneficial for the parties' future relationship. For example, Judge Charlesworth suggested that even if the disputing parties' positions had converged during the course of proceedings 'it was necessary and appropriate for the Court to issue a declaratory judgment recording the Parties' agreement' which would have been 'in the interest of legal certainty between the parties because it ensures that the parties commit to their

[210] Ibid [281]. See also Sep. Op. Greenwood [29]. The Court also emphasised the parties' strong record of cooperation in *Gulf of Maine*, a delimitation case that involved an area containing shared fisheries resources relied upon by both parties, where the Court refused to place the fisheries resources under the sole management of one of the parties: *Delimitation of the Maritime Boundary in the Gulf of Maine Area (Canada/United States of America)*, Judgment, ICJ Rep [1984] 286, [232], [240].

[211] See Pablo Sandonato de León, 'Diplomatic and Judicial Means of Dispute Settlement and How They Got Along in the *Pulp Mills* Case' in Laurence Boisson de Chazournes, Marcelo G Kohen and Jorge E Viñuales (eds), *Diplomatic and Judicial Means of Dispute Settlement* (Martinus Nijhoff 2013) 84–85; de Chazournes and Angelini (n 198) 23.

[212] See *Dispute over the Status and Use of the Waters of the Silala (Chile v Bolivia)*, Judgment, ICJ Rep [2022] 614, esp. [77]–[78], [87]–[88].

[213] Ibid [46], [64]–[65], [76], [85]–[86], [146]–[147], [154]–[155], [163].

positions'.[214] In contrast, as she noted, the majority judgment, in refusing to issue a declaratory judgment recording points where the parties agreed, raised questions about whether a party would be precluded from changing its position in future.[215] Similarly, Judge ad hoc Simma was 'perplexed as to why the Judgment' did not record the points of agreement reached by the parties in a declaratory judgment. He observed that 'States appearing before the Court have a legitimate interest in seeking declaratory judgments that may ensure recognition of a situation at law, once and for all and with binding force' and '[t]he Court owes it to the parties to render well-reasoned judgments which settle their disputes with binding force, and, where appropriate, offers them guidance on their rights and obligations'.[216]

There are also instances where the ICJ might have allowed greater space for post-adjudication negotiation between the parties and did not do so. An example is *Jan Mayen*, a delimitation case which had an environmental component with the parties 'in conflict over access to fishery resources'[217] and the Court deciding exceptionally to adjust the provisional delimitation line to achieve equitable access for both parties.[218] Norway, as respondent, argued that the Court should have given a 'declaratory' judgment, which indicated the bases for delimitation and left the task of drawing the boundary line to negotiation between the parties.[219] The Court rejected this approach, reasoning that it would 'not be a complete discharge of its duty to determine the dispute'.[220] Arguably the main issue at stake, delimiting a maritime boundary, was reasonably

[214] *Dispute over the Silala* (n 212) Dec. Charlesworth [20], [22]. See also [19] ('Declarations clarifying the legal situation between the parties can assist in stabilizing the legal relations between them').

[215] Ibid [15].

[216] *Dispute over the Silala* (n 212) Sep Op. Simma [18]–[20].

[217] *Maritime Delimitation in the Area between Greenland and Jan Mayen (Denmark v Norway)*, Judgment, ICJ Rep [1993] 38, [75]. On the environmental aspects of the case, see especially Sep. Op. Weeramantry [235]–[244].

[218] Ibid [76], [90], [92]. For criticism of the reasoning regarding equitable access to fisheries resources see Sep. Op. Schwebel 118–20; Sep. Op. Oda [93]–[94]; Diss. Op. Fischer [14]–[15].

[219] *Jan Mayen* (n 217) [88]. As Judge Shahabuddeen noted, the negotiations Norway envisaged would have been limited to the question of determining the delimitation line to give effect to the Court's 'descriptive statement' of where the boundary lay in the judgment. Norway was not arguing that the Court should only have indicated guidelines on the basis of which the parties would negotiate over the location of the boundary: *Jan Mayen* (n 217) Sep. Op. Shahabuddeen 202.

[220] *Jan Mayen* (n 217) [89]. See also Sep. Op. Shahabuddeen 202–04.

well suited to determination by a judicial pronouncement.[221] In contrast, disputes focused on the ongoing management of a shared resource, particularly those where the parties possess much of the relevant information and expertise, such as the *Fisheries Jurisdiction* cases, are arguably well suited to resolution through post-adjudication cooperation between the parties. However, the approach in *Jan Mayen*, a delimitation case brought under the optional clause, should be contrasted with the approach taken in some other delimitation disputes submitted by special agreements where the parties agreed that the Court would indicate the applicable rules of international law and the parties would conduct the delimitation by agreement on the basis of the judgment.[222] This different context has led the Court, as in *Fisheries Jurisdiction*, to emphasise the obligation to negotiate,[223] and indicate the factors to be taken into account by the parties in future negotiations.[224] Yet, as others have noted, the downside of this approach is that it requires more diplomatic effort to implement the judgment, and accordingly States have, in other delimitation disputes, agreed that the Court can go beyond indicating the applicable principles.[225] More broadly, these examples demonstrate that the ICJ's decisions frequently contribute to broader processes of dispute resolution.[226]

221 Contrast *Jan Mayen* (n 217) Sep. Op. Oda [75]–[90]. Note also that the treaty concluded by the parties to implement the judgment departed in certain respects from the coordinates in the Court's judgment and addressed an issue not covered by the judgment concerning exploitation of potential oil and gas resources: see Constanze Schulte, *Compliance with Decisions of the International Court of Justice* (OUP 2004) 222–24.

222 See e.g. *North Sea Continental Shelf (Federal Republic of Germany/Denmark, Federal Republic of Germany/Netherlands)*, Judgment, ICJ Rep [1969] 3, 5–6 (Article 1 of the relevant agreements).

223 Ibid [85(a)]–[87].

224 Ibid [101(C)–(D)]. See also [84], [92].

225 See Boisson de Chazournes and Angelini (n 198) 11–12 (discussing *Gulf of Maine* (above n 210) where the Court was entrusted to determine the boundary, and other examples where the Court was permitted to give practical guidance on how the relevant rules could be applied). Karel Wellens, *Negotiations in the Case Law of the International Court of Justice: A Functional Analysis* (Ashgate 2014) 297–99 (discussing these issues in relation to the Court's delimitation case law).

226 See e.g. de Chazournes and Angelini (n 198) esp. 18–31 (discussing numerous examples where ICJ judgments have informed a wider diplomatic process, sometimes involving a third party and often going beyond the issues before the Court, with the aim of resolving the wider dispute); Wellens (n 225) ch 8 (examining the interaction between ICJ litigation and negotiations in the post-adjudicative phase); Victor Stoica, *Remedies before the International Court of Justice: A Systemic Analysis* (CUP 2021) 167–68 (noting that the Court adjudicates with an eye to the post-adjudicatory phase, including by often inviting the parties to negotiate).

E. Conclusion

This chapter has analysed how within its environmental case law the ICJ has experienced and responded to the three cross-cutting challenges confronting international tribunals considered throughout this book: managing change in relevant legal norms or facts, determining the appropriate standard and method of review when scrutinising State conduct for compliance with international obligations, and contributing to broader processes of dispute resolution. The above analysis demonstrates that in many respects the ICJ's practices are shaped by contextual considerations that are specific to the Court and the legal settings in which it has an opportunity to adjudicate. Yet the practices reviewed also provide insights into wider challenges experienced by other international tribunals and possible legal responses with relevance beyond this context.

The diversity of the ICJ's work, reflecting that it lacks any compulsory jurisdiction and generally does not hear repeated disputes concerning the same legal framework or text, is an important factor apparent in many of the practices discussed. How the problem of responding to potential changes in international law arose and was managed partly depended on the particular treaty or other legal context in which the Court was adjudicating. For example, in the *Whaling* case the issue of whether the treaty exception for scientific whaling had narrowed over time had to be understood in light of the institutional structure created by the Whaling Convention, and developments within that setting that arguably shifted the balance in the Convention towards the interest of conservation. Similarly, in *Gabčikovo-Nagymaros* the Court's interpretation of the treaty in a manner that emphasised the obligation of the parties to take account of newly emerged environmental norms in implementing an existing project was possible because the relevant provisions were drafted in relatively open-ended terms and open to such a reading.[227] The relevant treaty provisions in *Pulp Mills* and *Navigational Rights* – concerning, respectively, an obligation to protect and preserve the environment and a right of free navigation for the purposes of 'commerce' – were relatively open ended and clearly open to being interpreted in a manner that would evolve in light of relevant developments in international law.

However, the problem arising in these disputes, namely how developments in wider international law might affect the meaning of existing treaty obligations, was also plainly of wider relevance, beyond the

[227] See above n 94.

particular treaty or legal context in which the ICJ was adjudicating. The best evidence of this was that in *Navigational Rights* the Court formulated a general rule regarding when treaty terms are to be interpreted in an evolutive manner which has proved highly influential in subsequent international legal discourse.[228] Similarly, the principle developed in *Gabčikovo-Nagymaros*, that new environmental norms need to be taken into account when continuing existing activities, has proved highly transferable to other contexts where international adjudicators have also incrementally adapted aging treaty frameworks.[229] The Court has also made important contributions to general international law concerning EIAs, including when deciding disputes under particular bilateral river treaties (as in *Pulp Mills*). As we saw in the last chapter, these contributions regarding the law of EIAs have been draw upon by UNCLOS adjudicators.[230] These examples demonstrate that there is a circulation of concepts across different sites of international dispute settlement, whereby concepts travel beyond the immediate context in which they are developed.[231]

Overall, the ICJ has repeatedly made important contributions in incrementally adapting aging treaty frameworks in light of relevant developments in international law and formulating more generalisable statements that have proved transferable to other contexts. An important part of what is occurring in this respect is that the ICJ is performing an informal coordination role within the wider system of international law, as has been suggested in fragmentation debates.[232] Other international tribunals sometimes perform a similar function of incorporating wider developments in international law into a relevant treaty framework against the background of decentralised international law-making – the WTO Appellate Body's interpretation in *US – Shrimp*, considered in Chapter 2,

228 See e.g. Appellate Body Report, *China – Measures Affecting Trading Rights and Distribution Services for Certain Publications and Audiovisual Entertainment Products*, WT/DS363/AB/R, adopted 19 January 2010, [396] fn 705.

229 See e.g. *Indus Waters Kishenganga Arbitration (Pakistan v India)*, Partial Award (18 February 2013) 154 ILR 1, [452]; *In the Arbitration Regarding the Iron Rhine ("Ijzeren Rijn") Railway (Belgium v Netherlands)*, Award (24 May 2005), 140 ILR 130, [59].

230 See further Chapter 3(B)(1) text at nn 134–135 and 145. Consider also the discussion of the ICJ's distinctive contribution to the development of the obligation of States to prevent transboundary harm, as compared to other law-developing actors, in Akhtarkhavari (n 181) 142–48.

231 See generally Hélène Ruiz Fabri and Lorenzo Gradoni (eds), *La circulation des concepts juridiques: Le droit international de l'environnement entre mondialisation et fragmentation* (Société de législation compare 2009).

232 See above n 43.

is one example.[233] Another example are the recent decisions of UNCLOS adjudicators considered in Chapter 3, which have added normative depth to Part XII of the Convention by reading it in light of wider developments in international environmental law (e.g. the *South China Sea Arbitration*).[234] Yet such a coordination or 'mainstreaming' role is particularly pronounced in the ICJ's work, reflecting its immense semantic authority, especially on matters of general international law.[235] That semantic authority, in turn, owes a great deal to being the oldest permanent international tribunal and having a general rather than subject-specific jurisdiction.

The ICJ's approach to the issue of factual changes that may affect the application of a legal norm was also shaped by contextual factors specific to the Court and yet provided insight into a wider issue that is often faced by international tribunals. For example, in *Request for an Examination of the Situation*, the fact that the Court was being asked by New Zealand to re-open a contentious case, in a situation where consent to jurisdiction no longer existed, was highly relevant to understanding the majority's refusal to take account of developments in scientific understanding since 1974. While the case demonstrated the ICJ's general bias towards consent on jurisdictional issues, at a more general level the Court was facing the problem seen in the other adjudication settings studied in this book that assumptions regarding risk can be thrown into doubt by new scientific evidence.

The ICJ's approach to the issues of the appropriate standard and method of review were also heavily shaped by the particular treaty and legal context in which it was adjudicating, but nevertheless provided insights into wider challenges that frequently confront international tribunals. For example, in the *Whaling* case the Court developed its reasonableness test that it applied to decide upon Japan's reliance on the treaty exception in light of a series of factors drawn from the parties' arguments and IWC resolutions. At one level, all of this could be seen as specific to the Whaling Convention. Yet that would miss several contributions the ICJ made regarding the wider issue of the standard and method of review in international adjudication. As Foster has noted, in *Whaling* 'the Court employed the terminology of standard of review as though it were already an established technique', and the submissions of the disputing parties and several of the individual opinions drew directly

[233] See discussion above Chapter 2(B)(1).
[234] See above Chapter 3(B)(1), esp. text at nn 138–139.
[235] See references cited above n 43.

upon WTO case law concerning the standard of review. In turn, this may reflect that the ICJ saw itself (and the parties saw the Court) as part of a wider group of international tribunals engaged in scrutinising State conduct, and specifically States' reliance on contested science-based determinations, for compliance with international norms.[236] Similarly to the other tribunals studied in this book, the ICJ avoided evaluating the scientific merit of Japan's research aims, which it was ill-equipped to do, but nevertheless made important normative choices regarding what would count as an acceptable decision-making process, in that case for issuing a permit for scientific whaling pursuant to the treaty exception. Furthermore, the reasonableness test developed by the ICJ to balance the competing interests under the Whaling Convention, although clearly shaped by the treaty context, operated in a functionally very similar manner to necessity or least restrictive means testing, which is frequently used as a method of review in the other settings studied in this book.

Staying with the issue of the method of review, the reasonableness test applied in *Navigational Rights*, although developed by the ICJ from the applicable treaty framework, operated in a manner analogous to least restrictive means testing to balance one State's right to regulate and another's right to freedom of navigation. The ICJ's reasoning in *Navigational Rights* that a regulating State will be best placed to assess the need for regulation, and that any alternative measures proposed by a complainant would need to be shown to be able to achieve the relevant regulatory aim, and be practically available, fits within a broader pattern regarding how international adjudicators are resolving such questions.[237] Like other international tribunals, the ICJ did not want to second-guess the choices made by a regulating State without clear evidence that any proposed alternative measures were equally effective and reasonably available in terms of cost.

The partly prospectively focused style of adjudication that was evident in many of the ICJ cases considered was also shaped in important ways by contextual factors. Within these cases the issues raised were often ones that required cooperation between neighbouring States or States interested in a particular shared resource. In many of these cases it was clear that cooperation would be needed after the judgment, for example to complete a project, conduct environmental monitoring, or adopt conservation measures. The ICJ did not always have sufficient knowledge or

[236] Foster (n 136) 16–18. See also Foster (n 133) 57.
[237] See also Foster (n 133) 58, 78.

expertise to resolve the issues in dispute, as the Court itself noted in *Fisheries Jurisdiction*.[238] In some of these disputes the relevant treaty also established an institutional framework for cooperation that could be used after the ICJ's judgment. For example, in the *Pulp Mills* case, cooperation after the judgment occurred through the bilateral river commission established under the relevant treaty.[239] As we saw, how a case comes to the ICJ matters because the parties may, if submitting the dispute via special agreement, decide that the Court is to indicate principles on the basis of which they will negotiate, or alternatively the parties may request that the Court make more specific determinations such as itself delimiting a maritime boundary.

While it is important to note the contextual considerations that explain why we see such a facilitative style of adjudication relatively frequently in ICJ case law, these developments should not be seen as unique to this setting. As demonstrated in the previous chapter, within UNCLOS adjudication there is substantial support, both in case law and commentary, for the idea that adjudication might complement a broader process of cooperation between the parties, and that such an approach can lead to more effective dispute resolution. UNCLOS cases, like the ICJ cases discussed, have often concerned disputes between neighbouring States or disputes concerning the management of shared resources, where the disputing parties will have an ongoing relationship after adjudication, and international tribunals do not necessarily have sufficient information to prescribe a solution. Similarly, while WTO adjudication occurs within a specific institutional setting, which creates comparatively clear avenues for pursuing compliance, a meaningful analogy exists with the ICJ practices considered. In both instances adjudication is operating to clarify the parties' legal obligations – including their obligations to have regard to affected foreign interests and pursue cooperative solutions – and to facilitate their future interactions. In both contexts we see examples of the disputing parties rebuilding their relationship after adjudication, assisted by the clarification that an authoritative third-party determination of contested legal issues can provide.

[238] See above text at nn 184–86.
[239] See above n 211.

5

Investment Treaty Arbitration

This chapter analyses the three challenges facing international tribunals traced throughout this book – managing change, scrutinising State conduct for compliance with international law, and contributing to wider processes of dispute resolution – in the decentralised but relatively comprehensive regime for investment treaty arbitration. The essential parameters of this regime are well known: there are some 2,219 Bilateral Investment Treaties (BITs) in force, the vast majority of which include advance consent by States to investor–State arbitration, and another 364 treaties with investment provisions in force.[1] The latter category largely consists of Preferential Trade Agreements (PTAs) with investment chapters – only some of which include State consent to investor–State arbitration – but also includes several multilateral investment agreements that operate on a regional or sectorial basis.[2] Collectively, BITs and other treaties with investment provisions are known as International Investment Agreements (IIAs). Currently, there are around 2,000 IIAs in force that provide advance State consent to investor–State arbitration.[3] While States have for several centuries concluded contractual agreements with foreign investors, what makes the past thirty years or so distinctive is the widespread emergence of general treaty-based State

[1] Figures from UNCTAD's International Investment Agreements Navigator <https://investmentpolicy.unctad.org/international-investment-agreements> as at 21 June 2023. Similar figures are found by searching the Electronic Database on Investment Treaties filtering by agreements in force <https://edit.wti.org/document/investment-treaty/search>.

[2] Eg Energy Charter Treaty (1994) 2080 UNTS 95; ASEAN Comprehensive Investment Agreement (2009); Agreement on Promotion, Protection and Guarantee of Investments amongst the Member States of the Organization of the Islamic Conference (1981).

[3] Daniel Behn, Ole Kristian Fauchald and Malcolm Langford, 'The International Investment Regime and Its Discontents' in Daniel Behn, Ole Kristian Fauchald and Malcolm Langford (eds), *The Legitimacy of Investment Arbitration: Empirical Perspectives* (CUP 2022) 44. The EDIT database returns some 2038 IIAs in force that include a general ISDS clause (n 1).

consent to adjudicate disputes with an indeterminate class of foreign investors.[4] For this reason, although this regime is largely bilaterally constructed, it operates with some resemblance to a multilateral structure, providing general standards for ordering States' behaviour in relation to foreign investments.[5] Since the first treaty-based dispute was filed in 1987, the total number of known treaty-based claims filed had risen to 1,257 by 31 December 2022. By that date, 890 known treaty-based arbitrations had been concluded, with another 343 pending.[6]

In terms of cases with an environmental component, UNCTAD counted some 175 treaty-based ISDS cases that had been brought against measures that were related to environmental protection up to the end of 2021, employing a deliberately wide definition of such measures.[7] In another survey that is not exhaustive but which also used a broad definition of what counts as a case with an environmental component, Viñuales counted some 117 such investor–State cases up to October 2015.[8] Strikingly, half of these disputes were filed since the year 2012, and all but a handful of the disputes were filed since the year 2000.[9] Using a narrower definition of an environmental dispute, including only those cases where a domestic environmental measure was directly challenged or the host State argued that at least one of its measures was justified for environmental reasons, Behn and Langford identified some forty-nine treaty-based cases up to October 2016.[10] In short, even

[4] Gus Van Harten and Martin Loughlin, 'Investment Treaty Arbitration as a Species of Global Administrative Law' (2006) 17 EJIL 121, 128; Campbell McLachlan, Laurence Shore and Matthew Weiniger, *International Investment Arbitration: Substantive Principles* (2nd ed, OUP 2017) 4–5.

[5] See below text at n 27.

[6] Figures from UNCTAD's ISDS navigator <https://investmentpolicy.unctad.org/investment-dispute-settlement> updated to 31 December 2022. There are also twenty-four cases where the outcome is unknown.

[7] UNCTAD, 'Treaty-based Investor–State Dispute Settlement Cases and Climate Action', IIA Issues Note No 4 (2022) 2.

[8] Jorge E Viñuales, 'Foreign Investment and the Environment in International Law: Current Trends' in Kate Miles (ed), *Research Handbook on Environment and Investment Law* (Edward Elgar 2019) 19–20. Note that Viñuales includes some contract-based disputes in his list, whereas all other figures cited in this chapter only cover treaty-based cases.

[9] Ibid 20–21. Similarly: Flavia Marisi, *Environmental Interests in Investment Arbitration: Challenges and Directions* (Kluwer Law International 2020) 20 and Annex.

[10] Daniel Behn and Malcolm Langford, 'Trumping the Environment? An Empirical Perspective on the Legitimacy of Investment Treaty Arbitration' (2017) 18 JWIT 14, 17–18.

employing a deliberately narrow definition of what constitutes an environmental case, there is no shortage of such disputes in this regime.[11]

The future of the investment treaty regime, and in particular advance treaty-based consent by States to investor–State arbitration, is far from clear. While a legitimacy crisis and reform proposals have been prominent in the regime for around fifteen to twenty years, in the last five years or so the political will to alter the shape of the existing regime in a more significant manner appears to have emerged.[12] In 2017, Working Group III of the UN Commission on International Trade Law (UNCITRAL) started work on a mandate concerning reform of investor–State dispute settlement (ISDS), and since 2019 has been addressing the final part of this mandate, developing solutions for areas where the Working Group has identified that reform of the existing system of ISDS is desirable. The reform options that are being addressed by the Working Group are numerous – although focused on procedural aspects of ISDS rather than the substantive standards contained in investment treaties – and include, among others, the development of a standing Multilateral Investment Court to replace the current system of ad hoc arbitration, or a multilateral appellate mechanism to sit above the existing system of arbitration, and an opt-in treaty to apply these reforms to existing investment treaties.[13] In addition to this multilateral reform process, in the last ten to fifteen years numerous States and economic groupings have rethought their approach towards ISDS and pursued various reform strategies. This has included terminating old agreements, negotiating fundamentally refashioned agreements to replace terminated treaties, omitting ISDS from some IIAs, and in the case of the European Union, opting for an alternative 'Investment Court System' in treaties for which an ISDS mechanism is desired.[14]

[11] See also discussion in Chapter 1(C)(1) regarding what constitutes an environmental case.

[12] For a periodisation of legitimacy discourses in the investment treaty regime see Behn, Fauchald and Langford (n 3) 61–78. They note '[f]rom around early 2017 when UNCITRAL was given this mandate, it appears that the life cycle of the legitimacy crisis in ISDS has reached a consensus point on the need to move away from the *status quo*': 77.

[13] See eg UNCITRAL Working Group III, 'Standing Multilateral Mechanism: Selection and Appointment of ISDS Tribunal Members and Related Matters', Note by the Secretariat, A/CN.9/WG.III/WP.213, 8 December 2021; UNCITRAL Working Group III, 'Appellate Mechanism', Note by the Secretariat, A/CN.9/WG.III/WP.224, 17 November 2022; UNCITRAL Working Group III, 'Multilateral Instrument on ISDS Reform', Note by the Secretariat, A/CN.9/WG.III/WP.221, 22 July 2022. Further documents are available on the Working Group III website.

[14] See eg Andreas Kulick (ed), *Reassertion of Control over the Investment Treaty Regime* (CUP 2016); Steffen Hindelang and Markus Krajewski (eds), *Shifting Paradigms in*

In this context it would be futile to predict the future shape of this regime, which remains a major site of political struggle and which may only become clear in a piecemeal fashion, similar to the manner in which the regime originally emerged.[15] Accordingly, this chapter is focused on investment treaty arbitration as it currently exists. Even if the future shape of this regime changes significantly, the large number of cases already concluded and the significant number afoot mean this is undoubtedly one of the most significant sites of contemporary public international law adjudication,[16] including for cases with an environmental component. Relatedly, even if fundamental reforms occur, such as the development of a Multilateral Investment Court, the existing system of investment treaty arbitration is likely to exist alongside it for some time to come, including because of the application of so-called sunset clauses.[17]

This chapter continues the book's overall inquiry into how international tribunals might discharge their functions given the demands that are being placed upon them and the limitations of their roles. It will develop a series of conclusions regarding how the practices of investment treaty tribunals are shaped by the particular context in which they

International Investment Law: More Balanced, Less Isolated, Increasingly Diversified (OUP 2016); Jean E Kalicki and Anna Joubin-Bret (eds), *Reshaping the Investor-State Dispute Settlement System: Journeys for the Twenty-first Century* (Brill Nijhoff 2015). The 'Investment Court System' can be found in the Comprehensive Economic and Trade Agreement between Canada and the European Union (CETA) (2016), the EU–Singapore Investment Protection Agreement (IPA) (2018), the EU–Vietnam IPA (2019), the EU-Chile Advanced Framework Agreement (2023), and the EU–Mexico Global Agreement update (not yet signed). As of February 2024, none of these agreements have entered into force with respect to their investment protection aspects. While the first four agreements have been signed, they will only enter into force once ratified by all EU member States.

15 On the piecemeal emergence of the current regime, see generally Taylor St John, *The Rise of Investor-State Arbitration: Politics, Law, and Unintended Consequences* (OUP 2018); Joost Pauwelyn, 'At the Edge of Chaos?: Foreign Investment Law as a Complex Adaptive System, How It Emerged and How It Can Be Reformed' (2014) 29 ICSID Review 372.

16 Frédéric Gilles Sourgens, *A Nascent Common Law: The Process of Decision-Making in International Legal Disputes between States and Foreign Investors* (Brill Nijhoff 2015) 8; José E Alvarez, *The Public International Law Regime Governing International Investment* (Martinus Nijhoff 2011) 495–96.

17 Stephan W Schill and Geraldo Vidigal, 'Investment Dispute Settlement à La Carte: A Proposal for the Reform of Investor–State Dispute Settlement' in Manfred Elsig, Rodrigo Polanco and Peter Van Den Bossche (eds), *International Economic Dispute Settlement: Demise or Transformation?* (CUP 2021) 252, 257–58.

operate. It will explain why some of the practices demonstrate significant differences with the other adjudication mechanisms studied. However, investment treaty arbitration is not truly incomparable or sui generis, and I will explain why the challenges faced by adjudicators in this regime, and legal techniques used in response, also display important similarities with those seen in the other contexts studied. The chapter proceeds as follows. Section A analyses key contextual features of this adjudication mechanism to provide a context-sensitive basis for the analysis. Section B analyses how investment treaty arbitrators have experienced and responded to the problem of balancing the competing interests of stability and change. It demonstrates that investment treaty arbitrators play a role in managing change in international legal norms, in a similar manner to how adjudicators in the other contexts studied in this book also contribute to processes of law-development alongside other actors in a regime. However, investment treaty tribunals, by applying investment treaty standards in particular disputes, also perform a distinct role of deciding on the permissible degree of change in host State regulation, in the context of an investor's interest in stability and a host State's need to adapt regulation to new demands. Section C considers how investment treaty arbitrators have responded to the interrelated issues of the appropriate standard and method of review when scrutinising States' compliance with investment treaty norms. While the context of investment treaty arbitration shapes how these issues arise, the responses developed by arbitrators exhibit important similarities with the other adjudication contexts studied in this book. Section D considers how investment treaty arbitration contributes to broader processes of dispute resolution. It demonstrates and seeks to explain why, as compared to the other international tribunals studied in this book, adjudication in this regime is largely retrospectively focused and there is comparatively little attention paid to providing guidance for the disputing parties' future interactions, including the potential rebuilding of their relationship after adjudication. Section E draws together the findings emerging from the analysis.

A. Institutional Context for Investment Treaty Arbitration

1. *The Investment Treaty Regime*

As Bonnitcha, Poulsen, and Waibel note '[t]he notion of an "investment treaty regime"' is helpful because it highlights 'the regularities across thousands of treaties and hundreds of arbitrations, which on the surface may otherwise appear diverse'.[18] This regime 'consists of three main components: (i) investment treaties; (ii) the set of treaties, rules, and institutions governing investment treaty arbitration; and (iii) the decisions of arbitral tribunals applying and interpreting investment treaties'.[19] The body of IIAs that is the foundation of the investment treaty regime was introduced above, as was substantial body of arbitral decisions interpreting and applying these treaties. As regards the procedural frameworks that govern investment treaty arbitration, many IIAs provide claimant investors with a choice of arbitral rules and institutions. The most commonly used are the ICSID Convention and its Arbitration Rules,[20] administered by the International Centre for Settlement of Investment Disputes (ICSID), a subsidiary body of the World Bank, the ICSID Additional Facility rules, which is a set of rules created to make ICSID's services available where the respondent State or the investor's State of nationality (or both) are not a Party to the ICSID Convention, and the UNCITRAL arbitration rules, which are not tied to a particular institution and are commonly administered by ICSID and the Permanent Court of Arbitration.[21] A minority of treaty-based investor–State cases have also used the arbitration rules of other commercial arbitration centres that are less frequently mentioned as an option in investment treaties (e.g. the Arbitration Institute of the Stockholm Chamber of Commerce or the International Chamber of Commerce).[22]

In addition to providing the procedural rules that govern arbitration, these procedural frameworks are tied to powerful multilateral enforcement mechanisms. Under the ICSID Convention, which currently has 158 Contracting States, States must recognise awards rendered under the Convention and enforce pecuniary obligations imposed by awards as if

[18] Jonathan Bonnitcha, Lauge N Skovgaard Poulsen and Michael Waibel, *The Political Economy of the Investment Treaty Regime* (OUP 2017) 3. Similarly: Jeswald W Salacuse, 'The Emerging Global Regime for Investment' (2010) 51 HILJ 427, 435–36.

[19] Bonnitcha, Poulsen and Waibel (n 18) 3. Note that the investment treaty regime, which is the focus of this chapter, is only one component of the much broader 'regime complex' that governs international investment, which includes, among other elements, investor–State contracts, domestic investment laws, relevant aspects of regional human rights regimes and international tax regulation: ibid 6–7.

[20] Convention on the Settlement of Investment Disputes between States and Nationals of Other States (1965) 575 UNTS 159 ('ICSID Convention'); ICSID Arbitration Rules (2022).

[21] ICSID Additional Facility Rules (2022) art 2(1); UNCITRAL Arbitration Rules (2010).

[22] See Behn, Fauchald and Langford (n 3) 58–59; UNCTAD, ISDS Investment Dispute Settlement Navigator (n 6) (cases viewed by administering institution).

they were a final judgment of a domestic court, subject to a limited annulment procedure established under the Convention.[23] Investor–State awards rendered outside of the ICSID Convention, including under the ICSID Additional Facility rules and the UNCITRAL rules, rely on the legal framework for recognition and enforcement of awards developed for international commercial arbitration.[24] This is based on the widely ratified 1958 New York Convention on Recognition and Enforcement of Foreign Arbitral Awards and the UNCITRAL Model Law on International Commercial Arbitration, both of which have shaped the arbitration laws of many jurisdictions.[25] Essentially, in arbitration outside the ICSID Convention, while the precise legal framework will vary depending on the law of the seat of arbitration and the law of the jurisdiction where recognition and enforcement of an award is sought, there are only limited grounds on which an award can be set aside at the seat of arbitration or a third jurisdiction can refuse to enforce the award.[26]

As others have highlighted, although the investment treaty regime is largely constructed on a bilateral basis, and there are important differences between treaties, it operates in its totality with certain features that resemble a multilateral regime, creating general standards for constraining States' conduct towards foreign investors.[27] There are several factors supporting such multilateralisation. First, many IIAs contain a small number of common substantive standards, such as the non-discrimination obligations of national treatment and most-favoured nation (MFN) treatment, the standards of fair and equitable treatment and full protection and security, protection against direct and indirect expropriation without payment of compensation, and a guarantee to permit free transfers of capital.[28] The vast majority of BITs and some PTAs combine these substantive standards with the powerful

[23] ICSID Convention arts 52, 54(1).

[24] CL Lim, Jean Ho and Martins Paparinskis, *International Investment Law and Arbitration: Commentary, Awards and Other Materials* (2nd ed., CUP 2021) 538.

[25] Convention on the Recognition and Enforcement of Foreign Arbitral Awards (1958) 330 UNTS 38; UNCITRAL Model Law on International Commercial Arbitration (1985, with amendments as adopted in 2006).

[26] For a succinct introduction, see Bonnitcha, Poulsen and Waibel (n 18) 77–81. In greater detail, see e.g. Borzu Sabahi, Noah D Rubins and Don Wallace Jr, *Investor-State Arbitration* (2nd ed., OUP 2019) ch XXII.

[27] Salacuse (n 18) 431–32; Stephan W Schill, *The Multilateralization of International Investment Law* (CUP 2009) 368–69, 372–73, 377; Van Harten and Loughlin (n 3) 124–25; McLachlan, Shore and Weiniger (n 3) 19–21.

[28] Schill (n 27) 74–75; Salacuse (n 18) 452–54.

enforcement mechanism of investor–State arbitration, without a requirement to exhaust local remedies.[29] Investment treaties also largely share the same object and purpose, which was initially one of protecting and promoting investment in order to increase investment flows and ultimately the economic prosperity of the treaty parties, and has evolved into a more balanced goal of promoting sustainable development.[30] Second, the commonality across investment treaties reflects that contemporary investment treaties have their origins in a small number of failed attempts to negotiate investment protection standards at a multilateral level, mostly in the late 1950s and early 1960s. While no multilateral framework was agreed, the same standards were carried into the existing regime, which was developed largely through the bilateral investment treaty programs of a limited number of capital exporting States.[31] Furthermore, many States use a model investment treaty or chapter, which acts as a default negotiating position, and which is typically revised periodically, including in response to wider developments in the investment treaty regime such as arbitral decisions under other formally unrelated agreements.[32]

Third, one of the most important pieces of evidence that investment treaties and the resulting arbitral decisions constitute a wider regime is that actors in this area (e.g. arbitral tribunals, disputing parties, or commentators) frequently refer to awards rendered under different, unrelated treaties, for example to support an argument regarding how a particular provision should be interpreted.[33] In short, it is extremely

[29] Salacuse (n 18) 446–47.

[30] See especially Federico Ortino, 'Investment Treaties, Sustainable Development and Reasonableness Review: A Case against Strict Proportionality Balancing' (2017) 30 LJIL 71, 76–83. See also Jeswald W Salacuse, *The Law of Investment Treaties* (3rd ed., OUP 2021) 142–49. See eg the preambles of the following recent treaties or models: Canada Model FIPA (2021); Netherlands Model BIT (2019); EU–Vietnam IPA. Hungary–UAE BIT (2021); Indonesia–Singapore BIT (2018).

[31] See e.g. Schill (n 27) 89–92; Salacuse (n 18) 464–66; Bonnitcha, Poulsen and Waibel (n 18) 19–21, 184–90; St John (n 15) 68–99, 201–33 (historical study covering failed proposals during the 1960s for a multilateral agreement on substantive standards and the BIT programs of capital exporting States).

[32] See e.g. Chester Brown, 'Introduction: The Development and Importance of the Model Bilateral Investment Treaty' in Chester Brown (ed), *Commentaries on Selected Model Investment Treaties* (OUP 2013) 2.

[33] See e.g. Salacuse (n 18) 432; Stephan W Schill, 'Sources of International Investment Law: Multilateralization, Arbitral Precedent, Comparativism, Soft Law' in Samantha Besson and Jean d'Aspremont (eds), *The Oxford Handbook of the Sources of International Law* (OUP 2018) 1102–03. On the appropriateness of this practice, see generally Andrew

common for participants to argue from the implicit assumption that investment treaties do constitute a wider regime.[34] Fourth, the vast majority of investment treaties include a most-favoured-nation (MFN) obligation, which historically has acted as a basis for claimant investors to import into the treaty the most favourable substantive standards extended by a host State under any of its investment treaties,[35] although the scope for this has reduced somewhat due to States preventing it in the drafting of newer MFN provisions, and shifts in the approaches of some arbitral tribunals to the permissibility of the practice.[36] Finally, historically the broad definition of investor and investment contained in investment treaties, combined with the ease of incorporation in many domestic legal systems, has meant that where an investor's State of nationality does not have an investment treaty with the host State, an investor may be able to gain protection, for example by structuring its investment via a subsidiary incorporated in a third State that has an investment treaty with the host State.[37] Again, however, the scope for this aspect of 'multilateralisation' has been narrowed because recent investment treaties increasingly include criteria beyond incorporation in order for a company to qualify as an investor of a treaty Party, such as requiring 'substantial business activities' in the territory of the home State.[38]

The above considerations nevertheless mean that it makes sense to speak of an 'investment treaty regime', consisting of the treaties themselves and the resulting arbitral decisions. Put differently, investment treaties and the resulting arbitrations give rise to a broader functionally oriented regime whose significance goes beyond the specific bilateral

D Mitchell and James Munro, 'Someone Else's Deal: Interpreting International Investment Agreements in the Light of Third-Party Agreements' (2017) 28 EJIL 669.

34 Salacuse (n 18) 436; Schill (n 27) 367–68.

35 Schill (n 27) 365–66 and ch iv.

36 See e.g. CETA art 8.7(4); 2021 Canada Model FIPA art 6(6)–(7); Yannick Radi, *Rules and Practices of International Investment Law and Arbitration* (CUP 2020) 125–35; Simon Batifort and J Benton Heath, 'The New Debate on the Interpretation of MFN Clauses in Investment Treaties: Putting the Brakes on Multilateralization' (2017) 111 AJIL 873.

37 Schill (n 27) 366 and ch v; Bonnitcha, Poulsen and Waibel (n 18) 53–55; Van Harten and Loughlin (n 3) 139.

38 See e.g. CETA art 8.1 (definition of 'enterprise of a Party'); EU–Vietnam IPA art 1.2(c), (i); EU–Singapore IPA art 1.2(2), (5); 2019 Netherlands Model BIT art 1(b)–(c). Additionally, arbitral tribunals have developed case law that prevents some forms of nationality planning where it occurs at a point in time where a specific dispute was foreseeable: see eg Rudolf Dolzer, Ursula Kriebaum and Christoph Schreuer, *Principles of International Investment Law* (3rd ed., OUP 2022) 72–73.

treaties at issue.[39] In a similar manner to the multilateral regimes studied in this book (e.g. the WTO or UNCLOS), the vast network of investment treaties creates a set of broadly similar standards for State conduct, backed up by the common dispute settlement mechanism of investor–State arbitration and common enforcement mechanisms.[40] Nevertheless, it must be kept in mind that there are significant differences between investment treaties and ultimately in any dispute it is the features of the specific investment treaty applicable that matters.

2. *The Adjudicators in Investment Treaty Arbitration*

Investor–State tribunals 'are nearly always composed of three arbitrators'.[41] The standard procedure, provided for in the ICSID Convention and many investment treaties, is that each party appoints one arbitrator, and the third, who is the president of the tribunal, is appointed by the agreement of the parties.[42] Under the ICSID Convention, where a tribunal is not constituted within ninety days of a request for arbitration being registered – for example because the parties cannot agree upon a president – either party can request the Chairman of ICSID's Administrative Council[43] to appoint the remaining arbitrators, who must consult both parties as far as possible.[44] Arbitrators appointed by the Chairman cannot be nationals of the State party to the dispute or the investor's State of nationality,[45] and must come from the Panel of Arbitrators, maintained by ICSID,[46] to which each Contracting State to the ICSID Convention can nominate four persons.[47] Under the ICSID Convention

[39] On the concept of regimes in international law and international relations literature, see e.g. Margaret A Young, 'Introduction: The Productive Friction between Regimes' in Margaret A Young (ed), *Regime Interaction in International Law: Facing Fragmentation* (CUP 2012) 4–11.

[40] See above n 27.

[41] Dolzer, Kriebaum and Schreuer (n 38) 401.

[42] ICSID Convention art 37(2)(b); Comprehensive and Progressive Agreement for Trans-Pacific Partnership (CPTPP) (2018) art 9.22(1).

[43] The Chairman is the President of the World Bank (ICSID Convention art 5), but in practice acts upon the recommendation of ICSID's Secretary General. ICSID's Secretary General is explicitly made the appointing authority under many investment treaties. Eg CPTPP arts 9.22(2), 9.1.

[44] ICSID Convention art 38.

[45] Ibid.

[46] Ibid art 40(1).

[47] Ibid arts 12–13. However, note that the ICSID secretariat has developed a practice that when it receives a request to appoint an arbitrator it first seeks to assist the parties to

and arbitration rules, parties cannot ordinarily appoint an individual who has the nationality of the State Party to the dispute or the investor's nationality; however, there is an exception if each member of the tribunal is appointed by the agreement of the parties.[48] Party-appointed arbitrators may, and often do, come from outside ICSID's Panel of Arbitrators, but must still possess the same characteristics,[49] which include that they are 'of high moral character and recognised competence in the fields of law, commerce, industry or finance' and can be relied upon to exercise independent judgment.[50] Arbitrators can be disqualified if they manifestly lack such qualities, and are often challenged on this basis.[51] More recent investment treaties often impose additional requirements through a code of conduct for arbitrators,[52] and the ICSID and UNCITRAL secretariats have recently developed codes of conduct for members of a future Multilateral Investment Court and for investor–State arbitrators.[53]

Several comprehensive empirical studies have shown that, to date, investment treaty arbitration has been dominated by a relatively small group of frequently appointed arbitrators, the majority of whom are

identify a mutually acceptable candidate (through a so-called 'ballot procedure') who if identified is then appointed by agreement of the disputing parties. Candidates appointed in this manner do not need to come from the ICSID Panel of Arbitrators: see e.g. Eloïse Obadia and Frauke Nitschke, 'Institutional Arbitration and the Role of the Secretariat' in Chiara Giorgetti (ed), *Litigating International Investment Disputes: A Practitioner's Guide* (Brill Nijhoff 2014) 112–13.

48 See ICSID Convention art 39; ICSID Arbitration Rules, rule 13(2)–(3).

49 ICSID Convention art 40.

50 ICSID Convention art 14(1).

51 Challenges are decided by the remaining arbitrators, or if they cannot agree or the majority of arbitrators is challenged, the Chairman of ICSID's Administrative Council: ICSID Convention art 58; ICSID Arbitration Rules rule 23. In non-ICSID arbitration, the procedure depends on the applicable arbitration rules. For example, under the UNCITRAL Arbitration Rules (2010) arts 12–13, the appointing authority decides on arbitrator challenges. On arbitrator challenges, see generally Lim, Ho and Paparinskis (n 24) 189–230.

52 See e.g. the Code of Conduct created for ISDS under CPTPP: Annex to CPTPP/COM/2019/D004.

53 UNCITRAL, 'Draft Code of Conduct for Arbitrators in International Investment Dispute Resolution and Commentary', A/CN.9/1148, 28 April 2023; UNCITRAL, Draft Code of Conduct for Judges in International Investment Dispute Resolution and Commentary', A/CN.9/1149, 28 April 2023. The former was adopted, and the latter adopted in principle, by UNCITRAL at its fifty-sixth session in July 2023: see Report of the United Nations Commission on International Trade Law, Fifty-sixth session (3–21 July 2023) A/78/17, [27]–[29], [41]–[90].

male, are nationals of a limited number of western developed States, and have a background in private practice or less commonly academia.[54] Compared to the other adjudication settings studied in this book the bench is more polarised with many of the most commonly appointed arbitrators being repeatedly appointed either by claimant investors or host States.[55] Arbitrators have a right to append an individual opinion,[56] and while the frequency of dissent is higher than in WTO adjudication, it is not clearly higher than in many other international tribunals nor as high as might be expected given the use of party-appointed arbitrators, the novelty of this legal field and its ideological divisions.[57] As there is no permanent bench or appellate mechanism and tribunals may operate in materially different treaty contexts, investment treaty arbitration does not exhibit the degree of consistency of jurisprudence seen in the other adjudication settings studied in this book. Nevertheless, tribunals and disputing parties engage in extensive consideration of prior awards, and the relatively small group of frequently appointed arbitrators enables certain common approaches to consolidate over time.[58]

3. *The Functions of Investment Treaty Arbitration*

Arbitral tribunals constituted under investment treaties clearly have the function of resolving disputes between foreign investors and host States. The preambles of the ICSID Convention and of certain investment treaties endorse this idea.[59] In a recent study of the history of the ICSID Convention, Zhang notes that 'the drafters' original assumption about the judicial function was a consciously narrow one, focusing on the resolution of specific disputes in relation to specific parties'.[60] Some

[54] See e.g. Joost Pauwelyn, 'The Rule of Law without the Rule of Lawyers? Why Investment Arbitrators Are from Mars, Trade Adjudicators from Venus' (2015) 109 AJIL 761, 769–83; Sergio Puig, 'Social Capital in the Arbitration Market' (2014) 25 EJIL 387, 404–22; Malcolm Langford, Daniel Behn and Runar Hilleren Lie, 'The Revolving Door in International Investment Arbitration' (2017) 20 JIEL 301, 309–10; Bonnitcha, Poulsen and Waibel (n 18) 28–29.

[55] Pauwelyn (n 54) 782; Puig (n 54) 404; Langford, Behn and Lie (n 54) 310.

[56] ICSID Convention art 48(4), generally art 48(1)–(4).

[57] Catherine A Rogers, 'The Politics of International Investment Arbitrators' (2013) 12 Santa Clara JIL 223, 242–46.

[58] E.g. Schill (n 33) 1102–06.

[59] See eg ICSID Convention preamble; US–Uruguay BIT (2005) preamble.

[60] Yanwen Zhang, 'The Judicial Function of Investment Tribunals: Taking Foundational Assumptions Seriously' (2022) 25 JIEL 129, 146. See also 145.

investment tribunals have also observed that their primary function is to decide the dispute before them given that they are constituted to hear a single, particular dispute between a protected investor and a host State.[61] The idea that dispute settlement is a central goal of investment treaty arbitration is also implicit in the oft-repeated claims that this form of dispute settlement was designed to provide foreign investors with an effective remedy that is independent of the host State and that is not subject (unlike diplomatic protection) to the political discretion of its home State, and, relatedly, to prevent investor–State disputes from undermining the broader inter-State relationship between the treaty parties.[62]

As regards the law-development function of investment treaty tribunals, as in the other adjudication settings studied in this book there is little in the relevant constitutive instruments that directly supports this function.[63] Nevertheless, there is wide acknowledgement that investment treaty tribunals, by deciding disputes, play an important role in clarifying and developing the standards contained in investment treaties.[64] Some investment tribunals have stated that while they are not bound by the decisions of other arbitral tribunals, and must keep in mind the specifics of the applicable treaty and the case at hand, they nevertheless do have a

[61] See e.g. *Glamis Gold Ltd v United States of America*, UNCITRAL, Award (8 June 2009) [3], [7].

[62] See e.g. Christoph Schreuer, 'Investment Arbitration' in Cesare PR Romano, Karen J Alter and Yuval Shany (eds), *The Oxford Handbook of International Adjudication* (OUP 2013) 296–97; Ursula Kriebaum, 'Evaluating Social Benefits and Costs of Investment Treaties: Depoliticization of Investment Disputes' (2018) 33 ICSID Review 14, 16–19; Daniel Behn, 'Performance of Investment Treaty Arbitration' in Theresa Squatrito and others (eds), *The Performance of International Courts and Tribunals* (CUP 2018) 78–85; Sergio Puig, 'Recasting ICSID's Legitimacy Debate: Towards a Goal-Based Empirical Agenda' (2013) 36 Fordham ILJ 465, 484–88. There are important criticisms of such claims of depoliticisation: see e.g. Bonnitcha, Poulsen and Waibel (n 18) 193–98; Geoffrey Gertz, Srividya Jandhyala and Lauge N Skovgaard Poulsen, 'Legalization, Diplomacy, and Development: Do Investment Treaties De-Politicize Investment Disputes?' (2018) 107 World Development 239; Joachim Pohl, 'Societal Benefits and Costs of International Investment Agreements: A Critical Review of Aspects and Available Empirical Evidence', OECD Working Papers on International Investment 2018/01 (2018) 50–55 <https://doi.org/10.1787/18151957>.

[63] See e.g. ICSID Convention art 53(1) ('The award shall be binding on the parties'); Zhang (n 60) 144–45 (emphasising the limited law-development role of ICSID tribunals intended by the Convention's drafters).

[64] See e.g. Stephan W Schill, 'System-Building in Investment Treaty Arbitration and Lawmaking' (2011) 12 German LJ 1083; Schill (n 33) 1103–07; Bonnitcha, Poulsen and Waibel (n 18) 246–47; Behn (n 62) 86; José E Alvarez, *The Impact of International Organizations on International Law* (Brill Nijhoff 2017) 289–92.

wider, systemic role in contributing to the development of investment law.[65] Certain tribunals have referred in this regard to a 'duty to contribute to the harmonious development of investment law and thereby to meet the legitimate expectations of the community of States and investors towards legal certainty and the rule of law'.[66] In *Glamis Gold v USA*, the Tribunal although beginning by noting its 'case specific mandate', in contrast to 'a standing adjudicative body which addresses multiple disputes', nevertheless emphasised that this was 'not license to ignore systemic implications' which required 'sensitivity to the position of future tribunals and awareness of other systemic implications'.[67] As the *Glamis* Tribunal observed, 'Chapter 11 of the NAFTA contains a significant public system of private investment protection', and the integrity of this system required 'a modicum of awareness of each of these tribunals for each other and the system as a whole' and for tribunals to give detailed reasons for their awards and for any 'departing from major trends present in previous decisions'.[68]

Investment treaty tribunals also perform a 'compliance monitoring' function by scrutinising State conduct for compliance with the substantive standards contained in investment treaties.[69] The compliance-monitoring function of investment treaty arbitration may also have significance beyond the particular dispute being decided. By issuing decisions that are typically published and are followed closely by a wider professional audience, investment treaty tribunals contribute incrementally to developing more generalised standards for acceptable State conduct, which may be picked up by other actors, for example third States that are concerned about litigation risk under their own IIAs.[70] This has

[65] *Mesa Power v Canada*, PCA Case No 2012-17, Award (24 March 2016) [222].

[66] Ibid; *Saipem S.p.A v Bangladesh*, ICSID Case No ARB/05/07, Decision on Jurisdiction and Provisional Measures (21 March 2007) [67]; *Mr Jürgen Wirtgen & Ors v Czech Republic*, PCA Case No 2014-03, Final Award (11 October 2017) [181]; For somewhat different formulations, see e.g. *Daimler Financial Services AG v Argentina*, ICSID Case No ARB/05/1, Award (22 August 2012) [52]; *Suez, Sociedad General de Aguas de Barcelona S.A. v Argentina*, ICSID Case No ARB/03/19, Decision on Liability (30 July 2010) [189]; *Bosh International, Inc v Ukraine*, ICSID Case No ARB/08/11, Award (25 October 2012) [211].

[67] *Glamis v USA* (n 61) [3], [6], and generally [3]–[9].

[68] Ibid [5], [8].

[69] On this function of international tribunals, see generally Chapter 1, text at nn 66–68.

[70] Benedict Kingsbury and Stephan Schill, 'Investor-State Arbitration as Governance: Fair and Equitable Treatment, Proportionality and the Emerging Global Administrative Law' in Albert Jan van den Berg (ed), *50 Years of the New York Convention* (Kluwer Law International 2009) 5–6, 23–26. See also Federico Ortino, 'The Investment Treaty System as Judicial Review' (2013) 24 Am. Rev. Int. Arb. 437, 443–46 (discussing the role of

been referred to, correctly, as investment treaty arbitration performing a 'governance function'.[71]

B. Balancing Stability and Change in Investment Treaty Arbitration

This section analyses the function of investment treaty tribunals in balancing the competing interests of stability and change when interpreting and applying applicable legal norms. At the outset, it is useful to distinguish between two distinct ways in which investment treaty arbitration involves balancing the competing interests of stability and change. First, investment treaty tribunals play a role in managing potential changes in international legal norms, in a similar manner to how adjudicators in the other contexts studied in this book also contribute to ongoing processes of law-development alongside other actors within a regime. Secondly, and more interestingly, investor–State tribunals play a crucial role in determining the permissible balance between the competing interests of stability and change within the host State's regulatory system by interpreting and applying standards of investment treaty protection in particular disputes.[72]

The above distinction helps us understand how investment arbitration is simultaneously quite similar to the other contexts studied in this book regarding the role of adjudicators in contributing to wider processes of law development, and distinct insofar as adjudication in this regime has an overriding focus on determining the 'acceptable margin of change' in host State regulation by interpreting and applying investment treaty obligations.[73] This distinction brings greater analytical clarity to understanding the role of investment treaty tribunals in balancing the competing interests of stability and change, whereas existing discussions of this issue have tended to conflate the questions of change in international

investment treaty arbitration in identifying and applying principles of 'good public governance').

[71] E.g. Bonnitcha, Poulsen and Waibel (n 18) 246–47; Kingsbury and Schill (n 70). On the idea of a governance function of international tribunals, with discussion of ISDS, see generally Alvarez (n 64) 310–40.

[72] Section B of this chapter partly draws on material from Joshua Paine, 'On Investment Law and Questions of Change' (2018) 19 JWIT 173.

[73] *El Paso Energy Int'l Co v Argentina*, ICSID Case No ARB/03/15, Award (31 October 2011) [402].

legal norms and change in host State regulation,[74] or only focused on one of these issues.[75] Of course, host States still retain the primary role of deciding upon and implementing their regulatory aims. What investment law does is to make host State regulation that affects protected investments subject to the international standards contained in an investment treaty.[76] Investment tribunals, by interpreting and applying those standards in particular disputes, exercise a form of international control over the permissible degree of change within host State regulation. While tribunals cannot prevent regulatory changes at the domestic level – their decisions not having direct effect – they can, by finding violations and awarding compensation, make adopting certain forms of regulatory change very expensive. As the *9REN v Spain* Tribunal recognised, investor–State tribunals through their decisions determine who should bear the costs of regulatory change: the investor or the host State and its taxpayers.[77]

1. *Managing Change in International Legal Norms: The Case of the International Minimum Standard*

The role of investment treaty tribunals in deciding on potential changes in applicable international legal norms is clearly demonstrated by debates

[74] See Thomas M Franck, *Fairness in International Law and Institutions* (OUP 1998) 438–41 (focusing on an investor's interest in stability and a host State's interest in change but recognising the discourse could concern general norms rather than being dispute-specific); Roland Kläger, *'Fair and Equitable Treatment' in International Investment Law* (CUP 2011) 148–53 (focusing on the law application stage and suggesting the investor's interest in stability is subject to balancing both given the host State's sovereignty and as investment norms need to be understood alongside other international norms with different objectives); Roland Kläger, 'Fair and Equitable Treatment: A Look at the Theoretical Underpinnings of Legitimacy and Fairness' (2010) 11 JWIT 435, 452–55; Anne van Aaken, 'International Investment Law between Commitment and Flexibility: A Contract Theory Analysis' (2009) 12 JIEL 507, 508–09, 522–31 (contract theory perspective suggesting that investment law faces the challenge of ensuring an optimal balance between commitment and flexibility in the face of uncertainty and this balance is realised both through treaty drafting and through tribunals' interpretation of investment treaties in specific disputes); Valentina Vadi, 'Crisis, Continuity, and Change in International Investment Law and Arbitration' (2021) 42 Mich. J. Int'l L. 321, esp. 365–67.

[75] See eg Moshe Hirsch, 'Between Fair and Equitable Treatment and Stabilization Clause: Stable Legal Environment and Regulatory Change in International Investment Law' (2011) 12 JWIT 783 (focusing on the implications of interpretations of the FET standard for the balance between stability and change in the host State's regulatory system).

[76] Franck (n 74) 446–47.

[77] *9REN Holding S.a.r.l v Spain*, ICSID Case No ARB/15/15, Award (31 May 2019) [253]. Similarly: Thomas W Wälde and Abba Kolo, 'Environmental Regulation, Investment Protection and "Regulatory Taking" in International Law' (2001) 50 ICLQ 811, 824–25.

over the evolution of the customary international minimum standard of treatment (MST) and its relationship to the fair and equitable treatment (FET) standard. As this debate is already covered extensively in the existing literature, it will not be treated exhaustively here.[78] Rather, this debate is considered briefly because it provides clear evidence of investor–State tribunals grappling with the question of potential change in applicable international legal norms, alongside other law-developing actors in this regime (particularly States).[79] This issue has been particularly prominent in jurisprudence under the North American Free Trade Agreement (NAFTA), as the three NAFTA States Parties, through a 2001 determination of the Free Trade Commission (FTC), clarified that the 'minimum standard of treatment' contained in NAFTA prescribes the customary MST owed to aliens, and that the reference in the provision to 'fair and equitable treatment' does 'not require treatment in addition to or beyond that which is required by the customary' standard.[80] This interpretation was issued by the treaty parties in response to several early expansive interpretations by tribunals of NAFTA's provision on the MST and FET.[81] The clarification has subsequently been included in many other treaties,[82] and non-NAFTA tribunals routinely take positions on whether the customary MST has evolved over time.[83]

[78] See e.g. Patrick Dumberry, 'Fair and Equitable Treatment: Its Interaction with the Minimum Standard and Its Customary Status' (2017) 1 Brill Research Perspectives in International Investment Law and Arbitration 1; Martins Paparinskis, *The International Minimum Standard and Fair and Equitable Treatment* (OUP 2013).

[79] For other discussions that frame the issue in similar terms, see eg W Michael Reisman, 'Canute Confronts the Tide: States versus Tribunals and the Evolution of the Minimum Standard in Customary International Law' (2015) 30 ICSID Review 616; Johannes Hendrik Fahner, 'Maximising Investment Protection under the Minimum Standard: A Case Study of the Evolutive Interpretation and Application of Customary International Law in Investment Arbitration' (2023) 12(1) ESIL Reflections.

[80] NAFTA Free Trade Commission, Notes of Interpretation of Certain Chapter 11 Provisions (31 July 2001), [B(1)–(2)]; NAFTA art 1105(1).

[81] See e.g. Dumberry (n 78) 30–31.

[82] From many, see eg CPTPP art 9.6(1)–(2); Dominican Republic–Central America–United States FTA (2004) art 10.5(1)–(2); Canada–China FIPA (2012) art 4(1)–(2); US–Korea FTA (2007) art 11.5(1)–(2); US–Colombia TPA (2006) art 10.5(1)–(2); United States–Mexico–Canada Agreement (2018) art 14.6(1)–(2); Canada–Korea FTA (2014) art 8.5 (1)–(2).

[83] See e.g. the following cases holding the standard had evolved: *Azurix Corp v Argentina*, ICSID Case No ARB/01/12, Award (14 July 2006) [365], [372]; *Gold Reserve Inc. v Venezuela*, ICSID Case No ARB(AF)/09/1, Award (22 September 2014) [567]; *Railroad Development Corporation v Guatemala*, ICSID Case No ARB/07/23, Award (29 June 2012), [218]. See also discussion of *Eco Oro v Colombia*, below text at nn 90–104.

The historical content of the customary MST, the evolution of which is debated, has often been equated with a statement by the US–Mexico Claims Commission in the *Neer* case, requiring, for breach of the standard that the conduct 'amount to an outrage, to bad faith, to wilful neglect of duty, or to an insufficiency of governmental action so far short of international standards that every reasonable and impartial man would readily recognize its insufficiency'.[84] In contemporary investment arbitration, two competing approaches to this question have emerged. The first approach recognises a substantial degree of change in the relevant international legal norm, while the second approach emphasises continuity in the norm whilst recognising that it now applies to a wider range of factual situations.

An initial example of the first approach comes from *Bilcon v Canada*, a dispute concerning a domestic environmental review process that denied an approval required for the claimant's construction project to proceed. In considering the parties' arguments regarding whether the customary MST had evolved, the *Bilcon* Tribunal accepted that '[t]he contemporary minimum international standard involves a more significant measure of protection' than was historically the case, as reflected in the *Neer* formulation.[85] Nevertheless, the Tribunal emphasised that 'the mere breach of domestic law or any kind of unfairness does not violate the international minimum standard'.[86] Ultimately, the *Bilcon* Tribunal endorsed an oft-

[84] *L.F.H. Neer and Pauline E. Neer v Mexico*, US–Mexico Claims Commission, Opinion (15 October 1926) IV RIAA 60, [4]. Commentators and certain tribunals have highlighted that the *Neer* formulation was only intended to cover cases of denial of justice, or failure of a State to redress wrongs suffered by a foreign national at the hands of another private actor, and a lower standard was applied by the US–Mexico Claims Commission to cases involving injury to an alien resulting directly from actions of the State's executive or legislature: e.g. Charalampos Giannakopoulos and Malvika Monga, 'History as Interpretative Context in the Evolutionary Interpretation of FET in International Investment Law' in Georges Abi-Saab and others (eds), *Evolutionary Interpretation and International Law* (Hart 2019) 300–01; Jan Paulsson and Georgios Petrochilos, '*Neer*-Ly Misled?' (2007) 22 ICSID Review 242, 242–47, 254–57; *ADF Group Inc v United States of America*, ICSID Case No ARB[AF]/00/1, (Award) (9 January 2003) [181].

[85] *William Ralph Clayton, William Richard Clayton, Douglas Clayton, Daniel Clayton and Bilcon of Delaware, Inc v Canada*, Award on Jurisdiction and Liability (17 March 2015) PCA Case No 2009-04, [433]–[434]. For other awards holding that the customary MST has evolved and provides a greater degree of protection than the *Neer* formulation, see eg *Mondev International Ltd v United States of America*, ICSID Case No ARB[AF]/99/2, Award (11 October 2002), [115]–[117], [123]–[125]; *ADF v USA* (n 84) [179]; *Mesa Power v Canada* (n 65) [500]; above n 83.

[86] *Bilcon v Canada* (n 85) [436].

cited statement of the *Waste Management II v Mexico* Tribunal concerning the content of the MST, accepting that while there is a 'high threshold' for a breach of the standard this did not require 'that the challenged conduct reaches the level of shocking or outrageous behaviour'.[87] This reflected that 'the *Neer* standard of indisputably outrageous misconduct is no longer applicable ... [given] the modern evolution of the standard'.[88] Notably, the *Bilcon* Tribunal also cited at length, apparently with approval, a review of this issue by the *Merrill & Ring Forestry v Canada* Tribunal, which took a particularly expansive view of how the customary MST had evolved, holding that it now 'protects against all such acts or behavior that might infringe a sense of fairness, equity and reasonableness'.[89]

Another notable example concerning whether the customary MST had evolved comes from the majority award and one of the dissenting opinions in *Eco Oro v Colombia*. This case was brought by a Canadian mining company under the Canada–Colombia FTA and concerned measures taken by Colombia to protect a *páramo* ecosystem, which had allegedly deprived the investor of a right to exploit a mining concession it held for an area that potentially fell partly within the *páramo*.[90] Importantly, the relevant treaty provision makes clear that the Parties are only obliged to afford covered investments treatment in accordance with the customary MST, with the reference to FET not requiring anything beyond this.[91] Moreover, the Parties had in a binding subsequent interpretation, issued a year after the arbitration was commenced, clarified that if an investor alleged a breach of the MST it bore the burden of proving the existence (and content) of any rule of customary international law relied upon.[92]

The majority of the Tribunal began by holding that the MST 'must be permitted to evolve as indeed international customary law itself evolves' and that the modern standard was broader than the formulation from the *Neer* case.[93] In addressing the content of the MST, the majority appears

87 Ibid [442]–[444], citing *Waste Management, Inc v Mexico*, ICSID Case No ARB(AF)/00/3, Award (30 April 2004), [98]–[99].

88 *Bilcon v Canada* (n 85) [441].

89 *Merrill & Ring Forestry LP v Canada*, ICSID Case No UNCT/07/1, Award (31 March 2010) [207]–[213], cited in ibid [435].

90 For the full chronology of the facts, see *Eco Oro v Colombia*, ICSID Case No ARB/16/41, Decision on Jurisdiction, Liability and Directions on Quantum (9 September 2021) [79]–[204].

91 Canada-Colombia FTA (2008) art 805(1).

92 *Eco Oro v Colombia* (n 90) [212]–[213].

93 Ibid [744].

to have conflated this standard with FET, holding that 'FET encompassing concepts of non-arbitrariness, transparency and fairness are recognised elements of customary international law within the confines of reasonableness'.[94] Indeed, two paragraphs later, the Tribunal spent a lengthy paragraph reciting various components of the FET standard recognised by prior arbitral decisions, including 'transparency, stability and the protection of the investor's legitimate expectations', without relating these to the customary MST that it had to apply.[95] Nonetheless, the majority accepted that 'there must be some aggravating factor such that the acts identified comprise more than a minor derogation from that which is deemed to be internationally acceptable'.[96] Accordingly, the majority held that to show a breach of the MST the claimant would need to show that Colombia either (i) breached the claimant's legitimate expectations 'or (ii) failed to provide at all times a stable and transparent investment environment; or (iii) did not act in good faith as required by international law', and additionally that Colombia's actions were 'unacceptable from an international law perspective'.[97] Ultimately, the majority held that Colombia's conduct amounted to a breach of the MST as Colombia had frustrated the investor's legitimate expectations and failed to provide 'a stable and predictable regulatory environment', and this conduct was 'unacceptable from an international law perspective' given Colombia had acted in an arbitrary manner.[98]

A markedly different approach to the question of potential change in the content of the MST, and the extent to which this standard includes protection of an investor's legitimate expectations or a guarantee of regulatory stability, was advanced by Arbitrator Sands in dissent. Arbitrator Sands viewed the majority approach as having incorrectly conflated the MST, which it had to apply under the FTA, with the FET standard such that, in Arbitrator Sands' view, the majority had applied the incorrect standard to find a breach of the FTA.[99] For Arbitrator Sands, the claimant had not shown that the MST had evolved to have a similar content to the FET standard, rather it retained its own distinct

[94] Ibid [752].
[95] Ibid [754].
[96] Ibid [755].
[97] Ibid [762].
[98] Ibid [804]–[806], [820]–[821].
[99] *Eco Oro v Colombia* (n 90) Partial Dissent of Professor Philippe Sands QC [8], [11], [35].

identity.[100] In relation to the majority's emphasis on legitimate expectations, Arbitrator Sands held that in the context of the customary MST this concept has a 'more limited role than in relation to FET' and would require a '"quasi-contractual" relationship or expectation', which did not exist on the facts.[101] Arbitrator Sands further held that the majority's emphasis on a lack of stability in the domestic regulatory framework was mistaken, as while this element was arguably part of the FET standard, no evidence had been provided that a failure to provide regulatory stability, without more, could give rise to a breach of the MST.[102] Accordingly, Arbitrator Sands viewed the majority as having 'effectively engaged in judicial law-making; it has invented a new element for the identification of the customary standard which no state has appeared to have articulated, in the total absence of any evidence of state practise or *opinio juris*'.[103] Finally, in rejecting the majority's conclusion that Colombia, through its conduct, had acted arbitrarily and thus violated the customary MST, Arbitrator Sands emphasised that given the challenges States increasingly face in striking 'complex trade-offs' between protection of the environment and competing social objectives, often of an economic nature, 'internal government debate – and changes of direction' were to be expected.[104] In short, Arbitrator Sands, in dissent, was unconvinced that the claimant had shown any evolution of the MST to include equivalent content to the FET standard regarding the protection of legitimate expectations and regulatory stability. He was also far more willing to tolerate a degree of regulatory uncertainty as to be expected given the complex trade-offs facing governments.

A significant example of a more restrained approach to whether the customary MST has evolved comes from *Glamis Gold v USA*. This case arose from the regulatory approval process applied to the claimant's proposed mining project, given concerns about protection of the environment and sites of indigenous cultural heritage. The *Glamis* Tribunal rejected the claimant's argument that the customary MST had converged with the FET standard under investment treaties.[105] The Tribunal held that the claimant had not proved that the MST had evolved beyond the

[100] Ibid [9]–[10].
[101] Ibid [14]–[18], citing *Glamis v USA* (n 61) [766] and *Cargill, Inc v Mexico*, ICSID Case No ARB(AF)/05/Z, Award (18 September 2009) [290].
[102] Ibid [21]–[23].
[103] Ibid [22].
[104] See ibid [29]–[34].
[105] *Glamis v USA* (n 61) [609]–[610].

statement in *Neer* and while the standard was being applied to 'more varied and complicated' situations, 'the level of scrutiny is the same' remaining 'as stringent as it was under *Neer*'.[106] Subsequently, the Tribunal interpreted the content of the MST to only impose relatively limited constraints on changes in host State regulation. Specifically, the Tribunal held that a violation of the MST on the basis of unsettling reasonable investment-backed expectations would only arise where there was 'at least a quasi-contractual relationship between the State and the investor, whereby the State has purposely and specifically induced the investment'.[107] On the facts, this was not found to exist as 'Claimant was operating in a climate that was becoming more and more sensitive to the environmental consequences of open-pit mining', and although the federal-level regulatory process had reached 'a different result than a reasonable investor might expect under the mining regulatory regime as it stood, the federal government did not make specific commitments to induce Claimant to persevere with its mining claims', nor guarantee that those claims would be approved.[108] Similarly, applying this standard to separate state-level legislation affecting the claimant's proposed project, the Tribunal noted that 'Respondent has presented a prima facie showing that California is a particularly highly regulated environment with respect to environmental measures in general, and mineral exploration in particular' and the claimant had not shown that it had received specific assurances regarding future regulation that might affect its proposed project.[109] In summary, the *Glamis* Tribunal grappled with two questions: had the MST evolved, and in what circumstances would a change in host State regulation rise to the level of breaching that standard?

2. *The Function of Investment Treaty Arbitration in Balancing Stability and Change in Host State Regulation*

As already noted, beyond the standard role of international tribunals in contributing to wider processes of law development, there is a more fundamental sense in which investor–State arbitration engages with questions of stability and change, which explains a great deal about the role of adjudication in this regime. In short, investment arbitrators, by

[106] Ibid [612]–[616], [627]. See also [604]. Similarly: *Cargill v Mexico* (n 101) [284]–[286].
[107] *Glamis v USA* (n 61) [766].
[108] Ibid [767].
[109] Ibid [800]–[802].

interpreting and applying investment treaty standards in particular disputes, also effectively determine the permissible balance between the investor's interest in the stability of the domestic regulatory system applying to its investment and the host State's interest in being able to adjust regulation to meet new circumstances. This function of investor–State arbitration is important because States frequently need to adjust regulation to meet new demands, for example in relation to newly appreciated environmental risks, and such measures are liable to be challenged before investment treaty tribunals.[110] In order to develop this argument, this subsection focuses on cases under the FET standard with an environmental component. Essentially, there are two strands of the FET obligation that can operate to limit a State's ability to change regulation in response to new demands. First, a line of case law has recognised that the FET standard includes a limited guarantee regarding the stability of the host State's regulatory system. Second, the FET standard is widely interpreted to include protection of an investor's objectively reasonable legitimate expectations.[111] It will be shown that approaches to these issues have evolved over time. While a few early awards posited an impossibly high standard of regulatory stability, the case law has become more accommodating of regulatory change as a normal occurrence, such that certain types of regulatory change will not ordinarily constitute an FET breach.[112] Nevertheless, there are notable variations even within the most recent jurisprudence, and these two aspects of the FET standard retain the potential to constrain States' ability to adjust regulation to meet evolving circumstances. As investor–State tribunals have themselves recognised, in applying these

[110] See e.g. *RENERGY S.à.r.l. v Spain*, ICSID Case No ARB/14/18, Dissent on Liability and Quantum Professor Philippe Sands QC (22 April 2022) [48]; *Mathias Kruck and Others v Spain*, ICSID Case No ARB/15/23, Partial Dissenting Opinion Prof. Zachary Douglas KC (13 September 2022) [57]; Gus Van Harten, 'Foreign Investor Protection and Climate Action: A New Price Tag for Urgent Policies' [2015] Osgoode Legal Studies Research Paper Series, Research Paper No 21/2016; Kate Miles, *The Origins of International Investment Law: Empire, Environment and the Safeguarding of Capital* (CUP 2013) 169.

[111] The point that legitimate expectations must be objectively reasonable, assessed in all the circumstances, is well established: see eg *Wirtgen v Czech Republic* (n 66) [407]; *Duke Energy Electroquil Partners v Ecuador*, ICSID Case No ARB/04/19, Award (18 August 2008) [340].

[112] Similarly: Federico Ortino, *The Origin and Evolution of Investment Treaty Standards: Stability, Value, and Reasonableness* (OUP 2019) 25; Ursula Kriebaum, 'FET and Expropriation in the (Invisible) EU Model BIT' (2014) 15 JWIT 454, 471.

aspects of the FET standard they are determining whether a State's measures fall 'outside the acceptable margin of change'[113] or 'outside the acceptable range of legislative and regulatory behaviour'.[114]

Certain early investment treaty arbitrations with an environmental component developed a particularly expansive interpretation of the FET standard, including a particularly expansive understanding of the protections it afforded vis-à-vis regulatory stability and legitimate expectations. For example, in *Tecmed v Mexico*, Mexico was found to have violated the FET standard by failing to provide clarity regarding the regulatory conditions affecting the investor's hazardous waste operation, including by refusing to renew the operating permit for reasons extraneous to the stated environmental reasons.[115] In an infamous formulation, the Tribunal viewed the FET provision as requiring:

> treatment that does not affect the basic expectations that were taken into account by the foreign investor to make the investment. The foreign investor expects the host State to act in a consistent manner, free from ambiguity and totally transparently in its relations with the foreign investor, so that it may know beforehand any and all rules and regulations that will govern its investments, as well as the goals of the relevant policies and administrative practices or directives, to be able to plan its investment and comply with such regulations.... The foreign investor also expects the host State to act consistently, i.e. without arbitrarily revoking any preexisting decisions or permits issued by the State that were relied upon by the investor to assume its commitments as well as to plan and launch its commercial and business activities.[116]

As Ortino has highlighted, the *Tecmed* formulation focuses on 'consistency' rather than 'stability' (which is not mentioned in the award) and is somewhat less unbalanced than several subsequent early awards which, drawing on *Tecmed*, did explicitly endorse a requirement of legal stability.[117] Nevertheless, the *Tecmed* formulation was rightly criticised in both

[113] *El Paso v Argentina* (n 73) [402].

[114] *AES Summit Generation Ltd and AES-Tisza Erömü Kft v Hungary*, ICSID Case No ARB/07/22, Award (23 September 2010) [9.3.73], applied eg in *Novenergia II – Energy & Environment (SCA), SICAR v Spain*, SCC Arbitration 2015/063, Final Arbitration Award (15 February 2018) [695].

[115] *Tecnicas Medioambientales Tecmed SA v Mexico*, ICSID Case No ARB(AF)/00/2, Award (29 May 2003) [162]–[172].

[116] Ibid [154].

[117] Ortino (n 112) 20–22. See eg *CMS Gas Transmission Co v Argentina*, ICSID Case No ARB/01/8, Award (12 May 2005) [274]–[280]; *Occidental Exploration and Production Company v Ecuador*, LCIA Case No 3467, UNCITRAL, Final Award

commentary and subsequent arbitral decisions.[118] There is a strong argument that it reflects an unrealistic standard of 'perfect public regulation in a perfect world' that few States are ever likely to attain.[119] A similarly unrealistic expectation of State behaviour was reflected in the *Metalclad* award, another case where Mexico was held liable for failing to ensure a predictable regulatory framework for an investor that was found to have invested on the understanding it had met all the legal requirements for the development of a hazardous waste facility, which was subsequently not permitted on environmental grounds.[120] In a move which led to its award being partially set aside in the Canadian courts, the Tribunal interpreted the FET obligation in light of the reference in NAFTA's preamble to transparency,[121] holding that:

> all relevant legal requirements for the purpose of initiating, completing and successfully operating investments made, or intended to be made, under the Agreement should be capable of being readily known to all affected investors of another Party. There should be no room for doubt or uncertainty on such matters.[122]

Obviously, if these early, extremely broad interpretations of the FET standard were widely endorsed it would impede States' ability to adopt or update environmental regulation to reflect 'advances in scientific knowledge or shifts in social values'.[123] These early awards represent one extreme within the role that investment treaty tribunals play in determining the permissible degree of change in the host State regulation.

In contrast, the interpretation of the FET standard that has generally prevailed in more recent cases has been more limited both in relation to any protection of regulatory stability included in the standard and

(1 July 2004) [183], [185]; *Enron Corp and Ponderosa Assets, LP v Argentina*, ICSID Case No ARB/01/3, Award (22 May 2007) [259]–[267]; *Sempra Energy International v Argentina*, ICSID Case No ARB/02/16, Award (28 September 2007) [298]–[300], [303]; *LG&E Energy Corp et al v Argentina*, ICSID Case No ARB/02/1, Decision on Liability (3 October 2006) [124]–[125], [131].

118 See e.g. *Biwater Gauff (Tanzania) Ltd v Tanzania*, ICSID Case No ARB/05/22, Award (24 July 2008) [600]; *MTD Equity Sdn Bhd v Chile*, ICSID Case No ARB/01/7, Decision on Annulment (21 March 2007) [66]–[67].

119 Zachary Douglas, 'Nothing If Not Critical for Investment Treaty Arbitration: *Occidental*, *Eureko* and *Methanex*' (2006) 22 Arb. Int. 27, 28.

120 *Metalclad Corp v Mexico*, ICSID Case No ARB(AF)/97/1, Award (30 August 2000) [99], generally [77]–[99].

121 See *United Mexican States v Metalclad* [2001] BCSC 664, [66]–[76], [133]–[136].

122 *Metalclad* (n 120) [76].

123 Miles (n 110) 169.

regarding the legitimate expectations aspect of the standard. This reflects that tribunals have become more sensitive to host States' need 'to maintain a reasonable degree of regulatory flexibility to respond to changing circumstances in the public interest'.[124] In general terms, the more recent jurisprudence has shifted away from any strict obligation of regulatory stability and has instead focused on whether, assessed in the totality of the circumstances including the public policy rationale for the change, the regulatory change was unreasonable or disproportionate.[125] Similarly, in relation to the legitimate expectations strand of FET, when determining whether any expectations were objectively reasonable, tribunals have frequently emphasised that ordinarily investors must expect that a State may adapt existing regulation to evolving public interests, and at times have accepted that a countervailing public interest can provide a justification for subsequently disappointing any legitimate expectations that are established.[126]

A good example of this more restrained approach to the protection which the FET standard provides in relation to changes of domestic regulation is *Mamidoil v Albania*, where the Tribunal viewed the FET standard as only protecting investors from 'inacceptable and inappropriate changes of conditions and circumstances by the State', given the 'State's legitimate interest and right to change conditions reasonably for public policy purposes'.[127] This case concerned an investment in the construction and operation of an oil container terminal at a port and the host State's decision to close the port to petroleum tankers as part of a rezoning aimed at environmental remediation. In finding that the zoning change was a legitimate exercise of sovereign power and 'did not lead to

[124] *Electrabel SA v Hungary*, ICSID Case No ARB/07/19, Decision on Jurisdiction, Applicable Law and Liability (30 November 2012) [7.77]. See also *Infracapital F1 S.à.r. l. v Spain*, ICSID Case No ARB/16/18, Decision on Jurisdiction, Liability and Directions on Quantum (13 September 2021) [565]; *Greentech Energy Systems A/S v Italy*, SCC Arbitration Case No V (2015/095), Diss. Op. Sacerdoti [10].

[125] Ortino (n 112) 31–32. Ortino rightly highlights that even in recent case law there is a lack of clarity regarding what exactly makes a regulatory change become unacceptable and thus breach the FET standard: ibid 41, 43, 46; *RENERGY S.à.r.l. v Spain*, ICSID Case No ARB/14/18, Award (6 May 2022) [642] (outlining the numerous different formulations used in past jurisprudence to express when a regulatory change will violate the FET standard).

[126] For a critical analysis of these two approaches to reconciling an investor's legitimate expectations and the host State's right to regulate, see Ortino (n 112) 145–49. See also *Mathias Kruck*, Partial Diss. Op. Douglas (n 110) [2]–[4], [44]–[46], [102]–[113].

[127] *Mamidoil Jetoil Greek Petroleum Products Societe SA v Albania*, ICSID Case No ARB/11/24, Award (30 March 2015) [634], [703]. See also [613]–[618].

unreasonable instability',[128] the Tribunal emphasised that Albania was a country in transition from a communist regime, which had a pressing need to modernise its infrastructure with limited resources.[129] Thus, investors could not expect the 'same results of stability as in Great Britain, USA or Japan'.[130] Furthermore, no specific assurances had been given to the investor regarding the use of the port,[131] and the measures were of a general nature, affecting all companies operating at the port.[132] Albania had in fact pursued its modernisation process 'in a gradual way' and the policy changes were first communicated to the investor at a point when it still retained significant flexibility, not having made the bulk of its investment.[133] Similarly, in the *Bilcon* case, although the majority held that Canada had breached the arbitrariness aspect of the FET standard through the failure of the domestic environmental review body to apply its mandate,[134] it emphasised that: '[a]s lessons of experience are learned, as new policy ideas are advanced, as governments change in response to democratic choice, State authorities with the power to change law or policy must have reasonable freedom to proceed without being tasked with having breached the minimum standard'. This freedom was however 'not absolute' and could be restricted in special circumstances, such as where regulatory changes were contrary to prior specific assurances given to the investor.[135]

A more realistic approach to appraising the permissibility of change in host State regulation was also adopted in *Plama v Bulgaria*. In this case, the investor alleged that Bulgaria had breached the FET standard by amending its environmental law to make the investor liable for past environmental damage at an oil refinery that the investor had acquired.[136] In rejecting this claim, the Tribunal emphasised that Bulgaria had not promised or represented to the investor that it would freeze its environmental legislation, and the investor could not have been sure upon investing that it would avoid liability for past environmental

[128] Ibid [657].
[129] Ibid [625]–[629].
[130] Ibid [626].
[131] Ibid [644], [651].
[132] Ibid [661].
[133] Ibid [660], [720]–[724]. See also [704]–[707].
[134] *Bilcon v Canada* (n 85) [573].
[135] Ibid [572].
[136] *Plama Consortium v Bulgaria*, ICSID Case No ARB/03/24, Award (27 August 2008) [149].

damage given the state of domestic law.[137] As the Tribunal observed, the FET standard 'does not protect investors against any and all changes in the host country's laws'.[138]

The large body of recent cases involving challenges to several European States' changes to renewable energy incentives have significantly advanced debates over the stability and legitimate expectations aspects of the FET standard.[139] Environmental considerations have generally only featured marginally in these cases.[140] Nevertheless, the main features of this case law will be discussed because it starkly highlights the role of investment arbitration in deciding on the permissible degree of change in host State regulation. The majority of tribunals in these cases have held that absent specific assurances, investors cannot expect that a regulatory regime, even where it is designed to incentivise investment in a particular economic sector, will remain completely unchanged over the life of an investment.[141] Rather, most tribunals in the renewables subsidy

[137] Ibid [218]–[222]. Note that the Tribunal had earlier rejected the case on the ground that the claimant was not entitled to rely on the investment protections in the ECT because the investment had been established through fraudulent misrepresentation: see [143]–[146]. Nevertheless, the Tribunal went on to consider the claims on the merits and explain why they would have failed: [147].

[138] Ibid [219].

[139] Similarly: August Reinisch and Christoph Schreuer, *International Protection of Investments: The Substantive Standards* (CUP 2020) 475, 514.

[140] See eg *Sevilla Beheer B.V. and Others v Spain*, ICSID Case No ARB/16/27, Decision on Jurisdiction, Liability and the Principles of Quantum (11 February 2022) [860]–[862]; *RREEF Infrastructure (GP) Limited v Spain*, ICSID Case No ARB/13/30, Decision on Responsibility and on the Principles of Quantum (30 November 2018) [87]–[88]; *OperaFund Eco-Invest SICAV PLC v Spain*, ICSID Case No ARB/15/36, Diss. Op. Sands (13 August 2019) [39], [42]; *RENERGY v Spain*, Dissent Sands (n 110) [1], [48].

[141] See eg *Infracapital v Spain* (n 124) [527]–[528], [565]–[569]; *Eurus Energy Holdings Corporation v Spain*, ICSID Case No ARB/16/4, Decision on Jurisdiction and Liability (17 March 2021) [315]–[317]; *PV Investors v Spain*, PCA Case No 2012-14, Final Award (28 February 2020) [570]; *RREEF v Spain* (n 140) [244]–[245], [261]–[263]; *RWE Innogy GmbH v Spain*, ICSID Case No ARB/14/34, Decision on Jurisdiction, Liability, and Certain Issues of Quantum (30 December 2019) [448]–[451]; *Eiser Infrastructure Ltd v Spain*, ICSID Case No ARB/13/36, Award (4 May 2017) [362]–[363]; *Cavalum SGPS, SA v Spain*, ICSID Case No ARB/15/34, Decision on Jurisdiction, Liability and Directions on Quantum (31 August 2020) [411], [418]–[420], [438]–[439]; *NextEra Energy Global Holdings B.V. & Ors v Spain*, ICSID Case No ARB/14/11, Decision on Jurisdiction, Liability and Principles of Quantum (12 March 2019) [584]–[601] (finding liability due to specific assurances given to the claimants and noting that 'legislation can be changed'); *Cube Infrastructure Fund SICAV and Others v Spain*, ICSID Case No ARB/15/20, Decision on Jurisdiction, Liability and Partial Decision on Quantum (19 February 2019) [397], [408], [411]; *Eskosol S.p.A. in liquidazione v Italy*, ICSID Case No ARB/15/50, Award (4 September 2020) [434].

cases have held that investors are only protected against regulatory changes that are unreasonable, disproportionate, arbitrary,[142] or which constitute an 'unpredictable radical transformation in the conditions of the investments'[143] 'in a manner that does not take account of the circumstances of existing investments made in reliance on the prior regime'.[144] Reviewing this case law, the majority in *RENERGY v Spain* held that the FET standard only protected investors against legislative changes that were 'radical'.[145] It outlined various criteria to be used to determine whether a regulatory change exceeded the '(wide) acceptable margin', including the 'magnitude of the change', its economic impact on the investor, the time given to the investor to adjust to the new regulatory regime, whether the change was 'triggered by a change of external circumstances, i.e. circumstances largely beyond the control of the host State', and the importance of the public interests involved.[146]

However, a minority of tribunals in the renewables cases have endorsed a more expansive concept of regulatory stability and legitimate expectations under the FET standard, with clear similarities to early, widely critiqued awards such as *Tecmed*. For example, the majority in

[142] See e.g. *Blusun SA v Italy*, ICSID Case No ARB/14/3, Award (27 December 2016) [318], [319(5)], [372]; *Infracapital v Spain* (n 124) [531], [566]; *PV Investors v Spain* (n 141) [580]–[583], [624]; *Eurus v Spain* (n 141) [335]–[336]; *RWE v Spain* (n 141) [451], [462], [570]; *BayWa.r.e. Renewable Energy GmbH v Spain*, ICSID Case No ARB/15/16, Decision on Jurisdiction, Liability and Directions on Quantum (2 December 2019) [463]; *Hydro Energy 1 S.À R.L. v Spain*, ICSID Case No ARB/15/42, Award (9 March 2020) [568], [582]–[590], [676(3)–(11)]; *Wirtgen v Czech Republic* (n 66) [408]–[409], [437].

[143] See eg *RREEF v Spain* (n 140) [315]–[317]; *Sevilla Beheer v Spain* (n 140) [713], [793], [799], [934]; *SolEs Badajoz GmbH v Spain*, ICSID Case No ARB/15/38, Award (31 July 2019) [315]–[318]; *Cavalum v Spain* (n 141) [406], [538]; *Foresight Luxembourg Solar 1 S.à.r.l. & Ors v Spain*, SCC Arbitration V 2015/150, Final Award (14 November 2018) [359]; *Infrastructure Services Luxembourg S.à.r.l. & ors v Spain*, ICSID Case No ARB/13/31, Award (15 June 2018) [532]; *Novenergia v Spain* (n 114) [654]–[656]; *Cube Infrastructure v Spain* (n 141) [397], [408]–[412] (holding that as Spain had represented that certain provisions would be maintained for a certain time, they could only be 'adjusted in a manner that does not significantly alter the fundamental economic basis of investments made in reliance on that representation'); *SunReserve Luxco Holdings S.À.R.L v Italy*, SCC Arbitration V 2016/32, Final Award (25 March 2020) [692]; *Silver Ridge Power BV v Italy*, ICSID Case No ARB/15/37, Award (26 February 2021) [417].

[144] *Eiser v Spain* (n 141) [363], [370], [382]; *InfraRed Environmental Infrastructure GP Limited and Others v Spain*, ICSID Case No ARB/14/12, Award (2 August 2019) [368].

[145] *RENERGY v Spain*, Award (n 125) [642], [682].

[146] Ibid [642], [681].

Watkins Holdings v Spain, drawing on *Tecmed* and other early investment treaty jurisprudence concerning regulatory stability and legitimate expectations, held that although Spain did not have to freeze its laws it could not 'substantially alter the regulatory framework that was applicable to the Claimants' investment'.[147] The majority in *Greentech v Italy* concluded on the facts that Italy had provided the claimants with 'non-waivable guarantees', meaning at most 'the investor might need to live with some minor adjustments'. In a part of its reasoning that is revealing of its emphasis on regulatory stability, the Tribunal remarked that the economic difficulties faced by Italy did not 'reach the level of *force majeure*'.[148] Similarly, the majority in *ESPF v Italy* held that Italy had, through the regulatory scheme establishing the incentives for qualifying solar facilities, provided specific commitments that the promised tariff would be paid for the full twenty-year term.[149] For the majority, as the investor's legitimate expectation of a constant tariff was reasonable and the result of a specific commitment, the size of the change was irrelevant, as was the question of whether the change was a proportionate and reasonable measure given the regulatory challenges faced by Italy.[150]

Nearly all the renewables subsidy cases have turned on Article 10(1) of the Energy Charter Treaty (ECT), which provides, insofar as relevant for present purposes:

> Each Contracting Party shall, in accordance with the provisions of this Treaty, encourage and create stable, equitable, favourable and transparent conditions for Investors of other Contracting Parties to make Investments in its Area. Such conditions shall include a commitment to accord at all

[147] *Watkins Holding S.À.R.L v Spain*, ICSID Case No ARB/15/44, Award (21 January 2020) [518], [521]–[522], [543]. Consider also *Masdar Solar & Wind Cooperatief U.A. v Spain*, ICSID Case No ARB/14/1, Award (16 May 2018) [520]–[522] (holding that due to specific commitments the claimant could expect that Spain's regulatory regime would remain unaltered); *9REN v Spain* (n 77) [292]–[299], [308]–[309] (holding that despite no specific commitments being given to the investor individually, the regulatory scheme was sufficiently clear and specific to give rise to a legitimate expectation that it would be maintained for the life of existing facilities); *Mathias Kruck and Others v Spain*, ICSID Case No ARB/15/23, Decision on Jurisdiction, Liability and Principles of Quantum (14 September 2022) [197]–[202] (holding that given the context of the relevant regulatory regime, while Spain could modify the incentive regime, it had agreed that it would not alter the 'fundamental characteristics' of the regime).

[148] See *Greentech Energy Systems A/S v Italy*, SCC Arbitration Case No V (2015/095), Award (23 December 2018), [446]–[455]. Cf Diss. Op. Sacerdoti [8]–[51].

[149] *ESPF Beteiligungs GmbH & Ors v Italy*, ICSID Case No ARB/16/5, Award (14 September 2020) [512]–[520], [529]–[531], [545]–[546].

[150] Ibid [577]–[582]. Cf [645] (Dissent Boisson de Chazournes).

> times to Investments of Investors of other Contracting Parties fair and equitable treatment.[151]

The dominant interpretation of this provision in the renewables cases has been that the first sentence of Article 10(1) does not create a separate obligation of stability but provides context that informs the interpretation of the FET obligation in the second sentence.[152] Notably, some tribunals have also rejected the argument that these features of Article 10 (1) of the ECT mean that it creates a more demanding obligation of regulatory stability than FET provisions in other investment treaties.[153] As the *PV Investors v Spain* Tribunal noted, in highlighting the need to take a balanced approach to interpreting the ECT: 'the requirement of stability is not absolute; it must be balanced with other principles, including those that are directly derived from "State sovereignty", e.g. the State's right to regulate and to adapt the regulatory framework to changed circumstances'.[154] However, several tribunals have drawn on the specific wording in the first sentence of Article 10(1) of the ECT, and the object and purpose of the ECT, to hold that it involves a stronger obligation of regulatory stability than other investment treaties.[155] In understanding the variations in outcomes across the large body of renewables cases it is also important to note that there are significant differences between the disputes on key factual issues, such as the time at which an investment was made and whether specific assurances were given to an investor.[156] Ultimately, this brief examination demonstrates that whatever stance a tribunal takes on the contested legal issues analysed above, this burgeoning body of jurisprudence highlights the crucial function of investment treaty arbitration in determining the permissible degree of change in domestic regulation, taking into account the circumstances in which an investment was made and the evolving policy problems faced by the host State.

151 ECT art 10(1).

152 *Eurus v Spain* (n 141) [314]–[317]; *Infracapital v Spain* (n 124) [520]–[521]; *Novenergia v Spain* (n 114) [646]; *Stadtwerke München GmbH v Spain*, ICSID Case No ARB/15/1, Award (2 December 2019) [195]–[198]. Contrast: *Hydro Energy v Spain* (n 142) [549].

153 *Infracapital v Spain* (n 124) [521]–[524]. See also *PV Investors v Spain* (n 141) [566]–[570]; *Eurus v Spain* (n 141) [314].

154 *PV Investors v Spain* (n 141) [570]. See also *RENERGY v Spain*, Dissent Sands (n 110) [27].

155 E.g. *Watkins Holding v Spain* (n 147) [540]–[543]; *Infrastructure Services v Spain* (n 143) [533], generally [518]–[533]. See also *Eiser v Spain* (n 141) [377]–[380].

156 *SolEs v Spain* (n 143) [334].

C. The Standard and Method of Review in Investment Treaty Arbitration

1. *Standard of Review in Investment Treaty Arbitration*

Similarly to the other adjudication contexts studied in this book, investment treaty arbitration frequently raises the problem of the appropriate intensity of international adjudicatory scrutiny of domestic-level determinations that are based on the application of non-legal expertise that arbitrators do not hold and/or that involve the exercise of discretion by domestic authorities, including over value-laden issues. This subsection will demonstrate that at least within cases with an environmental component, investment treaty jurisprudence has become increasingly consistent in endorsing the idea that an international tribunal owes the host State a significant although not unlimited degree of deference over such regulatory determinations.[157] Nevertheless, the wider case law and literature on this issue suggests that the trends identified here are not confined to cases with an environmental component, but reflect a broader mainstreaming of certain ideas around deference in investment treaty arbitration.[158]

A good starting point is provided by *Muszynianka spółka z ograniczoną odpowiedzialnością v Slovak Republic*, a case where the investor was challenging, among other measures, Slovakia's adoption of

[157] Note that signs of such deference were already present in some of the earliest investment treaty awards with an environmental component: see especially *SD Myers, Inc v Canada*, Partial Award (13 November 2000) UNCITRAL [261], [263].

[158] Aspects of Section (C)(1) of this chapter draw on Joshua Paine, 'Standard of Review: Investment Arbitration' in Hélène Ruiz Fabri (ed), *Max Planck Encyclopedia of International Procedural Law* (OUP 2019) and Joshua Paine, 'Standard of Review' in Hélène Ruiz Fabri and Edoardo Stoppioni (eds), *International Investment Law: An Analysis of Major Decisions* (Hart 2022) 327. The former includes an extensive bibliography current up to January 2018 and the latter chapter cites more recent literature. Among the extensive literature on deference and the standard of review in investment treaty arbitration, see eg Esmé Shirlow, *Judging at the Interface: Deference to State Decision-Making Authority in International Adjudication* (CUP 2021); Johannes Hendrik Fahner, *Judicial Deference in International Adjudication: A Comparative Analysis* (Hart 2020); Caroline Henckels, *Proportionality and Deference in Investor-State Arbitration: Balancing Investment Protection and Regulatory Autonomy* (CUP 2015); Stephan W Schill, 'Deference in Investment Treaty Arbitration: Re-conceptualizing the Standard of Review' (2012) 3 JIDS 577; Erlend M Leonhardsen, 'Designing Deference: Towards a Thin Margin of Appreciation Doctrine in International Investment Law?' in Jelena Bäumler and others (eds), *European Yearbook of International Economic Law 2021* (Springer 2022); Gary Born, Danielle Morris and Stephanie Forrest, '"A Margin of Appreciation": Appreciating Its Irrelevance in International Law' (2020) 61 HILJ 65.

a constitutional amendment that prohibited the cross-border transport of non-bottled water.[159] In determining whether the constitutional amendment complied with the reasonableness strand of the FET standard, the Tribunal began by emphasising that '[i]nvestment treaty arbitration tribunals owe deference to States in determining what serves as a legitimate public purpose ... the presumption is that State conduct seeks to attain a legitimate common good'.[160] At this initial stage of the analysis, the majority of the tribunal accepted that the constitutional amendment had pursued the legitimate aims of protecting the environment, public health, and regulating the use of Slovakia's water resources, even though parts of the record also indicated an intent of developing the local economy by ensuring bottling of water occurred in Slovakia.[161] Subsequently, in determining whether the constitutional amendment had a reasonable relationship with these legitimate policy aims, the majority emphasised that:

> it is not the role of an arbitral tribunal to "weigh the wisdom of legislation" ... arbitral tribunals must pay deference to the choices States make when deciding how to implement policy objectives. Such deference or margin of appreciation makes sense because arbitral tribunals are not embedded within the host State and State authorities are better placed to assess national the [sic] conditions, needs, sensitivities, priorities, technical specificities and interests of the stakeholders.[162]

On the facts, the Tribunal found that several features of the constitutional amendment demonstrated that it had a reasonable relationship to the legitimate policy aims of preserving Slovakia's water reserves, regulating the rational use of that resource and protecting public health.[163]

The large number of recent cases challenging reductions in the subsidies offered to renewable energy sources also demonstrate the mainstreaming of a significant but not unlimited notion of deference in investment treaty arbitration. For example, in *RENERGY v Spain*, in responding to the investor's argument that there were other ways Spain could have addressed the tariff deficit that had accumulated in its electricity system, without reducing incentives for renewable energy sources, the Tribunal noted that:

159 *Muszynianka spółka z ograniczoną odpowiedzialnością v Slovak Republic*, PCA Case No 2017-08, Award (7 October 2020).
160 Ibid [546].
161 Ibid [546]–[556].
162 Ibid [557]–[558] (citations omitted).
163 Ibid [559]–[565]. Cf Partial Diss. Op. Volterra [21]ff.

> it is not for the Tribunal to pass judgment on what would have been the best policy decision for the Respondent to take ... balancing competing public interests is one of the core responsibilities and prerogatives of a State. The Tribunal does not find it appropriate to second-guess the Respondent's assessment at the time that ... it was more important to bring the Tariff Deficit under control than to keep incentives for investment in green energy at the same level as before. This policy choice is not manifestly unreasonable ... Therefore, the Tribunal will defer to the Respondent's policy choice.[164]

Similarly, the *RREEF v Spain* Tribunal, in assessing the proportionality and reasonableness of Spain's measures, held that:

> the Respondent enjoys a margin of appreciation in conducting its economic policy; therefore, it will not substitute its own views either on the appropriateness of the measures at stake or on the characterization of the situation which prompted them; in particular, the Tribunal will abstain to take any position on the issue of the existence of other or more appropriate possible measures to face this situation.[165]

Unsurprisingly, immediately after this the Tribunal noted that the 'Respondent's margin of appreciation cannot be unlimited ... "discretionary" cannot be equated with "arbitrary"; margin of appreciation is different from unfettered discretion'.[166] The *Antaris v Czech Republic* Tribunal, in enunciating a series of propositions supported by prior jurisprudence concerning the FET standard, also noted that:

> The host State is not required to elevate the interests of the investor above all other considerations, and the application of the FET standard allows for a balancing or weighing exercise by the State and the determination of a breach of the FET standard must be made in the light of the high measure of deference which international law generally extends to the right of national authorities to regulate matters within their own borders.[167]

This statement regarding deference has subsequently been endorsed by several other tribunals in the renewables disputes.[168]

[164] *RENERGY v Spain*, Award (n 125) [899]–[901]. See also *RENERGY v Spain*, Dissent Sands (n 110) [34]. Similar: *BayWa.r.e. v Spain* (n 142) [480].

[165] *RREEF v Spain* (n 140) [468].

[166] Ibid.

[167] *Antaris GMBH & Ors v Czech Republic*, PCA Case No 2014-01, Award (2 May 2018) [360(9)]. Cf Diss. Op. Born [41]–[54].

[168] E.g. *Sevilla Beheer v Spain* (n 140) [929]–[930]; *CEF Energia B.V. v Italy*, SCC Arbitration V (2015/158), Award (16 January 2019) [236].

The *Bilcon* award also made an important contribution regarding the standard of review and the considerations that should inform this issue. As noted above, in this case the majority found that the domestic environmental review panel had failed to follow its mandate under the applicable Canadian legislation and in doing so violated the MST and the national treatment standard. Specifically, the review panel had applied a standard to the investor's project, emphasising community values, which the majority considered lacked a basis in the relevant domestic legislation and meant that the panel had failed to assess the project's adverse effects after potential mitigation measures, as required by the panel's mandate.[169] The majority found that what was at issue was 'not merely a matter of disputed judgments interpreting grey areas of the law, weighing contested points of evidence, or exercising scientific judgment'.[170] Rather, the review panel had 'departed in fundamental ways from the standard of evaluation required by the laws of Canada rather than merely being controversial in matters of detailed application'.[171] The majority highlighted that it was not purporting 'to conduct its own environmental assessment ... [nor] deciding what the actual outcome should have been'.[172] Instead, the key was that the investors had been denied a 'fair *opportunity* to have the specifics of that case considered, assessed and decided in accordance with applicable [Canadian] laws'.[173] The majority emphasised that 'mere error in legal or factual analysis' was insufficient to give rise to a breach of the MST.[174] Importantly, the majority addressed directly the policy considerations that underlie debates over the appropriate standard or intensity of review, noting that:

> third-party adjudicators must, in applying the international minimum standard, take into account that domestic authorities may have more familiarity with the factual and domestic legal complexities of a situation. Secondly, domestic authorities may also enjoy distinctive kinds of

169 *Bilcon v Canada* (n 85) [451]–[452], [525]–[528], [583], [591].

170 Ibid [454].

171 Ibid [594], see also [600]–[602].

172 Ibid [602].

173 Ibid [603] (emphasis in original), [571]. Also central to the finding of a breach of the international minimum standard was that the review panel had failed to provide the investor reasonable notice of the approach, based on community values, that would be applied to its project: [534], [543], [594]. The majority's finding of a breach of the national treatment standard depended on similar considerations, namely that unlike comparable projects, the investor's project was not assessed according to the standards established by the applicable Canadian legislation: [697], [700], [704]–[705].

174 Ibid [594].

> legitimacy, such as being elected or accountable to elected authorities. Thirdly, ... Third-party adjudicators may have their own advantages including independence and detachment from domestic pressures.[175]

The majority also observed that '[m]odern regulatory and social welfare states tackle complex problems.... The imprudent exercise of discretion or even outright mistakes do not, as a rule, lead to a breach of the international minimum standard.'[176] The inclusion of these more generalised statements in the *Bilcon* award supporting a degree of deference to the determinations of domestic authorities may reflect that it was an obviously controversial case, involving a finding of breach of the MST in relation to a determination of a domestic environmental review panel.[177]

The *Glamis v USA* Award, already discussed above, also made a significant intervention regarding the intensity with which an international tribunal should scrutinise determinations of domestic authorities that are based on the application of specialised forms of expertise. As noted above, this case involved a challenge to the regulatory approval process that was applied to the investor's proposed mining project due to concerns about the protection of sites of indigenous cultural heritage and environmental protection. Importantly, the Tribunal accepted the US' submission that '[i]t is simply not this Tribunal's task to become archaeologists and ethnographers' and answer de novo questions that were involved in the cultural review process applied to the investor's project.[178] More generally, it was 'not the role of this Tribunal, or any international tribunal, to supplant its own judgment of underlying factual material and support for that of a qualified domestic agency'.[179] Rather, the Tribunal could 'assess only whether there was reasonable evidence, and thus the government's reliance on such was not obviously and actionably misplaced'.[180] Specifically, in applying the MST the Tribunal asked whether 'the agency's review and conclusions exhibit a gross denial of justice, manifest arbitrariness, blatant unfairness, a complete lack of due process, evident discrimination, or a manifest lack of reasons'.[181] For example, in applying this standard to the cultural review process, the

[175] Ibid [439].
[176] Ibid [437].
[177] See also in this regard *Bilcon v Canada* (n 85) [595]–[600], [735]–[738].
[178] *Glamis v USA* (n 61) [779].
[179] Ibid.
[180] Ibid [786].
[181] Ibid [779]. See also [616]–[617] (disagreeing with the suggestion 'that domestic deference in national court systems is necessarily applicable to international tribunals' and

Tribunal noted that the US had relied on the advice of qualified professionals and had established a prima facie case regarding why particular aspects of the process were reasonable in the circumstances.[182] In rejecting the claimant's challenge to separate state-level legislation applied to its proposed project, the Tribunal also held that the fact that this legislation addressed some but not all of the harms posed by open-pit mining to indigenous sacred sites did not mean that the legislation was arbitrary, rather it simply reflected the normal role of government in striking a 'compromise between the interests of competing parties'.[183] To be sure, *Glamis* is at the deferential end of the existing jurisprudence, given its view on the high threshold for the MST to be breached.[184] Nevertheless, the Award highlights several reasons why some degree of deference to determinations made by domestic authorities can be appropriate, for example where those determinations were made on the basis of specialised forms of non-legal expertise that the international tribunal does not hold, or involve the exercise of discretion given the normal role of governments in compromising between different interests.

The majority Award in *Lone Pine v Canada* is another noteworthy example of deference in the reasoning of investment treaty tribunals. In this case the investor challenged a revocation of its rights to explore for shale gas under the St Lawrence River through a general legislative measure enacted by the Québec National Assembly.[185] The investor argued that Québec's revocation of its permit rights without compensation was a breach of the MST as, among other reasons, these acts were 'neither rationally connected nor necessary to serve the stated purposes of environmental protection and preservation of the St. Lawrence River'.[186] The majority of the Tribunal rejected these claims, noting that the legislation revoking the permits had been adopted by the Québec National Assembly 'following proper democratic procedures' and had 'the stated public policy objective of preservation of the fluvial environment under the St. Lawrence River'.[187] Noting the high threshold for

finding that deference was present within the international minimum standard rather than being additive to it).

182 Ibid [783], [787].

183 Ibid [803]–[805]. See also [817].

184 See above text at n 181.

185 *Lone Pine Resources Inc. v Canada*, ICSID Case No UNCT/15/2, Final Award (21 November 2022). See generally [142]–[238] for the factual background.

186 Ibid [615].

187 Ibid [620]–[622].

establishing a breach for the MST, the majority held '[i]n general, arbitral tribunals must grant significant deference to the host State's democratic process and public policy choices and may not substitute their own judgment for that of the host State'.[188] On this basis, the majority refused to undertake an analysis of whether the reports and studies relied on by the relevant regulatory agency supported the legislative measure enacted in response – involving revocation of permits – as '[t]his would be tantamount to substituting its decision for that of the legislature'.[189] The Tribunal suggested that showing a breach of the MST '[i]n the facts of this case ... would require Claimant to demonstrate that there was a complete disconnect between the impugned Act and the objective of protecting the fluvial environment under the St. Lawrence River', which it did not accept was established.[190] Ultimately, it is striking that the majority deliberately avoided engaging in any detailed scrutiny of whether the environmental studies that were before the Québec legislature provided sufficient support for the legislative measure adopted (involving revocation of permits). While the majority implicitly found that, based on the evidence on the record, the claimant had not demonstrated 'that there was a complete disconnect between the impugned Act and the objective of protecting the fluvial environment', its decision not to engage in further scrutiny of the measures adopted to pursue that aim is notable.[191] For example, the majority rejected the claimant's argument that the permanent revocation of the permit rights 'was "an unnecessary deprivation of rights" as there were other effective mechanisms' for protecting the fluvial environment, noting '[t]hat the Québec Government chose one option over another option in pursuance of its objective ... cannot be regarded as manifestly arbitrary conduct' and hence a breach of the MST.[192]

A final case worth considering in relation to the standard of review, particularly in the context of contested science-based determinations that are common in environmental disputes, is *Chemtura v Canada*, which concerned Canada's ban on lindane-based products that the investor produced. The Tribunal emphasised that the review involved in applying the international minimum standard was fact specific and it had to take 'into account all the circumstances, including the fact that certain

[188] Ibid [623]–[624].
[189] Ibid [625].
[190] See Ibid [626]–[629].
[191] Ibid [625]–[629].
[192] Ibid [628]. Cf the Partial Dissent of David R. Haigh [3]–[5].

agencies manage highly specialized domains involving scientific and public policy determinations'.[193] The Tribunal rejected the idea of a general doctrine of deference: 'This is not an abstract assessment circumscribed by a legal doctrine about the margin of appreciation of specialized regulatory agencies. It is an assessment that must be conducted *in concreto*.'[194] Nevertheless, in the approach applied, the Tribunal noted that it was 'not its task to determine whether certain uses of lindane are dangerous, whether in general or in the Canadian context'.[195] The Tribunal emphasised that 'lindane has raised increasingly serious concerns both in other countries and at the international level since the 1970s', citing numerous examples of national and international regulation.[196] Despite the existence of some divergence of views within the Canadian authorities, the Tribunal was not convinced that the national regulatory process was conducted in bad faith,[197] adding that it was not its role to 'judge the correctness or adequacy of the scientific results' relied upon.[198] The Tribunal's approach reflects that, as others have noted, the substantive standards contained in investment treaties generally only require that scientific claims relied on by a domestic regulator be reasonable rather than correct, and largely relate to the quality of the regulatory process employed.[199]

This subsection has demonstrated that at least within the universe of cases with an environmental component, a form of deference has been increasingly mainstreamed in investment treaty jurisprudence. On the

193 *Chemtura Corporation (formerly Crompton Corporation) v Canada*, UNCITRAL Award (2 August 2010) [123].

194 Ibid.

195 Ibid [134].

196 Ibid [135]–[136].

197 Ibid [137]–[138], [143], [148].

198 Ibid [153]. For a similar approach in the context of contested scientific evidence, see *Methanex Corporation v USA*, UNCITRAL Final Award (3 August 2005) pt III, ch A [101].

199 Lukasz Gruszczynski and Valentina Vadi, 'Standard of Review and Scientific Evidence in WTO Law and International Investment Arbitration: Converging Parallels?' in Lukasz Gruszczynski and Wouter Werner (eds), *Deference in International Courts and Tribunals: Standard of Review and Margin of Appreciation* (OUP 2014) 169–70; Yuka Fukunaga, 'Standard of Review and "Scientific Truths" in the WTO Dispute Settlement System and Investment Arbitration' (2012) 3 JIDS 559, 572–76; Federico Ortino and Nima Mersadi Tabari, 'International Dispute Settlement: The Settlement of Investment Disputes Concerning Natural Resources – Applicable Law and Standards of Review' in Elisa Morgera and Kati Kulovesi (eds), *Research Handbook on International Law and Natural Resources* (Edward Elgar 2016) 513–14.

whole, investment arbitrators are aware of the arguments in favour of a limited degree of deference, based both on the greater expertise of domestic authorities on certain issues and domestic authorities' greater legitimacy to make certain kinds of discretionary determinations that frequently confront governments. Other studies, not focusing specifically on environmental cases, have also demonstrated the increasing reception of arguments concerning a limited form of deference in investment treaty arbitration.[200]

2. *Methods of Review in Investment Treaty Arbitration*

This subsection analyses the most common methods of review, or balancing tests, that have been used in investment treaty arbitration. Focusing on cases with an environmental component, it will demonstrate that variants of proportionality analysis have become increasingly common in investment treaty jurisprudence. As Vadi has observed, of those investor–State tribunals that mention the concept of proportionality, most do not engage in the structured three-step test familiar from certain other courts and tribunals and from the literature. Rather, many investor–State tribunals mention proportionality in passing, alongside a collection of other concepts (eg reasonableness and non-arbitrariness), and understand proportionality to simply mean proportionality balancing stricto sensu, omitting the preceding steps of suitability and necessity.[201] Nevertheless, this subsection will demonstrate that a subset of investment treaty awards have engaged with proportionality analysis in a more detailed manner, applying its distinct stages. As in the other adjudication contexts studied in this book, the essential attraction of a structured three-step proportionality analysis as a method of review appears to be that it provides adjudicators with a ready-made structure or formula for balancing competing interests, in the context of being required to adjudicate over relatively open-ended treaty provisions.[202]

[200] See above n 158.

[201] Valentina Vadi, *Proportionality, Reasonableness and Standards of Review in International Investment Law and Arbitration* (Edward Elgar 2018) 88, 95–96, 99, 106.

[202] On the idea of regulatory standards or 'formulae' developed by international courts for this purpose, see Caroline E Foster, *Global Regulatory Standards in Environmental and Health Disputes: Regulatory Coherence, Due Regard, and Due Diligence* (OUP 2021) 20–21, 34–36, 349; Vadi (n 201) 242. Foster argues that a due regard test can provide the methodological structure that makes proportionality analysis attractive but has the major advantage of not drawing investment arbitrators into themselves weighing up

(a) Least Restrictive Means Testing in Investment Treaty Arbitration

Necessity or least restrictive means testing, which asks whether there was an alternative measure that could have feasibly been adopted by the regulating State that would have achieved the same regulatory aim but with a lesser restriction of other legally protected rights or interests, has been employed by a few investment treaty tribunals.[203] A good example is *SD Myers v Canada*, which concerned a Canadian measure purportedly adopted pursuant to the country's international environmental obligations that temporarily banned the cross-border movement of certain types of hazardous waste. In undertaking a wide-ranging analysis of the relevant trade, investment, and environmental obligations, the Tribunal emphasised that to the extent that the measure had a legitimate environmental objective – in preserving a domestic hazardous waste disposal industry – this could have been achieved by other less NAFTA-inconsistent alternative measures that were available.[204] The Tribunal found that Canada's measure operated to favour Canadian nationals over non-nationals, was enacted with protectionist intent,[205] and thus breached the national treatment and FET obligations.[206] The key principle applied by the Tribunal was that 'where a state can achieve its chosen level of environmental protection through a variety of equally effective and reasonable means, it is obliged to adopt the alternative that is most consistent with open trade'.[207] The cross-cutting nature of necessity or least restrictive means testing as a balancing test was further discussed by Arbitrator Schwartz, who noted:

> In both trade treaties and environmental treaties, a general approach is taken to reconciling the promotion of trade with the protection of the

the sort of value-laden factors involved in a proportionality analysis: see Caroline E Foster, 'Why Due Regard Is More Appropriate than Proportionality Testing in International Investment Law' (2022) 23 JWIT 388, esp. 397–99, 412–16.

203 Some tribunals that employed proportionality balancing stricto sensu also applied the prior stage of necessity testing and where relevant these decisions are discussed in Section C(2)(b). Sections C(2)(a) and (b) of this chapter partly draw on material from Joshua Paine, 'Autonomy to Set the Level of Regulatory Protection in International Investment Law' (2021) 70 ICLQ 696, esp. 722–30.

204 *SD Myers* (n 157) [215], [221], [255].

205 Ibid [193]–[194].

206 Ibid [256], [266], [268].

207 Ibid [221].

> environment. Governments have the unrestricted right to their environmental objectives. They can aim as high as they like. In pursuing those standards, however, governments should avoid measures that are discriminatory. Governments should also avoid measures that restrict trade more than is reasonably necessary in order to achieve the objectives they have freely chosen.[208]

Another interesting application of a least restrictive means test comes from *Muszynianka v Slovakia*, already discussed above, although as will be explained below the Tribunal subsequently went on to apply an additional proportionality stricto sensu stage. The focus here is on the Tribunal's reasoning within its FET analysis as to why it was satisfied that Slovakia's Constitutional Amendment – which prohibited the cross-border transport of non-bottled water – satisfied a least restrictive means test. The Tribunal rejected the claimant's argument that the alternative measure it proposed – an existing measure known as the 'Maximum Quantities Decisions', which regulated the maximum extractable quantity of mineral water – was a genuine alternative, as it would not have been as effective in achieving the Constitutional Amendment's aims of preserving water and regulating the use of this natural resource.[209] Similarly to the other courts and tribunals studied in this book, the Tribunal emphasised that the burden of identifying a less restrictive but equally available and effective alternative measure lay with the claimant: 'Host States cannot be expected to *ex officio* demonstrate, within a universe of options, that the measure at issue was the least restrictive and viable to achieve the intended public purpose.'[210] Nevertheless, the Tribunal further noted that 'given that mineral water represents only a small portion of Slovak water, the Tribunal has asked itself whether the Respondent should have carved out mineral water from the scope of the Constitutional Amendment or improved its maximum quantities decisions system to monitor the overall yield of Slovak water'.[211] While the Tribunal noted that such alternatives had been considered by Slovakia in the process of designing its measure, ultimately it was not satisfied the potential alternative measures had been shown to be:

> *available and equally effective*. Without any empirical evidence proving that these conditions are satisfied, engaging in such a scrutiny would

[208] Ibid Sep. Op. Schwartz [93]. See also [106], [114]–[115].
[209] *Muszynianka v Slovak Republic* (n 159) [549]–[553], [568]–[569].
[210] Ibid [569].
[211] Ibid [570].

> exceed the Tribunal's institutional capacity. It would blur the line between adjudication and policy-making, the latter being reserved to the State's legislative and regulatory organs. Thereby, it would fail to grant the deference owed to States on how to implement their policies.[212]

Furthermore, the Tribunal reasoned that water preservation was not the only aim pursued by the Constitutional Amendment, so that identifying an alternative that was equally effective in relation to achieving that aim would not necessarily be dispositive of the necessity analysis.[213] Thus, the Constitutional Amendment was found to satisfy the necessity test. This aspect of the award suggests that necessity or least restrictive means testing in investment treaty arbitration has substantial similarities with the same essential balancing test as seen in the other adjudicatory settings studied in this book. For example, as in WTO necessity jurisprudence, the *Muszynianka v Slovakia* Tribunal required a complainant to identify a proposed alternative measure and required evidence that the proposed alternative was reasonably available to the regulating State and would be equally effective at achieving the chosen regulatory aim(s).

(b) Proportionality Balancing Stricto Sensu in Investment Treaty Arbitration

A growing number of investment treaty tribunals have engaged in the final, controversial stage of proportionality analysis, known as proportionality balancing stricto sensu, which involves asking whether the costs imposed by measure were disproportionate to its benefits taking into account the relative importance of the competing legally protected interests being balanced. This subsection provides an analysis of this case law, focusing, as in the rest of the book, on cases with an environmental component.[214] *Muszynianka v Slovakia*, just considered in relation to a least restrictive means test, went on to apply a proportionality stricto sensu test as part of the FET standard.[215] The Tribunal noted that in

212 Ibid [571] (emphasis added).

213 Ibid [571].

214 For significant examples of proportionality balancing stricto sensu outside of an environmental context, see e.g. *Electrabel SA v Republic of Hungary*, ICSID Case No ARB/07/19, Award (25 November 2015) [179]–[180] (proportionality analysis including proportionality stricto sensu in the context of the FET standard). In the context of indirect expropriation analysis, see eg *PL Holdings S.à.r.l. v Poland*, SCC Arbitration No V 2014/163, Partial Award (28 June 2017) [354]–[391]; *Olympic Entertainment Group AS v Ukraine*, PCA Case No 2019-18, Award (15 April 2021) [87]–[90], [96]–[101].

215 *Muszynianka v Slovak Republic* (n 159) [461], [466], [566].

performing this step of the analysis it 'must exercise restraint. Consequently, proportionality stricto sensu would be lacking when a measure imposes an excessive burden on an investor's rights in relation to the aim of the measure'.[216] Ultimately, the *Muszynianka* Tribunal concluded very quickly that the Constitutional Amendment satisfied the proportionality stricto sensu test, since the specific objective of the measure 'protection and rational use of water' and the broader public purposes that prompted the measure 'environmental conservation, public health, and the regulation of natural resources, are far from negligible. The vital importance of this non-renewable resource cannot be overstated, especially in an era of alarming climate change.'[217] The Tribunal reasoned that the competing commercial interest of the claimant in the cross-border exploitation of the relevant mineral water sources, located in Slovakia, were not 'remotely capable of outweighing the public interests involved in the adoption of the Constitutional Amendment'.[218]

The concepts of proportionality or disproportionality have frequently been mentioned in the numerous renewables disputes of the last decade although only a few of these tribunals have articulated a structured three-stage proportionality analysis.[219] In general the renewables tribunals have asked, as part of an analysis under the FET standard, whether the regulatory change implemented by the State was proportionate, or was not disproportionate to the relevant policy aim(s), bearing in mind the reason for the change and the impact on investors who had invested in reliance on the prior incentive scheme.[220] One of the most detailed applications of a proportionality test in the renewables jurisprudence occurred in *RWE v Spain*. For this Tribunal, 'the question of disproportionality ... entails a consideration as to whether the changes were suitable and necessary to achieve the legislative intent, and whether an excessive financial burden was shifted to the Claimants'.[221] At the necessity stage of the analysis, the Tribunal found that the claimants had not established that there were other alternative, less restrictive measures

216 Ibid [574].
217 Ibid [575].
218 Ibid.
219 E.g. *Cavalum v Spain* (n 141) [414]–[415]; *Hydro Energy v Spain* (n 142) [573]–[574], [676(4), (6)]. See also *RREEF v Spain* (n 140) [460], [463]–[465].
220 See eg *PV Investors v Spain* (n 141)[582]–[583], [624]–[630]; *SolEs v Spain* (n 143) [316]–[318], [462]; *Stadtwerke v Spain* (n 152) [354]–[355]; *Silver Ridge v Italy* (n 143) [446], [458]–[474].
221 *RWE v Spain* (n 141) [551].

available that would have addressed the tariff deficit faced by Spain.[222] In asking whether Spain's regulatory change satisfied the proportionality stricto sensu test, the Tribunal reasoned that, given the context of the case as one concerning changes to a tariff regime designed to incentivise a particular sector, 'it is appropriate to identify the burden that has been borne by the Claimants when that regime undergoes radical change, and whether that burden is excessive in relation to the legitimate aim being pursued through the change'.[223] In light of evidence concerning the reduced profitability of several of the claimants' renewable energy plants the Tribunal concluded that an 'excessive and disproportionate burden is being borne by the Claimants'[224] 'relative to the policy objective of the Respondent'.[225] Accordingly, Spain's changes to the tariff regime violated the FET standard.[226] This is a controversial exercise for an international tribunal to engage in, as it involves directly weighing the impact of a measure on a claimant investor against the State's policy objective, including in light of the relative importance of that policy objective.[227]

Moreover, the *RWE v Spain* Tribunal held that the focus should be on the burden placed on the individual claimants, 'not on the question of burden more generally, even though the Disputed Measures plainly have far broader impacts than those before this Tribunal'.[228] In contrast, the *Eskosol v Italy* Tribunal, in assessing the question of disproportionality as part of the FET standard, held that '[t]he proportionality of a measure of general applicability must be evaluated in light of its overall features and impacts, and not through the narrow lens of its impact on a particular investor'.[229] The latter approach is the preferable one because, as Foster has argued, investment treaties ultimately remain inter-State bargains, despite the procedural rights conferred on investors, and claimant investors will typically be part of a wider class of foreign investors protected by an investment treaty.[230] Accordingly, while the impact of a host State measure on the claimant investor may be part of a proportionality

222 Ibid [566]–[567].
223 Ibid [570].
224 Ibid [589].
225 Ibid [600]. See generally [598]–[600]. See also [590]–[597] (regarding whether Spain had given due consideration to investors' interests in its decision-making process).
226 Ibid [600].
227 See below text at n 237.
228 *RWE v Spain* (n 141) [598].
229 *Eskosol v Italy* (n 141) [413].
230 Foster, *Global Regulatory Standards* (n 202) 259–61.

analysis, a tribunal should adopt a wider focus and consider the extent to which the measure restricts the relevant investment treaty obligations owed to the home State.[231]

One of the earliest investment treaty decisions to engage in proportionality balancing stricto sensu was *Tecmed v Mexico*. The case concerned Mexico's non-renewal of an operating permit for a hazardous waste facility, purportedly on the basis of certain violations of the permit conditions by the operator. The Tribunal stated that in order to determine whether the host State's regulatory actions constituted an indirect expropriation or a non-compensable exercise of police powers, it would consider 'whether such actions or measures are proportional to the public interest presumably protected thereby and to the protection legally granted to investments'.[232] The Tribunal recognised that 'the analysis starts at the due deference owing to the State when defining the issues that affect its public policy or the interests of society as a whole, as well as the actions that will be implemented to protect such values'. However, this did not prevent it from examining 'whether such measures are reasonable with respect to their goals, the deprivation of economic rights and the legitimate expectations of [those] who suffered such deprivation'.[233] Importantly, the Tribunal held that '[t]here must be a reasonable relationship of proportionality between the charge or weight imposed to the foreign investor and the aim sought to be realized by any expropriatory measure'.[234] The Tribunal's application of this test involved directly balancing the competing interests at stake. For example, the Tribunal, having determined that non-renewal of the permit was motivated by public opposition to the urban location of the landfill, not the operation of the landfill, recognised it would have to weigh the interest that the measure was pursuing, in responding to such public concern, against the impact on the investor's interests.[235] The Tribunal proceeded to find that the opposition to the location of the landfill was not massive, and did not justify the measure, which completely neutralised the investment without compensation.[236] In so doing, the

[231] Ibid; Foster, 'Why Due Regard' (n 202) 399–400, 415.
[232] *Tecmed v Mexico* (n 115) [122].
[233] Ibid [122].
[234] Ibid.
[235] Ibid [132]–[133], and generally [127]–[133].
[236] Ibid [144], [147]–[149] (also reasoning that there was no evidence that the investor's operations had actually endangered the environment or public health, despite minor infringements).

international tribunal itself engaged in weighing the relative importance of the interest being pursued by the impugned measure against the impact on a protected investor. This is controversial because it involves 'placing the competing interests on a scale and effectively determining whether one takes precedence over another'.[237] In contrast, if the method of review was limited to least restrictive means testing, the tribunal would not directly weigh the regulatory aim being pursued by the State against the impact of the measure on an investor, but would only ask whether there was an alternative, reasonably available means of securing the States' chosen regulatory aim that was less restrictive of the competing treaty-protected interest of investment protection.

A final stark example of investment treaty arbitrators engaging in proportionality balancing stricto sensu that warrants discussion is *Occidental v Ecuador*,[238] which concerned a penalty imposed on the investor in the form of having its oil exploration contract terminated after the investor, in contravention of Ecuador's hydrocarbons law, assigned some of its exploration rights without approval from Ecuador's authorities. In other words, as the Tribunal recognised, the case concerned Ecuador's rights as sovereign over its own natural resources, including deciding which parties would be given permission to exploit those resources.[239] The context for the Tribunal's lengthy analysis of the proportionality of the penalty was that Ecuadorian law included a requirement that administrative discretion be exercised proportionately.[240] However, the case is of much wider relevance because the Tribunal held that the principle of proportionality was 'applicable as a matter of general international law',[241] and thus Ecuador's penalty, being disproportionate, breached customary international law, as well as the treaty standard of FET and treatment according to the MST.[242]

Significantly, the Tribunal held that it had to assess the proportionality of Ecuador's conduct even if it found no meaningful alternatives were

237 Ortino (n 112) 159.

238 *Occidental Petroleum Corporation & Ors v Ecuador*, ICSID Case No ARB/06/11, Award (5 October 2012). The award was subject to a partially successful application for annulment; however, the Tribunal's application of the proportionality principle was upheld: see *Occidental Petroleum Corporation & Ors v Ecuador*, ICSID Case No ARB/06/11, Decision on Annulment of the Award (2 November 2015) [343]–[351].

239 *Occidental (Award)* (n 238) [446].

240 See ibid [424]–[425], [396]–[401].

241 Ibid [427], [402]–[409].

242 Ibid [452].

available to the State.[243] Thus, in addition to identifying three alternatives that were available to Ecuador,[244] the Tribunal explicitly weighed the relative importance of the regulatory aim pursued by the State against the impact on the investor's interests. The Tribunal found that the penalty imposed on the investor – which constituted 'total loss of an investment worth many hundreds of millions of dollars' – was disproportionate to its alleged wrongdoing and to 'the importance and effectiveness of the "deterrence message" which the Respondent [Ecuador] might have wished to send the wider oil and gas community'.[245] As a balancing technique, or method of review, this is fairly exceptional, with the international tribunal itself weighing the relative importance of the regulatory aim pursued by the State against the impact of the measure on the claimant investor.

Focusing on disputes with an environmental component, this subsection has demonstrated that variants of proportionality analysis, and in particular tests that endorse a final stage of proportionality balancing stricto sensu, have become increasingly common in investment treaty arbitration. As touched on in passing above, there is also reason to think that the increasing use of a structured three-step proportionality analysis in investment treaty arbitration is a trend present in disputes beyond those with an environmental component.[246]

D. The Contribution of Investment Treaty Arbitration to Broader Processes of Dispute Resolution

In the investment treaty context, it is much harder to find examples of tribunals acting in a facilitative manner and assisting the disputing parties to manage their relationship going forward, for example by providing guidance on the legal framework for their future interactions or by ordering the disputing parties to engage in post-adjudication cooperation. Instead, adjudication in this context largely functions as a backwards-looking compensation mechanism.[247] Thus, investment

243 Ibid [426]–[427].

244 Ibid [434], generally [428]–[436].

245 Ibid [450]. Note that the Tribunal took into account whether the State's interests, as sovereign over its natural resources, were actually harmed by the investor's misconduct: ibid [445]–[447].

246 See case law cited above n 214 and literature cited above nn 201–202.

247 Similarly: Benedikt Pirker, *Proportionality Analysis and Models of Judicial Review: A Theoretical and Comparative Study* (Europa Law Publishing 2013) 347; UNCTAD, 'Investor–State Disputes: Prevention and Alternatives to Arbitration' (UNCTAD Series

treaty arbitration differs significantly from the other adjudication contexts considered in this book in terms of the contribution of adjudicators' decisions to broader processes of dispute resolution.

Several features of investment treaty arbitration help explain why there is much less evidence in this context of a prospectively oriented and facilitative style of adjudication. First, in investment treaty arbitration, in contrast to the inter-State adjudication contexts studied, it is more common that by the time of a decision on the merits the disputing parties no longer have an ongoing relationship. Instead, in many (but not all) disputes the investor will have exited the host state and will be seeking to recover part of its losses.[248] However, there are exceptions and this factor alone does not fully explain the finding of difference. There is empirical evidence that a minority of investors continue to invest or reinvest in the host State even after a dispute involving investor–State arbitration.[249] Furthermore, there is clear evidence that even after an arbitral ruling is issued, some investors negotiate a broader settlement with the host State, particularly in the context of long-term investments, such as in oil and gas or infrastructure where an investor may have other investments in the host State and thus a broader relationship to preserve.[250] Yet importantly, even where post-adjudication bargaining occurs in this regime, it generally does not occur under the supervision

on International Investment Policies for Development 2010) xxiii (investor–State 'arbitration is focused entirely on the payment of compensation and not on maintaining a working relationship between the parties').

[248] Pirker (n 247) 347; Christoph Schreuer, 'Non-Pecuniary Remedies in ICSID Arbitration' (2004) 20 Arb. Int'l 325, 332.

[249] Rachel L Wellhausen, 'International Investment Law and Foreign Direct Reinvestment' (2019) 73 International Organization 839 (empirical study finding that in all investor–State arbitrations up to the end of 2014, in 31 per cent of cases a claimant investor either retained an investment in the host State or exited from and re-invested in the host State after an arbitration had occurred).

[250] See Emilie M Hafner-Burton, Sergio Puig and David G Victor, 'Against Secrecy: The Social Cost of International Dispute Settlement' (2017) 42 Yale J. Int'l L. 279, 310, 321–28 (discussing three such case studies); ibid 845–46 (analysing the proportion of cases where reinvestment occurs by sector). There is also empirical evidence that a minority of cases where a request for arbitration is registered are settled before a final award is issued: see generally Ana Ubilava, 'Amicable Settlements in Investor-State Disputes: Empirical Analysis of Patterns and Perceived Problems' (2020) 21 JWIT 528 (empirical study finding inter alia that of all known, treaty-based investor–State arbitrations concluded up to the end of 2017, 24 per cent were amicably settled before a final award, and disputes in sectors with long-term interests had a 10 per cent higher settlement rate).

of adjudicators.[251] A limited exception to this observation is that there is an increasingly common practice of investment treaty tribunals deciding issues of liability and the broad principles that should apply to issues of quantum, and then requiring the disputing parties to attempt to agree on the amount of quantum, with a possibility of the tribunal determining the amount where the parties cannot agree.[252]

Other contextual features of investment treaty arbitration help explain this finding of difference with the other adjudication contexts studied in this book. While investor–State tribunals under many investment treaties formally have the power to order a wide range of non-pecuniary remedies,[253] in practice, unlike the other settings studied, compensation is nearly always the only remedy that is requested by claimants and awarded by tribunals.[254] This preference of claimants likely reflects that under the ICSID Convention, the most commonly used procedural framework, only pecuniary obligations are subject to the powerful enforcement mechanism created,[255] and given the multi-year length of investment arbitrations, a claimant will typically have lost their place in the relevant market.[256] The dominance of compensation also reflects that, unlike in the inter-State adjudication settings studied, the claimants in this regime are generally driven solely by commercial motivations.[257] Furthermore, States as both treaty drafters and as respondents in arbitrations have often resisted the idea that investment treaty tribunals can order non-pecuniary remedies, reflecting sovereignty-based

[251] Ibid; Michael E Schneider, 'Investment Disputes – Moving beyond Arbitration' in Laurence Boisson de Chazournes, Marcelo G Kohen and Jorge E Viñuales (eds), *Diplomatic and Judicial Means of Dispute Settlement* (Martinus Nijhoff 2013) 140.

[252] See e.g. *RREEF v Spain* (n 140) [592]–[598], [600(5)–(7)]; *Cavalum v Spain* (n 141) [701]–[706]; *Eurus v Spain* (n 141) [460]–[461], [468]–[469]; *BayWa.r.e. v Spain* (n 142) [615]–[617], [630]-631]; *Sevilla Beheer v Spain* (n 140) [1019]–[1021], [1081].

[253] See *Bernhard von Pezold and Others v Zimbabwe*, ICSID Case No ARB/10/15, Award (28 July 2015) [695]–[700]; Schreuer (n 248) 331–32; Berk Demirkol, 'Reconsideration of Proper Remedies in Investment Arbitration in Light of Recent Cases: Should the Remedy Follow the Primary Obligation?' (2021) 22 JWIT 129, 139. Note, however, that newer investment treaties often limit the available remedies to monetary damages and provide that if a tribunal orders restitution of property it must provide the respondent State the option of paying monetary damages instead: see eg NAFTA art 1135(1); CETA art 8.39(1). Cf 2019 Netherlands Model BIT art 22(3); ECT art 26(8).

[254] Pirker (n 248) 346–47; Schreuer (n 248) 332.

[255] ICSID Convention art 54(1); Schreuer (n 248) 325–26.

[256] Berk Demirkol, 'Remedies in Investment Treaty Arbitration' (2015) 6 JIDS 403, 411.

[257] Demirkol (n 253) 133.

concerns.[258] Even in the small number of awards where tribunals have contemplated the option of awarding non-pecuniary remedies, they have typically provided the host State or the investor with the option of unilaterally selecting compensation instead.[259] Tribunals may also be reluctant to order non-pecuniary remedies due to the concern that they have no effective way of enforcing such remedies against an unwilling State,[260] and a tribunal will not necessarily remain in existence to monitor compliance unless it chooses to retain jurisdiction over a compliance phase.[261] The relative dominance of compensation in investment treaty arbitration also reflects that, as Demirkol has noted, the primary obligations in investment treaties create certain standards for State conduct that affects protected investments, which are in turn established under domestic law, rather than the treaty creating new property or contractual rights at the international level that could be subject to an order for restitution by a treaty-based investor–State tribunal.[262]

[258] See the treaty drafting choices mentioned above n 253. Regarding State attitudes as respondents, see eg *Enron Corporation and Ponderosa Assets, LP v Argentine Republic*, ICSID Case No ARB/01/3, Decision on Jurisdiction (14 January 2004) [76].

[259] Similarly: Demirkol (n 253) 142–43. See eg *Antoine Goetz and Others v Burundi*, ICSID Case No ARB/95/3, Award (10 February 1999) [133], [135]–[137]; English translation in 6 ICSID Reports 3 (Tribunal gave the respondent State the option of paying compensation to the investor or reinstating the benefits of the free zone certificate which had been revoked within four months, with provision for a return to the Tribunal to fix the appropriate reparation if Burundi did not take one of these steps. Subsequently, the parties reached a settlement by which their relationship was re-established: see 6 ICSID Reports 46ff); *Franck Charles Arif v Moldova*, ICSID Case No ARB/11/23, Award (8 April 2013) [570]–[572], [633(d)–(g)] (Tribunal ordered restitution and compensation as alternative remedies, with the parties to negotiate on the possibility of restitution and the investor having the option of electing to take compensation); *von Pezold* (n 253) [727]–[744], [874]–[877], [1020.1–3] (Tribunal ordered Zimbabwe to reinstate claimants' title to expropriated properties and provided a period of 90 days in which this could occur, with provision for an alternative award of compensation if the respondent did not effect restitution); *Occidental v Ecuador* (n 117) [213]–[214] (Tribunal offered disputes parties 'guidance as how to best conduct their future relations' if they wished to explore rebalancing the contract concerned). See also *CMS v Argentina* (n 117) [406]–[408].

[260] Demirkol (n 256) 408.

[261] Brooks E Allen, 'The Use of Non-Pecuniary Remedies in WTO Dispute Settlement: Lessons for Arbitral Practitioners' in Michael E Schneider and Joachim Knoll (eds), *Performance as a Remedy: Non-Monetary Relief in International Arbitration* (Juris 2011) 303. But see Demirkol (n 253) 144–45 (highlighting these considerations also apply to other international tribunals, e.g. State–State arbitration, so they are not entirely convincing).

[262] See Demirkol (n 253) 148–58.

The prevailing paradigm in which investment treaty arbitration occurs is also relevant. In a regime that has drawn many of its participants from a commercial arbitration background, the idea that arbitrators might play a facilitative role, aimed at assisting the disputing parties to resolve their dispute themselves, may be controversial.[263] It is often assumed that the entire point of investment arbitration is to obtain an order for compensation,[264] which can be enforced in domestic courts. A purely negotiation-based regime is said to be inappropriate given the inferior bargaining power of a foreign investor that has already sunk its capital in the host State.[265] All of these contextual factors help explain why investment treaty arbitration has a predominantly retrospective focus, aimed at assessing liability and awarding compensation, and we generally do not see adjudication in this context having a partly prospective focus aimed at assisting the parties to rebuild their relationship after adjudication.

E. Conclusion

This chapter has analysed the three challenges confronting international tribunals considered throughout this book in relation to investment treaty arbitration in a manner that is sensitive to the numerous contextual features that shape this adjudication mechanism. The largely retrospective focus of adjudication in this setting represents an obvious finding of difference with the other contexts studied where there are clear signs of tribunals at times providing guidance to assist the parties' future interactions and the potential rebuilding of their relationship after adjudication. As the contextual features of the investment treaty regime that help explain this finding have been considered above, this conclusion focuses on explaining the other findings of similarity and difference emerging from this chapter.

[263] Allen (n 261) 298. There is a large literature in the field of international commercial arbitration debating whether it is appropriate for arbitrators to attempt to facilitate settlements: see e.g. Klaus Peter Berger and J Ole Jensen, 'The Arbitrator's Mandate to Facilitate Settlement' (2017) 40 Fordham ILJ 887 (citing at fn 2 much of the existing literature).

[264] Christoph Schreuer, 'Alternative Remedies in Investment Arbitration' (2016) 3 The Journal of Damages in International Arbitration 1, 1.

[265] W Michael Reisman, 'International Investment Arbitration and ADR: Married but Best Living Apart' (2009) 24 ICSID Review 185, 190–91; Sergio Puig, 'No Right without a Remedy: Foundations of Investor-State Arbitration' (2014) 35 Univ. of Pennsylvania JIL 829, 841–48.

Similarly to the other courts and tribunals studied in this book, investment treaty arbitration contributes alongside other processes of law-development – especially treaty drafting by States – to broader processes of change in international legal norms. The case law analysed above concerning investment tribunals' differing views on whether the MST had evolved over time to provide a higher degree of investment protection, which was prompted by States' strategy of tying FET provisions to the customary standard, provided a clear illustration of this point. Yet in addition to contributing to broader processes of change in international legal norms, investment treaty tribunals, by interpreting and applying investment treaty standards in particular disputes, also effectively determine the permissible degree of change in host State regulation. This distinction highlights the two quite different, although interrelated, ways in which investment treaty tribunals confront the challenge of balancing stability and change. Contextual features of investment treaty arbitration help further explain these observations. In the investment treaty regime, States are able to exercise a prominent role, alongside adjudicators, in contributing to the development of international legal norms because the regime is largely bilaterally constructed. Accordingly, it is in some senses easier to change than major multilateral structures, such as the WTO Agreement or UNCLOS, where States face the difficulty of achieving compromise among a much more diverse set of treaty parties in order to agree to new treaty text, treaty amendments, or authoritative interpretations.[266] The decision of States to use ad hoc tribunals in the investment treaty regime, and (so far) largely avoid creating any permanent tribunal or appellate mechanism, also reduces the relative influence of any single tribunal in terms of development of the law.[267] On the other hand, the direct access that this regime provides non-State actors to international arbitration, without a requirement to exhaust local remedies, reduces enormously States' control over how investment treaty norms are interpreted and applied.

The goals or *telos* of the investment treaty regime also help explain why we frequently see investor–State tribunals performing a role of

[266] See e.g. Tom Ginsburg, 'Bounded Discretion in International Judicial Lawmaking' (2005) 45 Va. J. Int'l L. 631, 661–65. However, note that the bilaterally constructed nature of the investment treaty regime also means that any changes are piecemeal: see e.g. above text at nn 15–17.

[267] Santiago Montt, *State Liability in Investment Treaty Arbitration: Global Constitutional and Administrative Law in the BIT Generation* (Hart 2009) 157–59.

determining the permissible balance between an investor's interest in stability of the regulatory system applying to its investment and a host State's interest in being able to adjust regulation to new demands. Although stability is not an explicit aim of most investment treaties,[268] it is clear that the investment treaty regime was designed to exercise a degree of control over public decision-making in developing, capital-importing states, as a means of attracting foreign investment flows and ultimately promoting the economic development of the treaty parties.[269] Consistent with this aim, the substantive norms in this regime cut deeply into the regulatory sovereignty of host States. In short, an important part of the bias at play in this regime is a bias against change within the host State's regulatory system.[270] This bias has not been constant. For example, in relation to the key treaty standard of FET, it was shown that while early arbitral awards required an unrealistically high standard of stability, more recent awards have endorsed the State's right to adjust regulation over time, considering the proportionality of the relevant regulatory change in light of the policy rationale for it and any specific assurances given to the investor. Clearly, international norms in other regimes also cut deeply into certain areas of domestic decision-making where protected foreign interests are affected. The norms governing non-tariff barriers to trade contained in the SPS and TBT agreements, considered in Chapter 2 on WTO dispute settlement, are one example. Yet in none of the other contexts studied in this book did the wider international regime, and the case law generated by its adjudication mechanism, have the same overriding focus on controlling the permissible degree of change in the respondent State's regulatory system. This finding may also partly

268 Jonathan Bonnitcha, 'Investment Treaties and Transition from Authoritarian Rule' (2014) 15 JWIT 965, 966–68.

269 Ortino (n 70) 441–44; Jeswald W Salacuse and Nicholas P Sullivan, 'Do BITs Really Work: An Evaluation of Bilateral Investment Treaties and Their Grand Bargain' (2005) 46 HILJ 67, 77; Kenneth J Vandevelde, *Bilateral Investment Treaties: History, Policy, and Interpretation* (OUP 2010) 3–4; Jan Kleinheisterkamp, 'Investment Treaty Law and the Fear for Sovereignty: Transnational Challenges and Solutions' (2015) 78 MLR 793, 811–12.

270 Similarly: David Schneiderman, *Constitutionalizing Economic Globalization: Investment Rules and Democracy's Promise* (CUP 2008) 9, 37, 236; Gus Van Harten, 'Investment Rules and the Denial of Change' (2010) 60 University of Toronto Law Journal 893. On the idea that all regimes have certain biases, see e.g. Young (n 39) 10–11; Martti Koskenniemi, *From Apology to Utopia: The Structure of International Legal Argument* (reissue, CUP 2005) 608–10.

reflect that investment treaty arbitration, unlike the three inter-State adjudication contexts studied, confers direct standing to bring international claims on a non-State actor who typically has an ongoing presence (in the form of an investment) in the host State, meaning there is a particular focus on contesting regulatory changes within the host State.

Investor–State tribunals' approaches to the intensity with which they scrutinise determinations made by domestic authorities bear important similarities to the manner in which this issue arose and was addressed by adjudicators in the other contexts studied, although contextual features of this regime clearly shape the relevant practices. In this setting the relevant treaty texts do not rely on scientific determinations in the same way as provisions of the SPS Agreement, considered in the WTO context; however, investment tribunals nevertheless repeatedly faced fact-intensive determinations based on specialised forms of non-legal expertise. This reflects that the domestic regulatory measures affecting foreign investments often partly depended upon determinations based on specialised scientific or technical expertise, which arbitrators did not themselves hold. Given generally only investors bring claims in this setting, it was always the investor, as claimant, seeking to fault the host State's decision-making process, for example by showing that it was not scientifically or technically well-founded or was contrary to regulatory processes applied in equivalent cases. Investment tribunals frequently refrained from engaging in substitutionary de novo review of certain determinations made by host States, for example those concerning risk, often emphasising that they did not hold the specialist forms of expertise that had been relied on by national-level authorities.[271] Like other international tribunals, investment arbitrators are non-specialists in relation to the scientific and technical determinations that often lie at the heart of environmental disputes. Another reason arbitrators advanced for avoiding de novo review of certain determinations was that domestic-level authorities were better placed to balance competing interests, given their greater democratic legitimacy and familiarity with relevant local conditions. The observation by several of the investor–State decisions considered that modern regulatory States frequently must exercise discretion and strike a compromise between conflicting interests, and accordingly

[271] See case law discussed above Section C(1).

should not be too easily second-guessed by international tribunals, is a point with relevance beyond this context.[272]

Regarding the methods of review or balancing tests used in this setting, this chapter demonstrated that within environmental cases tribunals have repeatedly used variants of proportionality analysis in determining whether State measures that pursue a permissible regulatory interest but restrict the treaty-protected interest of investment protection comply with investment treaty disciplines. The wording of the relevant investment treaty obligations did not appear determinative of the methods of review used, with such tests frequently 'read into' the relevant treaty,[273] particularly in relation to the commonly invoked standards of FET and indirect expropriation. The use of variants of proportionality analysis may reflect that investment arbitrators, faced with striking a balance between the competing interests embodied in vaguely worded treaty provisions, have found it convenient to draw on balancing techniques that may be familiar from other international, regional, and national contexts, and from the abundant scholarly literature addressing proportionality analysis in the investment treaty context.[274] For example, in *SD Myers*, arbitrators drew on the fact that least restrictive means testing is utilised in other trade and environment treaties.[275] In *Muszynianka*, the Tribunal also directly engaged with some of the scholarly literature on proportionality analysis in investment treaty arbitration, an approach that is not uncommon in more recent awards.[276] As in the other adjudication contexts studied, the use of necessity or least restrictive means testing gave rise to the question of how readily an international tribunal should conclude that a proposed alternative measure would have been equally effective in achieving the relevant regulatory aim and was reasonably available to the regulating State. It is also noteworthy that an increasing number of investment treaty tribunals have engaged in the final, controversial step of proportionality balancing stricto sensu, asking whether the restriction of protected investor interests was disproportionate to the benefits of the regulatory measure, including in light of the relative importance of the relevant regulatory aim. There is reason to

272 See case law discussed above Section C(1), especially *Muszynianka*, *RENERGY v Spain*, *Glamis v USA* and *Lone Pine v Canada*.

273 Foster, *Global Regulatory Standards* (n 202) 33–35.

274 See also ibid 20, 33–35.

275 See above text at nn 204–208.

276 E.g. *Muszynianka v Slovak Republic* (n 159) [566]–[574].

question whether this method of review, which involves a tribunal potentially second-guessing the regulatory aim selected by the regulatory State, has any place in investment treaty arbitration.[277] A compromise position that has been suggested by some commentators and arbitrators may be to limit the proportionality stricto sensu stage to simply checking that a measure is not manifestly disproportionate to its aims.[278]

[277] See e.g. Paine (n 203) esp. 699–700, 735; Henckels (n 158) 164, 168; Ortino (n 30) 88–89.

[278] See e.g. Foster, *Global Regulatory Standards* (n 202) 267; Henckels (n 158) 161, 168; *Mathias Kruck*, Partial Diss. Op. Douglas (n 110) [104].

6

Conclusion

At the broadest level, this book has considered how international tribunals might perform their functions given the limitations of their roles and the demands being placed upon them across several different areas of international law. To explore this wide-ranging question, this book has used the focus of environmental disputes to analyse how international tribunals across the WTO, UNCLOS, ICJ, and investment treaty contexts manage the challenges of change, review of State conduct for compliance with international law, and dispute resolution, and why their practices differ. The analysis in the preceding chapters provides a basis for identifying convergences and divergences in how the selected international tribunals respond to these problems in environmental cases, and for identifying wider insights into how these tribunals perform various functions in the contemporary international legal order. This chapter draws together and extends the comparative analysis that has unfolded across the prior chapters, each focused on a specific institutional context. It explains why tribunals' practices differ across the contexts studied and assesses to what extent those practices provide insights into wider problems facing international adjudication and legal techniques that are potentially transferable across contexts. This chapter focuses consecutively on my findings in relation to the three challenges facing international tribunals analysed throughout this study: managing change in applicable international legal norms or relevant facts, calibrating the appropriate standard and method of review when scrutinising State conduct for compliance with international obligations, and contributing to broader processes of dispute resolution. The chapter finishes with some final remarks that close the book, concerning the contribution of this book to our understanding of the role of international adjudication in contemporary international law and its implications for future studies in this field.

A. Findings Regarding the Function of International Tribunals in Managing Change

This book has demonstrated and explained why across diverse areas of international law international tribunals frequently face the problem of responding to changes in international law or changes in relevant facts that may affect how they should interpret and apply applicable international legal norms. To a significant degree, such challenges stem from the fact that the international legal system has relatively under-developed processes for law adjustment. As is well known, international law lacks a central legislative mechanism and in some (although not all) areas lacks specialist regulators entrusted with adjusting rules over time.[1] While a treaty may formally remain unchanged, by the time it comes to be applied in a specific dispute it will frequently exist within a context in which wider international law, community concerns, and material facts have evolved significantly. Accordingly, international tribunals are often urged by litigants to adapt treaties in response to wider developments in international law, new social demands, or changed factual conditions.[2] Nevertheless, as we have seen, international tribunals are conscious of the need to provide legal certainty through their decisions, in particular for the parties bound by an obligation.[3]

As noted in Chapter 1, over the last century, various commentators who have reflected on the international adjudicative function have highlighted the role of international tribunals in balancing the competing interests of stability and change.[4] While interest in this aspect of international adjudication is longstanding, striking an appropriate balance

[1] Clearly there are some areas where international law has such regulators, for example in the form of conferences of the parties to multilateral environmental agreements, or the committees of domestic regulators often provided for in preferential trade agreements. For prior discussion of the point that international law has under-developed processes for law adjustment, see e.g. Hersch Lauterpacht, *The Function of Law in the International Community* (OUP 1933) 250–57.

[2] See also Thomas Kleinlein, 'Matters of Interpretation: How to Conceptualize and Evaluate Change of Norms and Values in the International Legal Order' in Heike Krieger and Andrea Liese (eds), *Tracing Value Change in the International Legal Order: Perspectives from Legal and Political Science* (OUP 2023) 74 ('Since process of formal international law-making ... is cumbersome, international courts simply correspond to an existing social need for change').

[3] See also the discussion of this issue in Henrik Palmer Olsen, 'International Courts and the Doctrinal Channels of Legal Diplomacy' (2015) 6 Transnational Legal Theory 661, 676–77.

[4] See Chapter 1, text at nn 53–54.

between stability and change is a key challenge at present because of the significant slow-down in treaty-making in recent decades, the large number of disputes being submitted to international tribunals, and the wide range of social demands that contemporary international law is expected to respond to.[5] The contribution made by this part of the book has been to interrogate the role of adjudicators in responding to the problem of change, in order to explain why this role varies across the contexts studied and precisely what is at stake.

Distinguishing between changes in international legal norms themselves and changes in facts that affect the application of a norm, or what a norm requires at a particular point in time, begins to provide a more nuanced picture of how this challenge plays out somewhat differently across the four contexts studied.[6] In relation to the role of adjudicators in managing potential changes in international legal norms themselves, one key variable is how active other processes of law-making are within a regime. This is because adjudicators are typically only one of several potential law-developing actors. In both the WTO and UNCLOS contexts, part of what was occurring was that with processes of treaty-making, amendment, or authoritative interpretation largely stalled, given the difficulty of reaching agreement in a large multilateral setting, adjudicators were being asked to adapt the relevant treaties incrementally in light of wider developments in international law. However, while treaty-making in a multilateral context remains difficult, such processes are not entirely stalled. For example, in the UNCLOS context, negotiations were completed in 2023 for a legally binding implementing agreement addressing the conservation and sustainable use of marine biological diversity in areas beyond national jurisdiction.[7] In the WTO context, the twelfth Ministerial Conference in mid-2022 saw the conclusion of decades-long negotiations on an agreement concerning fisheries subsidies, and negotiations regarding two plurilateral 'joint statement

[5] See Chapter 1, text at nn 55–58. As Kleinlein notes, the increased role of international adjudication in international law in recent decades has provided greater opportunities for evolutive interpretations: 'more adjudication and more judicial decision-making have now increased the chances for reinterpretations and re-evaluations of previous decisions. Thus, the structural change of judicialization contributes to a trend towards more evolutive interpretation': Kleinlein (n 2) 66.

[6] See further discussion in Chapter 1, text at nn 64–65.

[7] Agreement under the United Nations Convention on the Law of the Sea on the Conservation and Sustainable Use of Marine Biological Diversity of Areas beyond National Jurisdiction.

initiatives' – on services domestic regulation and investment facilitation – have concluded in recent years, while negotiations on several other plurilateral initiatives remain ongoing.[8] Despite these signs that treaty-making in these contexts is not entirely idle, it is notable that unlike some areas of contemporary international law – for example multilateral environmental agreements – the four adjudication settings studied in this book both lack a treaty body like a conference of the parties that is charged with adapting the relevant regime over time, and include a substantial grant of jurisdiction to international tribunals, meaning the role of the latter in incrementally adapting international norms becomes particularly pronounced.[9]

In terms of the demand for adjudicators to engage in incremental adaptation of legal norms, one relevant variable is the number of States parties to an agreement and thus whether treaty amendment or renegotiation is a realistic prospect. For example, in wide-ranging multilateral contexts, such as the WTO or UNCLOS, given the difficulty of reaching agreement on authoritative interpretations or treaty amendments among over 160 parties, and reluctance to re-open wide-ranging 'package deals', it is likely that we will continue to see demands for tribunals in these contexts to incrementally adapt the relevant treaties.[10] In contrast, as others have highlighted, the investment treaty regime, because it is largely

[8] WTO, 'Agreement on Fisheries Subsidies: Ministerial Declaration of 17 June 2022', WT/MIN(22)/33, WT/L/1144, 22 June 2022; WTO, 'Joint Initiative on Services Domestic Regulation: Reference Paper on Services Domestic Regulation', INF/SDR/2, 26 November 2021; WTO, 'WTO Structured Discussions on Investment Facilitation for Development: Statement by the Co-coordinators', INF/IFD/W/51, 6 July 2023. See Chapter 2(A)(2)(c), n 66 and accompanying text.

[9] On conferences of the parties (COPs) and similar treaty bodies and their role in developing the norms of relevant treaties, see eg Sebastián Rioseco, 'Conferences of the Parties beyond International Environmental Law: How COPs Influence the Content and Implementation of Their Parent Treaties' (2023) 36 LJIL 699, esp. 699–712; Geir Ulfstein, 'Treaty Bodies and Regimes' in Duncan B Hollis (ed), *The Oxford Guide to Treaties* (2nd ed., OUP 2020) 414–18, 420–24; Robin R Churchill and Geir Ulfstein, 'Autonomous Institutional Arrangements in Multilateral Environmental Agreements: A Little-Noticed Phenomenon in International Law' (2000) 94 AJIL 623, 636–42; Jutta Brunnée, 'COPing with Consent: Law-Making under Multilateral Environmental Agreements' (2002) 15 LJIL 1, 15–33.

[10] See eg Joost Pauwelyn and Manfred Elsig, 'The Politics of Treaty Interpretation: Variations and Explanations across International Tribunals' in Jeffrey L Dunoff and Mark Pollack (eds), *Interdisciplinary Perspectives on International Law and International Relations: The State of the Art* (CUP 2012) 463–64 and generally 459–68 (discussing how such factors affect the 'interpretation space' available to an international tribunal).

bilaterally constructed, is easier for States to change via treaty amendment, renegotiation, or authoritative interpretations.[11] Of course, the bilaterally constructed nature of the investment treaty regime also means that any changes adopted by States only have a piecemeal effect on the wider regime, and the resistance of the investment treaty regime to fundamental change has been a common theme arising from various reform processes in the last decade or so.[12]

Another relevant factor influencing the role of adjudicators in incrementally adapting treaty frameworks is the wording of relevant treaty provisions and any relationship the treaty may have with new developments in international law being drawn upon.[13] Essentially this reflects that the rules of treaty interpretation may provide a basis for referring to a wider body of international norms, for example if a treaty term is phrased in generic or open-ended terms, such that the ordinary meaning of the term can be informed by reference to other international norms.[14] Overall, the WTO cases considered in relation to the change theme suggest that the role of non-WTO law in that regime remains controversial. *US – Shrimp* is an important example of WTO adjudicators interpreting a generic term in the GATT – 'exhaustible natural resources' – which was clearly open to such a reading, in light of contemporary international law concerning conservation, even though, as we saw this approach was not necessary for the AB to reach its conclusion. However, the use of non-WTO law is far more controversial where it could alter or conflict with WTO obligations, as illustrated by *EC – Biotech* and to some degree *EC – Hormones*.[15] The contested nature of non-WTO law should be understood against the background of political processes having failed to settle the relationship between the WTO agreements and multilateral environmental agreements.[16] WTO adjudicators are understandably reluctant to resolve such controversial questions 'which have proved

[11] See e.g. Tom Ginsburg, 'Bounded Discretion in International Judicial Lawmaking' (2005) 45 Va. J. Int'l L. 631, 661–65; Anthea Roberts and Taylor St John, 'Complex Designers and Emergent Design: Reforming the Investment Treaty System' (2022) 116 AJIL 96, 148.

[12] See generally Roberts and St John (n 11) 129–31, 113–14.

[13] See also Pauwelyn and Elsig (n 10) 461–62.

[14] See eg Campbell McLachlan, 'The Principle of Systemic Integration and Article 31(3)(c) of the Vienna Convention' (2005) 54 ICLQ 279, 317–18.

[15] Andrew Lang, 'Twenty Years of the WTO Appellate Body's "Fragmentation Jurisprudence"' (2015) 14 J. Int'l Trade L. Policy 116, 118–20.

[16] See e.g. Henrik Horn and Petros C Mavroidis, 'Multilateral Environmental Agreements in the WTO: Silence Speaks Volumes' (2014) 10 Int'l J. Econ. Theory 147, esp. 147–50, 162–64.

too difficult for traditional political processes'.[17] In contrast, the analysis in Chapter 3 demonstrated that UNCLOS is particularly open to being affected by subsequent developments in international environmental law and regulation as marine environmental protection is a key goal of the Convention, which includes obligations to protect the marine environment framed in general terms, so-called rules of reference, and instructs tribunals to apply other relevant rules of international law.[18] Additionally, ITLOS and UNCLOS arbitral tribunals operate within a professional community that has consistently seen marine environmental protection as a key part of its mandate.

Key instances where the ICJ interpreted treaties in light of new norms of international environmental law – such as *Gabčikovo-Nagymaros* and *Pulp Mills* – partly reflect that the relevant treaties contained generally worded provisions requiring the parties to protect the environment, the precise content of which could evolve in light of changes in environmental standards.[19] These developments are also explained by the ICJ's interest in endorsing new norms of international environmental law both to demonstrate sensitivity to such developments and to influence them going forward. As Chapter 4 noted, the ICJ has often played an important role in coordinating or mainstreaming the concerns of different regimes within wider international law given its immense semantic authority and its general jurisdiction.[20] More broadly, the developments reviewed in this book demonstrate that while international law-making remains decentralised and sectorial, adjudication is an important site of regime interaction, including because statements by tribunals are an important influence on future understandings of the relationship between different areas of international law. In many of the disputes considered in this book where tribunals favoured an evolutionary or open-ended meaning of a treaty term, this was a gateway for referring to other international norms that could inform the meaning of the treaty term.[21] To some extent, this finding likely reflects the focus of this study on environmental disputes, because such disputes lack a dedicated

[17] Lang (n 15) 120–23.

[18] See Chapter 3(B), text at nn 103–115.

[19] See Chapter 4(B)(1), text at nn 92 and 94.

[20] See Chapter 4, text at nn 43, 232–235.

[21] See e.g. Chapter 2(B)(1), discussion of *US – Shrimp*, Chapter 4(B)(1) discussion of *Gabčikovo-Nagymaros* and *Pulp Mills* in text at nn 91–95, Chapter 3(B)(1) discussion of *South China Sea Arbitration* in text at nn 118–124. On the connection between evolutionary interpretation and taking account of relevant rules of international law

international tribunal and are instead litigated through a variety of 'borrowed' fora,[22] and the applicable law in environmental disputes often sits at the intersection of different regimes.[23]

The analysis in prior chapters also demonstrates that while adjudication makes an important contribution in incrementally updating international law, and State consent alone could not account for many of the developments considered,[24] adjudicators nevertheless continually sought to explain why their interpretations were consistent with what States had already agreed to, even where those interpretations strongly favoured legal change.[25] WTO adjudicators, as we saw, operate in the context of an explicit instruction that their rulings cannot add to or diminish the rights of members under the covered agreements. Faced with the question of whether relevant WTO norms might have evolved in light of wider developments in international law, adjudicators either explained how those new norms were already incorporated within existing WTO provisions (as in *US – Shrimp* or *EC – Hormones*) or emphasised that they could not alter the content of the relevant WTO norms (as the panels did in *EC – Biotech* and *India – Solar Cells*).[26] Similarly, in key examples where the ICJ favoured an evolutive meaning of relevant treaty terms, such as *Gabčikovo-Nagymaros* and *Navigational Rights*, it was careful to explain why the relevant treaty terms were intended to evolve with changes in the law.[27] The tendency of adjudicators to justify their interpretative arguments in terms of State consent reflects that international adjudicators are under pressure to demonstrate that their decisions respect legal certainty and stability and do not make law,[28] despite State consent being an inadequate explanation of the manner in which international law develops through ongoing processes of

pursuant to Article 31(3)(c) of the VCLT see generally Richard K Gardiner, *Treaty Interpretation* (2nd ed., OUP 2015) 332–33, 468, 470, 290–98.

22 Pierre-Marie Dupuy and Jorge E Viñuales, *International Environmental Law* (2nd ed., CUP 2018) 300, 303.

23 See also Justine Bendel, *Litigating the Environment: Process and Procedure before International Courts and Tribunals* (Edward Elgar 2023) 18, 25.

24 Eyal Benvenisti, *The Law of Global Governance* (Martinus Nijhoff 2014) 197.

25 For a similar observation see José E Alvarez, *International Organizations as Law-Makers* (OUP 2006) 532.

26 See Chapter 2(B)(1).

27 See Chapter 4(B)(1), esp. text at nn 94–95 and 100–104.

28 Ilmar Tammelo, *Treaty Interpretation and Practical Reason: Towards a General Theory of Legal Interpretation* (Law Book Company 1967) 53; Ingo Venzke, 'The Role of International Courts as Interpreters and Developers of the Law: Working Out the Jurisgenerative Practice of Interpretation' (2011) 34 Loy. L.A. Int'l & Comp. LR 99, 101.

interpretation.[29] Nevertheless, the contribution of international tribunals in operationalising international norms is unmistakable. As others have noted, in contemporary international adjudication tribunals often appear to be employing an approach that favours contextual and effective interpretation,[30] 'linking rights to corresponding obligations that are informed by the object and purpose of [a treaty] . . . its overall balance of interests, and sometimes also relevant obligations under general international law'.[31] One way to square such developments with State consent may be, as Roland Holst has suggested, to understand State consent in entering into treaties in less static terms '*as consent to a process of normative development*; to a legal framework that governs durable legal relationships that are intended to last, including under circumstances not expressly foreseen at the time initial consent was given'.[32] Such an approach is particularly appropriate for major law-making treaties (e.g. the WTO Agreement or UNCLOS), which are entered into for an indefinite duration, which include a significant grant of advance consent to the jurisdiction of an international tribunal or tribunals, and which are aimed at governing 'durable legal relationships that are intended to last'.[33]

The common practice of tribunals finding that the application of treaty terms would be affected by changes in relevant facts reflects that the provisions concerned were, given their content and the subject matter being regulated, open to being affected by certain types of factual change. For example, in the cases analysed where WTO adjudicators acknowledged the relevance of factual changes they were often applying provisions of the SPS Agreement that depended on the state of certain facts that were liable to change, such as scientific knowledge or the SPS characteristics of an area.[34] Similarly, ITLOS' Seabed Disputes

[29] See e.g. Ingo Venzke, *How Interpretation Makes International Law: On Semantic Change and Normative Twists* (OUP 2012).

[30] Caroline E Foster, *Global Regulatory Standards in Environmental and Health Disputes: Regulatory Coherence, Due Regard, and Due Diligence* (OUP 2021) 290–92.

[31] Rozemarijn J Roland Holst, *Change in the Law of the Sea: Context, Mechanisms and Practice* (Brill Nijhoff 2022) 311–12.

[32] Ibid 11–12 (emphasis added), 66–67, 184–89, drawing on Ellen Hey, *Teaching International Law: State-Consent as Consent to a Process of Normative Development and Ensuing Problems* (Kluwer Law International 2003).

[33] Roland Holst (n 31) 12, 187–88; Vaughan Lowe, 'The Law of Treaties; or, Should This Book Exist?' in Christian J Tams, Antonios Tzanakopoulos and Andreas Zimmermann (eds), *Research Handbook on the Law of Treaties* (Edward Elgar 2014) 7–9, 11–12; *Dispute regarding Navigational and Related Rights (Costa Rica v Nicaragua)*, Judgment, ICJ Rep [2009] 213, [66].

[34] See discussion in Chapter 2(B)(2).

Chamber held that the application of provisions requiring States to exercise due diligence would depend on the state of scientific knowledge and technical capacity at the time the provisions were applied.[35] As others have suggested, due diligence obligations effectively enable the evolution of a legal framework, including because what is sufficient to fulfil an obligation of due diligence may change depending on scientific and technical considerations,[36] and because subsequent normative developments (whether binding or not) can inform whether a State has complied with a due diligence obligation.[37] Due diligence obligations may therefore be a useful tool for treaty negotiators who want an international obligation to keep track with future changes, for example changes in scientific understanding and technical capacity. More broadly, environmental disputes, focused on by this book, frequently raise the issue of how changes in relevant facts affect the application of legal obligations.

This aspect of the book has also developed a strong claim of difference regarding the problem of change in investment treaty arbitration. Like international tribunals in the other contexts studied, investment treaty tribunals contribute to processes of change in international legal norms alongside other law-developing actors within the relevant regime. This was clearly demonstrated by debates over potential changes in the customary international minimum standard of treatment (MST), where States as treaty parties tried to limit the content of the fair and equitable treatment standard by tying it to the customary MST and tribunals took differing views over whether the customary standard had evolved over time. Importantly, however, by interpreting and applying relevant investment treaty standards, investment treaty arbitrators also determine the permissible degree of change in host State regulation.[38] Several factors help explain this distinct role of investment treaty arbitration. As explained in Chapter 5, investment treaties are designed to impose a degree of control over the host State's public decision-making.[39] The authoritative

[35] See Chapter 3(B)(2).

[36] For example International Law Commission, 'Draft Articles on Prevention of Transboundary Harm from Hazardous Activities' [2001] II ILC Ybk 148, 154, commentary to art 3, para 11.

[37] Yoshifumi Tanaka, 'Obligation to Conduct an Environmental Impact Assessment (EIA) in International Adjudication: Interaction between Law and Time' (2021) 90 Nordic JIL 86, 92, 120; Heike Krieger and Anne Peters, 'Due Diligence and Structural Change in the International Legal Order' in Heike Krieger and Anne Peters (eds), *Due Diligence in the International Legal Order* (OUP 2020) 380–81; Alan Boyle and Catherine Redgwell, *Birnie, Boyle, and Redgwell's International Law and the Environment* (4th ed., CUP 2021) 165–66.

[38] See Chapter 5(B).

[39] See Chapter 5, text at nn 268–269.

application function of arbitral tribunals, in deciding whether a change in host State regulation violates investment treaty standards and should be compensated, determines in particular disputes how onerous that degree of international control is.

The crucial role of investment treaty tribunals whereby they determine the permissible degree of regulatory change in the host State in the context of a specific dispute is likely to remain prominent. On the whole, States continue to provide access to treaty-based investor–State arbitration. Key contemporary regulatory challenges, such as the economic and social changes required in the transition to a low-carbon economy, require States to adjust domestic regulation, including in ways that may dramatically impact investors' interests.[40] Investors are likely to challenge such measures before investment treaty tribunals even under so-called 'new style' investment treaties, for example by arguing that regulatory changes are manifestly arbitrary and therefore breach the customary MST or FET standard,[41] or that rare circumstances exist that mean that a non-discriminatory regulatory change nevertheless constitutes an indirect expropriation.[42] The first wave of investor–State cases concerning climate measures, such as phase outs of coal-fired power plants or prohibitions on fossil fuel exploration and extraction activities, have emerged in recent years and claims regarding regulatory stability are at the heart of these disputes.[43] The large body of cases in the last decade concerning States' reductions in renewable energy incentives, considered in Chapter 5, also support the suggestion that a key role of investment treaty arbitration is determining the 'acceptable margin of change' in host

[40] See e.g. *RENERGY S.à.r.l. v Spain*, ICSID Case No ARB/14/18, Dissent on Liability and Quantum Professor Philippe Sands QC (22 April 2022) [48]; *Mathias Kruck and Others v Spain*, ICSID Case No ARB/15/23, Partial Dissenting Opinion Prof. Zachary Douglas KC (13 September 2022) [57]; Gus Van Harten, 'Foreign Investor Protection and Climate Action: A New Price Tag for Urgent Policies' [2015] Osgoode Legal Studies Research Paper Series, Research Paper No 21/2016.

[41] See e.g. CETA art 8.10(2)(c); 2021 Canada Model FIPA art 8(1)(c); Consider also Draft Interpretation of the CETA Joint Committee regarding Article 8.10, Annex 8-A, Article 8.9 and Article 8.39 of the Comprehensive Economic and Trade Agreement (CETA), 9 February 2024, [1(d)], <https://policy.trade.ec.europa.eu/news/joint-statement-sustainable-economic-growth-eu-and-canada-through-comprehensive-economic-and-trade-2024-02-09_en>.

[42] See e.g. CETA Annex 8–A(3) and also Draft Interpretation of the CETA Joint Committee, ibid [2(d)].

[43] See e.g. *TC Energy Corporation v USA*, ICSID Case No ARB/21/63, Request for Arbitration (22 November 2021) [1], [15], [68]–[69], [96]; *Uniper SE v the Netherlands*, ICSID Case No ARB/21/22, Claimants' Memorial (20 May 2022) [464]–[481]; *Westmoreland Mining Holdings LLC v Canada*, ICSID Case No UNCT/20/3, Notice of Arbitration and Statement of Claim (12 August 2019) [98]–[110].

State regulation,[44] and specifically who should bear the costs of regulatory change: the investor or the host State and its taxpayers.[45]

Clearly other international norms applied by other international tribunals also cut deeply into States' regulatory autonomy, for example the numerous disciplines on various forms of trade-restrictive regulation in the WTO covered agreements. Yet in none of the other adjudication settings considered in this book did the wider regime and the case law generated by its adjudication mechanism have the same overriding focus on controlling the permissible degree of change in domestic regulation of the respondent State. This book has suggested that a key bias apparent in investment treaty arbitration is a bias against change in host State regulation and has explained why we see this bias given the contextual features of the investment treaty regime.[46] As Chapter 5 explained, this bias appears to be shifting towards a position where tribunals are generally open to change in host State regulation, subject to certain conditions such as that prior specific assurances given to investors are respected and regulatory changes are not radical or disproportionate to the problem faced by a host State.[47] This reflects that tribunals are to some degree responding to concerns about the investment treaty regime constraining the ability of States to adopt legitimate regulatory changes given evolving circumstances.

B. Findings Regarding Tribunals' Function of Scrutinising State Conduct for Compliance with International Obligations

1. *Findings Regarding Tribunals' Approaches to the Standard of Review*

This book's analysis of tribunals' practices concerning the standard or intensity of review across the four contexts studied suggests that this is a pervasive problem in contemporary international adjudication. Across

[44] *El Paso Energy Int'l Co v Argentina*, ICSID Case No ARB/03/15, Award (31 October 2011) [402].

[45] *9REN Holding S.a.r.l v Spain*, ICSID Case No ARB/15/15, Award (31 May 2019), [253]; Thomas W Wälde and Abba Kolo, 'Environmental Regulation, Investment Protection and "Regulatory Taking" in International Law' (2001) 50 ICLQ 811, 824–25. See further discussion of these cases in Chapter 5(B)(2), text at nn 139–156.

[46] On the idea that all functional regimes, such as the investment treaty regime, have certain biases, see e.g. Martti Koskenniemi, *From Apology to Utopia: The Structure of International Legal Argument* (reissue, CUP 2005) 608–10; Margaret A Young, 'Introduction: The Productive Friction between Regimes' in Margaret A Young (ed), *Regime Interaction in International Law: Facing Fragmentation* (CUP 2012) 10–11.

[47] See Chapter 5(B)(2), esp. text at nn 124–146.

diverse settings, international tribunals are routinely faced with scrutinising determinations made by domestic authorities where the latter may have applied specialised forms of non-legal expertise that adjudicators do not hold, have greater familiarity with relevant local circumstances, or enjoy greater legitimacy to make the relevant determination, for example if it involves exercising discretion over value-laden matters such as determining what is in the domestic public interest.[48] While a substantial body of existing literature considers these issues in the WTO and investment treaty contexts, this book has connected these debates to the same fundamental problems arising in the jurisprudence of UNCLOS tribunals and the ICJ, which have only more recently been the subject of sustained scholarly attention.

The different treaty contexts in which tribunals were operating clearly influenced how the standard of review arose as an issue, although most treaties do not explicitly address this issue. For example, because provisions of the SPS Agreement require WTO members' measures to be based on a risk assessment and available scientific evidence, the question of the standard of review was unsurprisingly a crucial issue in cases where measures were challenged as lacking a sufficient scientific basis. In the UNCLOS cases analysed, the question of the appropriate standard of review arose in the context of the Convention conferring upon the coastal State, within various maritime zones, broad but not unlimited discretionary powers. In short, while the standard of review is a cross-cutting problem in contemporary international adjudication, like other challenges it is always 'fitted into' the particular context in which a tribunal operates.[49]

Despite clear differences in treaty context, a significant element of similarity across the studied contexts was that adjudicators sought to avoid substitutionary de novo review of determinations based on scientific or other forms of non-legal expertise that they did not hold.[50] Tribunals instead repeatedly sought to exercise other more procedural forms of control over the determinations of domestic authorities, for example by considering whether a determination came from a respected source or by scrutinising the process employed for arriving at the

[48] For literature supporting these points see Chapter 1, text at nn 80–83.

[49] See generally Georges Abi-Saab, 'The Normalization of International Adjudication: Convergence and Divergencies' (2010) 43 NYUJILP 1, 7–10.

[50] Similarly: Johannes Hendrik Fahner, *Judicial Deference in International Adjudication: A Comparative Analysis* (Hart 2020) 151–52 (concluding 'deference on this ground is relatively uncontroversial').

determination. This reflects that international tribunals do not hold the specialised forms of scientific or technical expertise that often lie at the heart of international disputes concerning domestic regulatory measures, including in environmental cases. As Henckels has argued, for certain types of decisions such as those involving 'gathering and evaluating complex information (including in relation to risk or harm), monitoring developing situations, engaging in consultation and investigating alternative courses of action', domestic decision-makers will possess greater 'institutional competence and expertise'.[51] This has led others to suggest that adjudicators are, by their training, better equipped to scrutinise the decision-making procedure a State has followed, rather than the merits of a determination based on specialised expertise.[52]

Viewed in comparative perspective, the significance of the debate concerning the standard of review in the SPS context is that it highlights that more procedurally focused forms of scrutiny still require adjudicators to make important normative judgments 'in order to determine what amounts to an adequate [domestic] process'.[53] In many of the cases considered across the four contexts studied, while adjudicators sought to avoid substitutionary de novo review of certain domestic-level determinations, their decisions clearly made normative judgments regarding what would count as an acceptable domestic process. A good example is the ICJ's judgment in the *Whaling* case, considered in Chapter 4, where the

[51] Caroline Henckels, *Proportionality and Deference in Investor-State Arbitration: Balancing Investment Protection and Regulatory Autonomy* (CUP 2015) 39, generally 38–41; Yuval Shany, 'Toward a General Margin of Appreciation Doctrine in International Law?' (2005) 16 EJIL 907, 918.

[52] See e.g. Joel P Trachtman, 'International Legal Control of Domestic Administrative Action' (2014) 17 JIEL 753, 754–56; Michael Ioannidis, 'Beyond the Standard of Review: Deference Criteria in WTO Law and the Case for a Procedural Approach' in Lukasz Gruszczynski and Wouter Werner (eds), *Deference in International Courts and Tribunals: Standard of Review and Margin of Appreciation* (OUP 2014) 109–11; Jürgen Kurtz, 'Adjudging the Exceptional at International Investment Law: Security, Public Order and Financial Crisis' (2010) 59 ICLQ 325, 367.

[53] Jacqueline Peel, *Science and Risk Regulation in International Law* (CUP 2010) 354–55; Jacqueline Peel, 'The Use of Science in Environment-Related Investor-State Arbitration' in Kate Miles (ed), *Research Handbook on Environment and Investment Law* (Edward Elgar 2019) 259–60; Andrew Lang, *World Trade Law after Neoliberalism: Reimagining the Global Economic Order* (OUP 2011) 346. Note that those advocating a more procedural form of review do not claim to avoid difficult normative choices: eg Michael Ioannidis, 'A Procedural Approach to the Legitimacy of International Adjudication: Developing Standards of Participation in WTO Law' (2011) 12 German LJ 1175, 1181–82.

Court developed a series of criteria that had to be satisfied in order for the permits granted by a State to be covered by the treaty exception for scientific whaling.[54]

A related element of similarity that emerged across very different contexts was that adjudicators often acknowledged that domestic decision-makers may have greater familiarity with relevant local circumstances or enjoy greater legitimacy in making certain kinds of determinations. Such considerations were evident in several of the UNCLOS cases reviewed, where adjudicators emphasised that in relation to measures for conserving and managing living resources in the Exclusive Economic Zone, 'national courts or authorities are better placed to appreciate all the relevant considerations of law and fact . . . Hence, they should be given a broad "margin of appreciation"'.[55] Numerous investment treaty tribunals also recognised the comparatively greater legitimacy of domestic authorities and noted the normal role of government in striking a compromise between conflicting interests. These have emerged as standard tropes that are routinely invoked by investor–State tribunals faced with scrutinising domestic regulatory measures.[56] This reflects that investors have used the direct access to international arbitration that this regime provides to challenge a vast range of domestic measures and tribunals are aware of the need to respond to widespread concerns about the potential impact on States' regulatory autonomy.

Another way of reflecting on the case law considered in this part of the book would be to ask whether the standard or intensity of review applied varies depending on the sensitivity of the domestic regulatory interests at stake. For example, in the WTO SPS context some commentators have suggested a difference, in terms of the intensity of adjudicatory scrutiny applied, between '"high level" cases in which the risks at issue have a high degree of political and cultural salience in the regulating country, and the underlying science is highly contested', and '"low level" cases' which do not have the same political sensitivity.[57] Several of the investment treaty

[54] See discussion in Chapter 4(C)(1), esp. text at nn 134–141.

[55] *M/V 'Virginia G' (Panama/Guinea-Bissau)*, Judgment, ITLOS Reports 2014, p. 4, Diss. Op. Hoffmann, Marotta Rangel, Chandrasekhara Rao, Kateka, Gao and Bouguetaia [50]. Further cases discussed in Chapter 3(C)(1).

[56] See discussion in Chapter 5(C)(1).

[57] Lang (n 53) 337–38; Jacqueline Peel, 'Of Apples and Oranges (and Hormones in Beef): Science and the Standard of Review in WTO Disputes under the SPS Agreement' (2012) 61 ICLQ 427, 452–57 (proposing a differentiated standard of review in SPS cases based on the considerations of uncertainty and socio-political contestation of the issues involved).

awards reviewed where tribunals emphasised the deference owed to domestic authorities – such as *Glamis Gold*, *Lone Pine*, *Chemtura*, or *Bilcon* – were disputes with high political salience and contested claims based on scientific or other technical expertise.[58] Nevertheless, discussions of deference in the investment treaty regime are not confined to such high controversy disputes, rather ideas around deference and the standard of review have been mainstreamed in investment treaty case law and are routinely applied in a wide range of disputes. The broader point worth noting is that, as Shirlow has argued, deference is a multifaceted tool used by international adjudicators 'to settle conflicts about the interface between international and domestic decision-making authority', and, just as importantly, 'to build, maintain or defend their legitimacy'.[59]

More generally, as a wide-ranging and 'inward-looking' international law of cooperation continues to be litigated, the main grounds for avoiding substitutionary de novo review of domestic determinations encountered in this book – namely domestic authorities' application of specialised forms of non-legal expertise that adjudicators do not hold, their greater proximity to local conditions, and their greater legitimacy – are likely to remain important.[60] It might be argued that these rationales for some degree of deference are particularly relevant in the WTO and investment treaty contexts, as the international norms in those regimes are frequently focused on issues occurring inside a State's borders. Yet as we have seen, the issue of the standard or intensity of review is also a significant issue in recent environmental disputes in the UNCLOS and ICJ contexts, where the relevant international norms frequently place certain restrictions on the exercise of discretion by a regulating State (eg regarding enforcement measures adopted by coastal States).[61] As others have noted, in contemporary international law determining whether States have complied with their treaty obligations often requires consideration of specialist forms of non-legal expertise that adjudicators do not

[58] See discussion in Chapter 5(C)(1).

[59] Esmé Shirlow, *Judging at the Interface: Deference to State Decision-Making Authority in International Adjudication* (CUP 2021) 5, 31–32. See also 16.

[60] See also ibid 253–54 (discussing the relationship between the subject matter regulated by international law and deference and noting: 'Deference is therefore particularly likely to be relevant where a treaty puts into issue domestic decisions or matters likely to be regulated at the domestic level'); Shany (n 51) 920–21.

[61] See further Chapters 3(C)(1) and 4(C)(1).

possess,[62] or an evaluation of local conditions that detached international adjudicators are not well placed to make.[63] While there are good normative reasons for adjudicators to avoid substitutionary de novo review of certain types of domestic determinations, it is also important that these are evaluated in the particular circumstances of a case.[64] The result of an overly deferential standard of review is that the treaty disciplines that adjudicators are tasked with applying may be undermined,[65] and international adjudication may be weakened as a mechanism for securing shared international interests.[66] For example, in the WTO context, others have noted that an overly deferential standard of review may lead to the treaty-protected interests of other WTO members in trade liberalisation being undermined.[67] It is also important to remember that the rationales for judicial deference in certain systems of domestic public law cannot simply be transposed to the international level, as was explained in the introductory chapter with reference to recent scholarship on this point.[68]

2. *Findings Regarding the Methods of Review Employed*

This study has demonstrated that the method of review, or balancing test, used in determining State compliance with international norms is a fundamental issue in contemporary international adjudication because tribunals are frequently faced with scrutinising the legality of measures that further one protected interest under the relevant legal regime but also restrict other legally protected interests. All the legal regimes studied protect a variety of partially competing goals and contain treaty provisions drafted at a high level of generality, for example requiring measures be 'reasonable' or 'necessary'. The effect of such design features is that for those disputes where they have jurisdiction, adjudicators determine

62 Makane Moïse Mbengue and Rukmini Das, 'The ICJ's Engagement with Science: To Interpret or Not to Interpret?' (2015) 6 JIDS 568, 568–69, 576; Trachtman (n 52) 754–56, 784.

63 See e.g. Henckels (n 51) 37; Shany (n 51) 919.

64 Henckels (n 51) 190.

65 Ibid 30.

66 Caroline E Foster, 'Diminished Ambitions? Public International Legal Authority in the Transnational Economic Era' (2014) 17 JIEL 355, 374–75; Caroline E Foster, 'Adjudication, Arbitration and the Turn to Public Law "Standards of Review": Putting the Precautionary Principle in the Crucible' (2012) 3 JIDS 525, 557–58.

67 Stefan Zleptnig, *Non-Economic Objectives in WTO Law* (Martinus Nijhoff 2010) 97–100, 361–62, 390.

68 See Chapter 1, text at nn 69–72.

where the precise balance between the partially competing interests embodied in the relevant provisions lies.[69] As Foster has argued, while '[t]he applicable legal rules and provisions set the basic parameters', increasingly elaborate 'regulatory standards' such as WTO-style necessity testing or three-step proportionality analysis are 'read into the law' by international courts and tribunals and refined over successive disputes.[70] Such 'regulatory standards' are 'elaborated . . . due to the practical need for international courts and tribunals to deploy reasoning that will enable decisions giving effect to the balance of legal interests among the parties that is written into the relevant international legal provisions'.[71]

Overall, the analysis in prior chapters suggests that two methods of review or balancing tests are commonly used across the four settings considered in this book in scrutinising State compliance with international obligations. Adjudicators frequently use some variation of necessity or least restrictive means testing, and, in some of the contexts studied, particularly investment treaty arbitration, have increasingly engaged in proportionality balancing stricto sensu. At one level, this reflects that these are both balancing techniques of wider relevance, which have been used in numerous international, regional, and national adjudication settings.[72] The existence of such established balancing techniques, which may be familiar from previous experience in other contexts and from an abundant scholarly literature,[73] is likely convenient for international adjudicators faced with scrutinising States' measures under treaties that do not fully resolve how to mediate between competing, legally protected interests. While these issues are addressed by a significant literature in the trade and investment contexts, this book has extended such debates by also providing a thorough analysis of the

[69] For this point in the law of the sea context, see e.g. James Harrison, 'Safeguards against Excessive Enforcement Measures in the Exclusive Economic Zone – Law and Practice' in Henrik Ringbom (ed), *Jurisdiction over Ships: Post-UNCLOS Developments in the Law of the Sea* (Brill Nijhoff 2015) 218, 248; For analysis of this aspect of WTO adjudication, in light of literature concerning incomplete contracts, see Joel P Trachtman, 'The Domain of WTO Dispute Resolution' (1999) 40 HILJ 333, 344ff.

[70] See Foster (n 30) 23, 34–35, 152–53.

[71] Ibid 20.

[72] See generally Alec Stone Sweet and Jud Mathews, 'Proportionality Balancing and Global Constitutionalism' (2008) 47 Colum. J. Transnat'l L. 72; Alec Stone Sweet and Jud Mathews, *Proportionality Balancing and Constitutional Governance: A Comparative and Global Approach* (OUP 2019).

[73] Foster, 'Diminished Ambitions?' (n 66) 374 (on the potential influence of scholarly literature).

equivalent problems in ICJ and UNCLOS adjudication. Importantly, the analysis was sensitive to the different contextual factors that shape how the issue of the method of review arises in each setting.

To be sure, in the ICJ cases reviewed, and some of the UNCLOS cases, tribunals used a test phrased in terms of reasonableness and developed from the specific treaty context, rather than consistently referring to necessity testing or proportionality balancing stricto sensu. However, the way such reasonableness-based tests were developed and applied was functionally very similar to necessity testing. For example, in *Whaling* and *Navigational Rights*, the ICJ considered whether the regulating State could have achieved its aims through measures that were less restrictive of other legally protected interests, and whether alternative measures proposed by the complainant would have achieved the relevant regulatory aims and were practically available.[74] Other commentators have also noted that such case law, although expressed in terms of a reasonableness test, effectively amounts to applying elements of proportionality analysis such as a necessity or least restrictive means test.[75] In the UNCLOS context, as explained in Chapter 3, some of the most recent case law has suggested that '[t]he exercise of enforcement powers by a (coastal) State in situations where the State derives these powers from provisions of the Convention' is subject to the requirement of reasonableness, which 'encompasses the principles of necessity and proportionality'.[76] In scrutinising the exercise of coastal State enforcement powers for compliance with treaty provisions that required such measures be 'reasonable' or 'necessary', on several occasions UNCLOS adjudicators have asked whether the same regulatory aim could be achieved through a less restrictive measure or even noted the parallel with WTO necessity testing.[77]

[74] See further Chapter 4(C)(2)(a).

[75] Pasquale De Sena and Lorenzo Acconciamessa, 'Balancing Test' in Hélène Ruiz-Fabri (ed), *Max Planck Encyclopedia of International Procedural Law* (OUP 2021) [16], [40]; Asier Garrido-Muñoz, 'Managing Uncertainty: The International Court of Justice, "Objective Reasonableness" and the Judicial Function' (2017) 30 LJIL 457, 467–71; Enzo Cannizzaro, 'Proportionality and Margin of Appreciation in the *Whaling* Case: Reconciling Antithetical Doctrines?' (2016) 27 EJIL 1061, 1062–64, 1068–69; Kevin Crow, 'The Opacity of Proportionality in International Courts: Could Categories Clarify?' (2019) 51 GWILR 289, 302.

[76] *Duzgit Integrity Arbitration* (*Malta v São Tomé and Príncipe*), Award (2016) 173 ILR 95, [209]. See also discussion of *Arctic Sunrise* in Chapter 3(C)(2), text at nn 228–230.

[77] See case law discussed in Chapter 3(C)(2), esp. text at n 207 and nn 216–221.

Two key questions arising from the case law reviewed in earlier chapters concern the appropriateness of proportionality balancing stricto sensu and, relatedly, how adjudicators can apply the methods of review being developed in a manner that does not undermine the regulatory autonomy of respondent States. This book has suggested that in the four adjudication contexts studied, necessity or least restrictive means testing is a more appropriate method of review than the more demanding test of proportionality stricto sensu. Necessity or least reactive means testing has the major advantage that it does not involve international tribunals second-guessing the relative importance of the aim pursued by a regulating State.[78] Under this method of review, adjudicators only treat as genuine alternatives those measures that would make an equivalent contribution to the regulatory aim selected by a regulating State and that were practically available at reasonable cost.[79] The key argument in favour of engaging in proportionality balancing stricto sensu is that without it a legally protected right or interest might be severely restricted by a measure pursuing another relatively unimportant but legally protected interest.[80] Such a measure might pass a least restrictive means test but fail the proportionality stricto sensu stage given the greater importance of the restricted right or interest. This argument is not without merit. However, it presumes an agreed hierarchy of values, whereby some rights or interests protected by a legal regime can be judged as more important than other competing legally protected interests pursued by a regulating State. As commentators have highlighted in the WTO context, that regime is not designed to impose any comprehensive normative vision on members, but is meant to leave them free to choose which regulatory aims they pursue.[81] Overall, the other adjudication settings considered exhibit even less evidence of any agreed hierarchy between

[78] See e.g. Kurtz (n 52) 368–69; Federico Ortino, 'Investment Treaties, Sustainable Development and Reasonableness Review: A Case against Strict Proportionality Balancing' (2017) 30 LJIL 71, 88–89; Csongor István Nagy, 'Clash of Trade and National Public Interest in WTO Law: The Illusion of "Weighing and Balancing" and the Theory of Reservation' (2020) 23 JIEL 143, 148–49.

[79] See the discussion of these aspects of WTO necessity jurisprudence in Chapter 2(C)(2), text at nn 240, 267–270 and 282.

[80] See eg Alec Stone Sweet and Florian Grisel, *The Evolution of International Arbitration: Judicialization, Governance, Legitimacy* (OUP 2017) 249–50; Stone Sweet and Mathews, *Proportionality Balancing* (n 72) 37; Aharon Barak, *Proportionality: Constitutional Rights and Their Limitations* (CUP 2012) 342–43.

[81] See Chapter 2, text at n 251.

competing legally protected interests.[82] Where adjudicators are appointed on an ad hoc basis and concerns exist about their representativeness, as in the existing relatively polarised system of investor–State arbitration, this adds weight to the argument that they are not well placed to engage in the value-laden exercise of proportionality balancing stricto sensu.[83]

The case law considered in the preceding chapters highlights that a significant risk of proportionality balancing stricto sensu is that it creates additional space, beyond a necessity test, for regulatory measures to be challenged and found not to be proportionate through a controversial weighing of arguably incommensurable values.[84] Most obviously, in some of the investment treaty cases considered, the public interests pursued by a regulating State were arguably undermined through the application of a proportionality stricto sensu test that weighed the aim furthered by the relevant measure (in light of the relative importance of that aim) against the measure's impact on a claimant investor. A stark example was *Occidental v Ecuador*, where the Tribunal itself weighed the impact of the measure on the claimant investor against the interests of Ecuador as sovereign over its natural resources with the right to decide on what conditions such resources could be exploited.[85] As demonstrated in Chapter 5, some of the renewables disputes have also directly weighed the policy aim being pursued by the State in those cases (addressing a 'tariff deficit' and an unsustainably costly electricity system) against the burden placed on the claimant investor(s).[86] *Tecmed* was also a case where the impact of a measure on the claimant investor was directly weighed against the policy aim being pursued by the host State (in that case, responding to public opposition to the location of the landfill).[87]

Ultimately, as Foster has noted, the key challenge with proportionality balancing stricto sensu is that it 'elevate[s] decision-making concerning the relative priorities of different values and policies from the domestic to the international legal plane' and specifically invites international

82 For similar arguments regarding investment arbitration, see Henckels (n 51) 160, 164–65; Kurtz (n 52) 367–68. See also Crow (n 75) 317–18.

83 Prabhash Ranjan, 'Using the Public Law Concept of Proportionality to Balance Investment Protection with Regulation in International Investment Law: A Critical Reappraisal' (2014) 3 Cambridge JICL 853, 862–64; Henckels (n 51) 164.

84 Henckels (n 51) 27–29, 168.

85 See further discussion in Chapter 5(C)(2)(b), text at nn 238–45.

86 See Chapter 5(C)(2)(b), text at nn 219–31.

87 See Chapter 5(C)(2)(b), text at nn 232–37.

tribunals to 'weigh the relative value of the legal interests at issue'.[88] The above difficulties with proportionality balancing stricto sensu should be borne in mind by adjudicators who may be tempted to extend this concept into new areas. States, as system designers, may also wish to protect their regulatory autonomy by specifying in greater detail in future treaties the methods of review to be used by adjudicators when scrutinising State conduct for compliance with particular provisions.[89]

There are also alternatives to proportionality balancing stricto sensu that warrant further consideration. For example, as noted in Chapter 5, one variation on a proportionality balancing stricto sensu test that has been suggested by some commentators and certain investment treaty arbitrators is to limit this aspect of the inquiry to checking whether a measure is not manifestly disproportionate to the regulatory aim pursued, taking account of the measure's impact on other legally protected interests.[90] There is precedent for such a reframing of the proportionality stricto sensu stage of the analysis as a test that simply checks that a measure is not manifestly disproportionate in some areas of European Union (EU) law, in which the EU courts have been faced with scrutinising the discretionary policy choices of EU authorities.[91] Similarly, Rivers, writing in the context of European and UK human rights law, has argued that in certain circumstances it may be appropriate to frame the test as one of disproportionality, whereby a measure that has been shown by the regulating State to pursue a legitimate aim and to be capable of contributing to that aim is presumed to comply with the necessity and proportionality stricto sensu stages of analysis, with the burden of proving the measure fails these steps placed on the claimant.[92] Such an approach is to some extent already present in the case law reviewed in this book – for example in the approach of WTO tribunals and some investment treaty

[88] Foster (n 30) 26, 323–25; Caroline E Foster, 'Why Due Regard Is More Appropriate than Proportionality Testing in International Investment Law' (2022) 23 JWIT 388, 394, 413–14.

[89] One possible precedent in this regard is the footnote to Article 5.6 of the SPS agreement: see Chapter 2(C)(2)(c), text at nn 281–82. See also Foster (n 88) 391 (suggesting States in future investment treaties incorporate a due regard standard, which 'would oblige treaty parties to carry out advance consideration of the effect of regulatory action on protected investment interests').

[90] Foster (n 30) 267–68; Henckels (n 51) 161, 168; *Mathias Kruck and Others v Spain*, ICSID Case No ARB/15/23, Partial Dissenting Opinion Prof. Zachary Douglas KC (13 September 2022) [104].

[91] See Paul Craig, *EU Administrative Law* (3rd ed., OUP 2018) 644–55.

[92] See Julian Rivers, 'The Presumption of Proportionality' (2014) 77 MLR 409.

tribunals of requiring that a claimant must identify a less restrictive measure that was reasonably available and would make an equivalent contribution to the relevant regulatory aim, rather than requiring the regulating State to establish that out of the universe of possible measures the impugned measure was the least restrictive available.[93] Similarly, the ICJ in *Navigational Rights* framed its test of reasonableness in negative terms, namely that a regulation 'must not be unreasonable, which means that its negative impact on the exercise of the right in question must not be manifestly excessive when measured against the protection afforded to the purpose invoked', and emphasised that the Court would require a claimant to point to '[c]oncrete and specific facts' to establish that a regulation was unreasonable.[94]

If a test of requiring that a measure is not manifestly disproportionate to the regulatory aim pursued is further developed in future, one challenge may be to give greater determinacy to what the 'manifest' qualifier does in such a test, because the qualifier on its own does not make a lot clearer the test to be applied by adjudicators.[95] Indeed, of investor–State tribunals in the many renewables cases that have framed their approach as a test for disproportionality, there are a variety of approaches.[96] A related idea is to limit proportionality analysis to a form of procedural proportionality review, in which the international tribunal asks whether the domestic authority has carried out a proportionality analysis in designing its measures – and thus considered the negative impact on other legally protected interests – but does not itself engage in weighing the competing interests.[97] Another approach, suggested by Foster, may be to leave the concept of proportionality behind altogether and instead employ a test based on the concept of due regard, which is a more procedurally focused determination of whether a State has engaged in an adequate consideration, before adopting a measure, of the impacts of the measure on the competing legally protected interests of other States.[98]

93 See further Chapter 2(C)(2)(a), text at nn 240 and 293–95 and Chapter 5(C)(2)(a), text at n 210.

94 *Dispute regarding Navigational Rights* (n 33) [87], [101], affirmed and applied in *Certain Iranian Assets (Islamic Republic of Iran v United States of America)*, Judgment, 30 March 2023, [146], [149].

95 Henckels (n 51) 168.

96 See Chapter 5(C)(2)(b), text at nn 219–229.

97 See e.g. Tor-Inge Harbo, *The Function of Proportionality Analysis in European Law* (Brill Nijhoff 2015) 307–14; Foster (n 88) 411–12.

98 See Foster (n 30) 327–35; Foster (n 88) esp. 413–15.

C. Findings Regarding Tribunals' Contributions to Broader Processes of Dispute Resolution

This book has analysed to what extent international tribunals across the four contexts studied seek to contribute to broader processes of dispute resolution through their decisions. Specifically, it has considered whether adjudication is largely retrospective and aims to dispose entirely of the parties' dispute, or alternatively whether it also has a partly prospective focus and attempts to provide guidance to the disputing parties to assist them in their future interactions, including in rebuilding their relationship after adjudication. As explained in Chapter 1, this aspect of the book builds on several strands of existing literature, including those who have argued that as a general matter international adjudication may be most effective in terms of dispute resolution where it complements a broader process driven by the parties.[99] Other commentators with a focus on one of the adjudication contexts studied (eg WTO or UNCLOS dispute settlement) have praised examples in existing case law of international adjudication playing a more facilitative role, which clarifies the law applicable to the parties' relationship and pushes them to resolve the dispute through further negotiation or cooperation.[100] This aspect of the analysis gives rise to several findings.

At one level, such developments are clearly shaped by the particular treaty or legal context concerned. For example, in considering the relevant GATT Article XX jurisprudence in Chapter 2, we saw that the duty to pursue cooperative solutions or consider the interests of other affected WTO members is not free-standing but has been developed as part of determining whether there is arbitrary or unjustifiable discrimination, which remains the focus of the 'chapeau' test.[101] Similarly, in the ICJ cases that exhibited a forward-looking and facilitative style of adjudication, the obligations of the parties were often developed from the particular legal context concerned, such as through the monitoring obligations and concept of preferential rights in *Fisheries Jurisdiction*, or through the relevant bilateral river treaties, read in light of customary international law on the duty to prevent environmental harm, in *Gabčikovo-Nagymaros*, *Pulp Mills*, and the *Certain Activities* and *Construction of a Road* cases.[102] The prominence of a facilitative

[99] See Chapter 1, text at n 101.

[100] See Chapter 2(D), text at nn 301–303 and Chapter 3(D), text at nn 240–42.

[101] See Chapter 2(D), text at nn 326–29.

[102] See Chapter 4(D).

approach to adjudication in UNCLOS dispute settlement is also partly explained by the fact that the Convention contains numerous obligations to cooperate, including with regard to protection of the marine environment. Focusing on this level of specificity tends to support the suggestion made by others who have compared obligations to cooperate across different areas of international law that such obligations are generally 'treaty-based. The ensuing consequences cannot be generalized'.[103]

However, if we move the analysis to a slightly higher level of generality, the comparison undertaken reveals a significant difference, namely that in contrast to the three inter-State adjudication contexts studied, in investor–State arbitration there is far less attention paid to the disputing parties' future interactions and the focus is largely retrospective and compensatory. The contextual features of investment treaty arbitration that help explain this finding were analysed in the last chapter. Here the focus is on comparing those features to contextual features of the other adjudication settings studied to explain fully this finding of difference. Whether the disputing parties have an ongoing need to deal with each other after adjudication influences why adjudication in some contexts, and not others, has a partly facilitative and prospective focus. As explained in Chapter 5, in the investor–State context it is less common that the disputing parties have an ongoing relationship by the time a dispute is decided by an arbitral tribunal, although this is the case in a minority of disputes.[104] In contrast, in the three inter-State adjudication contexts considered in this book the disputing parties will nearly always have an ongoing need to interact with each other after the adjudication is over.[105] For example, the UNCLOS and ICJ cases that exhibited

[103] Rüdiger Wolfrum, 'International Law of Cooperation' in Rüdiger Wolfrum (ed), *Max Planck Encyclopedia of Public International Law* (OUP 2010) [40]; Jost Delbrück, 'The International Obligation to Cooperate – An Empty Shell or a Hard Law Principle of International Law? – A Critical Look at a Much Debated Paradigm of Modern International Law' in Holger P Hestermeyer and others (ed), *Coexistence, Cooperation and Solidarity: Liber Amicorum Rüdiger Wolfrum*, vol 1 (Martinus Nijhoff 2012) 4, 16; Neil Craik, 'The Duty to Cooperate in International Environmental Law: Constraining State Discretion through Due Respect' (2019) 30 Ybk IEL 22, 43.

[104] See Chapter 5(D), text at nn 248–250.

[105] Bill Mansfield, 'Compulsory Dispute Settlement after the Southern Bluefin Tuna Award' in Alex G Oude Elferink and Donald R Rothwell (eds), *Oceans Management in the Twenty-first Century: Institutional Frameworks and Responses* (Martinus Nijhoff 2004) 255–56 (discussing this aspect of inter-State disputes). Similarly: Kenneth Keith, 'The Role of an ICJ Judge' in Carlos Espósito and Kate Parlett (eds), *The Cambridge Companion to the International Court of Justice* (CUP 2023) 63.

a forward-looking and facilitative style of adjudication typically concerned disputes between neighbouring States or States interested in a shared resource.[106] In such circumstances, the parties may have a collective interest that will benefit from the dispute being resolved, for example if that enables a shared resource to be exploited or removes an irritant from otherwise close bilateral relations.[107] In several of these cases adjudicators also did not have sufficient knowledge or information to dispose fully of the dispute, and the parties were better placed to determine appropriate management and conservation measures going forward.[108]

Another key contextual factor that explains whether adjudication has a prospective focus is the type of remedies that are commonly awarded by a court or tribunal. The system for remedies in WTO dispute settlement, considered in Chapter 2,[109] is 'inherently forward-looking' and concerned with inducing future compliance rather than providing retrospective compensation.[110] It 'gives the parties an unusually prominent role in fashioning the remedies to be applied'.[111] In a context where a losing party gets a chance to redesign its measure in a way that complies with the relevant obligations, and post-adjudication bargaining between the parties is standard, it is particularly plausible to suggest that tribunals might provide authoritative guidance on the applicable legal framework but leave the parties some room to resolve their dispute. This is why the GATT Article XX cases discussed in Chapter 2 can be read as instances where the Appellate Body effectively established certain other-regarding procedural values that a regulating State must observe but refrained from resolving the underlying clash of trade and non-trade values that divided the disputing parties.[112]

106 See generally discussion in Chapters 3(D) and 4(D).

107 See Heather L Jones, 'Why Comply? An Analysis of Trends in Compliance with Judgments of the International Court of Justice Since Nicaragua' (2012) 12 Chi.-Kent J. Int'l & Comp. L. 57, 68–70.

108 See e.g. discussion of *Fisheries Jurisdiction* in Chapter 4(D), text at n 185 and *Land Reclamation* in Chapter 3(D), text at nn 247–251.

109 See Chapter 2(A)(2)(e).

110 Brooks E Allen, 'The Use of Non-Pecuniary Remedies in WTO Dispute Settlement: Lessons for Arbitral Practitioners' in Michael E Schneider and Joachim Knoll (eds), *Performance as a Remedy: Non-Monetary Relief in International Arbitration* (Juris 2011) 289–90; Chester Brown, *A Common Law of International Adjudication* (OUP 2007) 220.

111 Allen (n 110) 297.

112 See further Chapter 2(D), text at nn 301–303.

The ICJ cases analysed in Chapter 4 demonstrate that the Court has repeatedly placed the parties under obligations to cooperate either as part of the remedies ordered in the operative part of the judgment,[113] or through remarks in its reasoning.[114] In terms of the remedies employed, such instances could either be categorised as the Court issuing a declaratory judgment clarifying the legal obligations of the parties or, in certain instances, as orders for specific performance where the Court left the parties a wide degree of discretion regarding how the relevant obligations were to be performed.[115] Overall the cases reviewed are significant because they provide clear and repeated examples of the ICJ seeking to assist the parties to manage their relationship going forward.[116] Such examples have much in common with several of the UNCLOS cases considered in Chapter 3 where tribunals were quite clearly performing a facilitative or conflict management role, clarifying the legal framework applicable to the parties' relationship and ordering them to engage in further cooperation.[117]

Overall, the type of remedies used in investment treaty arbitration differ significantly from the other three adjudication contexts. As is well known, compensation is by far the dominant remedy used and it is rare for investment treaty tribunals to mandate future negotiation or other cooperation between the disputing parties.[118] At most we see investment arbitrators occasionally offering the parties 'guidance' if they wish to

[113] See e.g. discussion of *Fisheries Jurisdiction* and *Gabčikovo-Nagymaros* in Chapter 4(D), text at nn 186–88 and nn 190–91.

[114] See e.g. discussion of *Certain Activities/Construction of a Road* and *Pulp Mills* in Chapter 4(D), text at nn 200–205 and nn 207–210.

[115] In a study of remedies before the ICJ, Stoica argues that although declaratory judgments are the most common remedy requested from and ordered by the Court, the ICJ has ordered specific performance in certain cases, and highlights *Gabčikovo-Nagymaros* as a significant example, with the Court finding that the parties had to perform the obligations in the applicable treaty: Victor Stoica, *Remedies before the International Court of Justice: A Systemic Analysis* (CUP 2021) 21–22, ch 4 esp. 46–49, 57–59, 169. See also Christine Gray, 'Remedies' in Cesare PR Romano, Karen J Alter and Yuval Shany (eds), *The Oxford Handbook of International Adjudication* (OUP 2013) 876–79; James Crawford, 'Flexibility in the Award of Reparation: The Role of the Parties and the Tribunal' in Rüdiger Wolfrum, Maja Sersic and Trpimir M Šošić (eds), *Contemporary Developments in International Law: Essays in Honour of Budislav Vukas* (Brill Nijhoff 2016) 692, 696–700.

[116] See generally discussion in Chapter 4(D). See also Stoica (n 115) 167–68.

[117] See generally Chapter 3(D).

[118] See discussion in Chapter 5(D), text at nn 253–59.

explore rebuilding their relationship,[119] or making remarks about 'expecting' the parties to negotiate in good faith as to the possibility of restitution while nevertheless giving the investor a unilateral option to request compensation.[120] As noted in Chapter 5, there are practical reasons why investors and States typically prefer pecuniary remedies in investment arbitration, including, respectively, avenues for enforcement and sovereignty-based sensitivities.[121] The current reliance on ad hoc tribunals in investment treaties means that a tribunal will not necessarily remain in existence to monitor future compliance with a non-pecuniary order,[122] although this point is also true of State–State arbitration.[123] Arbitrators would need to opt to retain jurisdiction over a compliance phase, a practice that is not entirely unheard of but results in increased time and cost.[124] The emerging use of permanent courts or tribunals in investor–State dispute settlement may in due course remove this contextual difference.[125]

A final consideration that helps explain why adjudicators may (or may not) play a partly facilitative, conflict management role is the prevailing paradigm in which adjudication occurs. As explained in Chapter 5, consistent with a commercial arbitration paradigm, many view the point of investment treaty arbitration as enabling an investor, which enjoys markedly less bargaining power after it has sunk its capital in the host State, to obtain an order for compensation that can be enforced in domestic courts.[126] In contrast, the more forward-looking style of adjudication apparent in WTO dispute settlement partly reflects a regime with strong diplomatic origins,[127] where members retain significant control

[119] *Occidental Exploration and Production Company v Ecuador*, LCIA Case No 3467, UNCITRAL, Final Award (1 July 2004) [213]–[214].

[120] *Franck Charles Arif v Moldova*, ICSID Case No ARB/11/23, Award (8 April 2013) [572]. Additional case law discussed above Chapter 5(D), text at n 259.

[121] See above Chapter 5(D), text at nn 255–261.

[122] Allen (n 110) 303. See *Arif* (n 120) [571] (noting restitution, although the preferable remedy, could not be supervised by the Tribunal).

[123] Berk Demirkol, 'Reconsideration of Proper Remedies in Investment Arbitration in Light of Recent Cases: Should the Remedy Follow the Primary Obligation?' (2021) 22 JWIT 129, 144.

[124] Allen (n 110) 303. See also discussion of *Goetz v Burundi* in Chapter 5(D), text at n 259.

[125] As noted briefly below, regional human rights courts may also be an interesting comparator in this regard because some of them include dedicated processes to oversee compliance: see below n 144.

[126] See discussion in Chapter 5(D), text at nn 263–65.

[127] Robert E Hudec, 'Broadening the Scope of Remedies in WTO Dispute Settlement' in Friedl Weiss (ed), *Improving WTO Dispute Settlement Procedures: Issues and Lessons*

over the dispute settlement system, and specifically how disputes are resolved after a finding of non-compliance is made.[128] Similarly, the forward-looking and facilitative style of adjudication apparent in many of the UNCLOS and ICJ cases considered reflects that in those contexts it is widely accepted that adjudication can complement a broader diplomatic-driven dispute resolution process. In short, both States and other actors (eg litigators and adjudicators) appear to conceive of the three inter-State adjudication settings studied in this book as having a more diplomatic orientation, whereas a commercial arbitration paradigm has been influential in understanding investment treaty arbitration.[129]

There is reason to ask whether investment treaty arbitration may benefit from making greater use of a more facilitative and prospectively oriented style of adjudication. As explained in Chapter 1, many have suggested that international adjudication can sometimes be most effective in terms of dispute resolution where it complements a wider process driven by the parties.[130] Whether a prospectively focused adjudicatory approach is appropriate will depend on the particular facts of a dispute, such as whether there is any hope of re-establishing a relationship between the disputing parties, and whether they have any interest in future cooperation (eg because the investor has other existing or potential investments in the host State).[131] As noted in Chapter 5, there is evidence that some investors who are involved in investor–State arbitration have a wider relationship with the host State spanning multiple or long-term investments.[132] These considerations are relevant because although arbitrators enjoy discretion in awarding remedies, they are ultimately limited by the requests of the disputing parties.[133] Given that the disputing parties will typically have explored the possibility of a negotiated solution

from the Practice of Other International Courts and Tribunals (Cameron May 2000) 383 (practice of setting aside past conduct and focusing on forward-looking remedies reflects a diplomatic mode of dispute settlement).

128 Allen (n 110) 289–90, 297.

129 On the influence of a commercial arbitration paradigm in investment treaty arbitration, see eg Stephan W Schill, 'W(h)ither Fragmentation? On the Literature and Sociology of International Investment Law', 22 EJIL 875 (2011) at 887–89; Jonathan Bonnitcha, Lauge N Skovgaard Poulsen and Michael Waibel, *The Political Economy of the Investment Treaty Regime* (OUP 2017) 28–29; Anthea Roberts, 'Clash of Paradigms: Actors and Analogies Shaping the Investment Treaty System' (2013) 107 AJIL 45, 54–63.

130 See Chapter 1, text at n 101.

131 Allen (n 110) 307–08.

132 See Chapter 5(D), text at nn 249–250.

133 Known as the *non ultra petita* rule: Crawford (n 115) 706.

prior to submission of a claim to arbitration (eg during a 'cooling-off' period), investor–State tribunals would need to provide significant clarity on contested issues of law and fact, which might lead the parties to re-evaluate their positions.[134] Whether arbitration could realistically be expected to do this in a timely manner would also be a relevant consideration.

Within the investment treaty regime there are clear indications that States, as ultimate principals of the regime, are interested in making greater use of more facilitative modes of dispute settlement to resolve investor–State disputes.[135] For example, recent investment treaties often include strengthened language around the initial obligation to seek an amicable settlement and provide additional details on how such consultations are to occur.[136] A growing minority of investment treaties also provide for mediation as a mechanism for resolving investor–State disputes, although in most (but not all) such treaties mediation requires the agreement of the disputing parties, rather than mediation being an alternative to arbitration or a mandatory step before arbitration.[137] Many States have also raised the issue of improving means of dispute

[134] For this point in an inter-State context, see David Anderson, 'Negotiation and Dispute Settlement' in Malcolm D Evans (ed), *Remedies in International Law: The Institutional Dilemma* (Hart 1998) 119. However, note that where a State is strongly committed to maintaining the impugned measures this may reduce its willingness to negotiate with a claimant investor.

[135] See generally the contributions to the special issue 'Innovative Strategies for Conflict Management: Improving Investor-State Relations to Propel Global Growth Symposium' (2021) 17(2) University of St Thomas Law Journal 201–480.

[136] For example, EU investment treaties typically provide that '[a] dispute should as far as possible be settled amicably' and provide certain details regarding how consultations are to occur: eg EU–Vietnam IPA art 3.29, 3.30(3)–(4); CETA art 8.19(1)–(4). See also 2021 Canada Model FIPA art 25;. 2019 Netherlands Model BIT arts 17–18; Indonesia–Australia CEPA art 14.22(1)–(2); Indonesia–Singapore BIT 2018 arts 14(1), 15.

[137] See generally UNCITRAL, 'Draft Provisions on Mediation', Note by the Secretariat, A/CN.9/WG.III/WP.217, 13 July 2022, [7]–[10]; Romesh Weeramantry, Brian Chang and Joel Sherard-Chow, 'Conciliation and Mediation in Investor-State Dispute Settlement Provisions: A Quantitative and Qualitative Analysis' (2023) 38 ICSID Review 201, 224–29, 210–14 (finding in forty-three of fifty-three IIAs that refer to mediation, mediation requires the agreement of the disputing parties). ICSID has recently adopted a set of rules for investor–State mediation and other arbitral institutions or professional bodies have also developed similar rules: see generally UNCITRAL, 'Dispute Prevention and Mitigation – Means of Alternative Dispute Resolution', Note by the Secretariat, A/CN.9/WG.III/WP.190, 15 January 2020, [38]–[42]. There is a substantial literature on investor–State mediation. See e.g. Esmé Shirlow, 'The Promises and Pitfalls of Investor-State Mediation' in Lisa Sachs, Lise Johnson and Jesse Coleman (eds), *Yearbook on International Investment Law & Policy 2019* (OUP 2021); '[Special Issue] Alternative Dispute Resolution in Investment Disputes' (2014) 29(1) ICSID Review 1–141; Jeswald

prevention and alternative means of settling investor–State disputes in the UNCITRAL Working Group III process, leading to the development of a set of model provisions and guidelines on investor–State mediation adopted by UNCITRAL, which may be endorsed by future investment treaties or a multilateral reform instrument.[138] Besides increased interest in investor–State mediation, there is also significant interest in other forms of dispute prevention and management, such as the ombudsperson or contact point institutions that certain States use at the domestic level in an effort to resolve investor–State disputes before they progress to international arbitration.[139] Another alternative means for settling investor–State disputes that has received some attention is to provide for a joint committee, constituted by representatives of the treaty parties, tasked with resolving investor–State disputes,[140] an approach that Brazil has used in its post-2015 investment treaties.[141]

While there are significant variations in States' approaches to these alternative means of dispute settlement, collectively they demonstrate States' desire to 'detect, prevent and manage' disputes with foreign investors given States' increased familiarity with the significant costs of

W Salacuse, 'Is There a Better Way? Alternative Methods of Treaty-Based, Investor-State Dispute Resolution' (2007) 31 Fordham Int'l LJ 138; Andrea Kupfer Schneider and Nancy A Welsh, 'Bargaining in the Shadow of Investor-State Mediation: How the Threat of Mediation Will Improve Parties' Conflict Management' (2021) 17 University of St. Thomas Law Journal 373; Ignacio de la Rasilla, '"The Greatest Victory"? Challenges and Opportunities for Mediation in Investor-State Dispute Settlement' (2023) 38 ICSID Review 169; Catherine Kessedjian and others, 'Mediation in Future Investor–State Dispute Settlement' (2023) 14 JIDS 192.

138 UNCITRAL Secretariat, 'Draft Provisions on Mediation', A/CN.9/1150, 25 April 2023; UNCITRAL Secretariat, 'Draft UNCITRAL Guidelines on Investment Mediation', A/CN.9/1151, 21 April 2023. These draft provisions were adopted at UNCITRAL's fifty-sixth session in July 2023: Report of the United Nations Commission on International Trade Law, Fifty-sixth session (3–21 July 2023) A/78/17, [28]–[40].

139 See the examples cited in Catharine Titi, 'Between Utopia and Realism: Mediation and the Settlement of Investment Disputes' in Catharine Titi and Katia Fach Gómez (eds), *Mediation in International Commercial and Investment Disputes* (OUP 2019) 29–30; UNCITRAL, 'Dispute Prevention and Mitigation', A/CN.9/WG.III/WP.190 (n 137) [12]–[13]; Silvia Constain, 'Mediation in Investor-State Dispute Settlement: Government Policy and the Changing Landscape' (2014) 29 ICSID Review 25, 30–31.

140 UNCITRAL, 'Dispute Prevention and Mitigation', A/CN.9/WG.III/WP.190 (n 137) [25] fn 31 (citing certain investment treaties other than those of Brazil that use this approach).

141 See eg Brazil–India BIT (2020) arts 13, 18; Brazil–United Arab Emirates BIT (2018) arts 18, 24; 2015 Brazil Model BIT arts 17, 23.

investor–State arbitration.[142] My findings are relevant to these developments because they suggest that investor–State arbitration itself might be conducted in a more facilitative and a forward-looking manner. This is a significant area for potential comparatively informed learning in light of the practices of the three inter-State adjudication contexts studied in this book, where adjudication has frequently operated in a complementary manner with other forms of dispute resolution, such as negotiation. While there are obviously major contextual differences between investor–State arbitration and the inter-State adjudication contexts considered in this book, such differences do not warrant dismissing outright the relevance of insights emerging from the latter regarding the potential promises (and pitfalls) of a more facilitative approach to adjudication, which complements subsequent negotiation or cooperation between the disputing parties. Beyond the adjudicatory settings studied in this book, regional human rights courts may also provide a useful comparator for considering whether investor–State arbitration could be performed in a more facilitative and forward-looking manner. This is for several reasons, including that regional human rights courts largely hear cases with non-State actors as claimants, meaning the disputing parties may have less need to interact going forward than an inter-State context; frequently award compensation (which dominates investment arbitration) but also use a range of other remedies aimed at bringing domestic practices into compliance;[143] and in some contexts include highly developed processes designed to oversee compliance.[144]

142 Constain (n 139) 25.

143 Commentators have highlighted significant differences between the practice of the European Court of Human Rights and the Inter-American Court of Human Rights, with the latter in general far more willing to order non-monetary remedies aimed at bringing domestic practices into compliance. See e.g. Veronika Fikfak, 'Structural Remedies: Human Rights Law' in Hélène Ruiz-Fabri (ed), *Max Planck Encyclopedia of International Procedural Law* (OUP 2022); Gray (n 115) 890–95; Angelika Nussberger, *The European Court of Human Rights* (OUP 2020) 161–72. See generally Dinah Shelton, *Remedies in International Human Rights Law* (3rd ed., OUP 2015).

144 In particular, the European Convention on Human Rights includes highly developed procedures for oversight of compliance with judgments through the Committee of Ministers and the secretariat body that assists it, the Department for the Execution of Judgments of the European Court of Human Rights. See generally Loris Marotti, 'Remedies Against Non-Compliance with International Judgments' in Hélène Ruiz-Fabri (ed), *Max Planck Encyclopedia of International Procedural Law* (OUP 2021) [42]–[45]; Başak Çali and Anne Koch, 'Foxes Guarding the Foxes? The Peer Review of Human Rights Judgments by the Committee of Ministers of the Council of Europe' (2014) 14 Human Rights Law Review 301; Elisabeth Lambert, 'Execution of Judgment:

While this aspect of the book has highlighted the potential for adjudication to complement broader processes of dispute resolution, it is important that any approach is tailored to the specific circumstances of a dispute and that the potential downsides of a more facilitative approach to adjudication are kept in mind. A risk of facilitative approaches to adjudication is that they may involve a tribunal refraining from fully enforcing the international obligations at issue, which may pursue important shared international interests (e.g. environmental protection).[145] Additionally, if an international tribunal does not provide sufficient guidance when handing back parts of a dispute to the parties for further negotiation or cooperation, the dispute may remain unresolved, for example as occurred in *Gabčikovo-Nagymaros*.[146] In polarised disputes, where one or more of the parties is completely unwilling to re-evaluate its position in light of a tribunal's determination of contested legal or factual issues (e.g. the *South China Sea Arbitration*) then obviously the scope for adjudication to contribute to a broader process of dispute resolution is greatly reduced. Finally, as has been suggested at throughout this book, there should be no doubt that more procedural forms of adjudicatory scrutiny still require difficult normative choices to be made. Specifically, adjudicators face important decisions regarding which affected foreign interests a regulating State must consider and how far a regulating State must go in pursuing cooperative (rather than unilateral) solutions.[147]

D. Final Remarks

This book has demonstrated and explained why across diverse areas of contemporary international law international tribunals perform several key functions, namely incrementally adapting international legal norms to relevant changes in law or facts, scrutinising State conduct for compliance with international obligations, and contributing to broader processes of dispute resolution. The book has emphasised the various constraints under which the tribunals studied operate, which include formal and informal legal and political constraints and other more

European Court of Human Rights (ECtHR)' in Hélène Ruiz-Fabri (ed), *Max Planck Encyclopedia of International Procedural Law* (OUP 2018).

145 Tim Stephens, *International Courts and Environmental Protection* (CUP 2009) 100–02. Above n 66 and text.

146 See further Chapter 4(D), text at nn 196–98.

147 Lang (n 53) 345–47.

practical limitations that have become increasingly apparent with the increased adjudicatory activity of the past twenty-five to thirty years. As we have seen, international tribunals often lack the legitimacy, specialist knowledge, or familiarity with relevant facts needed to engage in substantial law-making, to second-guess determinations made by regulating States, or to dispose entirely of a dispute.

Importantly, this book's analysis of the functions performed by international tribunals has been attentive to the specific context of each of the four adjudicatory settings studied. Our understanding of the possibilities and limits of international adjudication must be sensitive to the markedly different contexts in which international tribunals operate. Admittedly, focusing on cases in a different issue area (besides disputes with an environmental component), or focusing on different cross-cutting challenges would be likely to produce a somewhat different account of the state of contemporary international adjudication. For example, studies focusing on more procedural topics, including the internal working practices of courts and tribunals, have provided important insights in recent years.[148] Despite these caveats, this book has provided a thorough interrogation of three key challenges confronting international tribunals across diverse areas of international law and has considered to what extent these challenges, and the responses by tribunals, provide broader insights into the functions of international adjudication with relevance beyond the specific context in which they were identified. Environmental cases were used as a focus for this comparative study because they lack a dedicated tribunal and are heard across a range of adjudicatory fora with markedly different design features and functional orientations.[149] Accordingly, this category of cases is representative of the sectorial and decentralised nature of contemporary international adjudication.[150]

[148] See e.g. Jeffrey L Dunoff and Mark A Pollack, 'International Judicial Practices: Opening the "Black Box" of International Courts' (2018) 40 Mich. J. Int'l L. 47; Jeffrey L Dunoff and Mark A Pollack, 'The Judicial Trilemma' (2017) 111 AJIL 225; Freya Baetens (ed), *Identity and Diversity on the International Bench: Who Is the Judge?* (OUP 2020); Freya Baetens (ed), *Legitimacy of Unseen Actors in International Adjudication* (CUP 2019); Eric De Brabandere (ed), *International Procedure in Interstate Litigation and Arbitration: A Comparative Approach* (CUP 2021); Chester Brown, *A Common Law of International Adjudication* (OUP 2007).

[149] See Chapter 1, text at nn 22–25.

[150] Ellen Hey, *Reflections on an International Environmental Court* (Kluwer Law International 2000) 24.

The comparative study undertaken in this book suggests that there is further scope for careful comparative analysis of how various challenges arise and are addressed by international tribunals across different sites of international adjudication. Too often different areas of international adjudication have remained separated by artificial academic or bureaucratic barriers, although the tide has turned somewhat in the last decade or so.[151] As international lawyers continue to confront these issues, they can benefit from considering methodological insights from comparative law given that field's long experience with explaining similarities and differences between legal systems. A key challenge in comparing the practices of different international tribunals is not only to identify how the practices of tribunals differ, but, crucially, to explain why such differences exist. To be sure, a comparative approach introduces a challenging number of variables and raises the question of whether different international tribunals have a sufficient core of similarity to be truly comparable. Yet the common functional challenges identified in the case law of the four adjudicatory settings covered in this book, and the significant commonalities in tribunals' responses to these challenges, suggest that the tribunals studied are not so different as to be incomparable.[152] While different regimes and their dispute settlement mechanisms clearly have distinct purposes and orientations, the analysis in this book demonstrates that 'a regime transcendent discourse' is possible and indeed continues to develop apace. Such a discourse is possible because all the tribunals considered share a common set of concepts, argumentative techniques and 'pre-understandings' developed from general international law.[153]

[151] See e.g. Anne Peters, 'The Refinement of International Law: From Fragmentation to Regime Interaction and Politicization' (2017) 15 ICON 671; Mads Andenas and Eirik Bjorge, 'Introduction: From Fragmentation to Convergence in International Law' in Mads Andenas and Eirik Bjorge (eds), *A Farewell to Fragmentation: Reassertion and Convergence in International Law* (CUP 2015); Shirlow (n 59); Fahner (n 50).

[152] Contrast Leslie Johns, *Strengthening International Courts: The Hidden Costs of Legalization* (University of Michigan Press 2015) 8 (eschewing such a comparison and suggesting it would be 'vacuous').

[153] Dirk Pulkowski, *The Law and Politics of International Regime Conflict* (OUP 2014) 255–56, 271 and generally ch 6; International Law Commission, 'Fragmentation of International Law: Difficulties Arising from the Diversification and Expansion of International Law – Report of the Study Group of the International Law Commission Finalized by Martti Koskenniemi' (13 April 2006) UN Doc A/CN4/L682, [493(3)]; Pierre-Marie Dupuy, 'A Doctrinal Debate in the Globalisation Era: On the "Fragmentation" of International Law' (2007) 1 EJLS 25, 28; James Crawford, *International Law as an Open System: Selected Essays* (Cameron May 2002) 17, 37;

The introduction to this book suggested that international adjudication is at a crossroads. Important questions have arisen about whether the increase in adjudicatory activity in recent decades has been a positive development, or whether, among other concerns, it has led to an over-reliance on law-development by international tribunals and whether more flexible modes of dispute settlement would be more appropriate for resolving some of the disputes currently being submitted to adjudication.[154] The most visible manifestation of this rethinking of the desirability of international adjudication has been the phenomenon of 'backlash' against international tribunals in the last decade, with some examples of existing tribunals being shut down, most notably the WTO Appellate Body.[155] However, the underlying questions and concerns extend beyond particular episodes of backlash and at times opportunistic behaviour by certain States.[156] Despite these significant concerns and instances of backlash, international adjudication is not about to disappear. On the contrary, across a variety of contexts, including the four considered in this book, many cases continued to be submitted to international tribunals. However, international adjudication is likely to adapt, as international tribunals seek to address existing or new concerns through their decisions and as States seek to adjust exiting institutions or even create new ones.[157]

Mario Prost, *The Concept of Unity in Public International Law* (Hart 2012) 138, 140–41, 159–60 and generally ch 6 (suggesting international law exhibits a weak form of unity in the form of a shared internal legal culture amongst its professionals); Shirlow (n 59) 56 (suggesting different regimes share a loose form of unity being 'conceptually related to general international law').

154 See e.g. Daniel Bethlehem, 'The Greening of International Dispute Settlement? Stepping Back a Little' (2020) 114 ASIL Proceedings 225, 230–34; Vaughan Lowe, 'The Function of Litigation in International Society' (2012) 61 ICLQ 209, 220–22; Anna Spain, 'Integration Matters: Rethinking the Architecture of International Dispute Resolution' (2010) 32 Univ. of Pennsylvania JIL 1.

155 See generally Joost Pauwelyn and Rebecca J Hamilton, 'Exit from International Tribunals' (2018) 9 JIDS 679; Karen J Alter, James T Gathii and Laurence R Helfer, 'Backlash against International Courts in West, East and Southern Africa: Causes and Consequences' (2016) 27 EJIL 293; Mikael Rask Madsen, Pola Cebulak and Micha Wiebusch, 'Backlash against International Courts: Explaining the Forms and Patterns of Resistance to International Courts' (2018) 14 International Journal of Law in Context 197.

156 Bethlehem (n 154) 231.

157 See generally, e.g., Karen J Alter, 'The High Water Mark of International Judicialization?', iCourts Working Paper Series no 250, 2021.

Against this backdrop, this book has approached the task of the international lawyer as a practical, creative, and, above all, problem-solving craft.[158] Under the constructive approach employed in this book, international adjudication is an evolving set of institutions and legal techniques that should be refined as shortcomings and limitations become apparent and as social needs change.[159] The main contribution of this book has been to provide a context-sensitive analysis of three key challenges arising from the practice of contemporary international adjudication – change, review of State conduct for compliance with international law, and dispute settlement – the legal techniques which might be utilised in response, and the functions that are being performed by international tribunals.

[158] Martti Koskenniemi, 'Law, Teleology and International Relations: An Essay in Counterdisciplinarity' (2011) 26 International Relations 3, 19–20.

[159] In a similar vein, see David D Caron, 'The Nature of the Iran-United States Claims Tribunal and the Evolving Structure of International Dispute Resolution' (1990) 84 AJIL 104, 152, 156 (suggesting international dispute settlement mechanisms evolve 'in response to the needs of the community controlling it'). More generally see C Wilfred Jenks, *The Prospects of International Adjudication* (Stevens & Sons 1964) 771–77. For approaches to international courts in light of practice theory which highlight that such practices can evolve, see eg Tommaso Soave, 'The Social Field of International Adjudication: Structures and Practices of a Conflictive Professional Universe' (2023) 36 LJIL 565, 567, 589–90; Dunoff and Pollack, 'International Judicial Practices' (n 148) esp. 55, 113.

BIBLIOGRAPHY

Abi-Saab G, 'The Normalization of International Adjudication: Convergence and Divergencies' (2010) 43 NYUJILP 1.

Adede AO, *The System for Settlement of Disputes under the UN Convention on the Law of the Sea* (Martinus Nijhoff 1987).

Akhtarkhavari A, *Global Governance of the Environment: Environmental Principles and Change in International Law and Politics* (Edward Elgar 2011).

Aljaghoub MM, *The Advisory Function of the International Court of Justice 1946–2005* (Springer 2006).

Allen BE, 'The Use of Non-Pecuniary Remedies in WTO Dispute Settlement: Lessons for Arbitral Practitioners' in Michael E Schneider and Joachim Knoll (eds), *Performance as a Remedy: Non-monetary Relief in International Arbitration* (Juris 2011).

Allott P, '*Mare Nostrum:* A New International Law of the Sea' (1992) 86 AJIL 764.

Alter KJ, *The New Terrain of International Law: Courts, Politics, Rights* (Princeton University Press 2014).

'The High Water Mark of International Judicialization?', iCourts Working Paper Series no 250, 2021.

'The International Court of Justice in Comparison: Understanding the Court's Limited Influence' (2021) 21 MJIL 676.

Alter KJ, Gathii JT and Helfer LR, 'Backlash against International Courts in West, East and Southern Africa: Causes and Consequences' (2016) 27 EJIL 293.

Alvarez JE, *International Organizations as Law-Makers* (OUP 2006).

The Public International Law Regime Governing International Investment (Martinus Nijhoff 2011).

'Is Investor-State Arbitration "Public"?' (2016) 7 JIDS 534.

The Impact of International Organizations on International Law (Brill Nijhoff 2017).

Anand RP, *Studies in International Adjudication* (Vikas Publications 1969).

Andenas M, 'Reassertion and Transformation: From Fragmentation to Convergence in International Law' (2015) 36 Georgetown JIL 685.

Andenas M and Bjorge E, 'Introduction: From Fragmentation to Convergence in International Law' in Mads Andenas and Eirik Bjorge (eds), *A Farewell to*

Fragmentation: Reassertion and Convergence in International Law (CUP 2015).

Andenas M and Zleptnig S, 'Proportionality: WTO Law in Comparative Perspective' (2007) 42 Texas ILJ 371.

Anderson D, 'Negotiation and Dispute Settlement' in Malcolm D Evans (ed), *Remedies in International Law: The Institutional Dilemma* (Hart 1998).

Anderson DH, 'Prompt Release of Vessels and Crews' in Rüdiger Wolfrum (ed), *Max Planck Encyclopedia of International Law* (OUP 2008).

Asmelash H, 'The First Ten Years of WTO Jurisprudence on Renewable Energy Support Measures: Has the Dust Settled Yet?' (2022) 21 WTR 455.

Baetens F (ed), *Legitimacy of Unseen Actors in International Adjudication* (CUP 2019).

Identity and Diversity on the International Bench: Who Is the Judge? (OUP 2020).

Barak A, *Proportionality: Constitutional Rights and Their Limitations* (CUP 2012).

Baranyai G and Bartus G, 'Anatomy of a Deadlock: A Systemic Analysis of Why the Gabčíkovo–Nagymaros Dam Dispute Is Still Unresolved' (2016) 18 Water Policy 39.

Barnes R, 'The Continuing Vitality of UNCLOS' in Jill Barrett and Richard Barnes (eds), *Law of the Sea: UNCLOS as a Living Treaty* (BIICL 2016).

Barrett J, 'The UN Convention on the Law of the Sea: A "Living" Treaty?' in Jill Barrett and Richard Barnes (eds), *Law of the Sea: UNCLOS as a Living Treaty* (BIICL 2016).

Bartels L, 'The Chapeau of the General Exceptions in the WTO GATT and GATS Agreements: A Reconstruction' (2015) 109 AJIL 95.

Batifort S and Heath JB, 'The New Debate on the Interpretation of MFN Clauses in Investment Treaties: Putting the Brakes on Multilateralization' (2017) 111 AJIL 873.

Behn D, 'Performance of Investment Treaty Arbitration' in Theresa Squatrito and others (eds), *The Performance of International Courts and Tribunals* (CUP 2018).

Behn D and Fauchald OK, 'Governments under Cross-Fire? Renewable Energy and International Economic Tribunals' (2015) 12 Manchester JIEL 117.

Behn D, Fauchald OK and Langford M, 'The International Investment Regime and Its Discontents' in Daniel Behn, Ole Kristian Fauchald and Malcolm Langford (eds), *The Legitimacy of Investment Arbitration: Empirical Perspectives* (CUP 2022).

Behn D and Langford M, 'Trumping the Environment? An Empirical Perspective on the Legitimacy of Investment Treaty Arbitration' (2017) 18 JWIT 14.

Bekker PH, 'Gabcikovo-Nagymaros Project (Hungary/Slovakia), Judgement' (1998) 92 AJIL 273.

Bendel J, *Litigating the Environment: Process and Procedure before International Courts and Tribunals* (Edward Elgar 2023).

Benvenisti E, *The Law of Global Governance* (Martinus Nijhoff 2014).

Berger KP and Jensen JO, 'The Arbitrator's Mandate to Facilitate Settlement' (2017) 40 Fordham ILJ 887.

Berman F, 'The International Court of Justice as an "Agent" of Legal Development' in Christian J Tams and James Sloan (eds), *The Development of International Law by the International Court of Justice* (OUP 2013).

Bethlehem D, 'The Greening of International Dispute Settlement? Stepping Back a Little' (2020) 114 ASIL Proceedings 225.

Beviglia Zampetti A, Low P and Mavroidis PC, 'Consensus Decision-Making and Legislative Inertia at the WTO: Can International Law Help?' (2022) 56 JWT 1.

Biermann F, *Earth System Governance: World Politics in the Anthropocene* (MIT Press 2014).

Bilder R, 'The Settlement of Disputes in the Field of the International Law of the Environment' (1975) 144 RdC 140.

Bjorge E, *The Evolutionary Interpretation of Treaties* (OUP 2014).

Bodansky D, *The Art and Craft of International Environmental Law* (Harvard University Press 2010).

Boisson de Chazournes L, 'Subsequent Practice, Practices, and "Family-Resemblance": Towards Embedding Subsequent Practice in Its Operative Milieu' in Georg Nolte (ed), *Treaties and Subsequent Practice* (OUP 2013).

Boisson de Chazournes L and Angelini A, 'After "The Court Rose": The Rise of Diplomatic Means to Implement the Pronouncements of the International Court of Justice' (2012) 11 LPICT 1.

Bonnitcha J, 'Investment Treaties and Transition from Authoritarian Rule' (2014) 15 JWIT 965.

Bonnitcha J, Poulsen LNS and Waibel M, *The Political Economy of the Investment Treaty Regime* (OUP 2017).

Born G, 'A New Generation of International Adjudication' (2012) 61 Duke LJ 775.

Born G, Morris D and Forrest S, '"A Margin of Appreciation": Appreciating Its Irrelevance in International Law' (2020) 61 HILJ 65.

Botkin DB, *The Moon in the Nautilus Shell: Discordant Harmonies Reconsidered from Climate Change to Species Extinction, How Life Persists in an Ever-Changing World* (OUP 2012).

Bown CP and Trachtman JP, '*Brazil – Measures Affecting Imports of Retreaded Tyres*: A Balancing Act' (2009) 8 WTR 85.

Boyle A, 'Further Development of the 1982 Convention on the Law of the Sea: Mechanisms for Change' in David Freestone, Richard Barnes and David Ong (eds), *The Law of the Sea: Progress and Prospects* (OUP 2006).

'The Environmental Jurisprudence of the International Tribunal for the Law of the Sea' (2007) 22 IJMCL 369.

'Developments in the International Law of Environmental Impact Assessments and Their Relation to the Espoo Convention' (2011) 20 RECIEL 227.

'Human Rights and the Environment: Where Next?' (2012) 23 EJIL 613.

'UNCLOS Dispute Settlement and the Uses and Abuses of Part XV' (2014) 47 Revue Belge de Droit International 182.

'The Tribunal and the Rule of Law' in ITLOS (ed), *The Contribution of the International Tribunal for the Law of the Sea to the Rule of Law: 1996–2016* (Brill Nijhoff 2018).

'Progressive Development of International Environmental Law: Legislate or Litigate?' (2019) 62 German Ybk. Int'l L. 305.

Boyle A and Harrison J, 'Judicial Settlement of International Environmental Disputes: Current Problems' (2013) 4 JIDS 245.

Boyle A and Redgwell C, *Birnie, Boyle, and Redgwell's International Law and the Environment* (4th ed., CUP 2021).

Boyle AE, 'Dispute Settlement and the Law of the Sea Convention: Problems of Fragmentation and Jurisdiction' (1997) 46 ICLQ 37.

Brown C, *A Common Law of International Adjudication* (OUP 2007).

'Introduction: The Development and Importance of the Model Bilateral Investment Treaty' in Chester Brown (ed), *Commentaries on Selected Model Investment Treaties* (OUP 2013).

Brunnée J, 'COPing with Consent: Law-Making under Multilateral Environmental Agreements' (2002) 15 LJIL 1.

'Procedure and Substance in International Environmental Law' (2020) 405 RdC 81.

Buga I, 'Between Stability and Change in the Law of the Sea Convention: Subsequent Practice, Treaty Modification, and Regime Interaction' in Donald R Rothwell and others (eds), *The Oxford Handbook of the Law of the Sea* (OUP 2015).

Modification of Treaties by Subsequent Practice (OUP 2018).

Buggenhoudt C, *Common Interests in International Litigation: A Case Study on Natural Resource Exploitation Disputes* (Intersentia 2017).

Burchardt D, 'The Functions of Law and Their Challenges: The Differentiated Functionality of International Law' (2019) 20 German LJ 409.

Button C, *The Power to Protect: Trade, Health and Uncertainty in the WTO* (Hart 2004).

Çalı B, 'International Judicial Review' in Anthony Lang and Antje Wiener (eds), *Handbook on Global Constitutionalism* (Edward Elgar 2017).

Çalı B and Koch A, 'Foxes Guarding the Foxes? The Peer Review of Human Rights Judgments by the Committee of Ministers of the Council of Europe' (2014) 14 Human Rights Law Review 301.

Cannizzaro E, 'Proportionality and Margin of Appreciation in the *Whaling* Case: Reconciling Antithetical Doctrines?' (2016) 27 EJIL 1061.

Caron DD, 'The Nature of the Iran-United States Claims Tribunal and the Evolving Structure of International Dispute Resolution' (1990) 84 AJIL 104.

'Towards a Political Theory of International Courts and Tribunals' (2006) 24 Berkeley JIL 401.

'The Multiple Functions of International Courts and the Singular Task of the Adjudicator' (2017) 111 ASIL Proceedings 231.

Caserta S and Madsen MR, 'The Situated and Bounded Rationality of International Courts: A Structuralist Approach to International Adjudicative Practices' (2022) 35 LJIL 931.

Charney JI, 'Entry Into Force of the 1982 Convention on the Law of the Sea' (1995) 35 Va. J. Int'l L 381.

Charnovitz S, 'The WTO's Environmental Progress' (2007) 10 JIEL 685.

Cho S, 'Of the World Trade Court's Burden' (2009) 20 EJIL 675.

The Social Foundations of World Trade: Norms, Community and Constitution (CUP 2014).

Churchill R, 'Some Reflections on the Operation of the Dispute Settlement System of the UN Convention on the Law of the Sea During Its First Decade' in David Freestone, Richard Barnes and David Ong (eds), *The Law of the Sea: Progress and Prospects* (OUP 2006).

'The 1982 United Nations Convention on the Law of the Sea' in Donald R Rothwell and others (eds), *The Oxford Handbook of the Law of the Sea* (OUP 2015).

Churchill RR and Ulfstein G, 'Autonomous Institutional Arrangements in Multilateral Environmental Agreements: A Little-Noticed Phenomenon in International Law' (2000) 94 AJIL 623.

Condon BJ, *Environmental Sovereignty and the WTO: Trade Sanctions and International Law* (Transnational Publishers 2006).

'Does International Economic Law Impose a Duty to Negotiate?' (2018) 17 Chinese JIL 73.

Constain S, 'Mediation in Investor-State Dispute Settlement: Government Policy and the Changing Landscape' (2014) 29 ICSID Review 25.

Cook G, 'The Illusion of "Evolutionary Interpretation" in WTO Dispute Settlement' in Georges Abi-Saab and others (eds), *Evolutionary Interpretation and International Law* (Hart 2019).

Cooper CA, 'The Management of International Environmental Disputes in the Context of Canada-United States Relations: A Survey and Evaluation of Techniques and Mechanisms' (1986) 24 Can YB Int'l L 247.

Corten O, 'The Notion of "Reasonable" in International Law: Legal Discourse, Reason and Contradictions' (1999) 48 ICLQ 613.

Craig P, *EU Administrative Law* (3rd ed., OUP 2018).

Craik AN, 'Recalcitrant Reality and Chosen Ideals: The Public Function of Dispute Settlement in International Environmental Law' (1997) 10 Georgetown Int'l Envtl. L. Rev. 551.

Craik N, 'The Duty to Cooperate in International Environmental Law: Constraining State Discretion through Due Respect' (2019) 30 Ybk IEL 22.

'The Duty to Cooperate in the Customary Law of Environmental Impact Assessment' (2020) 69 ICLQ 239.

Crawford J, *International Law as an Open System: Selected Essays* (Cameron May 2002).

State Responsibility: The General Part (CUP 2013).

'Flexibility in the Award of Reparation: The Role of the Parties and the Tribunal' in Rüdiger Wolfrum, Maja Sersic and Trpimir M Šošić (eds), *Contemporary Developments in International Law: Essays in Honour of Budislav Vukas* (Brill Nijhoff 2016).

Crawford J, Baetens F and Cameron R, 'Functions of the International Court of Justice' in Carlos Espósito and Kate Parlett (eds), *The Cambridge Companion to the International Court of Justice* (CUP 2023).

Crow K, 'The Opacity of Proportionality in International Courts: Could Categories Clarify?' (2019) 51 GWILR 289.

Czybulka D, 'Article 194' in Alexander Proelss (ed), *United Nations Convention on the Law of the Sea: A Commentary* (CH Beck 2017).

Davey WJ, 'WTO Dispute Settlement: Crown Jewel or Costume Jewelry?' (2022) 21 WTR 291.

De Baere G, Chane; A-L and Wouters J, 'International Courts as Keepers of the Rule of Law: Achievements, Challenges, and Opportunities' (2016) 48 NYUJILP 715.

De Brabandere E (ed), *International Procedure in Interstate Litigation and Arbitration: A Comparative Approach* (CUP 2021).

De Sena P and Acconciamessa L, 'Balancing Test' in Hélène Ruiz-Fabri (ed), *Max Planck Encyclopedia of International Procedural Law* (OUP 2021).

De Visscher C, *Theory and Reality in Public International Law* (PE Corbett tr, Revised ed, Princeton University Press 1968).

Delbrück J, 'The International Obligation to Cooperate–An Empty Shell or a Hard Law Principle of International Law?–A Critical Look at a Much Debated Paradigm of Modern International Law' in Holger P Hestermeyer et al (ed), *Coexistence, Cooperation and Solidarity: Liber Amicorum Rüdiger Wolfrum*, vol 1 (Martinus Nijhoff 2012).

Demirkol B, 'Remedies in Investment Treaty Arbitration' (2015) 6 JIDS 403.

'Reconsideration of Proper Remedies in Investment Arbitration in Light of Recent Cases: Should the Remedy Follow the Primary Obligation?' (2021) 22 JWIT 129.

Desmedt A, 'Proportionality in WTO Law' (2001) 4 JIEL 441.

Di Benedetto S, *International Investment Law and the Environment* (Edward Elgar 2013).

Diehl PF and Ku C, *The Dynamics of International Law* (CUP 2010).

Djeffal C, *Static and Evolutive Treaty Interpretation: A Functional Reconstruction* (CUP 2015).

Doelle M, 'Non-compliance Procedures' in Lavanya Rajamani and Jacqueline Peel (eds), *The Oxford Handbook of International Environmental Law* (2nd ed., OUP 2021).

Dolzer R, Kriebaum U and Schreuer C, *Principles of International Investment Law* (3rd ed., OUP 2022).

Donoghue JE, 'The Role of the World Court Today' (2012) 47 Georgia Law Review 181.

Dothan S, *International Judicial Review: When Should International Courts Intervene?* (CUP 2020).

Downes C, 'Worth Shopping Around? Defending Regulatory Autonomy under the SPS and TBT Agreements' (2015) 14 WTR 553.

Du M, 'The Necessity Test in World Trade Law: What Now?' (2016) 15 Chinese JIL 817.

Dumberry P, 'Fair and Equitable Treatment: Its Interaction with the Minimum Standard and Its Customary Status' (2017) 1 Brill Research Perspectives in International Investment Law and Arbitration 1.

Dunoff JL and Pollack MA, 'The Judicial Trilemma' (2017) 111 AJIL 225.

'International Judicial Practices: Opening the "Black Box" of International Courts' (2018) 40 Mich. J. Int'l L. 47.

Dupuy P-M, 'A Doctrinal Debate in the Globalisation Era: On the "Fragmentation" of International Law' (2007) 1 EJLS 25.

Dupuy P-M and Viñuales JE, *International Environmental Law* (2nd ed., CUP 2018).

Ehlermann C-D and Ehring L, 'The Authoritative Interpretation under Article IX:2 of the Agreement Establishing the World Trade Organization: Current Law, Practice and Possible Improvements' (2005) 8 JIEL 803.

Ehlermann C-D and Lockhart N, 'Standard of Review in WTO Law' (2004) 7 JIEL 491.

Elsig M and Pollack MA, 'Agents, Trustees, and International Courts: The Politics of Judicial Appointment at The World Trade Organization' (2014) 20 European Journal of International Relations 391.

Epps T, 'Recent Developments in WTO Jurisprudence: Has the Appellate Body Resolved the Issue of an Appropriate Standard of Review in SPS Cases?' (2012) 62 Univ. Toronto LJ 201.

Fahner JH, *Judicial Deference in International Adjudication: A Comparative Analysis* (Hart 2020).

'The Limited Utility of Deference in International Dispute Settlement' (2022) 21 LPICT 467.

'Maximising Investment Protection under the Minimum Standard: A Case Study of the Evolutive Interpretation and Application of Customary International Law in Investment Arbitration' (2023) 12(1) ESIL Reflections.

Fassbender B, 'Article 9' in Andreas Zimmermann and others (eds), *The Statute of the International Court of Justice: A Commentary* (3rd ed., OUP 2019).

Feria-Tinta M and Milnes SC, 'The Rise of Environmental Law in International Dispute Resolution: The Inter-American Court of Human Rights Issues a Landmark Advisory Opinion on the Environment and Human Rights' (2016) 27 Ybk IEL 64.

Fikfak V, 'Structural Remedies: Human Rights Law' in Hélène Ruiz-Fabri (ed), *Max Planck Encyclopedia of International Procedural Law* (OUP 2022).

Fitzmaurice M, 'The International Court of Justice and International Environmental Law' in Christian J Tams and James Sloan (eds), *The Development of International Law by the International Court of Justice* (OUP 2013).

'International Protection of the Environment' (2001) 293 RdC 9.

Fontanelli F, 'Necessity Killed the GATT: Art XX GATT and the Misleading Rhetoric about "Weighing and Balancing"' (2012) 4 EJLS 39.

Foster CE, 'Adjudication, Arbitration and the Turn to Public Law "Standards of Review": Putting the Precautionary Principle in the Crucible' (2012) 3 JIDS 525.

'International Adjudication–Standard of Review and Burden of Proof: *Australia-Apples* and *Whaling in the Antarctic*' (2012) 21 RECIEL 80.

'Diminished Ambitions? Public International Legal Authority in the Transnational Economic Era' (2014) 17 JIEL 355.

Global Regulatory Standards in Environmental and Health Disputes: Regulatory Coherence, Due Regard, and Due Diligence (OUP 2021).

'Why Due Regard Is More Appropriate than Proportionality Testing in International Investment Law' (2022) 23 JWIT 388.

Franck TM, *Fairness in International Law and Institutions* (OUP 1998).

Franckx E, '"Reasonable Bond" in the Practice of the International Tribunal for the Law of the Sea' (2002) 32 Calif WILJ 303.

Frankenberg G, 'Critical Comparisons: Re-thinking Comparative Law' (1985) 26 HILJ 411.

Freestone D, 'Caution or Precaution: "A Rose By Any Other Name…"?' (1999) 10 Ybk IEL 25.

Fukunaga Y, 'Standard of Review and "Scientific Truths" in the WTO Dispute Settlement System and Investment Arbitration' (2012) 3 JIDS 559.

Gao J, 'The ITLOS Advisory Opinion for the SRFC' (2015) 14 Chinese JIL 735.

Gardiner RK, *Treaty Interpretation* (2nd ed., OUP 2015).

Garrido-Muñoz A, 'Managing Uncertainty: The International Court of Justice, "Objective Reasonableness" and the Judicial Function' (2017) 30 LJIL 457.

Gautier P, 'The International Tribunal for the Law of the Sea: Activities in 2003' (2004) 3 Chinese JIL 241.

Gavouneli M, 'Protection Standards for the Marine Environment: Updating Part XII of the Law of the Sea Convention?' in Stephen Minas and H Jordan Diamond (eds), *Stress Testing the Law of the Sea: Dispute Resolution, Disasters & Emerging Challenges* (Brill Nijhoff 2018).

Gertz G, Jandhyala S and Poulsen LNS, 'Legalization, Diplomacy, and Development: Do Investment Treaties De-politicize Investment Disputes?' (2018) 107 World Development 239.

Giacco LL, *Judicial Decisions in International Law Argumentation: Between Entrapment and Creativity* (Hart 2022).

Giannakopoulos C and Monga M, 'History as Interpretative Context in the Evolutionary Interpretation of FET in International Investment Law' in Georges Abi-Saab and others (eds), *Evolutionary Interpretation and International Law* (Hart 2019).

Giladi R and Shany Y, 'The International Court of Justice' in Yuval Shany, *Assessing the Effectiveness of International Courts* (OUP 2014).

'Assessing the Effectiveness of the International Court of Justice' in Carlos Espósito and Kate Parlett (eds), *The Cambridge Companion to the International Court of Justice* (CUP 2023).

Gillett M, *Prosecuting Environmental Harm before the International Criminal Court* (CUP 2022).

Ginsburg T, 'Bounded Discretion in International Judicial Lawmaking' (2005) 45 Va. J. Int'l L. 631.

'The Institutional Context of the International Court of Justice' in Carlos Espósito and Kate Parlett (eds), *The Cambridge Companion to the International Court of Justice* (CUP 2023).

Ginsburg T and McAdams RH, 'Adjudicating in Anarchy: An Expressive Theory of International Dispute Resolution' (2004) 45 W&MLR 1229.

Godden L and Peel J, *Environmental Law: Scientific, Policy and Regulatory Dimensions* (OUP 2010).

Goodman C, 'Rights, Obligations, Prohibitions: A Practical Guide to Understanding Judicial Decisions on Coastal State Jurisdiction over Living Resources in the Exclusive Economic Zone' (2018) 33 IJMCL 558.

Gourgourinis A, 'The Distinction between Interpretation and Application of Norms in International Adjudication' (2011) 2 JIDS 31.

Gray C, 'Remedies' in Cesare PR Romano, Karen J Alter and Yuval Shany (eds), *The Oxford Handbook of International Adjudication* (OUP 2013).

Gros G, 'The ICJ's Handling of Science in the Whaling in the Antarctic Case: A Whale of a Case?' (2015) 6 JIDS 578.

Grossman N, 'The Normative Legitimacy of International Courts' (2013) 86 Temple Law Review 61.

Gruszczynski L, *Regulating Health and Environmental Risks under WTO Law: A Critical Analysis of the SPS Agreement* (OUP 2010).

'Standard of Review of Health and Environmental Regulations by WTO Panels' in Geert Van Calster and Denise Prévost (eds), *Research Handbook on Environment, Health and the WTO* (Edward Elgar 2013).

Gruszczynski L and Vadi V, 'Standard of Review and Scientific Evidence in WTO Law and International Investment Arbitration: Converging Parallels?' in Lukasz Gruszczynski and Wouter Werner (eds), *Deference in International Courts and Tribunals: Standard of Review and Margin of Appreciation* (OUP 2014).

Guzman AT, 'International Tribunals: A Rational Choice Analysis' (2008) 157 Univ. of Pennsylvania LR 171.

Hafner-Burton EM, Puig S and Victor DG, 'Against Secrecy: The Social Cost of International Dispute Settlement' (2017) 42 Yale J. Int'l L. 279.

Hamamoto S, 'From the Requirement of Reasonableness to a "Comply and Explain" Rule: The Standard of Review in the Whaling Judgment' in Malgosia Fitzmaurice and Dai Tamada (eds), *Whaling in the Antarctic: Significance and Implications of the ICJ Judgment* (Brill Nijhoff 2016).

Harbo T-I, *The Function of Proportionality Analysis in European Law* (Brill Nijhoff 2015).

Harrison J, 'Judicial Law-Making and the Developing Order of the Oceans' (2007) 22 IJMCL 283.

Making the Law of the Sea: A Study in the Development of International Law (CUP 2011).

'Reflections on the Role of International Courts and Tribunals in the Settlement of Environmental Disputes and the Development of International Environmental Law' (2013) 25 Journal of Environmental Law 501.

'Safeguards against Excessive Enforcement Measures in the Exclusive Economic Zone – Law and Practice' in Henrik Ringbom (ed), *Jurisdiction Over Ships: Post-UNCLOS Developments in the Law of the Sea* (Brill Nijhoff 2015).

'Patrolling the Boundaries of Coastal State Enforcement Powers: The Interpretation and Application of UNCLOS Safeguards Relating to the Arrest of Foreign-Flagged Ships' (2017) 42 L'Observateur des Nations Unies 117.

Saving the Oceans through Law: The International Legal Framework for the Protection of the Marine Environment (OUP 2017).

Heidar T, 'Introduction: How Does the Law of the Sea Adapt to New Knowledge and Changing Circumstances?' in Tomas Heidar (ed), *New Knowledge and Changing Circumstances in the Law of the Sea* (Brill Nijhoff 2020).

Helfer LR and Slaughter A-M, 'Why States Create International Tribunals: A Response to Professors Posner and Yoo' (2005) 93 Calif LR 899.

Helmersen ST, 'Evolutive Treaty Interpretation: Legality, Semantics and Distinctions' (2013) 6 EJLS 161.

'The Evolutionary Treaty Interpretation by the WTO Appellate Body' in Georges Abi-Saab and others (eds), *Evolutionary Interpretation and International Law* (Hart 2019).

Henckels C, 'Balancing Investment Protection and the Public Interest: The Role of the Standard of Review and the Importance of Deference in Investor-State Arbitration' (2013) 4 JIDS 197.

Proportionality and Deference in Investor-State Arbitration: Balancing Investment Protection and Regulatory Autonomy (CUP 2015).

Hernández GI, *The International Court of Justice and the Judicial Function* (OUP 2014).

'International Judicial Lawmaking' in Catherine Brölmann and Yannick Radi (eds), *Research Handbook on the Theory and Practice of International Lawmaking* (Edward Elgar 2016).

Hey E, *Teaching International Law: State-Consent as Consent to a Process of Normative Development and Ensuing Problems* (Kluwer Law International 2003).

Reflections on an International Environmental Court (Kluwer Law International 2000).

Hindelang S and Krajewski M (eds), *Shifting Paradigms in International Investment Law: More Balanced, Less Isolated, Increasingly Diversified* (OUP 2016).

Hirsch M, 'Between Fair and Equitable Treatment and Stabilization Clause: Stable Legal Environment and Regulatory Change in International Investment Law' (2011) 12 JWIT 783.

Hofmann R and Karl L, 'Article 57' in Andreas Zimmermann and others (eds), *The Statute of the International Court of Justice: A Commentary* (3rd ed., OUP 2019).

Horn H and Mavroidis PC, 'Multilateral Environmental Agreements in the WTO: Silence Speaks Volumes' (2014) 10 International Journal of Economic Theory 147.

Howse R, 'The Appellate Body Rulings in the *Shrimp/Turtle* Case: A New Legal Baseline for the Trade and Environment Debate' (2002) 27 Columbia JEL 491.

'Moving the WTO Forward-One Case at a Time' (2009) 42 Cornell ILJ 223.

'The World Trade Organization 20 Years On: Global Governance by Judiciary' (2016) 27 EJIL 9.

Howse R and Langille J, 'Continuity and Change in the World Trade Organization: Pluralism Past, Present, and Future' (2023) 117 AJIL 1.

Howse R, Langille J and Sykes K, 'Pluralism in Practice: Moral Legislation and the Law of the WTO after *Seal Products*' (2015) 48 GWILR 81.

Howse R and Türk E, 'The WTO Impact on Internal Regulations: A Case Study of the *Canada–EC Asbestos* Dispute' in George A Bermann and Petros C Mavroidis (eds), *Trade and Human Health and Safety* (CUP 2006).

Hudec RE, 'Broadening the Scope of Remedies in WTO Dispute Settlement' in Friedl Weiss (ed), *Improving WTO Dispute Settlement Procedures: Issues and Lessons from the Practice of Other International Courts and Tribunals* (Cameron May 2000).

Hudson MO, *International Tribunals: Past and Future* (Carnegie Endowment for International Peace 1944).

Husa J, 'Methodology of Comparative Law Today: From Paradoxes to Flexibility?' (2006) 58 Revue internationale de droit comparé 1095.

'Research Designs of Comparative Law – Methodology or Heuristics?' in Maurice Adams and Dirk Heirbaut (eds), *The Method and Culture of Comparative Law: Essays in Honour of Mark Van Hoecke* (Hart 2014).

Introduction to Comparative Law (2nd ed., Hart 2023).

Ioannidis M, 'A Procedural Approach to the Legitimacy of International Adjudication: Developing Standards of Participation in WTO Law' (2011) 12 German LJ 1175.

'Beyond the Standard of Review: Deference Criteria in WTO Law and the Case for a Procedural Approach' in Lukasz Gruszczynski and Wouter Werner (eds), *Deference in International Courts and Tribunals: Standard of Review and Margin of Appreciation* (OUP 2014).

Jackson JH, *Sovereignty, the WTO, and Changing Fundamentals of International Law* (CUP 2006).

Jackson VC, 'Comparative Constitutional Law: Methodologies' in Michel Rosenfeld and András Sajó (eds), *The Oxford Handbook of Comparative Constitutional Law* (OUP 2012).

Jenks CW, *The Prospects of International Adjudication* (Stevens & Sons 1964).

'Orthodoxy and Innovation in the Law of Nations' (1971) 57 Proceedings of the British Academy 215.

Jennings RY, 'The Judicial Function and the Rule of Law in International Relations' in Robert Y Jennings (ed), *Collected Writings of Sir Robert Jennings*, vol 1 (Kluwer Law International 1998).

Johns L, *Strengthening International Courts: The Hidden Costs of Legalization* (University of Michigan Press 2015).

Johnston DM, 'Fishery Diplomacy and Science and the Judicial Function' (2000) 10 Ybk IEL 33.

Jones HL, 'Why Comply? An Analysis of Trends in Compliance with Judgments of the International Court of Justice since Nicaragua' (2012) 12 Chi.-Kent J. Int'l & Comp. L. 57.

Kalicki JE and Joubin-Bret A (eds), *Reshaping the Investor-State Dispute Settlement System: Journeys for the 21st Century* (Brill Nijhoff 2015).

Kapterian G, 'A Critique of the WTO Jurisprudence on "Necessity"' (2010) 59 ICLQ 89.

Karaman IV, *Dispute Resolution in the Law of the Sea* (Martinus Nijhoff 2012).

Katz Cogan J, 'Competition and Control in International Adjudication' (2008) 48 Va. J. Int'l L 411.

Kavanagh A, *Constitutional Review under the UK Human Rights Act* (CUP 2009).

Keith K, 'The Role of an ICJ Judge' in Carlos Espósito and Kate Parlett (eds), *The Cambridge Companion to the International Court of Justice* (CUP 2023).

Kessedjian C and others, 'Mediation in Future Investor–State Dispute Settlement' (2023) 14 JIDS 192.

Kingsbury B, 'International Courts: Uneven Judicialisation in Global Order' in James Crawford and Martti Koskenniemi (eds), *The Cambridge Companion to International Law* (CUP 2012).

Kingsbury B and Schill S, 'Investor-State Arbitration as Governance: Fair and Equitable Treatment, Proportionality and the Emerging Global Administrative Law' in Albert Jan van den Berg (ed), *Fifty Years of the New York Convention* (Kluwer Law International 2009).

Kittichaisaree K, *The International Tribunal for the Law of the Sea* (OUP 2021).

Klabbers J, 'On Rationalism in Politics: Interpretation of Treaties and the World Trade Organization' (2005) 74 Nordic JIL 405.

Kläger R, 'Fair and Equitable Treatment: A Look at the Theoretical Underpinnings of Legitimacy and Fairness' (2010) 11 JWIT 435.

'Fair and Equitable Treatment' in International Investment Law (CUP 2011).

Klein N, *Dispute Settlement in the UN Convention on the Law of the Sea* (CUP 2005).

Klein N and Kroon D, 'Settlement of International Environmental Law Disputes' in Malgosia Fitzmaurice, Marcel Brus and Panos Merkouris (eds), *Research Handbook on International Environmental Law* (2nd ed., Edward Elgar 2021).

Klein N and Parlett K, *Judging the Law of the Sea: Judicial Contributions to the UN Convention on the Law of the Sea* (OUP 2022).

Kleinheisterkamp J, 'Investment Treaty Law and the Fear for Sovereignty: Transnational Challenges and Solutions' (2015) 78 MLR 793.

Kleinlein T, 'Matters of Interpretation: How to Conceptualize and Evaluate Change of Norms and Values in the International Legal Order' in Heike Krieger and Andrea Liese (eds), *Tracing Value Change in the International Legal Order: Perspectives from Legal and Political Science* (OUP 2023).

Koh T and Lin J, 'The Land Reclamation Case: Thoughts and Reflections' (2006) 10 Singapore YBIL 1.

Kojima C, 'South China Sea Arbitration and the Protection of the Marine Environment: Evolution of UNCLOS Part XII through Interpretation and the Duty to Cooperate' (2015) 21 Asian Yearbook of International Law 166.

Kolb R, *The International Court of Justice* (Alan Perry tr, Hart 2013).

'Short Reflections on the ICJ's Whaling Case and the Review by International Courts and Tribunals of "Discretionary Powers"' (2014) 32 AYBIL 135.

'Evolutionary Interpretation in International Law: Some Short and Less than Trail-Blazing Reflections' in Georges Abi-Saab and others (eds), *Evolutionary Interpretation and International Law* (Hart 2019).

Kooijmans P, 'The ICJ in the 21st Century: Judicial Restraint, Judicial Activism, or Proactive Judicial Policy' (2007) 56 ICLQ 741.

Koon Hean C, Koh T and Yee L, *Malaysia & Singapore The Land Reclamation Case: From Dispute to Settlement* (Straits Times Press 2013).

Kopar R, *Stability and Legitimate Expectations in International Energy Investments* (Hart 2021).

Koremenos B, Lipson C and Snidal D, 'The Rational Design of International Institutions' (2001) 55 International Organization 761.

Koskenniemi M, 'Peaceful Settlement of Environmental Disputes' (1991) 60 Nordic JIL 73.

From Apology to Utopia: The Structure of International Legal Argument (reissue, CUP 2005).

'The Case for Comparative International Law' (2011) 20 Finnish YBIL 1.

'Law, Teleology and International Relations: An Essay in Counterdisciplinarity' (2011) 26 International Relations 3.

Kotzé LJ, *Global Environmental Constitutionalism in the Anthropocene* (Hart 2016).

Kotzé LJ and others, 'Earth System Law: Exploring New Frontiers in Legal Science' (2022) 11 Earth System Governance 100126.

Krämer L, 'The Environment before the European Court of Justice' in Christina Voigt (ed), *International Judicial Practice on the Environment* (CUP 2019).

Kriebaum U, 'FET and Expropriation in the (Invisible) EU Model BIT' (2014) 15 JWIT 454.

'Evaluating Social Benefits and Costs of Investment Treaties: Depoliticization of Investment Disputes' (2018) 33 ICSID Review 14.

Krieger H and Peters A, 'Due Diligence and Structural Change in the International Legal Order' in Heike Krieger and Anne Peters (eds), *Due Diligence in the International Legal Order* (OUP 2020).

Krisch N, 'The Dynamics of International Law Redux' (2021) 74 Current Legal Problems 269.

Kulick A (ed), *Reassertion of Control over the Investment Treaty Regime* (CUP 2016).

Kulovesi K, *The WTO Dispute Settlement System: Challenges of the Environment, Legitimacy and Fragmentation* (Kluwer Law International 2011).

Kuokkanen T, *International Law and the Environment: Variations on a Theme* (Brill 2002).

Kurtz J, 'Adjudging the Exceptional at International Investment Law: Security, Public Order and Financial Crisis' (2010) 59 ICLQ 325.

'The Merits and Limits of Comparativism: National Treatment in International Investment Law and the WTO' in Stephan W Schill (ed), *International Investment Law and Comparative Public Law* (OUP 2010).

Lambert E, 'Execution of Judgment: European Court of Human Rights (ECtHR)' in Hélène Ruiz-Fabri (ed), *Max Planck Encyclopedia of International Procedural Law* (OUP 2018).

Lang A, *World Trade Law after Neoliberalism: Reimagining the Global Economic Order* (OUP 2011).

'The Role of the International Court of Justice in a Context of Fragmentation' (2013) 62 ICLQ 777.

'Twenty Years of the WTO Appellate Body's "Fragmentation Jurisprudence"' (2015) 14 Journal of International Trade Law and Policy 116.

Langford M, Behn D and Lie RH, 'The Revolving Door in International Investment Arbitration' (2017) 20 JIEL 301.

Lanovoy V, 'Standards of Review in the Practice of International Courts and Tribunals' in Gábor Kajtár, Basak Çali and Marko Milanovic (eds), *Secondary Rules of Primary Importance in International Law* (OUP 2022).

Lauterpacht H, *The Function of Law in the International Community* (OUP 1933).

The Development of International Law by the International Court (rev. ed., Stevens & Sons 1958).

Legrand P, 'The Impossibility of Legal Transplants' (1997) 4 Maastricht J. Eur. & Comp. L. 111.

Leonelli GC, *Transnational Narratives and Regulation of GMO Risks* (Hart 2021).

Leonhardsen EM, 'Designing Deference: Towards a Thin Margin of Appreciation Doctrine in International Investment Law?' in Jelena Bäumler and others (eds), *European Yearbook of International Economic Law 2021* (Springer 2022).

Lim CL, Ho J and Paparinskis M, *International Investment Law and Arbitration: Commentary, Awards and Other Materials* (2nd ed., CUP 2021).

Linton S and Kebede Tiba F, 'The International Judge in an Age of Multiple International Courts and Tribunals' (2008) 9 Chicago JIL 407.

Lissitzyn OJ, *The International Court of Justice: Its Role in the Maintenance of International Peace and Security* (Carnegie Endowment for International Peace 1951).

Lo C, Nakagawa J and Lin T (eds), *The Appellate Body of the WTO and Its Reform* (Springer 2020).

Loft P, 'British Indian Ocean Territory: UK to Negotiate Sovereignty 2022/23', House of Commons Library Research Briefing, 22 November 2022.

Lowe V, 'The Interplay between Negotiation and Litigation in International Dispute Settlement' in Tafsir Malick Ndiaye and Rüdiger Wolfrum (eds), *Law of the Sea, Environmental Law, and Settlement of Disputes: Liber Amicorum Judge Thomas A. Mensah* (Martinus Nijhoff 2007).

'The Function of Litigation in International Society' (2012) 61 ICLQ 209.

'The "Complementary Role" of ITLOS in the Development of Ocean Law' in Harry N Scheiber and Jin-Hyun Paik (eds), *Regions, Institutions, and Law of the Sea: Studies in Ocean Governance* (Martinus Nijhoff 2013).

'The Law of Treaties; or, Should This Book Exist?' in Christian J Tams, Antonios Tzanakopoulos and Andreas Zimmermann (eds), *Research Handbook on the Law of Treaties* (Edward Elgar 2014).

Lowe V and Churchill R, 'The International Tribunal for the Law of the Sea: Survey for 2001' (2002) 17 IJMCL 463.

Mackenzie R and others, *Selecting International Judges: Principle, Process, and Politics* (OUP 2010).

Madsen MR, Cebulak P and Wiebusch M, 'Backlash against International Courts: Explaining the Forms and Patterns of Resistance to International Courts' (2018) 14 International Journal of Law in Context 197.

Malacrida R, 'WTO Panel Composition: Searching Far and Wide for Administrators of World Trade Justice' in Gabrielle Marceau (ed), *A History of Law and Lawyers in the GATT/WTO: The Development of the Rule of Law in the Multilateral Trading System* (CUP 2015).

Mansfield B, 'Compulsory Dispute Settlement after the Southern Bluefin Tuna Award' in Alex G Oude Elferink and Donald R Rothwell (eds), *Oceans Management in the 21st Century: Institutional Frameworks and Responses* (Martinus Nijhoff 2004).

Marceau G, 'Evolutive Interpretation by the WTO Adjudicator' (2018) 21 JIEL 791.

Marceau G and Trachtman JP, 'A Map of the World Trade Organization Law of Domestic Regulation of Goods: The Technical Barriers to Trade Agreement, the Sanitary and Phytosanitary Measures Agreement, and the General Agreement on Tariffs and Trade' (2014) 48 JWT 351.

Marisi F, *Environmental Interests in Investment Arbitration: Challenges and Directions* (Kluwer Law International 2020).

Marotti L, 'Remedies against Non-compliance with International Judgments' in Hélène Ruiz-Fabri (ed), *Max Planck Encyclopedia of International Procedural Law* (OUP 2021).

Marotti L and Palchetti P, 'Of Restoring Compliance, Lex Specialis and Intersecting Wrongs: The Question of "Remedies" in *Gabčikovo-Nagymaros*' in Serena Forlati, Makane Moïse Mbengue and Brian McGarry (eds), *The Gabčíkovo-Nagymaros Judgment and Its Contribution to the Development of International Law* (Brill Nijhoff 2020).

Marr S, 'The Southern Bluefin Tuna Cases: The Precautionary Approach and Conservation and Management of Fish Resources' (2000) 11 EJIL 815.

Matz-Lück N and Van Doorn E, 'Due Diligence Obligations and the Protection of the Marine Environment' (2017) 42 L'Observateur des Nations Unies 177.

Mavroidis PC, 'Dispute Settlement in the WTO: Mind over Matter' in Kyle Bagwell and Robert W Staiger (eds), *Handbook of Commercial Policy*, vol 1A (North-Holland 2016).

The Regulation of International Trade, vol 1 (MIT Press 2016).

The WTO Dispute Settlement System: How, Why and Where? (Edward Elgar 2022).

Mayer B, 'The Pitfalls of Ineffective Conceptualization: The Case of the Distinction between Procedure and Substance' (2022) 33 EJIL 1307.

Mbengue MM, 'The South China Sea Arbitration: Innovations in Marine Environmental Fact-Finding and Due Diligence Obligations' (2016) 110 AJIL Unbound 285.

Mbengue MM and Das R, 'The ICJ's Engagement with Science: To Interpret or Not to Interpret?' (2015) 6 JIDS 568.

McDougall R, 'The Crisis in WTO Dispute Settlement: Fixing Birth Defects to Restore Balance' (2018) 52 JWT 867.

McGrady B, 'Necessity Exceptions in WTO Law: Retreaded Tyres, Regulatory Purpose and Cumulative Regulatory Measures' (2009) 12 JIEL 153.

McLachlan C, 'The Principle of Systemic Integration and Article 31(3)(c) of the Vienna Convention' (2005) 54 ICLQ 279.

'The Evolution of Treaty Obligations in International Law' in Georg Nolte (ed), *Treaties and Subsequent Practice* (OUP 2013).

McLachlan C, Shore L and Weiniger M, *International Investment Arbitration: Substantive Principles* (2nd ed, OUP 2017).

Merkouris P, '(Inter)Temporal Considerations in the Interpretative Process of the VCLT: Do Treaties Endure, Perdure or Exdure?' (2014) 45 Netherlands YBIL 121.

Article 31(3)(c) VCLT and the Principle of Systemic Integration: Normative Shadows in Plato's Cave (Brill Nijhoff 2015).

Meshel T, 'Unmasking the Substance behind the Process: Why the Duty to Cooperate in International Water Law Is Really a Substantive Principle' (2019) 47 Denver JILP 29.

Messenger G, *The Development of World Trade Organization Law: Examining Change in International Law* (OUP 2016).

'The Development of International Law, Perception, and the Problem of Time' in Luca Pasquet, León Castellanos-Jankiewicz and Klara Polackova Van der Ploeg (eds), *International Law and Time: Narratives and Techniques* (Springer 2022).

Messineo F, 'The Functions of The International Court of Justice: Tending to the Law While Settling Disputes?' in Avidan Kent, Nikos Skoutaris and Jamie Trinidad (eds), *The Future of International Courts: Regional, Institutional and Procedural Challenges* (Routledge 2019).

Michaels R, 'The Functional Method of Comparative Law' in Mathias Reimann and Reinhard Zimmermann (eds), *The Oxford Handbook of Comparative Law* (2nd ed., OUP 2019).

Miles K, *The Origins of International Investment Law: Empire, Environment and the Safeguarding of Capital* (CUP 2013).

(ed), *Research Handbook on Environment and Investment Law* (Edward Elgar 2019).

Mitchell AD and Henckels C, 'Variations on a Theme: Comparing the Concept of "Necessity" in International Investment Law and WTO Law' (2013) 14 Chicago Journal of International Law 93.

Mitchell AD and Munro J, 'Someone Else's Deal: Interpreting International Investment Agreements in the Light of Third-Party Agreements' (2017) 28 EJIL 669.

Mitchell AD and Sheargold E, *Principles of International Trade and Investment Law* (Edward Elgar 2021).

Mitchell SM and Owsiak AP, 'The International Court of Justice' in Robert M Howard and Kirk A Randazzo (eds), *Routledge Handbook of Judicial Behavior* (Routledge 2018).

'Judicialization of the Sea: Bargaining in the Shadow of UNCLOS' (2021) 115 AJIL 579.

Monti A, *Promoting Renewable Energy: The Mutual Supportiveness of Climate and Trade Law* (Edward Elgar 2023).

Montt S, *State Liability in Investment Treaty Arbitration: Global Constitutional and Administrative Law in the BIT Generation* (Hart 2009).

Motzfeldt Kravik A, 'An Analysis of Stagnation in Multilateral Law-Making – and Why the Law of the Sea Has Transcended the Stagnation Trend' (2021) 34 LJIL 935.

Murphy SD, 'International Judicial Bodies for Resolving Disputes between States' in Cesare PR Romano, Karen J Alter and Yuval Shany (eds), *The Oxford Handbook of International Adjudication* (OUP 2013).

Nagy B, 'The ICJ Judgment in the Gabčíkovo-Nagymaros Project Case and Its Aftermath: Success or Failure?' in Hélène Ruiz Fabri and others (eds), *A Bridge over Troubled Waters: Dispute Resolution in the Law of International Watercourses and the Law of the Sea* (Brill Nijhoff 2021).

Nagy CI, 'Clash of Trade and National Public Interest in WTO Law: The Illusion of "Weighing and Balancing" and the Theory of Reservation' (2020) 23 JIEL 143.

Neumann J and Türk E, 'Necessity Revisited: Proportionality in World Trade Organization Law after *Korea – Beef, EC – Asbestos* and *EC – Sardines* (2003) 37 JWT 199.

Nguyen LN, 'Expanding the Environmental Regulatory Scope of UNCLOS through the Rule of Reference: Potentials and Limits' (2021) 52 ODIL 419.

'Jurisdiction and Applicable Law in the Settlement of Marine Environmental Disputes under UNCLOS' (2021) 9 Korean J. Int. Comp. Law 337.

The Development of the Law of the Sea by UNCLOS Dispute Settlement Bodies (CUP 2023).

Nottage H and Sebastian T, 'Giving Legal Effect to the Results of WTO Trade Negotiations: An Analysis of the Methods of Changing WTO Law' (2006) 9 JIEL 989.

Noyes JE, 'Compulsory Third-Party Adjudication and the 1982 United Nations Convention on the Law the Sea' (1989) 4 Connecticut JIL 675.

Nussberger A, *The European Court of Human Rights* (OUP 2020).

O'Connell DP, *International Law* (2nd ed., Stevens & Sons 1970).

O'Hara C, 'Consensus Decision-Making and Democratic Discourse in the General Agreement on Tariffs and Trade 1947 and World Trade Organisation' (2021) 9 London Review of International Law 37.

Obadia E and Nitschke F, 'Institutional Arbitration and the Role of the Secretariat' in Chiara Giorgetti (ed), *Litigating International Investment Disputes: A Practitioner's Guide* (Brill Nijhoff 2014).

Oda S, 'Dispute Settlement Prospects in the Law of the Sea' (1995) 44 ICLQ 863.

Olsen HP, 'International Courts and the Doctrinal Channels of Legal Diplomacy' (2015) 6 Transnational Legal Theory 661.

Ortino F, 'The Investment Treaty System as Judicial Review' (2013) 24 Am. Rev. Int. Arb. 437.

'Investment Treaties, Sustainable Development and Reasonableness Review: A Case against Strict Proportionality Balancing' (2017) 30 LJIL 71.

The Origin and Evolution of Investment Treaty Standards: Stability, Value, and Reasonableness (OUP 2019).

Ortino F and Tabari NM, 'International Dispute Settlement: The Settlement of Investment Disputes Concerning Natural Resources – Applicable Law and Standards of Review' in Elisa Morgera and Kati Kulovesi (eds), *Research Handbook on International Law and Natural Resources* (Edward Elgar 2016).

Örücü AE, 'Methodology of Comparative Law' in Jan M Smits (ed), *Elgar Encyclopedia of Comparative Law* (2nd ed., Edward Elgar 2012).

Oude Elferink AG and others, 'Compulsory Jurisdiction as the DNA of LOSC Dispute Settlement: An Evolutionary Path' (2023) 38 IJMCL 185.

Oxman BH, 'The Duty to Respect Generally Accepted International Standards' (1991) 24 NYUJILP 109.

'Complementary Agreements and Compulsory Jurisdiction' (2001) 95 AJIL 277.

'Courts and Tribunals: The ICJ, ITLOS, and Arbitral Tribunals' in Donald R Rothwell and others (eds), *The Oxford Handbook of the Law of the Sea* (OUP 2015).

Paine J, 'The WTO's Dispute Settlement Body as a Voice Mechanism' (2019) 20 JWIT 820.

'Autonomy to Set the Level of Regulatory Protection in International Investment Law' (2021) 70 ICLQ 696.

Palmeter D and Alexandrov SA, '"Inducing Compliance" in WTO Dispute Settlement' in Daniel LM Kennedy and James D Southwick (eds), *The Political Economy of International Trade Law: Essays in Honor of Robert E. Hudec* (CUP 2002).

Palmeter D, Mavroidis PC and Meagher N, *Dispute Settlement in the World Trade Organization: Practice and Procedure* (3rd ed., CUP 2022).

Paparinskis M, *The International Minimum Standard and Fair and Equitable Treatment* (OUP 2013).

'Substantive Standards of Investment Protection under EU Law and International Investment Law' in Emmanuel Gaillard and Hélène Ruiz-Fabri (eds), *EU Law and International Investment Arbitration* (Juris 2018).

Park WW and Walsh TW, 'Review Essay: The Uses of Comparative Arbitration Law' (2008) 24 Arb. Int'l 615.

Paulsson J and Petrochilos G, '*Neer*-Ly Misled?' (2007) 22 ICSID Review 242.

Paulus A, 'International Adjudication' in Samantha Besson and John Tasioulas (eds), *The Philosophy of International Law* (OUP 2010).

Pauwelyn J, 'Enforcement and Countermeasures in the WTO: Rules Are Rules-toward a More Collective Approach' (2000) 94 AJIL 335.

'The Calculation and Design of Trade Retaliation in Context: What Is the Goal of Suspending WTO Obligations?' in Chad P Bown and Joost Pauwelyn (eds), *The Law, Economics and Politics of Retaliation in WTO Dispute Settlement* (CUP 2010).

'At the Edge of Chaos?: Foreign Investment Law as a Complex Adaptive System, How It Emerged and How It Can Be Reformed' (2014) 29 ICSID Review 372.

'The Rule of Law without the Rule of Lawyers? Why Investment Arbitrators Are from Mars, Trade Adjudicators from Venus' (2015) 109 AJIL 761.

Pauwelyn J and Elsig M, 'The Politics of Treaty Interpretation: Variations and Explanations across International Tribunals' in Jeffrey L Dunoff and Mark Pollack (eds), *Interdisciplinary Perspectives on International Law and International Relations: The State of the Art* (CUP 2012).

Pauwelyn J and Hamilton RJ, 'Exit from International Tribunals' (2018) 9 JIDS 679.

Pauwelyn J and Pelc K, 'Who Guards the "Guardians of the System"? The Role of the Secretariat in WTO Dispute Settlement' (2022) 116 AJIL 534.

Pauwelyn J, Wessel RA and Wouters J, 'When Structures Become Shackles: Stagnation and Dynamics in International Lawmaking' (2014) 25 EJIL 733.

Peel J, *Science and Risk Regulation in International Law* (CUP 2010).

'Of Apples and Oranges (and Hormones in Beef): Science and the Standard of Review in WTO Disputes under the SPS Agreement' (2012) 61 ICLQ 427.

'The Use of Science in Environment-Related Investor-State Arbitration' in Kate Miles (ed), *Research Handbook on Environment and Investment Law* (Edward Elgar 2019).

Peters A, 'The Refinement of International Law: From Fragmentation to Regime Interaction and Politicization' (2017) 15 ICON 671.

Petersmann M-C, 'When Environmental Protection and Human Rights Collide: Four Heuristics of Conflict Resolution' in Christina Voigt (ed), *International Judicial Practice on the Environment* (CUP 2019).

When Environmental Protection and Human Rights Collide: The Politics of Conflict Management by Regional Courts (CUP 2022).

Phan HD, 'International Courts and State Compliance: An Investigation of the Law of the Sea Cases' (2019) 50 ODIL 70.

Pirker B, *Proportionality Analysis and Models of Judicial Review: A Theoretical and Comparative Study* (Europa Law Publishing 2013).

Pitea C and Tanzi A, 'Non-compliance Mechanisms: Lessons Learned and the Way Forward' in Tullio Treves and others (eds), *Non-compliance Procedures and Mechanisms and the Effectiveness of International Environmental Agreements* (TMC Asser Press 2008).

Polonskaya K, 'Selecting Candidates to the Bench of the World Court: (Inevitable) Politicization and Its Consequences' (2020) 33 LJIL 409.

Proelss A, 'The Contribution of the ITLOS to Strengthening the Regime for the Protection of the Marine Environment' in Angela Del Vecchio and Roberto Virzo (eds), *Interpretations of the United Nations Convention on the Law of the Sea by International Courts and Tribunals* (Springer 2019).

Prost M, *The Concept of Unity in Public International Law* (Hart 2012).

Puig S, 'Recasting ICSID's Legitimacy Debate: Towards a Goal-Based Empirical Agenda' (2013) 36 Fordham ILJ 465.

'No Right without a Remedy: Foundations of Investor-State Arbitration' (2014) 35 Univ. of Pennsylvania JIL 829.

'Social Capital in the Arbitration Market' (2014) 25 EJIL 387.

Pulkowski D, *The Law and Politics of International Regime Conflict* (OUP 2014).

Radi Y, *Rules and Practices of International Investment Law and Arbitration* (CUP 2020).

Rajesh Babu R, 'State Responsibility for Illegal, Unreported and Unrelated Fishing and Sustainable Fisheries in the EEZ: Some Reflections on the ITLOS Advisory Opinion of 2015' (2015) 55 Indian JIL 239.

Ranjan P, 'Using the Public Law Concept of Proportionality to Balance Investment Protection with Regulation in International Investment Law: A Critical Reappraisal' (2014) 3 CJICL 853.

Rao PC and Gautier P, *The International Tribunal for the Law of the Sea: Law, Practice and Procedure* (Edward Elgar 2018).

Rasilla I de la, '"The Greatest Victory"? Challenges and Opportunities for Mediation in Investor-State Dispute Settlement' (2023) 38 ICSID Review 169.

Ratner SR, 'Regulatory Takings in Institutional Context: Beyond the Fear of Fragmented International Law' (2008) 102 AJIL 475.

Rayfuse R, 'The Future of Compulsory Dispute Settlement under the Law of the Sea Convention' (2005) 36 VUWLR 683.

'Standard of Review in the International Tribunal for the Law of the Sea' in Lukasz Gruszczynski and Wouter Werner (eds), *Deference in International Courts and Tribunals* (OUP 2014).

Redgwell C, 'Treaty Evolution, Adaptation and Change: Is the LOSC "Enough" to Address Climate Change Impacts on the Marine Environment?' (2019) 34 IJMCL 440.

Regan DH, 'The Meaning of "Necessary" in GATT Article XX and GATS Article XIV: The Myth of Cost–Benefit Balancing' (2007) 6 WTR 347.

Reimann M, 'Beyond National Systems: A Comparative Law for the International Age' (2001) 75 Tulane LR 1103.

'The Progress and Failure of Comparative Law in the Second Half of the Twentieth Century' (2002) 50 American Journal of Comparative Law 671.

Reinisch A and Schreuer C, *International Protection of Investments: The Substantive Standards* (CUP 2020).

Reisman WM, 'International Investment Arbitration and ADR: Married but Best Living Apart' (2009) 24 ICSID Review 185.

'Canute Confronts the Tide: States versus Tribunals and the Evolution of the Minimum Standard in Customary International Law' (2015) 30 ICSID Review 616.

Riles A, 'Wigmore's Treasure Box: Comparative Law in the Era of Information' (1999) 40 HILJ 221.

Rioseco S, 'Conferences of the Parties beyond International Environmental Law: How COPs Influence the Content and Implementation of Their Parent Treaties' (2023) 36 LJIL 699.

Rivers J, 'Proportionality and Discretion in International and European Law' in Nicholas Tsagourias (ed), *Transnational Constitutionalism: International and European Perspectives* (CUP 2007).

'The Presumption of Proportionality' (2014) 77 MLR 409.

Roberts A, 'Clash of Paradigms: Actors and Analogies Shaping the Investment Treaty System' (2013) 107 AJIL 45.

Roberts A and others, 'Comparative International Law: Framing the Field' (2015) 109 AJIL 467.

Roberts A and St John T, 'Complex Designers and Emergent Design: Reforming the Investment Treaty System' (2022) 116 AJIL 96.

Rogers CA, 'The Politics of International Investment Arbitrators' (2013) 12 Santa Clara JIL 223.

Roland Holst RJ, *Change in the Law of the Sea: Context, Mechanisms and Practice* (Brill Nijhoff 2022).

'Reflections on the Governance Function of Compulsory Dispute Settlement in the Legal Order for the Ocean' (2023) 38 IJMCL 283.

Romano CPR, *The Peaceful Settlement of International Environmental Disputes: A Pragmatic Approach* (Kluwer Law International 2000).

'A Taxonomy of International Rule of Law Institutions' (2011) 2 JIDS 241.

Romano CPR, Alter KJ and Shany Y, 'Mapping International Adjudicative Bodies, the Issues, and Players' in Cesare PR Romano, Karen J Alter and Yuval Shany (eds), *The Oxford Handbook of International Adjudication* (OUP 2013).

Ronen Y, 'Functions and Access' in William A Schabas and Shannonbrooke Murphy (eds), *Research Handbook on International Courts and Tribunals* (Edward Elgar 2017).

Rosenne S and Sohn LB (eds), *United Nations Convention on the Law of the Sea 1982: A Commentary*, vol 5 (Martinus Nijhoff 1989).

Rovnov Y, 'Appropriate Level of Protection: The Most Misconceived Notion of WTO Law' (2020) 31 EJIL 1343.

Sabahi B, Rubins ND and Wallace D Jr, *Investor–State Arbitration* (2nd ed., OUP 2019).

Sacerdoti G, 'Appeal and Judicial Review in International Arbitration and Adjudication: The Case of the WTO Appellate Review' in Ernst-Ulrich Petersmann (ed), *International Trade Law and the GATT/WTO Dispute Settlement System* (Kluwer Law International 1997).

Salacuse JW, 'Is There a Better Way? Alternative Methods of Treaty-Based, Investor-State Dispute Resolution' (2007) 31 Fordham Int'l LJ 138.

'The Emerging Global Regime for Investment' (2010) 51 HILJ 427.

The Law of Investment Treaties (3rd ed., OUP 2021).

Salacuse JW and Sullivan NP, 'Do BITs Really Work: An Evaluation of Bilateral Investment Treaties and Their Grand Bargain' (2005) 46 HILJ 67.

Sands P, 'Litigating Environmental Disputes: Courts, Tribunals and the Progressive Development of International Environmental Law' in Tafsir Malick Ndiaye, Rüdiger Wolfrum and Chie Kojima (eds), *Law of the Sea, Environmental Law, and Settlement of Disputes: Liber Amicorum Judge Thomas A. Mensah* (Martinus Nijhoff 2007).

Sands P and Peel J, *Principles of International Environmental Law* (4th ed., CUP 2018).

Sandonato de León P, 'Diplomatic and Judicial Means of Dispute Settlement and How They Got Along in the *Pulp Mills* Case' in Laurence Boisson de Chazournes, Marcelo G Kohen and Jorge E Viñuales (eds), *Diplomatic and Judicial Means of Dispute Settlement* (Martinus Nijhoff 2013).

Scalieri E, 'Discretionary Power of Coastal States and the Control of Its Compliance with International Law by International Tribunals' in Angela Del Vecchio and Roberto Virzo (eds), *Interpretations of the United Nations Convention on the Law of the Sea by International Courts and Tribunals* (Springer 2019).

Scanlon Z, 'Upsetting the Balance? The Legality of Vessel Confiscation under the LOSC after the *M/V Virginia G* Case' (2018) 33 IJMCL 166.

Scanlon Z and Beckman R, 'Assessing Environmental Impact and the Duty to Cooperate: Environmental Aspects of the Philippines v China Award' (2018) 3 Asia-Pacific Journal of Ocean Law and Policy 5.

Schatz V, 'Fishing for Interpretation: The ITLOS Advisory Opinion on Flag State Responsibility for Illegal Fishing in the EEZ' (2016) 47 ODIL 327.

Schebesta H and Sinopoli D, 'The Potency of the SPS Agreement's Excessivity Test: The Impact of Article 5.6 on Trade Liberalization and the Regulatory Power of WTO Members to Take Sanitary and Phytosanitary Measures' (2018) 21 JIEL 123.

Schill SW, *The Multilateralization of International Investment Law* (CUP 2009).

'System-Building in Investment Treaty Arbitration and Lawmaking' (2011) 12 German LJ 1083.

'W(h)ither Fragmentation? On the Literature and Sociology of International Investment Law' (2011) 22 EJIL 875.

'Deference in Investment Treaty Arbitration: Re-conceptualizing the Standard of Review' (2012) 3 JIDS 577.

'Sources of International Investment Law: Multilateralization, Arbitral Precedent, Comparativism, Soft Law' in Samantha Besson and Jean d'Aspremont (eds), *The Oxford Handbook of the Sources of International Law* (OUP 2018).

Schill SW and Vidigal G, 'Investment Dispute Settlement à La Carte: A Proposal for the Reform of Investor–State Dispute Settlement' in Manfred Elsig, Rodrigo Polanco and Peter Van Den Bossche (eds), *International Economic Dispute Settlement: Demise or Transformation?* (CUP 2021).

Schneider AK, 'Bargaining in the Shadow of (International) Law: What the Normalization of Adjudication in International Governance Regimes Means for Dispute Resolution' (2008) 41 NYUJILP 789.

Schneider AK and Welsh NA, 'Bargaining in the Shadow of Investor-State Mediation: How the Threat of Mediation Will Improve Parties' Conflict Management' (2021) 17 Univ. St. Thomas LJ 373.

Schneider ME, 'Investment Disputes – Moving beyond Arbitration' in Laurence Boisson de Chazournes' in Marcelo G Kohen and Jorge E Viñuales (eds), *Diplomatic and Judicial Means of Dispute Settlement* (Martinus Nijhoff 2013).

Schneiderman D, *Constitutionalizing Economic Globalization: Investment Rules and Democracy's Promise* (CUP 2008).

Schreuer C, 'Non-Pecuniary Remedies in ICSID Arbitration' (2004) 20 Arb. Int'l 325.

'Investment Arbitration' in Cesare PR Romano, Karen J Alter and Yuval Shany (eds), *The Oxford Handbook of International Adjudication* (OUP 2013).

'Alternative Remedies in Investment Arbitration' (2016) 3 The Journal of Damages in International Arbitration 1.

Schulte C, *Compliance with Decisions of the International Court of Justice* (OUP 2004).

Scott J, *The WTO Agreement on Sanitary and Phytosanitary Measures: A Commentary* (OUP 2009).

Scott S, 'The Contribution of the LOS Convention Organizations to Its Harmonious Implementation' in Alex G Oude Elferink and Donald R Rothwell (eds), *Oceans Management in the Twenty-first Century: Institutional Frameworks and Responses* (Martinus Nijhoff 2004).

Shaffer G, 'Developing Country Use of the WTO Dispute Settlement System: Why It Matters, the Barriers Posed' in James C Hartigan (ed), *Trade Disputes and the Dispute Settlement Understanding of the WTO: An Interdisciplinary Assessment* (Emerald Group Publishing 2009).

Shaffer G, Elsig M and Puig S, 'The Law and Politics of WTO Dispute Settlement' in Wayne Sandholtz and Christopher A Whytock (eds), *Handbook on the Politics of International Law* (Edward Elgar 2017).

Shaffer G and Trachtman JP, 'Interpretation and Institutional Choice at the WTO' (2011) 52 Va. J. Int'l L 103.

Shany Y, 'Toward a General Margin of Appreciation Doctrine in International Law?' (2005) 16 EJIL 907.

'No Longer a Weak Department of Power? Reflections on the Emergence of a New International Judiciary' (2009) 20 EJIL 73.

'One Law to Rule Them All: Should International Courts Be Viewed as Guardians of Procedural Order and Legal Uniformity?' in Ole Kristian Fauchald and André Nollkaemper (eds), *The Practice of International and National Courts and the (De-)Fragmentation of International Law* (Hart 2012).

Assessing the Effectiveness of International Courts (OUP 2014).

'Effectiveness of International Adjudication: Assessing Functions and Performance' (2014) 108 ASIL Proceedings 113.

Shaw MN, *Rosenne's Law and Practice of the International Court: 1920–2015* (5th ed., Brill Nijhoff 2016).

Shelton D, 'Form, Function, and the Powers of International Courts' (2008) 9 Chicago JIL 537.

Remedies in International Human Rights Law (3rd ed., OUP 2015).

Shigeta Y, *International Judicial Control of Environmental Protection: Standard Setting, Compliance Control, and the Development of International Environmental Law by the International Judiciary* (Kluwer Law International 2010).

Shirlow E, *Judging at the Interface: Deference to State Decision-Making Authority in International Adjudication* (CUP 2021).

'The Promises and Pitfalls of Investor-State Mediation' in Lisa Sachs, Lise Johnson and Jesse Coleman (eds), *Yearbook on International Investment Law & Policy 2019* (OUP 2021).

Shlomo-Agon S, 'Clearing the Smoke: The Legitimation of Judicial Power at the WTO' (2015) 49 JWT 539.

Shlomo-Agon S and Shany Y, 'The WTO Dispute Settlement System' in Yuval Shany, *Assessing the Effectiveness of International Courts* (OUP 2014).

Shlomo Agon S, *International Adjudication on Trial: The Effectiveness of the WTO Dispute Settlement System* (OUP 2019).

Shlomo Agon S and Benvenisti E, 'The Law of Strangers: The Form and Substance of Other-Regarding International Adjudication' (2018) 68 Univ. Toronto LJ 598.

Sifonios D, *Environmental Process and Production Methods (PPMs) in WTO Law* (Springer 2018).

Soave T, 'Who Controls WTO Dispute Settlement? Socio-Professional Practices and the Crisis of the Appellate Body' (2020) 29 Italian YBIL 13.

'The Social Field of International Adjudication: Structures and Practices of a Conflictive Professional Universe' (2023) 36 LJIL 565.

Sourgens FG, *A Nascent Common Law: The Process of Decision-Making in International Legal Disputes between States and Foreign Investors* (Brill Nijhoff 2015).

Spain A, 'Integration Matters: Rethinking the Architecture of International Dispute Resolution' (2010) 32 Univ. of Pennsylvania JIL 1.

'Beyond Adjudication: Resolving International Resource Disputes in an Era of Climate Change' (2011) 30 Stanford Environmental LJ 343.

'Examining the International Judicial Function: International Courts as Dispute Resolvers' (2011) 34 Loy L.A. Int'l & Comp. LR 5.

Squatrito T and others, 'A Framework for Evaluating the Performance of International Courts and Tribunals' in Theresa Squatrito and others (eds), *The Performance of International Courts and Tribunals* (CUP 2018).

St John T, *The Rise of Investor-State Arbitration: Politics, Law, and Unintended Consequences* (OUP 2018).

Stec S, 'Do Two Wrongs Make a Right? Adjudicating Sustainable Development in the Danube Dam Case' (1999) 29 Golden Gate University Law Review 317.

Steger DP, 'The Founding of the Appellate Body' in Gabrielle Marceau (ed), *A History of Law and Lawyers in the GATT/WTO: The Development of the Rule of Law in the Multilateral Trading System* (CUP 2015).

Stephens T, 'The Limits of International Adjudication in International Environmental Law: Another Perspective on the Southern Bluefin Tuna Case' (2004) 19 IJMCL 177.

International Courts and Environmental Protection (CUP 2009).

'What Is the Point of International Environmental Law Scholarship in the Anthropocene?' in Ole W Pedersen (ed), *Perspectives on Environmental Law Scholarship: Essays on Purpose, Shape and Direction* (CUP 2018).

Stoica V, *Remedies before the International Court of Justice: A Systemic Analysis* (CUP 2021).

Stone Sweet A and Mathews J, 'Proportionality Balancing and Global Constitutionalism' (2008) 47 Colum. J. Transnat'l L. 72.

Proportionality Balancing and Constitutional Governance: A Comparative and Global Approach (OUP 2019).

Sulyok K, *Science and Judicial Reasoning: The Legitimacy of International Environmental Adjudication* (CUP 2020).

Sweet AS and Grisel F, *The Evolution of International Arbitration: Judicialization, Governance, Legitimacy* (OUP 2017).

Sykes AO, 'The Least Restrictive Means' (2003) 70 The University of Chicago Law Review 625.

Tammelo I, *Treaty Interpretation and Practical Reason: Towards a General Theory of Legal Interpretation* (Law Book Company 1967).

Tams CJ, 'The ICJ as a "Law-Formative Agency": Summary and Synthesis' in Christian J Tams and James Sloan (eds), *The Development of International Law by the International Court of Justice* (OUP 2013).

Tams CJ and Tzanakopoulos A, '*Barcelona Traction* at 40: The ICJ as an Agent of Legal Development' (2010) 23 LJIL 781.

Tanaka Y, 'Prompt Release in the United Nations Convention on the Law of the Sea: Some Reflections on the ITLOS Jurisprudence' (2004) 51 Netherlands ILR 237.

'Unilateral Exploration and Exploitation of Natural Resources in Disputed Areas: A Note on the *Ghana/Côte d'Ivoire* Order of 25 April 2015 before the Special Chamber of ITLOS' (2015) 46 ODIL 315.

'Reflections on the Philippines/China Arbitration Award on Jurisdiction and Admissibility' (2016) 15 LPICT 305.

The International Law of the Sea (3rd ed., CUP 2019).

The South China Sea Arbitration: Toward an International Legal Order in the Oceans (Hart 2019).

'Obligation to Conduct an Environmental Impact Assessment (EIA) in International Adjudication: Interaction between Law and Time' (2021) 90 Nordic JIL 86.

Teitel R and Howse R, 'Cross-Judging: Tribunalization in a Fragmented but Interconnected Global Order' (2009) 41 NYUJILP 959.

Thirlway H, *The International Court of Justice* (OUP 2016).

Titi C, 'Between Utopia and Realism: Mediation and the Settlement of Investment Disputes' in Catharine Titi and Katia Fach Gómez (eds), *Mediation in International Commercial and Investment Disputes* (OUP 2019).

Tomuschat C, 'Article 36' in Andreas Zimmermann and others (eds), *The Statute of the International Court of Justice: A Commentary* (3rd ed., OUP 2019).

Trachtman JP, 'Trade and . . . Problems, Cost–Benefit Analysis and Subsidiarity' (1998) 9 EJIL 32.

'The Domain of WTO Dispute Resolution' (1999) 40 HILJ 333.

'International Legal Control of Domestic Administrative Action' (2014) 17 JIEL 753.

'WTO Trade and Environment Jurisprudence: Avoiding Environmental Catastrophe' (2017) 58 HILJ 273.

Treves T, 'A System for Law of the Sea Dispute Settlement' in David Freestone, Richard Barnes and David Ong (eds), *The Law of the Sea: Progress and Prospects* (OUP 2006).

Treves T and others (eds), *Non-compliance Procedures and Mechanisms and the Effectiveness of International Environmental Agreements* (TMC Asser Press 2008).

Trevisanut S, 'The Exercise of Administrative Functions by ITLOS: A Comment on Prompt Release Cases' in Nerina Boschiero and others (eds), *International Courts and the Development of International Law: Essays in Honour of Tullio Treves* (TMC Asser Press 2013).

'Twenty Years of Prompt Release of Vessels: Admissibility, Jurisdiction, and Recent Trends' (2017) 48 ODIL 300.

Ubilava A, 'Amicable Settlements in Investor-State Disputes: Empirical Analysis of Patterns and Perceived Problems' (2020) 21 JWIT 528.

Ulfstein G, 'Treaty Bodies and Regimes' in Duncan B Hollis (ed), *The Oxford Guide to Treaties* (2nd ed., OUP 2020).

UNCTAD, 'Treaty-based Investor–State Dispute Settlement Cases and Climate Action', IIA Issues Note No 4 (2022).

Vadi V, *Analogies in International Investment Law and Arbitration* (CUP 2015).

Proportionality, Reasonableness and Standards of Review in International Investment Law and Arbitration (Edward Elgar 2018).

'Crisis, Continuity, and Change in International Investment Law and Arbitration' (2021) 42 Mich. J. Int'l L. 321.

Valcke C and Grellette M, 'Three Functions of Function in Comparative Legal Studies' in Maurice Adams and Dirk Heirbaut (eds), *The Method and Culture of Comparative Law: Essays in Honour of Mark Van Hoecke* (Hart 2014).

van Aaken A, 'International Investment Law between Commitment and Flexibility: A Contract Theory Analysis' (2009) 12 JIEL 507.

Van den Bossche P, 'From Afterthought to Centerpiece: The WTO Appellate Body and Its Rise to Prominence in the World Trading System' in Giorgio Sacerdoti, Alan Yanovich and Jan Bohanes (eds), *The WTO at Ten: The Contribution of the Dispute Settlement System* (CUP 2006).

'Looking for Proportionality in WTO Law' (2008) 35 Legal Issues of Economic Integration 283.

'Is There Evolution in the Evolutionary Interpretation of WTO Law?' in Georges Abi-Saab and others (eds), *Evolutionary Interpretation and International Law* (Hart 2019).

'The Demise of the WTO Appellate Body: Lessons for Governance of International Adjudication?', WTI Working Paper No 02/2021.

Van den Bossche P and Zdouc W, *The Law and Policy of the World Trade Organization: Texts, Cases and Materials* (5th ed, CUP 2021).

Van der Ploeg KP, 'International Law through Time: On Change and Facticity of International Law' in Luca Pasquet, León Castellanos-Jankiewicz and Klara Polackova Van der Ploeg (eds), *International Law and Time: Narratives and Techniques* (Springer 2022).

Van Harten G, 'Investment Rules and the Denial of Change' (2010) 60 Univ. Toronto LJ 893.

'Foreign Investor Protection and Climate Action: A New Price Tag for Urgent Policies' [2015] Osgoode Legal Studies Research Paper Series, Research Paper No 21/2016.

Van Harten G and Loughlin M, 'Investment Treaty Arbitration as a Species of Global Administrative Law' (2006) 17 EJIL 121.

Vandevelde KJ, *Bilateral Investment Treaties: History, Policy, and Interpretation* (OUP 2010).

Venzke I, 'The Role of International Courts as Interpreters and Developers of the Law: Working Out the Jurisgenerative Practice of Interpretation' (2011) 34 Loy. L.A. Int'l & Comp. LR 99.

How Interpretation Makes International Law: On Semantic Change and Normative Twists (OUP 2012).

Viñuales JE, 'The Contribution of the International Court of Justice to the Development of International Environmental Law: A Contemporary Assessment' (2008) 32 Fordham ILJ 232.

Foreign Investment and the Environment in International Law (CUP 2012).

'The Organisation of the Anthropocene' (2018) 1 Brill Research Perspectives in International Legal Theory and Practice 1.

'Foreign Investment and the Environment in International Law: The Current State of Play' in Kate Miles (ed), *Research Handbook on Environment and Investment Law* (Edward Elgar 2019).

Voigt C, 'International Courts and the Environment: The Quest for Legitimacy' in Christina Voigt (ed), *International Judicial Practice on the Environment* (CUP 2019).

von Bogdandy A, 'Law and Politics in the WTO – Strategies to Cope with a Deficient Relationship' (2001) 5 Max Planck Ybk UN Law 609.

'Legitimacy of International Economic Governance: Interpretative Approaches to WTO Law and the Prospects of Its Proceduralization' in Stefan Griller (ed), *International Economic Governance and Non-economic Concerns: New Challenges for the International Legal Order* (Springer 2003).

von Bogdandy A and Venzke I, 'On the Functions of International Courts: An Appraisal in Light of Their Burgeoning Public Authority' (2013) 26 LJIL 49.

In Whose Name? A Public Law Theory of International Adjudication (OUP 2014).

von Staden A, 'The Democratic Legitimacy of Judicial Review beyond the State: Normative Subsidiarity and Judicial Standards of Review' (2012) 10 ICON 1023.

Vordermayer M, '"Gardening the Great Transformation": The Anthropocene Concept's Impact on International Environmental Law Doctrine' (2014) 25 Ybk IEL 79.

Vranes E, *Trade and the Environment: Fundamental Issues in International Law, WTO Law, and Legal Theory* (OUP 2009).

Wälde TW and Kolo A, 'Environmental Regulation, Investment Protection and "Regulatory Taking" in International Law' (2001) 50 ICLQ 811.

Webb P, *International Judicial Integration and Fragmentation* (OUP 2013).

Weeramantry CG, 'The Function of the International Court of Justice in the Development of International Law' (1997) 10 LJIL 309.

Weeramantry R, Chang B and Sherard-Chow J, 'Conciliation and Mediation in Investor-State Dispute Settlement Provisions: A Quantitative and Qualitative Analysis' (2023) 38 ICSID Review 201.

Weiler JH, 'The Rule of Lawyers and the Ethos of Diplomats Reflections on the Internal and External Legitimacy of WTO Dispute Settlement' (2001) 35 JWT 191.

Weimer M, 'Reconciling Regulatory Space with External Accountability through WTO Adjudication – Trade, Environment and Development' (2017) 30 LJIL 901.

Wellens K, *Negotiations in the Case Law of the International Court of Justice: A Functional Analysis* (Ashgate 2014).

Wellhausen RL, 'International Investment Law and Foreign Direct Reinvestment' (2019) 73 International Organization 839.

Werner W and Gruszczynski L, 'Introduction' in Lukasz Gruszczynski and Wouter Werner (eds), *Deference in International Courts and Tribunals: Standard of Review and Margin of Appreciation* (OUP 2014).

Whytock CA, 'Legal Origins, Functionalism, and the Future of Comparative Law' [2009] Brigham Young ULR 1879.

Wiener JB, 'Law and the New Ecology: Evolution, Categories, and Consequences' (1995) 22 Ecology LQ 325.

Wittich S, 'The Judicial Functions of the International Court of Justice' in Isabelle Buffard and others (eds), *International Law between Universalism and Fragmentation: Festschrift in Honour of Gerhard Hafner* (Martinus Nijhoff 2008).

Wolfrum R, 'International Law of Cooperation' in Rüdiger Wolfrum (ed), *Max Planck Encyclopedia of Public International Law* (OUP 2010).

Wyatt J, *Intertemporal Linguistics in International Law: Beyond Contemporaneous and Evolutionary Treaty Interpretation* (Hart 2020).

Yanovich A, 'The Evolving WTO Dispute Settlement System' in Yasuhei Taniguchi, Alan Yanovich and Jan Bohanes (eds), *The WTO in the Twenty-First Century: Dispute Settlement, Negotiations, and Regionalism in Asia* (CUP 2007).

Young MA, 'Introduction: The Productive Friction between Regimes' in Margaret A Young (ed), *Regime Interaction in International Law: Facing Fragmentation* (CUP 2012).

'Regime Interaction in Creating, Implementing and Enforcing International Law' in Margaret A Young (ed), *Regime Interaction in International Law: Facing Fragmentation* (CUP 2012).

Young MA and Sullivan SR, 'Evolution through the Duty to Cooperate: Implications of the *Whaling* Case at the International Court of Justice' (2015) 16 MJIL 311.

Zhang Y, 'The Judicial Function of Investment Tribunals: Taking Foundational Assumptions Seriously' (2022) 25 JIEL 129.

Zleptnig S, *Non-economic Objectives in WTO Law* (Martinus Nijhoff 2010).

Zweigert K and Kötz H, *Introduction to Comparative Law* (Tony Weir tr, OUP 1998).

INDEX

CAMBRIDGE STUDIES IN INTERNATIONAL AND COMPARATIVE LAW

Books in the Series

189 *The Functions of International Adjudication and International Environmental Litigation*
Joshua Paine

188 *Demystifying Treaty Interpretation*
Andrea Bianchi and Fuad Zarbiyev

187 *International Law-Making by the International Court of Justice and International Law Commission: Partnership for Purpose in a Decentralized Legal Order*
Omri Sender

186 *The Rebirth of Territory*
Gail Lythgoe

185 *Reimagining Sustainable Development in International Law: Perspectives from African Legal Cosmologies*
Godwin Eli Kwadzo Dzah

184 *Collective Self-Defence in International Law*
James A. Green

183 *Weaponising Evidence: A History of Tobacco Control in International Law*
Margherita Melillo

182 *The Justice Factory: Management Practices at the International Criminal Court*
Richard Clements

181 *A Communitarian Theory of WTO Law*
Chi Carmody

180 *Drones and International Law: A Techno-Legal Machinery*
Mignot-Mahdavi

179 *The Necessity of Nature: God, Science and Money in 17th Century English Law of Nature*
Mónica García-Salmones

178 *Making the World Safe for Investment: The Protection of Foreign Property 1922–1959*
Andrea Leiter

177 *National Governance and Investment Treaties*
Josef Ostřanský and Facundo Pérez Aznar

176 *Who Owns Outer Space? International Law, Astrophysics, and the Sustainable Development of Space*
Michael Byers and Aaron Boley

175 *Intervening in International Justice: Third States before Courts and Tribunals*
Brian McGarry

174 *Reciprocity in Public International Law*
Arianna Whelan

173 *When Environmental Protection and Human Rights Collide*
Marie-Catherine Petersmann Drones and International Law

172 *The International Law of Sovereign Debt Dispute Settlement*
Kei Nakajima

171 *The Everyday Makers of International Law: From Great Halls to Back Rooms*
Tommaso Soave

170 *Virtue in Global Governance: Judgment and Discretion*
Jan Klabbers

169 *The Effects of Armed Conflict on Investment Treaties*
Tobias Ackermann

168 *Investment Law's Alibis: Colonialism, Imperialism, Debt and Development*
David Schneiderman

167 *Negative Comparative Law: A Strong Programme for Weak Thought*
Pierre Legrand

166 *Detention by Non-State Armed Groups under International Law*
Ezequiel Heffes

165 *Rebellions and Civil Wars: State Responsibility for the Conduct of Insurgents*
Patrick Dumberry

164 *The International Law of Energy*
Jorge Viñuales

163 *The Three Ages of International Commercial Arbitration*
Mikaël Schinazi

162 *Repetition and International Law*
Wouter Werner

161 *State Responsibility and Rebels: The History and Legacy of Protecting Investment Against Revolution*
Kathryn Greenman

160 *Rewriting Histories of the Use of Force: The Narrative of 'Indifference'*
Agatha Verdebout

159 *The League of Nations and the Protection of the Environment*
Omer Aloni

158 *International Investment Law and Legal Theory: Expropriation and the Fragmentation of Sources*
Jörg Kammerhofer

157 *Legal Barbarians: Identity, Modern Comparative Law and the Global South*
Daniel Bonilla Maldonado

156 *International Human Rights Law Beyond State Territorial Control*
Antal Berkes

155 *The Crime of Aggression under the Rome Statute of the International Criminal Court*
Carrie McDougall

154 *Minorities and the Making of Postcolonial States in International Law*
Mohammad Shahabuddin

153 *Preclassical Conflict of Laws*
Nikitas E. Hatzimihail

152 *International Law and History: Modern Interfaces*
Ignacio de la Rasilla

151 *Marketing Global Justice: The Political Economy of International Criminal Law*
Christine Schwöbel-Patel

150 *International Status in the Shadow of Empire*
Cait Storr

149 *Treaties in Motion: The Evolution of Treaties from Formation to Termination*
Edited by Malgosia Fitzmaurice and Panos Merkouris

148 *Humanitarian Disarmament: An Historical Enquiry*
Treasa Dunworth

147 *Complementarity, Catalysts, Compliance: The International Criminal Court in Uganda, Kenya, and the Democratic Republic of Congo*
Christian M. De Vos

146 *Cyber Operations and International Law*
François Delerue

145 *Comparative Reasoning in International Courts and Tribunals*
Daniel Peat

144 *Maritime Delimitation as a Judicial Process*
Massimo Lando

143 *Prosecuting Sexual and Gender-Based Crimes at the International Criminal Court: Practice, Progress and Potential*
Rosemary Grey

142 *Capitalism As Civilisation: A History of International Law*
Ntina Tzouvala

141 *Sovereignty in China: A Genealogy of a Concept Since 1840*
Adele Carrai

140 *Narratives of Hunger in International Law: Feeding the World in Times of Climate Change*
Anne Saab

139 *Victim Reparation under the Ius Post Bellum: An Historical and Normative Perspective*
Shavana Musa

138 *The Analogy between States and International Organizations*
Fernando Lusa Bordin

137 *The Process of International Legal Reproduction: Inequality, Historiography, Resistance*
Rose Parfitt

136 *State Responsibility for Breaches of Investment Contracts*
Jean Ho

135 *Coalitions of the Willing and International Law: The Interplay between Formality and Informality*
Alejandro Rodiles

134 *Self-Determination in Disputed Colonial Territories*
Jamie Trinidad

133 *International Law as a Belief System*
Jean d'Aspremont

132 *Legal Consequences of Peremptory Norms in International Law*
Daniel Costelloe

131 *Third-Party Countermeasures in International Law*
Martin Dawidowicz

130 *Justification and Excuse in International Law: Concept and Theory of General Defences*
Federica Paddeu

129 *Exclusion from Public Space: A Comparative Constitutional Analysis*
Daniel Moeckli

128 *Provisional Measures before International Courts and Tribunals*
Cameron A. Miles

127 *Humanity at Sea: Maritime Migration and the Foundations of International Law*
Itamar Mann

126 *Beyond Human Rights: The Legal Status of the Individual in International Law*
Anne Peters

125 *The Doctrine of Odious Debt in International Law: A Restatement*
Jeff King

124 *Static and Evolutive Treaty Interpretation: A Functional Reconstruction*
Christian Djeffal

123 *Civil Liability in Europe for Terrorism-Related Risk*
Lucas Bergkamp, Michael Faure, Monika Hinteregger and Niels Philipsen

122 *Proportionality and Deference in Investor-State Arbitration: Balancing Investment Protection and Regulatory Autonomy*
Caroline Henckels

121 *International Law and Governance of Natural Resources in Conflict and Post-Conflict Situations*
Daniëlla Dam-de Jong

120 *Proof of Causation in Tort Law*
Sandy Steel

119 *The Formation and Identification of Rules of Customary International Law in International Investment Law*
Patrick Dumberry

118 *Religious Hatred and International Law: The Prohibition of Incitement to Violence or Discrimination*
Jeroen Temperman

117 *Taking Economic, Social and Cultural Rights Seriously in International Criminal Law*
Evelyne Schmid

116 *Climate Change Litigation: Regulatory Pathways to Cleaner Energy*
Jacqueline Peel and Hari M. Osofsky

115 *Mestizo International Law: A Global Intellectual History 1842–1933*
Arnulf Becker Lorca

114 *Sugar and the Making of International Trade Law*
Michael Fakhri

113 *Strategically Created Treaty Conflicts and the Politics of International Law*
Surabhi Ranganathan

112 *Investment Treaty Arbitration As Public International Law: Procedural Aspects and Implications*
Eric De Brabandere

111 *The New Entrants Problem in International Fisheries Law*
Andrew Serdy

110 *Substantive Protection under Investment Treaties: A Legal and Economic Analysis*
Jonathan Bonnitcha

109 *Popular Governance of Post-Conflict Reconstruction: The Role of International Law*
Matthew Saul

108 *Evolution of International Environmental Regimes: The Case of Climate Change*
Simone Schiele

107 *Judges, Law and War: The Judicial Development of International Humanitarian Law*
Shane Darcy

106 *Religious Offence and Human Rights: The Implications of Defamation of Religions*
Lorenz Langer

105 *Forum Shopping in International Adjudication: The Role of Preliminary Objections*
Luiz Eduardo Salles

104 *Domestic Politics and International Human Rights Tribunals: The Problem of Compliance*
Courtney Hillebrecht

103 *International Law and the Arctic*
Michael Byers

102 *Cooperation in the Law of Transboundary Water Resources*
Christina Leb

101 *Underwater Cultural Heritage and International Law*
Sarah Dromgoole

100 *State Responsibility: The General Part*
James Crawford

99 *The Origins of International Investment Law: Empire, Environment and the Safeguarding of Capital*
Kate Miles

98 *The Crime of Aggression under the Rome Statute of the International Criminal Court*
Carrie McDougall

97 *'Crimes against Peace' and International Law*
Kirsten Sellars

96 *Non-Legality in International Law: Unruly Law*
Fleur Johns

95 *Armed Conflict and Displacement: The Protection of Refugees and Displaced Persons under International Humanitarian Law*
Mélanie Jacques

94 *Foreign Investment and the Environment in International Law*
Jorge E. Viñuales

93 *The Human Rights Treaty Obligations of Peacekeepers*
Kjetil Mujezinović Larsen

92 *Cyber Warfare and the Laws of War*
Heather Harrison Dinniss

91 *The Right to Reparation in International Law for Victims of Armed Conflict*
Christine Evans

90 *Global Public Interest in International Investment Law*
Andreas Kulick

89 *State Immunity in International Law*
Xiaodong Yang

88 *Reparations and Victim Support in the International Criminal Court*
Conor McCarthy

87 *Reducing Genocide to Law: Definition, Meaning, and the Ultimate Crime*
Payam Akhavan

86 *Decolonising International Law: Development, Economic Growth and the Politics of Universality*
Sundhya Pahuja

85 *Complicity and the Law of State Responsibility*
Helmut Philipp Aust

84 *State Control over Private Military and Security Companies in Armed Conflict*
Hannah Tonkin

83 *'Fair and Equitable Treatment' in International Investment Law*
Roland Kläger

82 *The UN and Human Rights: Who Guards the Guardians?*
Guglielmo Verdirame

81 *Sovereign Defaults before International Courts and Tribunals*
Michael Waibel

80 *Making the Law of the Sea: A Study in the Development of International Law*
James Harrison

79 *Science and the Precautionary Principle in International Courts and Tribunals: Expert Evidence, Burden of Proof and Finality*
Caroline E. Foster

78 *Transition from Illegal Regimes under International Law*
Yaël Ronen

77 *Access to Asylum: International Refugee Law and the Globalisation of Migration Control*
Thomas Gammeltoft-Hansen

76 *Trading Fish, Saving Fish: The Interaction between Regimes in International Law*
Margaret A. Young

75 *The Individual in the International Legal System: Continuity and Change in International Law*
Kate Parlett

74 *'Armed Attack' and Article 51 of the UN Charter: Evolutions in Customary Law and Practice*
Tom Ruys

73 *Theatre of the Rule of Law: Transnational Legal Intervention in Theory and Practice*
Stephen Humphreys

72 *Science and Risk Regulation in International Law*
Jacqueline Peel

71 *The Participation of States in International Organisations: The Role of Human Rights and Democracy*
Alison Duxbury

70 *Legal Personality in International Law*
Roland Portmann

69 *Vicarious Liability in Tort: A Comparative Perspective*
Paula Giliker

68 *The Public International Law Theory of Hans Kelsen: Believing in Universal Law*
Jochen von Bernstorff

67 *Legitimacy and Legality in International Law: An Interactional Account*
Jutta Brunnée and Stephen J. Toope

66 *The Concept of Non-International Armed Conflict in International Humanitarian Law*
Anthony Cullen

65 *The Principle of Legality in International and Comparative Criminal Law*
Kenneth S. Gallant

64 *The Challenge of Child Labour in International Law*
Franziska Humbert

63 *Shipping Interdiction and the Law of the Sea*
Douglas Guilfoyle

62 *International Courts and Environmental Protection*
Tim Stephens

61 *Legal Principles in WTO Disputes*
Andrew D. Mitchell

60 *War Crimes in Internal Armed Conflicts*
Eve La Haye

59 *Humanitarian Occupation*
Gregory H. Fox

58 *The International Law of Environmental Impact Assessment: Process, Substance and Integration*
Neil Craik

57 *The Law and Practice of International Territorial Administration: Versailles to Iraq and Beyond*
Carsten Stahn

56 *United Nations Sanctions and the Rule of Law*
Jeremy Matam Farrall

55 *National Law in WTO Law: Effectiveness and Good Governance in the World Trading System*
Sharif Bhuiyan

54 *Cultural Products and the World Trade Organization*
Tania Voon

53 *The Threat of Force in International Law*
Nikolas Stürchler

52 *Indigenous Rights and United Nations Standards: Self-Determination, Culture and Land*
Alexandra Xanthaki

51 *International Refugee Law and Socio-Economic Rights: Refuge from Deprivation*
Michelle Foster

50 *The Protection of Cultural Property in Armed Conflict*
Roger O'Keefe

49 *Interpretation and Revision of International Boundary Decisions*
Kaiyan Homi Kaikobad

48 *Multinationals and Corporate Social Responsibility: Limitations and Opportunities in International Law*
Jennifer A. Zerk

47 *Judiciaries within Europe: A Comparative Review*
John Bell

46 *Law in Times of Crisis: Emergency Powers in Theory and Practice*
Oren Gross and Fionnuala Ní Aoláin

45 *Vessel-Source Marine Pollution: The Law and Politics of International Regulation*
Alan Khee-Jin Tan

44 *Enforcing Obligations Erga Omnes in International Law*
Christian J. Tams

43 *Non-Governmental Organisations in International Law*
Anna-Karin Lindblom

42 *Democracy, Minorities and International Law*
Steven Wheatley

41 *Prosecuting International Crimes: Selectivity and the International Criminal Law Regime*
Robert Cryer

40 *Compensation for Personal Injury in English, German and Italian Law: A Comparative Outline*
Basil Markesinis, Michael Coester, Guido Alpa and Augustus Ullstein

39 *Dispute Settlement in the UN Convention on the Law of the Sea*
Natalie Klein

38 *The International Protection of Internally Displaced Persons*
Catherine Phuong

37 *Imperialism, Sovereignty and the Making of International Law*
Antony Anghie

36 *Principles of the Institutional Law of International Organizations*
C. F. Amerasinghe

35 *Necessity, Proportionality and the Use of Force by States*
Judith Gardam

34 *International Legal Argument in the Permanent Court of International Justice: The Rise of the International Judiciary*
Ole Spiermann

33 -

32 *Great Powers and Outlaw States: Unequal Sovereigns in the International Legal Order*
Gerry Simpson

31 *Local Remedies in International Law* (second edition)
Chittharanjan Felix Amerasinghe

30 *Reading Humanitarian Intervention: Human Rights and the Use of Force in International Law*
Anne Orford

29 *Conflict of Norms in Public International Law: How WTO Law Relates to Other Rules of International Law*
Joost Pauwelyn

28 -

27 *Transboundary Damage in International Law*
Hanqin Xue

26 -

25 *European Criminal Procedures*
Edited by Mireille Delmas-Marty and J. R. Spencer

24 *Accountability of Armed Opposition Groups in International Law*
Liesbeth Zegveld

23 *Sharing Transboundary Resources: International Law and Optimal Resource Use*
Eyal Benvenisti

22 *International Human Rights and Humanitarian Law*
René Provost

21 *Remedies against International Organisations*
Karel Wellens

20 *Diversity and Self-Determination in International Law*
Karen Knop

19 *The Law of Internal Armed Conflict*
Lindsay Moir

18 *International Commercial Arbitration and African States: Practice, Participation and Institutional Development*
Amazu A. Asouzu

17 *The Enforceability of Promises in European Contract Law*
James Gordley

16 *International Law in Antiquity*
David J. Bederman

15 *Money Laundering: A New International Law Enforcement Model*
Guy Stessens

14 *Good Faith in European Contract Law*
Reinhard Zimmermann and Simon Whittaker

13 *On Civil Procedure*
J. A. Jolowicz

12 *Trusts: A Comparative Study*
Maurizio Lupoi and Simon Dix

11 *The Right to Property in Commonwealth Constitutions*
Tom Allen

10 *International Organizations before National Courts*
August Reinisch

9 *The Changing International Law of High Seas Fisheries*
Francisco Orrego Vicuña

8 *Trade and the Environment: A Comparative Study of EC and US Law*
Damien Geradin

7 *Unjust Enrichment: A Study of Private Law and Public Values*
Hanoch Dagan

6 *Religious Liberty and International Law in Europe*
Malcolm D. Evans

5 *Ethics and Authority in International Law*
Alfred P. Rubin

4 *Sovereignty over Natural Resources: Balancing Rights and Duties*
Nico Schrijver

3 *The Polar Regions and the Development of International Law*
Donald R. Rothwell

2 *Fragmentation and the International Relations of Micro-States: Self-Determination and Statehood*
Jorri C. Duursma

1 *Principles of the Institutional Law of International Organizations*
C. F. Amerasinghe

Printed in the USA
CPSIA information can be obtained
at www.ICGtesting.com
CBHW060735191024
15870CB00036B/243

9 781108 493499